LONGING FOR LIMITLESS LIGHT

LONGING FOR LIMITLESS LIGHT

C. R. LAMA & JAMES LOW

Published by Simply Being *www.simplybeing.co.uk*

British Library Cataloguing in Publication Data. A catalogue record for this book is available from the British Library.

ISBN: 978-1-7399381-0-9

All the images used in this book including the cover art are taken from the *Himalayan Art Resources* (*https://www.himalayanart.org/*) which kindly makes art work available for personal, educational and non-commercial use. With many thanks for their enormous generosity and good work they do in making Buddhist art available.

Layout by Sarah Allen.

འོད་དཔག་མེད་

Contents

Homage

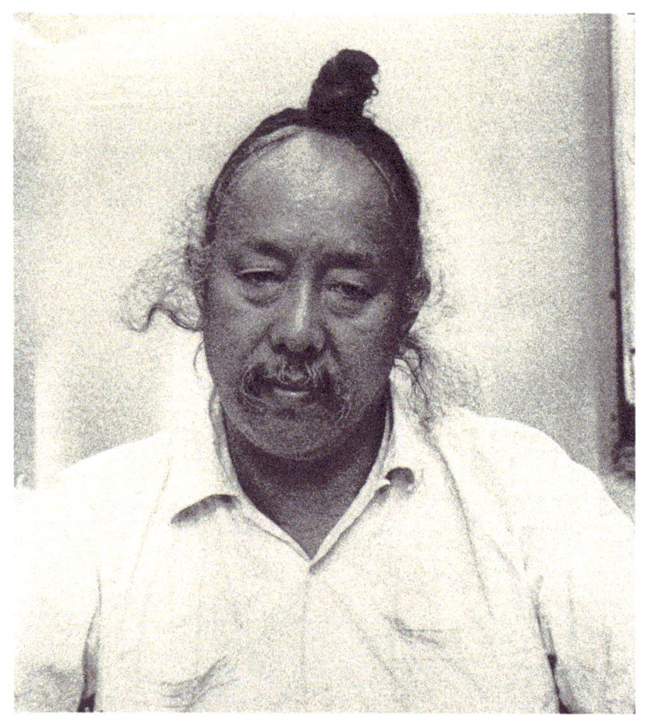

With kind eyes
And deep love
You poured amrita
Into the cracked vessel
Of my wounded heart

So much leaked away

Yet this flow of light
Never ceased
And drops of your blessing
Still moisten my face
As tears

Preface

The texts in this book provide a range of antidotes to loneliness and isolation. Due to the arising of a moment of ignoring the basic openness that hosts everyone and everything, whatever arises loses its bright clarity. This loss of clarity causes light to 'thicken' so that the appearance of light is taken to be the appearance of inherently existing entities. Thus, we live in a world of reified everyone and everything where each of us is looking for the specific 'things' that will make us complete and happy. Our yearning for the special people and things we want and need is so familiar for us that it can seem to be the valid driving force of our existence – getting what we want and avoiding what we do not want. The yearning for what will complete us is here inside us, yet we are often unskilled in managing the choices we make from the options that occur for us. Then we experience the two forms of suffering described by the Buddha: getting what we do not want and not getting what we do want.

This suffering arises because we refuse to recognise the impermanence and unreliability of the phenomena we seek to rely on. This impermanence and unreliability is not a punishment. It is a simple fact – and if we accept that this is the case, then we can cease from the ludicrous task of trying to make the impermanent permanent. If the phenomena we take to be entities are not actually entities, then what are they? Our eyes see light. In contrast to this, our habits of dualistic reifying interpretation construct the illusion of self-existing entities so that we 'see' what we imagine is there. By releasing ourselves from the prison of concepts, from the beliefs which dull bright appearance into the opacity of things, we find ourselves as light in a world of light. Then we see that our yearning for things was simply a mistake, a deluded form of our inherent yearning for wholeness, our longing for Limitless Light.

Limitless Light is the all-inclusive heart of the Buddha, the radiance within which the illusion of isolated existence dissolves. All phenomena are light within the infinite field of light and we, as phenomena, share that pure ground and expression. The heart pulse of the infinite openness of unchanging presence manifests as light and sound giving rise to the diverse appearances we encounter. If this integrity is not attended to, we find experience structured through binary oppositions. Then dark is seemingly excluded from light and the residual dualised light manifests as opacity – and thus we find ourselves as a thing amongst things. Amitabha, the Buddha Limitless Light, releases us from the delusion of thing-ness so that we awaken to our unique specific presence within infinite integrity.

All the texts in this book were translated with the guidance and encouragement of C.R. Lama, the Khordong Terchen Tulku Chimed Rigdzin. This work was done almost fifty years ago in the backyard of his small house in Shantiniketan, West Bengal. No initiation is needed to practise any of these texts. Rinpoche, this precious guru, was very insistent that faith and devotion are central to the Buddhist path. Mere intellectual interest will not cut through the thick skin of our deluding ego formation.

The prayers and aspirations presented here are precise methods for orienting our life-energy towards the task of universal awakening. As such, these prayers do not rest on the mere hope that they might be heard. The Buddhas and Bodhisattvas are always awake and ready to respond. Our aspirations build our connection with our own potential, our intrinsic Buddha nature. As we develop confidence in the availability of the Buddhas and the immediacy of their response we are freed from doubt and hesitation and prepared for non-dual practice.

The heart has to open in longing and in desperation – for this is the quick way for all the energy to gather in the heart and then enter the central channel, the open space of awareness already present within us. The Buddhas ceaselessly watch for the first awakening of interest in true awakening. When they see our hearts tremble they smile and shower us with the light of their love. If these translations can bring about such an initial longing, then Rinpoche's commitment to this work will not have been in vain. The translations have been revised in recent years by James Low. They were retyped by Barbara Terris and set up for this book by Sarah Allen.

May our longing for Limitless Light be fulfilled!

Introduction

The light of awareness is like the sun in the ever-open sky. Light shines forth, bringing illumination. If we see without looking for things, we will see that we see patterns of colour and light. This is the clarity or bright display which arises as the pure Buddha Realms. The Buddha Amitabha, 'Od-dPag-Med, 'Limitless Light' resides in Sukhavati, bDe-Ba-Can, Dewachen, 'The Happy'. At the beginning of his career as a Bodhisattva, the Universal Emperor Wheel Rim (as Amitabha was then) made a vow that he would accumulate so much merit that by the mere remembrance of him or his name, any being would be reborn close to him in his Buddha Realm where their progress to enlightenment would be easy. To long for Limitless Light is to long for enlightenment, to reside at the very source of light. For most of us simply becoming light is too subtle because of the opacity and density of our habits. Therefore the great vow of Amitabha, Limitless Light, has provided us with a wonderful halfway house, his own Happy realm where we can be purified on ever more subtle levels by his presence and instructions. How wonderful to be in a realm where every occurrence is an encouragement to awakening!

The sequence of texts in this book provides a progressive path for freeing ourselves from the sorrow-inducing delusions of being a separate entity burdened with inherent existence. By developing faith that deepens and widens into an uninterrupted confidence free of the turbulence of hopes and fears we are released from the imprisoning power of our own thoughts. Thoughts, feelings, sensations, memories and so on arise and pass with no inherent power to limit us. It is our own belief in the substantial reality and truth of our mental experiences that gives them their power. Faith and devotion allow us to shift our reliance away from both the outer reified objects of the world and the inner concepts shaping our dualistic intentions. Releasing the energy of our mind from its fixations, it is freed to be in the service of awakening rather than maintaining the limitations of samsara. Doubt, hesitancy, uncertainty are great enemies for those seeking liberation from duality. Being in two minds about something feeds the separation of self and other, subject and object, and this leads to further fragmentation of self and world. So we need to gather ourselves into one-pointed attention so that we can remain focused on our path and goal and resist all temptation to distraction. The texts offered here provide a way to remove both the obscuration of the root afflictions (opacity, desire, aversion, pride and jealousy) and the obscuration of cognising things. Moreover, they provide the basis for gathering the two accumulations of merit and wisdom which give us access to the realms of purity.

The first text is the short *Refuge and Bodhicitta* on page 17. The Buddhas always offer refuge – so it is always available whenever we turn towards them. We are saying: "I need your help, your protection, your inspiration. I want to be close to you." With their support, with the ongoing sense that there is a benign presence on my side, by my side, I can develop the courage to follow Amitabha in making the Bodhisattva vow and dedicating all my time, energy and intention towards the benefit of others. More detail on this is available later in the sections on the *Bodhisattva Vow*. But the key point at the beginning is the sense that: 'Now my life is meaningful.' The winds of desire and aversion that have us running towards our passing fancies and away from the emergent fears are forces of destabilising intensity. We let go of this immersion in the carnival of human life and settle into confidence in being part of the great work of bringing all sentient beings to liberation.

Then on page 18 we have the first version of the *Seven Branch Practice* which is contained in many of the texts in this volume. This version follows the method of offering employed by Bodhisattva Samantabhadra at the beginning of his career. His vision is so vast that it collapses all thought. His inconceivable generosity is to offer to as many Buddhas as there are particles of dust in the universe, each surrounded by just as many Bodhisattvas, an amazing array of all that brings pleasure. Gift giving is, among other functions, a way of making and deepening connection – and through following his method we have a vast way of linking ourselves with all that is good and wholesome. We offer our salutations to all the pure ones, those rich in wisdom and compassion, and make our offerings. Trusting their non-judgmental kindness towards us, we offer confession, distancing ourselves from both outer negatives acts and inner negative impulses. Then we rejoice in the virtue performed by others, and the merit arising from it. This is the great antidote to pride and envy. Others practise virtue, not only us. If we can celebrate what they do, then we can relax and open to being a small rivulet joining in the great river of Dharma.

Next, by asking of the Buddhas to teach the Dharma we make our half of the bridge of transmission. Buddhism is not an evangelical religion. If the karmic connection is not ripe, then Dharma is unlikely to be of interest, and so we have to show our interest by requesting teaching. When the generous giver meets the grateful recipient, the circle is completed. Following this we request the Buddhas not to die, not to leave, not to become unavailable. Although Buddhas are not impermanent we are advised to think of them as passing on in order to avoid complacency. For worldly life we need many things – and if one item is finished we can always get another. But when a Buddha leaves the world, it is a great loss and the periods between one Buddha and the next can be very long. The Dharma can stand in the place of the Buddha, yet we still need a teacher or guru to make it come alive for us.

Finally, there is the 7th branch, the dedication of the merit arising from the previous six branches, along with all other merit we have, for the sake of all beings. Beings in the three lower realms of hells, hungry ghosts and animals have very little capacity to create merit, while beings in the god realms are preoccupied with pleasure and the jealous gods are consumed with jealousy. We human beings have great opportunities – yet they are easily lost. Merit is the ethical and spiritual value generated by good actions. It is not a substance, yet it can be thought of as if it were in order to give us the sense that this is a resource that can be accumulated and put to good use for the benefit of all.

This is followed on page 34 by *Honouring True Value,* taken from ENTERING THE PATH OF ENLIGHTENMENT by Santideva. This famous beautiful section supports us in making many further offerings to the Buddhas. The offerings conjure up a sense of ease and plenty, and so match the mind of the Buddha, which is always relaxed and full of beauty and light. We offer beauty in order to find our own beauty. For our confessions we rely on the power of those we confess to, the Buddhas and great Bodhisattvas, for they can see our intrinsic purity, which for us is hidden at the moment by our adventitious obscurations. We also rely on the power of effective application of the antidotes of virtue and meditation. We invite the light of the Buddhas to flow into us and wash out all defilements and limitations so that we are translucent and sparkling like crystal glass. We activate the power of total renunciation, cutting ourselves free from the structures, beliefs and activity which have predisposed us to act in ways that were detrimental to the well-being of others and ourselves. Lastly, we employ the power of abandoning the return to error. We block the way back to worldliness by seeing the dangers that lie there, and by emphasising our commitment to change and by developing an unwavering alignment with the path to liberation. These are the famous 'four powers of purification' and they are vital for practice as they wash away the glue of our identification with limiting patterns

Having prepared the ground, we move on to the specific preparations for *Taking the Bodhisattva Vow*, page 56. To vow from the depths of our heart to work for the benefit of others from now on until all beings are fully liberated is profound and transforming, and therefore one should be aware of all that is involved. This is a vow that the ego cannot make. The ego says 'me first'. The Bodhisattva says 'you first'. With this vow our connection with all beings is illuminated, and our intention towards them starts to be purified of the distorting motives of the five afflicting poisons of opacity, aversion, desire, jealousy and pride. This vow is too onerous to be carried by oneself alone so we make it in front of all Buddhas and Bodhisattvas, including our own gurus and teachers. We will need their ongoing support and companionship if we are to remain true to our vow and become an enlightening presence in the many realms of darkness. Therefore we invite the Buddha to come with all his followers and through offerings and praise, we bind ourselves to them.

The term 'Bodhisattva' indicates a being (*sattva*) who is oriented towards awakening (*bodhi*) for all sentient beings. The Bodhisattva's view is narrow in that she is not focused on worldly concerns such as fame, wealth, or being liked. Yet her view is wide, indeed vast, because of her concern for the welfare of all beings without exception. She has renounced the categories of friend and foe, liked and not liked, near and distant, helpful and unhelpful. However beings are, she is for them as they are. This amazing orientation rests on her capacity to perceive the seed of enlightenment in all beings. Whoever is sentient has a mind, and if the actual nature of the mind is seen, then that is itself the act of awakening. To take the Bodhisattva vow is to enter the company of the great beings who have renounced all selfish concerns and find their fulfilment in the welfare of others. On an outer level, this means providing food, shelter, medicine and so on. On an inner level, it means staying present for the other however they are, in their emotions, bigotry and so on. On a secret or invisible level, it is simply staying open and without intention regarding whatever occurs. On this secret level, there is no longer striving for the benefit of others – their benefit lies in effortless inclusion in the ever-bright Buddha mind.

What we can do with the support of the Buddhas and Bodhisattvas is much more than what we can do on our own. In fact, the text is subtly pointing to the delusion of duality, to the separation of self and other. We are not, and have never been, separate from the Buddhas nor from all sentient beings, nor from all that emerges. The Buddhas already always include us in their company – and now we include all beings in ours. The entities which constitute samsara are being softened as we see that the fragmentation we experience is not intrinsic, but is simply the delusion arising from not seeing the light as light.

Taking the Bodhisattva Vow, page 74, sets out the actual ritual which you can use to take the vow. If possible, we receive the vow directly from someone who is fully in the practice and has previously received it from their teacher so that the blessing of the entire lineage strengthens our own resolve. If this is not possible in person, then prepare a small shrine with an image of the Buddha and scatter it with flower petals and open your heart to the ritual.

Firstly we recite prayers to the various lineages of the Bodhisattva vow. We call to mind all those who have gone before us in this great undertaking. May the power of their selfless intention feed our own so that we will not falter in our commitment to always act for the benefit of others. The final Guru in each of these lineages is Chimed Rigdzin, the great scholar and guru whom I assisted in the translation of these texts.

Having recollected our debt of gratitude to these great beings for having sustained the lineage so that we can now be supported by it, we direct the merit arising from this remembrance towards the flourishing of the Dharma. Dharma, the teachings and practices of Buddhism, is not something out there that will survive and thrive by itself. At this time of great change and increasing anxiety, the calming clarity of Dharma could be of great benefit to many. The presence of the Dharma is nourished by our faith, devotion and energy – without this, on a relative level, it will weaken and fade. Although on an absolute level Dharma is unchanging and freely available in all times and places, in our world of duality the polarity of increase/decrease is in play and so if we do not offer our life-energy to Dharma, it will not be available in future for ourselves and for others. Thus, we can see that even as beginners, our love and kindness can fuel the flames of Dharma which burn up all obscurations and ignorance and illuminate the path to freedom.

Then we again take refuge to link ourselves with the truly virtuous. We strengthen this by expressing our commitment to renounce harming others in anyway, and to focus on practising virtue with our body, speech, and mind. Selfishness and self-cherishing have become so habitual for us that we believe our ego-self identity to be the truth of how we actually are. In fact, the ego is not a thing, but a way of patterning experience around the delusion of a continuous self-entity. Hence it is necessary to outwardly shift our behaviour away from its function of affirming our 'self' as an existent entity; and to inwardly shift our thoughts and feelings away from self-confirmation; and more deeply to dissolve our self-reflexive consciousness in the ocean of awareness.

The central practice of *Taking the Bodhisattvas Vows* begins on page 106 with our direct request to the officiating teacher to raise within us the altruistic intention to gain unsurpassed supreme and complete enlightenment. They know how to raise this intention, and we're going to learn from them – again and again in this book we are encouraged to rely on the Three Jewels, to learn from the experience of the wise and to follow this well-trodden path. Inclusion, membership, participation and belonging constitute this path. Having lost our way in the jungle of samsara, it is only sensible to rely on the experienced guides who can point the way. Life is too short to keep entering dead ends in this labyrinth of karmic patterns.

The actual vow has various stages. Firstly, we *Develop the Bodhicitta of Aspiration*, our wish to become a Bodhisattva, a being (*sattva*) who works for the enlightenment (*bodhi*) of all, page 109. This is often compared to how we prepare for going on a journey. We gather information about the destination, collect what we might need for the journey, and ready ourselves for the challenges which might occur – particularly those manifesting from our fears, laziness and lack of belief in the fundamental goodness of ourselves and all beings. Just as all Bodhisattvas have done at the beginning of their careers, we express our intention to free all beings by taking them out of samsara and to give hope and confidence to all so that they can pass from suffering. How vast and comprehensive this vow is! How amazing that we can aspire to such a task! The aspiration itself begins our rebirth as we let go of our worldly concerns and become focused on the welfare of others.

The second stage is the bodhicitta, the mind (*citta*) of awakening (*bodhi*), manifesting as *Engagement in Actual Practice*, page 115. Now we are on the journey. We have left the familiar landmarks that remind us of our samsaric identity and are starting to find our way in the openness of the limitless path accommodating all beings. We commit to the actual training taken on by all Bodhisattvas, in particular we commit to training in the six paramita or transcendent qualities of generosity, morality, patience, diligence, meditation and true discernment. The first five qualities developed in the service of others become transcendent through the presence of the sixth. True discernment is the acuity, the bright sharpness of the mind, that reveals the absence of inherent existence in phenomena. All that appears, whether seemingly material or mental is empty of self-substance, self-existence and self-identity. All occurrence is like a dream – something seems to be experienced and yet no-thing has actually been experienced. This is the key quality that differentiates the great vehicle (*mahayana*) from the lesser vehicle (*hinayana*). Only the mind inseparable from emptiness is vast enough to encompass the welfare of all beings. Our human ego-self striving to do its best will only ever have limited capacity since although it may see the absence of inherent existence in beings, it cannot let go of the idea of fundamental entities. This dualistic reliance is its inherent structural limitation, restricting both wisdom and compassion.

The third stage is *Developing the Absolute Bodhicitta,* page 121. Here 'absolute' refers to sky-like emptiness, free of reification, objectification and duality. From the very beginning there has been not one atom of real existence. All beings are inseparable from the ever-open ground, the unborn presence of un-graspable spaciousness. All beings are essentially Buddhas because it is the awakening to this unborn ground that marks the 'birth' of each unborn Buddha. We are already in the Buddha mandala yet cannot see this due to our unborn obscurations. Neither beings, nor obscurations, nor awakenings, nor Buddhas really exist – this is the absolute bodhicitta.

The three stages of the Bodhisattva vows have been engaged with. There follows reiteration of the key points in the *Unified Teaching for Simple People,* page 122. Even if life is very busy or difficult, whatever we do and whatever happens to us, if we simply maintain recollection of our vow and include the welfare of all in our every experience, rejoicing in their virtue, and dedicating all merit to others, this will be sufficient.

Then on page 125 we recite verses which remind us of our new identity and the new values and tasks that come with it. The verse on page 130 is particularly illuminating of our new orientation: "*Whenever I am glad I will dedicate that joy to the happiness of all beings – may their happiness fill the sky! Whenever I get trouble, I will take the suffering of all beings as my own burden – may the oceans of suffering become dry!*" This is a beautiful expression of the principle of giving one's happiness to others and taking on their suffering. To give one's happiness to others may seem reasonable and virtuous. But to intensify one's own misery by adding the troubles of all beings to my own may seem punitive. It is here that we have to remember the absolute bodhicitta. All suffering is empty of inherent existence: the kindness of alleviating the suffering of others, if it is vast and unconditional, will bring with it the loosening of egoic self-referencing and the consequent revelation of the ungraspability of all experience.

The next section, page 133, *Honouring the Buddha's Speech*, highlights the ungraspable nature of all experience as it actually is. This is the wisdom of emptiness, which the *Heart sutra* makes available to each of us. Firstly, there is a tantric style practice which brings us into direct communication with Buddha Shakyamuni. We're not just thinking about or talking about the Buddha, we are entering into his unmediated presence. This shift is enacted through the purifying and equalising mantra, which indicates: "*Om, Pure nature. All phenomena have very pure nature – this is my nature.*" On the basis of this all conceptualised forms are resolved into their open ground. Within this vast expensive space, by saying *Om Mani Padme Hung*, I arise as Chenrezi, the Bodhisattva particularly associated with compassion, and in this form I attend to the words of pure Dharma streaming from Buddha Shakyamuni. Thus, the *Heart sutra* arises and I, as Chenrezi, participate in its unfolding. In this way, the revelation of true Dharma is appearing here and now, as direct contact with the source of clarity.

The *Heart sutra* has a simple structure and its words make clear that whatever is taken to be separate and really existing is actually always inseparable from, and non-dual with, ungraspable no-thing-ness. All that we know, see, taste, remember and so on is actually not what we take it to be. It is our deluded perception which generates the illusion of separate entities, including ourselves. When this unnecessary excessive effort is given up there is the naked simplicity of empty appearance. The less we do, the more the actual is revealed. It is revealed not as a work in progress, but as always already complete. When this is clear, the egoic formation is redundant and dissolves.

Honouring the Buddha's Speech concludes with some verses highlighting the power of emptiness to overcome all difficulties and render all negative forces ineffective. The verse that begins at the bottom of page 159 is a beautiful summation of the de-reification of all phenomena. All the appearances that we take to be fixed entities are in fact dynamic moments of experience which arise in collaboration with other moments of experience. They originate or arise or display dependent on the origination or arising or display of other aspects of the field of occurrence. The tree arises due to the soil, the rain, the sun, the absence of the chainsaw, and so on – there is no self-existing tree. Thus the key organising binaries of stopping and starting, annihilation and permanence, coming and going, diverse meanings and one fixed meaning are all groundless, being mere concepts without actual referent. To see this is to observe all the concepts you have used to construct your world losing their life force. This life force was nothing other than your belief in them. When the emptiness of these beliefs is seen, everything is pacified and the mind is at ease.

Following this, we have two prayers to ripen the mood of trust and devotion which is vital for arriving in Dewachen and seeing Amitabha. Devotion begins with inspiration as we gain the vivid faith of appreciation of the good qualities of the object of our yearning. This appreciation and inspiration makes us aware of the gap between where we are and where we want to be. This feeds our faith and eager aspiration to strive to end suffering and gain liberation. With this we can develop the faith of certainty or full confidence in the teachings and with that we find a commitment to empty samsara. Your heart opens and judgement falls away so that your separation from the Dharma diminishes as irreversible faith is born. These four aspects of faith support each other and help to keep us on track. The first short prayer, page 162, is a reminder of the great yogis and scholars who established the Dharma in Tibet. Without their effort and generosity we would not be able to access the teachings. So whether we know a lot or a little about the history of Buddhism in Tibet, we owe a debt of gratitude to these great ones and so this prayer lets us express this. To recognise our dependence on the good works of others is no diminution of ourselves. To depend on others is to be part of the unfolding field of revelation – we take our place within it through our devotion. How much sweeter to become part of the open Buddha field than to be endlessly ploughing our own deep furrow?

The second prayer, page 167, is by Padmasambhava and revealed as a treasure text by Chogyur Dechen Lingpa. It includes the *Seven Branch Practice* that has occurred in earlier texts and builds on this to make aspirations for success in learning, and for the long life and good health of the teachers who illuminate the world with the precious teachings. Teachers, students, sponsors, yogis – so many personalities, skills, interests and energies go towards creating and sustaining a flourishing Dharma culture. In the West, this process is just beginning as fragile shoots of study and practice start to extend roots downwards. This whole endeavour depends on goodwill, a profound commitment to the common good and the benefit of all. As we know, conflicts arise easily in human society. The concept of shared humanity has not been strong enough to end wars and exploitation. The concept of Buddhism or Buddhadharma has not been strong enough to prevent sectarian rivalries and hostility. Separation and differentiation is rapidly followed by hierarchical ordering leading to pride and jealousy. This brief prayer by the great Lotus Born is an encouragement to inclusivity, fellow feeling and benefit of all free of the fragility of dependence on concepts.

From page 176 to page 306, there are a series of aspirations for being born in the Buddha Realm of Amitabha, known as Dewachen in Tibetan and as Sukhavati in Sanskrit. This name translates as Happy Land or simply Happy. As *Appendix 1* on page 230 points out, this realm of Dewachen was generated by the fulfilment of the vow made by the Universal Emperor Wheel Rim. He vowed that as a result of his diligent practice, he would accumulate sufficient merit to manifest the highest Buddha Realm. Moreover, "*Whoever remembers me and my name and realm or hears of them will not be born again, but will come to my realm. If this does not occur, then I will not become a Buddha.*" The word of a Buddha is vajra, indestructible – whatever is said must come to pass. This great king Wheel Rim is stating that if his words are not fulfilled he will not enter enlightenment. The power of the spoken word used to be considered to rest in its truth and reliability: 'My word is my bond.' Nowadays when lying and spin seem to be inseparable from power, it can be difficult for us to comprehend the power of truth and the power of the commitment to the fulfilment of an aspiration. To make a vow to all beings for all time is to step free of strategy and tactics. The path is straight and clear: to free oneself from selfishness and judgement and to work for the benefit of all. To follow this is to approach ever closer to the honour and dignity of the Buddha.

Due to the fulfilment of his vow, the Universal Emperor Wheel Rim became the Buddha Amitabha residing in Dewachen, the Buddha realm his merit has generated. Such is the power of his vow that even today total reliance on his name and presence acts as a ring of faith by which his hook of compassion can catch us and bring us to Dewachen. We can ripen our faith by developing the four causes for being born in Dewachen, page 231. Firstly, we need to learn of the good qualities of this Buddha Realm otherwise why would we want to go there? We need to be clear that it is much superior to the god realms within samsara. Secondly, we need to accumulate much merit through the practise of virtue and the avoidance of non-virtue. The practice of virtue helps us to become simple and straightforward with less to hide and less need to pretend. We gain the dignity of open presence, of being available to and for others, with a heart full of affection and a mind suffused with active kindness. The Seven Branch Practice presented in various forms in this book is a key method for doing this. Our recollection of the generosity of the Buddhas, and our gratitude for all that they bring to our lives, is strengthened by offering them reverent salutation, myriad offerings and the confession of our faults and limitations. With this we can rejoice in the virtue done by others, request the Buddhas and Bodhisattvas to teach and to not become unavailable for us. By dedicating the merit of this for the benefit of others we diminish our selfishness and increase our loving concern.

The third cause of gaining birth in Dewachen is the generation of an altruistic intention towards enlightenment. The motive of seeking only one's own liberation is like a feeble torch on a dark night. If we want to enter the Realm of Limitless Light, we need to generate a bright light in our own heart, the light of love and commitment to the well-being of all, unconditional and without judgement. The fourth cause is to dedicate all the merit of all that we have ever done to the benefit and enlightenment of all beings. Without keeping even one atom of merit for ourselves, if our intention is totally altruistic, we will find that we actually have all the merit needed to live and thrive in Dewachen.

The Aspiration that Brings Birth in Dewachen, page 176, begins by describing the location of Dewachen. It is to be found far, far to the West, beyond innumerable lands. We cannot travel there by walking, by car, by plane – the only vehicle that will bring us there is the union of Amitabha's Vow and the adequacy of our four causes. It lies to the West, which is also the direction of the section in the mandala where Amitabha resides, the arena of the purification of desire where each appearance is clearly discerned, exactly as it is. Generally love is blind and desire is blind because they are over-focused on the objects of our selective attention. Panoramic appreciation reveals the specific display of each aspect of the field of clarity, the field of limitless light.

The beauty of the environment in this Buddha Realm is highlighted so that all its charming qualities can arouse in us a great and one-pointed yearning to go there. What in samsara could compare with such beauty, a beauty that effortlessly encourages awakening? In samsara beauty is a restricted commodity and this gives rise to desire, ambition, selfishness and hostility. But in Dewachen everything is light and bright, facilitating ease and attention, free of desire and appropriation. Our birth there is magical as we manifest in the centre of a lotus. This pure birth is a true rebirth and all our old self-centred habits are left far behind. There is no need for womb birth and so no one there has a female body. There is no sexual desire and no competition – how different that would be from the world we know! With constant remembrance of the marvellous qualities of this realm of pure light may it guide our actions in this life so that everything we do prepares us for birth there!

A Swift Path to Cross Easily to the Excellent Realm, page 187, offers a complete practice to achieve our goal. Each text focused on Dewachen has its own mood and style which helps us to find the form of this aspiration that is most fitting with our current circumstances. With the *Swift Path* we have the *dharani* or long mantra of the *Offering Cloud,* page 190, which increases the volume, variety and purity of the offerings we make. The mahayana view is vast – we fill the sky with offerings to myriad Buddhas filling the sky, and then dedicating the merit for the well-being of all. Vast and inclusive, generosity, love and compassion are freely available to all, regardless of their qualities. This view takes us away from the reward approach of narrowly considering cause and effect. We share the merit equally with all , with persecutors and with victims, with predators and with their prey. Good and bad are relative terms. Awakening is awakening from the relative and the dualised to the absolute and the non-dual. When we directly open to non-duality we see that there are no really existing entities, no actual people who are truly good or bad. All that appears is the radiance or clarity of the openness of presence.

On page 233 there is a further method of accumulating merit – the offering of food. We offer what we have actually assembled as well as all that we can imagine. We are asking the Buddhas for help, help to escape the endless suffering of samsara. This is a big request. Luckily for us, they are willing and happy to connect with us and help us. We offer food in order to give us the confidence that we have something to offer. This is actually just a comforting notion to ease our ego in its sense of its own lack. In fact, we are totally reliant on the kindness of the Buddha. Why is this? The Buddhas see the actual while we imagine the deceitful to be true. We deceive ourselves and others with our mistaken beliefs in the true existence of people and things. Living in the hazy maze of deception we cannot find the way out. The exit does not lie in concepts, in memories, in plans, nor in any of the other transient contents of the mind. We need the help of the Buddhas. They do not need our offerings. The less pride we have, the less defended we are and so are able to lessen the strength of our assertions of true existence. Then we have more space to receive the light of the Buddhas into our hearts. It is the light of the Buddha that lets us see that we also are Buddhas.

Being uncertain of being loved, we make offerings to try to ensure that the Buddhas will be willing to think of us. This is a transaction or deal that we as ego-self need to make – it is not required by the Buddhas. How generous they are to meet us within the drama of our illusory existence! Like a child's make-believe tea party, we pour imaginary tea and eat imaginary cakes, telling each other how good they are. But at least with this benign mental activity we open the way to belonging and to free participation.

On page 237 we have the famous *Dechen Monlam*, the aspiration to reach Dewachen, written by Raga Asya. Clearly written in a very inviting style, the text draws us into an exquisite vision of the life we will lead once we depart this life in the certainty of taking lotus birth in Amitabha's Buddha Realm. He begins by helping us to imagine Amitabha and his entourage, and how Amitabha is ceaselessly looking with compassion at all sentient beings in their diverse activity. This gaze manifests as his sambhogakaya form, Chenrezi/ Avalokitesvara, whose quick eye sees all the suffering of samsara. He also manifests Arya Tara and Padmasambhava. These three active saviours, the warmth of the Lotus family, also radiate out countless forms to move in samsara, bringing comfort and encouragement to all. All our thoughts, words and actions are known by Amitabha - for we are all already included in his enveloping care. Trusting this allows us to relax, cease from striving, and start to receive the love that has always flowed from the heart of the Buddha.

After an extensive Seven Branch Practice we prepare ourselves for our journey to Dewachen. At precisely the moment of death, as our consciousness eases free of its embodiment, we find Amitabha present before us ready to safely guide us to Dewachen. May we be happy to go there and easily resist being deflected to any of the six realms of samsara where only sorrow would await us! Yet old habits die hard and we have had many many lifetimes of deceiving ourselves with the belief that transient moments of happiness could be made permanent. Seeing that all these lives with their hopes and fears have been nothing more than dreams, we can let them go and turn towards the permanent satisfaction of awakening.

All beings who are born there are born from a lotus – but if one has doubted that one would actually be born there, then the petals of the lotus remain closed and one must wait five hundred years before they open. One will still be able to hear Amitabha teaching and will have no suffering except the frustration of not being able to see this blessed land. Doubt, hesitation, anxiety and uncertainty are signs of being in two minds, being divided in oneself, and this inner splitting maintains the structure of duality, and so is a great impediment.

Life in Dewachen page 282 is easy, pleasurable and fulfilling. Freed from the many tasks necessary for survival in samsara, our attention is available for deep study and practice – both of which are now easy to engage with. Raga Asya goes on to describe many beautiful features of the easy path to awakening that is available there. He has written this text for us as a concise summary of several sutras. His sources are reliable, his writing is clear – it is up to us to put it into practice.

This text is followed by two short texts by Mingyur Dorje page 301 which provide succinct summaries of the essence of this view. If we have become familiar with the longer texts, then these two brief summations can maintain our pure intention when we are pressed for time. Mingyur Dorje's words help to transform worldly dualistic longing into the profound emotion of one-pointed longing for light.

The book comes to an end with prayers for the flourishing of the Dharma with reminders of the depth and variety of the teachings.

> *May there be peace in the world for all beings, with freedom from war, illness and catastrophe! May all have the wish to practise Dharma and the opportunity to fulfil that wish!*

སྐྱབས་འགྲོ་དང་སེམས་བསྐྱེད།

Refuge and Bodhicitta

སངས་རྒྱས་ཆོས་དང་ཚོགས་ཀྱི་མཆོག་རྣམས་ལ།

SANG GYE	**CHO**	**DANG**	**TSOG**	**KYI**	**CHOG**	**NAM**	**LA**
buddha	*dharma*	*and*	*sangha* *(the assembly of committed practitioners)*	*of*	*supreme*	*(plural)*	*to*

To the Buddha, Dharma and Assembly of the Excellent Ones

བྱང་ཆུབ་བར་དུ་བདག་ནི་སྐྱབས་སུ་མཆི།

JANG CHUB	**BAR DU**	**DAG NI**	**KYAB**	**SU**	**CHI**
enlightenment	*until*	*I*	*refuge*	*for*	*go*

I go for refuge until enlightenment is gained.

བདག་གིས་སྦྱིན་སོགས་བགྱིས་པའི་བསོད་ནམས་ཀྱིས།

DAG	**GI**	**JIN**	**SOG**	**GYI PAI**	**SO NAM**	**KYI**
I	*by*	*generosity*	*other perfections**	*doing, practising*	*virtue*	*through*

*discipline, patience, diligence, meditation, wisdom

Through the virtue of practising generosity and the other perfections

འགྲོ་ལ་ཕན་ཕྱིར་སངས་རྒྱས་འགྲུབ་པར་ཤོག།

DRO	**LA**	**PHEN**	**CHIR**	**SANG GYE**	**DRUB PAR**	**SHO**
all beings	*to*	*benefit*	*in order to*	*buddha*	*accomplish*	*may it happen*

May I attain buddhahood for the benefit of all beings

I go for refuge to the Buddha, Dharma and Assembly of the Excellent Ones until enlightenment is gained. Through the virtue of practising generosity and the other perfections may I attain buddhahood for the benefit of all beings.

ལན་གསུམ་རྫེས༔ [Recite this three times.]

འཕགས་པ་བཟང་པོ་སྤྱོད་པའི་སྨོན་ལམ་གྱི་རྒྱལ་པོ་ལས་ཕྱུང་བའི་ཡན་ལག་བདུན་པ་བཞུགས་སོ།།

The Seven Branch Practice from 'Pure Good Conduct', the King of Aspirations

[This practice of the Bodhisattva Samantabhadra has the additional mandala offering inserted within it.]

འཕགས་པ་འཇམ་དཔལ་གཞོན་ནུར་གྱུར་པ་ལ་ཕྱག་འཚལ་ལོ།

PHAG PA	**JAM PAL**	**ZHON NUR GYUR PA**	**LA**	**CHAG TSHAL LO**
noble	*Manjushri*	*who is young, never gets old or ill*	*to*	*salutation*

Salutation to the Noble Manjushri who is always young.

ཇི་སྙེད་སུ་དག་ཕྱོགས་བཅུའི་འཇིག་རྟེན་ན།

JI NYED	**SU DAG**	**CHOG CHUI**	**JIG TEN**	**NA**
as many as there are	*those, them*	*ten directions//of (i.e. everywhere)*	*world*	*in*

As many as there are in the ten directions of the world,

དུས་གསུམ་གཤེགས་པ་མི་ཡི་སེང་གེ་ཀུན།

DU	**SUM**	**SHEG PA**	**MI**	**YI**	**SENG GE**	**KUN**
time (past, present, future)	*three*	*going*	*men*	*of (Buddha's title)*	*lions**	*all*

*just as the lion dominates all animals by its roar, so the Buddha's teaching on sunyata silences all false views of men.

All those lions among men, the Buddhas of the three times,

བདག་གིས་མ་ལུས་དེ་དག་ཐམས་ཅད་ལ།

DAG	**GI**	**MA LU**	**DE DAG**	**THAM CHE**	**LA**
me	*by*	*without exception*	*them*	*all*	*to*

To all of them without exception,

ལུས་དང་ངག་ཡིད་དང་བས་ཕྱག་བགྱིའོ།

LU	**DANG**	**NGAG**	**YID**	**DANG WAE**	**CHAG GYI O**
body	*and*	*speech*	*mind*	*faith, //by sincerity*	*make salutation, obeisance*

I sincerely make salutation with body, speech and mind.

Salutation to the Noble Manjushri who is always young. As many as there are in the ten directions of the world, all those lions among men, the Buddhas of the three times, to all of them without exception, I sincerely make salutation with body, speech and mind.

བཟང་པོ་སྤྱོད་པའི་སྨོན་ལམ་སྟོབས་དག་གིས།

ZANG PO	**CHO PAI**	**MON LAM**	**TOB DAG**	**GI**
the bodhisattva Samantabhadra *	*conduct,*	*prayer of aspiration*	*strength*	*by*

*The bodhisattva Samantabhadra completed the two necessary accumulations of merit and wisdom and gained Buddhahood by meditating that he had an infinite number of bodies, thus destroying body-centred egoism and so gaining wisdom. With these bodies he made an unending stream of offerings to all the Buddhas, thus destroying selfishness and gaining merit. By praying according to the same system we get his blessing and help.

By the power of aspiration following the practice of Samantabhadra,

རྒྱལ་བ་ཐམས་ཅད་ཡིད་ཀྱི་མངོན་སུམ་དུ།

GYAL WA	**THAM CHE**	**YID**	**KYI**	**NGON SUM**	**DU**
jinas,victors Buddhas	*all*	*mind*	*of*	*clarity (clearly imagining)*	*with*

With all the Buddhas clearly in mind,

ཞིང་གི་རྡུལ་སྙེད་ལུས་རབ་བཏུད་པ་ཡིས།

ZHING	**GI**	**DUL**	**NYED**	**LU**	**RAB TUD PA**	**YI**
realm, world, universe	*of*	*dust particle*	*as many as there are*	*body*	*manifesting bodies which make obeisance*	*by*

By manifesting as many bodies as there are dust particles in the universe,

རྒྱལ་བ་ཀུན་ལ་རབ་ཏུ་ཕྱག་འཚལ་ལོ།

GYAL WA	**KUN**	**LA**	**RAB TU**	**CHAG TSHAL LO**
jinas, victors	*all*	*to*	*fully, deeply*	*make salutation*

I truly make salutation to all the Buddhas.

By the power of aspiration following the practice of Samantabhadra, with all the Buddhas clearly in mind, by manifesting as many bodies as there are dust particles in the universe, I sincerely make salutation to all the Buddhas.

རྡུལ་གཅིག་སྟེང་ན་རྡུལ་སྙེད་སངས་རྒྱས་རྣམས།

DUL	**CHIG**	**TENG NA**	**DUL**	**NYED**	**SANG GYE**	**NAM**
particle of dust	*one, each*	*on top of*	*dust*	*as many there are*	*buddha*	*(plural)*

On each particle of dust in the universe there are as many Buddhas as there are particles of dust in the universe.

སངས་རྒྱས་སྲས་ཀྱི་དབུས་ན་བཞུགས་པ་དག།

SANG GYE SAE	**KYI U NA**	**ZHUG PA**	**DAG**
buddha's sons, bodhisattvas	*in the middle of*	*staying, sitting*	*them*

Each sitting in the midst of a host of Bodhisattvas.

དེ་ཏྟར་ཆོས་ཀྱི་དབྱིངས་རྣམས་མ་ལུས་པ།

DE TAR	**CHO KYI YING**	**NAM**	**MA LU PA**
like that	*dharmadhatu (everywhere)*	*(plural)*	*without exception*

In that way, I believe that every possible space for appearance

ཐམས་ཅད་རྒྱལ་བ་དག་གིས་གང་བར་མོས།

THAM CHE	**GYAL WA**	**DAG**	**GI**	**GANG WAR**	**MOE**
all	*jinas, Buddhas*	*(plural)*	*by*	*filled //as*	*believe*

Is filled with all the Buddhas.

On each particle of dust in the universe there are as many Buddhas as there are particles of dust in the universe, each sitting in the midst of a host of Bodhisattvas. In that way I believe that every possible space for appearance is filled with all the Buddhas.

དེ་དག་བསྔགས་པ་མི་ཟད་རྒྱ་མཚོ་རྣམས།

DE DAG	**NGAG PA**	**MI ZAD**	**GYAM TSHO NAM**
them	*praise*	*inexhaustible*	*oceans*

With inexhaustible oceans of praise,

དབྱངས་ཀྱི་ཡན་ལག་རྒྱ་མཚོ་སྒྲ་ཀུན་གྱིས།

YANG	**KYI**	**YAN LAG**	**GYAM TSO**	**DRA**	**KUN**	**GYI**
melodies	*of*	*branches,*	*ocean*	*sounds*	*all*	*by*

Employing all the sounds of an ocean of different melodies,

རྒྱལ་བ་ཀུན་གྱི་ཡོན་ཏན་རབ་བརྗོད་ཅིང༌།

GYAL WA	**KUN**	**GYI**	**YON TAN**	**RAB**	**JOD CHING**
jina, Buddha	*all*	*of*	*good qualities*	*fully*	*expressing, saying*

By fully proclaiming the good qualities of all the Buddhas,

བདེ་བར་གཤེགས་པ་ཐམས་ཅད་བདག་གིས་བསྟོད།

DE WAR SHEG PA	**THAM CHE**	**DAG**	**GI**	**TOD**
sugatas, happily gone buddhas	*all*	*me*	*by*	*praised*

I praise all the Buddhas, the Happily Gone.

With inexhaustible oceans of praise, employing all the sounds of an ocean of different melodies, by fully proclaiming the good qualities of all the Buddhas, I praise all the Buddhas, the Happily Gone.

མེ་ཏོག་དམ་པ་ཕྲེང་བ་དམ་པ་དང་།

ME TOG	DAM PA	TRENG WA	DAM PA	DANG
flowers	*excellent*	*garlands, necklaces etc.*	*the very best*	*and*

Splendid flowers and excellent garlands,

སིལ་སྙན་རྣམས་དང་བྱུག་པ་གདུགས་མཆོག་དང་།

SIL NYEN NAM	DANG	JUG PA	DUG	CHOG	DANG
music	*and*	*perfume*	*parasol*	*finest*	*and*

Music, perfumes, and the finest parasols,

མར་མེ་མཆོག་དང་བདུག་སྤོས་དམ་པ་ཡིས།

MAR ME	CHOG	DANG	DUG POE	DAM PA	YI
*butter lamps**	*best*	*and*	*incense*	*excellent*	*by*

*symbol of the Dharma which dispels the darkness of ignorance

Excellent lamps and the best incense, with these

རྒྱལ་བ་དེ་དག་ལ་ནི་མཆོད་པར་བགྱི།

GYAL WA	DE DAG	LA NI	CHOD PAR GYI
jina, buddha	*these*	*to*	*offer, make offering*

I make offerings to these Buddhas.

Splendid flowers and excellent garlands; music, perfumes and the finest parasols; excellent lamps and the best incense, with these I make offerings to these Buddhas.

ན་བཟའ་དམ་པ་རྣམས་དང་དྲི་མཆོག་དང་།

NAB ZA	DAM PA	NAM	DANG	DRI	CHOG	DANG
clothes, garments	*excellent*	*(plural)*	*and*	*scent*	*excellent, finest*	*and*

Excellent garments and the finest scent, and

ཕྱེ་མ་ཕུར་མ་རི་རབ་མཉམ་པ་དང་།

CHE MA	PHUR MA	RI RAB	NYAM PA	DANG
pieces of cloth	*pleated, folded cloth*	*Mt Meru**	*equalling*	*and*

*the vast mountain at the centre of the world

Pieces of cloth and folded cloth equalling Mt Meru –

བཀོད་པ་ཁྱད་པར་འཕགས་པའི་མཆོག་ཀུན་གྱིས།

KON PA	KHYE PAR	PHAG PAI	CHOG	KUN	GYI
display, set up	*special*	*noble, distinguished*	*excellent*	*all*	*by*

With all that is excellent and exquisite perfectly arranged

རྒྱལ་བ་དེ་དག་ལ་ནི་མཆོད་པར་བགྱི།

GYAL WA	**DE DAG**	**LA NI**	**CHOD PAR GYI**
jina, buddha	*these*	*to*	*make offerings*

I make offerings to these Buddhas.

Excellent garments and the finest scent; and pieces of cloth and folded cloth equalling Mt Meru – with all that is excellent and exquisite perfectly arranged, I make offerings to these Buddhas.

OFFERING THE MANDALA

ཨོཾ་བཛྲ་བྷཱུ་མི་ཨཱཿཧཱུྃཿ

OM	**BENZA**	**BHUMI**	**A HUNG**
five wisdoms	*vajra, indestructible*	*ground, foundation*	*sunyata, emptiness*

Five wisdoms. The indestructible foundation is not a graspable entity.

གཞི་ཡོངས་སུ་དག་པ་དབང་ཆེན་གསེར་གྱི་ས་གཞི།

ZHI	**YONG SU**	**DAG PA**	**WANG CHEN**	**SER**	**GYI**	**SA ZHI**
foundation, basis	*vast completely*	*pure*	*very strong (nothing can pass through it)*	*golden*		*ground, foundation*

(This vast flat ground lies beneath all the oceans and land masses of the world. It survives the destruction of the world at the end of the aeon. Try to clearly imagine it and all the following items.)

The golden foundation of the earth is of great strength and completely pure.

ཨོཾ་བཛྲ་རེ་ཁེ་ཨཱཿཧཱུྃ།

OM	**BENZA**	**RE KHE**	**A HUNG**
five wisdoms	*vajra, indestructible*	*outer wall that keeps everything inside*	*its nature is empty of inherent existence*

Five wisdoms. The indestructible outer wall is inherently empty.

ཕྱི་ལྕགས་རི་ཁོར་ཡུག་གི་རྭ་བས་

CHI	**CHAG RI**	**KHOR YUG**	**GI**	**RI WAE**
outer	*iron mountain*	*circumference, periphery marker*	*of*	*wall*

The outer periphery is completely surrounded

ཡོངས་སུ་བསྐོར་བའི་དབུས་སུ།

YONG SU	**KOR WAI**	**WU SU**
completely	*surrounding*	*in the centre of*

(there is a double ring of iron mountains which keeps everything inside)

By a wall of iron mountains and in the centre

ཧཱུྃ་རི་ཡི་རྒྱལ་པོ་རི་རབ།

HUNG **RI YI** **GYAL PO** **RI RAB**
five wisdoms *mountains* *king* *Mt Meru*
(the bija of Mt Meru)

The syllable Hung manifests Mt Meru, the king of mountains.

ཤར་ལུས་འཕགས་པོ།

SHA **LU PHAG PO**
east *Purvavideha (large healthy body)*

In the east is Purvavideha.

ལྷོ་འཛམ་བུ་གླིང་།

LHO **DZAM BU LING**
south *Jambudvipa ('the island of the Jambu tree')*

In the south is Jamudvipa,

ནུབ་བ་གླང་སྤྱོད།

NUB **BA LANG CHOD**
west *Godaniya ('having many cattle')*

In the west is Godaniya.

བྱང་སྒྲ་མི་སྙན།

JANG **DRA MI NYAM**
north *Uttarakuru ('unpleasant sound' people there have rough voices)*

In the north is Uttarakuru.

[The above are the four large continents]

ལུས་དང་ལུས་འཕགས།

LU **DANG** **LU PHAG**
Deha *and* *Viideha*
(flanking Lhuphagpo in the east)

Then comes Lhu and Lhupag,

རྔ་ཡབ་དང་རྔ་ཡབ་གཞན།

NGA YAB **DANG** **NGA YAB ZHAN**
Camara *and* *Aparacamara*
(flanking Dzambuling in the south)

Ngayab and Ngayabzhan.

གཡོ་ལྡན་དང་ལམ་མཆོག་འགྲོ།

YO DEN **DANG** **LAM CHOG DRO**
Shatha *and* *Uttaramantrina*
(flanking Balangchod in the west)

Yoden and Lamchogdro, and

སྒྲ་མི་སྙན་དང་སྒྲ་མི་སྙན་གྱི་ཟླ།

DRA MI NYEN **DANG** **DRA NI NYEN GYI DA**
Kurava *and* *Kaurava*
(flanking Draminyen in the north)

Draminyen and Draminyengyida.

[The above are the eight lesser continents.]

རིན་པོ་ཆེའི་རི་བོ།

RIN PO CHE **RI WO**
precious *mountain*
(made of jewels)

Here is the precious mountain,

དཔག་བསམ་གྱི་ཤིང་།

PAG SAM **GYI** **SHING**
many wishes *of* *tree*
(it fulfils all wishes)

the wish-granting tree,

འདོད་འཇོའི་བ། མ་རྨོས་པའི་ལོ་ཏོག།

DOD	JO	BA	MA	MO PAI	LO TOG
desires, likes	*always giving milk*	*cow*	*not*	*cultivating*	*harvest*
			(no effort required)		

The cow which gives milk at all times, the spontaneously bountiful harvest

འཁོར་ལོ་རིན་པོ་ཆེ། ནོར་བུ་རིན་པོ་ཆེ། བཙུན་མོ་རིན་པོ་ཆེ།

KHOR LO	RIN PO CHE	NOR BU	RIN PO CHE	TSUN MO	RIN PO CHE
wheel	*precious*	*jewel*	*precious*	*queen*	*precious*

Here is the precious wheel, the precious gem, the precious queen,

བློན་པོ་རིན་པོ་ཆེ། གླང་པོ་རིན་པོ་ཆེ། རྟ་མཆོག་རིན་པོ་ཆེ།

LON PO	RIN PO CHE	LANG PO	RIN PO CHE	TAM CHOG	RIN PO CHE
minister	*precious*	*elephant*	*precious*	*horse*	*precious*

The precious minister, the precious elephant, the precious horse,

དམག་དཔོན་རིན་པོ་ཆེ། གཏེར་ཆེན་པོ་ཡི་བུམ་པ།

MAG PON	RIN PO CHE	TER	CHEN PO	YI	BUM PA
general, field marshal	*precious*	*treasures*	*great*	*of*	*pot, urn*

[the seven symbols of the universal monarch]

The precious general, and the vessel of great treasures.

སྒེག་མོ་མ། ཕྲེང་བ་མ། གླུ་མ། གར་མ། མེ་ཏོག་མ།

GEG MO	MA	TRENG WA	MA	LU MA	GAR MA	ME TOG MA
beautiful	*lady*	*garland*	*lady*	*song lady*	*dance lady*	*flowers lady*
(Lasya)		*(Mala)*		*(Gita)*	*(Nrita)*	*(Puspa)*

Here is the mistress of charm, the mistress of garlands, the mistress of songs, the mistress of dance, the mistress of flowers,

བདུག་སྤོས་མ། སྣང་གསལ་མ། དྲི་ཆབ་མ།

DUG PO	MA	NANG SAL	MA	DRI CHAB	MA
incense	*lady*	*lamps, illumination*	*lady*	*scented water, perfume*	*lady*
(Dhupa)		*(Dipa)*		*(Gandha)*	

[the eight offering ladies who please the senses]

The mistress of scents, the mistress of lamps, and the mistress of perfumes.

ཉི་མ། ཟླ་བ། རིན་པོ་ཆེའི་གདུགས།

NYI MA	DA WA	RIN PO CHEI	DUG
sun	*moon*	*precious, jewelled*	*parasol*

Here are the sun and moon, the jewelled parasol,

ཕྱོགས་ལས་རྣམ་པར་རྒྱལ་བའི་རྒྱལ་མཚན།

CHOG	**LAE**	**NAM PAR**	**GYAL WAI**	**GYAL TSHAN**
directions	*in, from*	*completely*	*victorious, triumphant*	*victory banner*

The victory banner which is completely triumphant in every direction.

The five wisdoms. The indestructible foundation is not a graspable entity. The golden foundation of the earth is of great strength and completely pure.

The five wisdoms. The indestructible outer wall is inherently empty. The outer periphery is completely surrounded by a wall of iron mountains, and in the centre the syllable Hung manifests Mt Meru, the king of mountains.

In the east is Luphagpo. In the south is Dzambuling. In the west is Blangchod. In the north is Draminyan. (Then come) Lu and Luphag, Ngayab and Ngayabzhan, Yoden and Lamchogdro, Draminyan and Draminyangyida.

Here is the precious jewel-like mountain, the wish-granting tree, the cow which gives milk at all times, and the spontaneously bountiful harvest.

Here is the precious wheel, the precious gem, the precious queen, the precious minister, the precious elephant, the precious horse, the precious general, and the vessel of great treasures.

Here is the mistress of charm, the mistress of garlands, the mistress of songs, the mistress of dance, the mistress of flowers, the mistress of scents, the mistress of lamps, and the mistress of perfumes.

Here is the sun and the moon, the jewelled parasol, and the victory banner which is completely triumphant in every direction.

དབུས་སུ་ལྷ་དང་མིའི་དཔལ་འབྱོར་ཕུན་སུམ་ཚོགས་པ་

WU	**SU**	**LHA**	**DANG**	**MII**	**PAL JOR**	**PHUN SUM TSHOG PA**
middle, midst	*in*	*gods'*	*and*	*men's*	*wealth*	*good things, all that brings joy*

In the midst of this is all the wealth and pleasures of gods and men

གང་ཡང་མ་ཚང་བ་མེད་པ་ཚང་ཞིང་ཡིད་དུ་འོང་བ་

GANG YANG	**MA**	**TSHANG WA**	**ME PA**	**TSHANG ZHING**	**YID DU ONG WA**
whatever, something	*not*	*full*	*without, not*	*fully*	*fascinating, attractive*

With nothing whatsoever withheld, all the most fascinating things,

དང་བཅས་པ་དངོས་སུ་འབྱོར་བ་དང་།

DANG CHE PA NGO SU JOR WA DANG
and so on actual gathered and
Both my actual possessions and

ཡིད་ཀྱིས་རྣམ་པར་སྤྲུལ་པ་ལས་ཀུན་ཏུ་བཟང་པོའི་

YID KYI NAM PAR TRUL PA LAE KUN TU ZANG POI
mind by fully emanating from Bodhisattva Samantabhadra
(according to his offering system as in the aspiration this mandala offering is embedded in)
Whatever I imagine and create in my mind in the manner of Kuntuzangpo

མཆོད་སྤྲིན་ལྟ་བུར་མཛེས་པར་ཁྱབ་ཅིང་

CHOD TRIN TA BUR DZE PAR KHYAB CHING
offering cloud (i.e. vast) like, as beautiful pervading, vast
Like clouds of offerings which are beautiful and vast,

བཀྲམ་པའི་ཞིང་ཁམས་རབ་འབྱམས་ཡོངས་སུ་བཀོད་པ་འདི་ཉིད།

TRAM PAI ZHING KHAM RAB JAM YONG SU KOD PA DI NYID
arranged realms vast fully set up, construct this
(It comprises everything in the entire universe)
Perfectly designed as an infinitely vast and well-proportioned celestial realm.

In the midst of this is all the wealth and pleasures of gods and men with nothing whatsoever withheld, all the most fascinating things, both my actual possessions and whatever I imagine and create in my mind in the manner of Kuntuzangpo like clouds of offerings which are beautiful and vast, perfectly designed as an infinitely vast and well-proportioned celestial realm.

ས་གཞི་སྤོས་ཆུས་བྱུགས་ཤིང་མེ་ཏོག་བཀྲམ།

SA ZHI POE CHU JUG SHING ME TOG TRAM
the foundation of the earth perfumed water anointing flowers scatter, pattern
Anointing the foundation of the world with perfumed water, we pattern it with flowers, and

རི་རབ་གླིང་བཞི་ཉི་ཟླས་བརྒྱན་པ་འདི།

RI RAB LING ZHI NYI DA GYEN PA DI
Mt Meru the 4 continents sun moon adorn, ornament this
Adorn it with Mt Meru, the four continents and the sun and moon.

སངས་རྒྱས་ཞིང་དུ་དམིགས་ཏེ་ཕུལ་བ་ཡིས།

SANG GYE	ZHING	DU	MIG	TE	PHUL WA	YI
buddhas	*realm*	*to*	*imagine*	*then, thus*	*offer it there*	*by this*

Imagining the Buddha's realm we offer it there –

འགྲོ་ཀུན་རྣམ་དག་ཞིང་ལ་སྤྱོད་པར་ཤོག།

DRO	KUN	NAM DAG	ZHING	LA	CHOD PAR	SHOG
beings	*all*	*completely pure (enlightenment, dharmakaya)*	*realm*	*to*	*use, get*	*they must*

By this all beings must gain the completely pure realm.

Anointing the foundation of the world with perfumed water, we pattern it with flowers and adorn it with Mt Meru, the four continents and the sun and moon. Imagining the Buddha's realm we offer it there – by this all beings must gain the completely pure realm.

མཉེས་ཕྱིར་མཎྜལ་བཟང་པོ་འདི་ཕུལ་བས།

NYE	CHIR	MAN DAL	ZANG PO	DI	PHUL WAE
gladden	*for the sake of*	*mandala*	*good*	*this*	*by offering*

By offering this excellent mandala which brings joy,

བྱང་ཆུབ་ལམ་ལ་བར་ཆད་མི་འབྱུང་ཞིང་།

JANG CHUB	LAM	LA	BAR CHAD	MI JUNG	ZHING
enlightenment	*path*	*on*	*obstacles*	*not*	*arising*

With no obstacles arising on the path to enlightenment,

དུས་གསུམ་རྒྱལ་བའི་དགོངས་རྟོགས་པ་དང་།

DU	SUM	GYAL WAI	GONG	TOG PA	DANG
times	*three*	*Jinas', Buddhas'*	*inclusivity*	*awaken to*	*and*

May we awaken to the inclusivity of the Buddhas of the three time and,

སྲིད་པར་མི་འཁྲུལ་ཞི་བར་མི་གནས་པར།

SI PAR	MI	THRUL	ZHI BAR	MI	NAE PAR
in samsara	*not*	*confused*	*peace, nirvana of the Arhats*	*not*	*settle down*

Without being confused in samsara's becoming and without settling down in nirvana's limiting tranquillity,

ནམ་མཁའ་དང་མཉམ་པའི་འགྲོ་རྣམས་སྒྲོལ་བར་ཤོག།

NAM KHA	DANG	NYAM PAI	DRO NAM	DROL WAR	SHOG
sky	*and*	*equal*	*sentient beings*	*liberate*	*must*

May all we beings whose number equals the sky be liberated!

By offering this excellent mandala which brings joy, with no obstacles arising on the path to enlightenment, may we awaken to the inclusivity of the Buddhas of the three times, and without being confused in samsara's becoming and without settling down in nirvana's limiting tranquillity, may all of us beings, whose number equals the sky, be liberated!

སྐུ་གསུམ་ཡོངས་རྫོགས་བླ་མའི་ཚོགས་རྣམས་ལ།

KU	SUM	YONG DZOG	LA MAI	TSHOG NAM	LA
body	*three**	*fully*	*gurus'*	*host*	*to*

* dharmakaya, sambhogakaya, nirmanakaya

To the host of Gurus who are fully perfect with the three aspects of buddha,

ཕྱི་ནང་གསང་གསུམ་དེ་བཞིན་ཉིད་ཀྱིས་མཆོད།

CHI	NANG	SANG	SUM	DE ZHIN NYID	KYI	CHOD
outer	*inner*	*secret*	*three*	*thusness, how it is*	*by*	*offer*

We make the outer (universe), inner (possessions and relatives) and secret (own body) offerings within thusness.

བདག་ལུས་ལོངས་སྤྱོད་སྣང་སྲིད་ཡོངས་བཞེས་ནས།

DAG	LU	LONG CHOD	NANG SI	YONG	ZHE	NAE
I	*body*	*wealth*	*all that appears*	*fully*	*accept*	*then*

Please fully accept me, my body, my wealth and everything imaginable and then

བླ་མེད་མཆོག་གི་དངོས་གྲུབ་སྩལ་དུ་གསོལ།། ||

LA ME	CHO	GI	NGO DRUB	TSAL DU	SOL
unsurpassed	*supreme*	*of*	*siddhi, attainment*	*bestow*	*please*

Bestow the most excellent, unsurpassed attainment of enlightenment.

To the host of Gurus who are fully perfect with the three aspects of buddha, we make the outer (universe), inner (possessions and relatives) and secret (own body) offerings within thusness. Please fully accept me, my body, my wealth and everything imaginable, and then bestow the most excellent, unsurpassed attainment of enlightenment.

མཆོད་པ་གང་རྣམས་བླ་མེད་རྒྱ་ཆེ་བ།

CHOD PA	GANG NAM	LA ME	GYA CHE WA
offerings	*whatever has has been offered*	*unsurpassed (in quality)*	*very vast (in quantity)*

With all these offering things, unsurpassed in quality and vast in quantity,

དེ་དག་རྒྱལ་བ་ཐམས་ཅད་ལ་ཡང་མོས།

DE DAG GYAL WA THAM CHE LA YANG MOE
these jinas, buddhas all to also happy
(the Victors are pleased with these offerings)

All those Buddhas are pleased.

བཟང་པོ་སྤྱོད་ལ་དད་པའི་སྟོབས་དག་གིས།

ZANG PO CHO LA DAE PAI TOB DAG GI
Samantabhadra's practice system to faith's strength by

By the power of faith in Samantabhadra's offering system,

རྒྱལ་བ་ཀུན་ལ་ཕྱག་འཚལ་མཆོད་པར་བགྱི།

GYAL WA KUN LA CHAG TSHAL CHOD PAR GYI
jinas all to salutation offer do

I make salutation and offerings to all the Buddhas.

With all these offering things, unsurpassed in quality and vast in quantity, all those Buddhas are pleased. By the power of faith in Samantabhadra's offering system, I make salutation and offerings to all the Buddhas.

འདོད་ཆགས་ཞེ་སྡང་གཏི་མུག་དབང་གིས་ནི།

DOD CHAG ZHE DANG TI MUG WANG GI NI
desire anger stupidity power by*

*This stupidity or obscurity arises from ignorance of the actual truth and it affects all beings in samsara no matter how intelligent they may seem.

Due to the power of desire, anger and stupidity,

ལུས་དང་ངག་དང་དེ་བཞིན་ཡིད་ཀྱིས་ཀྱང་།

LU DANG NGAG DANG DE ZHIN YID KYI KYANG
body and speech and likewise similarly mind by also

By body and speech, and likewise by mind

སྡིག་པ་བདག་གིས་བགྱིས་པ་ཅི་མཆིས་པ།

DIG PA DAG GI GYI PA CHI CHII PA
sin,error me by done whatever I did

I have done sin. Whatever sins I have done,

དེ་དག་ཐམས་ཅད་བདག་གིས་སོ་སོར་བཤགས།

DE DAG THAM CHE DAG GI SO SOR SHAG
these all I, me by each confess and beg forgiveness

All and each of them I now confess and beg to be excused.

Whatever sins of body, speech and mind I have done due to the power of desire, anger and stupidity, each and all of them I now confess and beg to be excused.

ཕྱོགས་བཅུའི་རྒྱལ་བ་ཀུན་དང་སངས་རྒྱས་སྲས།

CHOG CHUI — GYAL WA — KUN — DANG — SANG GYE SAE
ten directions (everywhere) — jinas, victors — all — and — buddha's sons, bodhisattvas

All the Buddhas and Bodhisattvas of the ten directions,

རང་རྒྱལ་རྣམས་དང་སློབ་དང་མི་སློབ་དང་།

RANG GYAL NAM — DANG — LOB — DANG — MI LOB — DANG
pratekabuddhas — and — saiksa# — and — asaiksa + — and*

* pratekabuddhas and 'self victorious' Buddhas who practised in order to free themselves from suffering and who, on gaining that goal, just enjoy it by themselves without helping others.

'students', those practising the Dharma up till the 4th Way (Marga) and 9th Stage (Bhumi). They still require a teacher.

+ 'graduates' or 'non-students' are those who have reached the 5th Way and 10th Stage. They will now progress easily without danger of confusion or of falling back, and so do not require a teacher.

The Pratekabuddhas, Saiksas, and Asaiksas, and

འགྲོ་བ་ཀུན་གྱི་བསོད་ནམས་གང་ལ་ཡང་།

DRO WA — KUN — GYI — SO NAM — GANG LA YANG
beings — all — of — merit, virtues — whatever they have*

*the positive results of good deeds

All beings in samsara – at all the merit they have gathered whatsoever

དེ་དག་ཀུན་གྱི་རྗེས་སུ་བདག་ཡི་རང་།

DE DAG — KUN — GYI — JE SU — DAG — YI RANG
these — all — of — after — I — feel, have
(I am not jealous of their virtue and happiness)

I feel happy and joyful.

All the Buddhas and the Bodhisattvas in the ten directions, the Pratekabuddhas, Saiksas, and Asaiksas, and all beings in samsara – at all the merit they have gathered whatsoever I feel happy and joyful.

གང་རྣམས་ཕྱོགས་བཅུའི་འཇིག་རྟེན་སྒྲོན་མ་རྣམས།

GANG NAM — CHOG — CHUI — JIG TEN — DRON MA NAM
however many there are — directions (i.e. everywhere) — ten — world — lamps (i.e. buddhas)

Lamps of the world, however may there are in the ten directions, and

བྱང་ཆུབ་རིམ་པར་སངས་རྒྱས་མ་ཆགས་བརྙེས།

JANG CHUB	**RIM PAR**	**SANG GYE**	**MA CHAG**	**NYE**
enlightenment	*stages*	*buddhahood*	*free of desire*	*getting*

Those on the stages leading to enlightenment, those gaining buddhahood free of desire-

མགོན་པོ་དེ་དག་བདག་གིས་ཐམས་ཅད་ལ།

GON PO	**DE DAG**	**GI**	**THAM CHE**	**LA**
protectors, benefactors	*these*	*by*	*all*	*to*

I beseech all you protectors

འཁོར་ལོ་བླ་ན་མེད་པ་བསྐོར་བར་བསྐུལ།

KHOR LO	**LA NA ME PA**	**KOR WAR**	**KUL**
dharmachakra wheel of dharma	*unsurpassed (i.e. teach the mahayana doctrines)*	*turn*	*request, beseech, encourage*

To turn the unsurpassed dharmachakra.

Lamps of the world, however many you are in the ten directions, and those of you on the stages leading to enlightenment, and those of you gaining buddhahood free of desire – I beseech all of you protectors to turn the unsurpassed wheel of dharma.

མྱ་ངན་འདའ་སྟོན་གང་བཞེད་དེ་དག་ལ།

NYA NGAN DA	**TON**	**GANG**	**ZHE**	**DE DAG**	**LA**
pass from sorrow, die, enter nirvana	*showing*	*whoever*	*like to*	*them*	*to*

All you Buddhas who wish to show the passing away of your forms,

འགྲོ་བ་ཀུན་ལ་ཕན་ཞིང་བདེ་བའི་ཕྱིར།

DRO WA	**KUN**	**LA**	**PHEN ZHING**	**DE WAI**	**CHIR**
beings	*all*	*to*	*benefiting*	*happiness*	*in order to*

In order to benefit all beings and make them happy,

བསྐལ་པ་ཞིང་གི་རྡུལ་སྙེད་བཞུགས་པར་ཡང་།

KAL PA	**ZHING GI**	**DUL**	**NYED**	**ZHUG PAR**	**YANG**
aeons, kalpas	*realms, worlds*	*dust*	*as many as*	*stay*	*thus*

Please stay for as many kalpas as there are particles of dust in the universe.

བདག་གིས་ཐལ་མོ་རབ་སྦྱར་གསོལ་བར་བགྱི།

DAG	**GI**	**THAL MO RAB JAR**	**SOL WAR**	**GYI**
I	*by*	*with hands held in prayer (i.e. very sincerely)*	*pray*	*do*

With hands held in prayer I request this of you.

In order to benefit all beings and make us happy, may all you Buddhas who wish to show the passing away of your forms, please stay for as many kalpas as there are particles of dust in the universe. With hands held in prayer I request this of you.

ཕྱག་འཚལ་བ་དང་མཆོད་ཅིང་བཤགས་པ་དང་།

CHAG TSHAL WA	DANG	CHO CHING	SHAG PA	DANG
salutation	*and*	*offerings*	*confession*	*and*

By salutations, offerings, and confession, and

རྗེས་སུ་ཡི་རང་བསྐུལ་ཞིང་གསོལ་བ་ཡི།

JE SU YI RANG	KUL ZHING	SOL WA YI
rejoicing at the merit of others	*requesting dharma teaching*	*praying, requesting the buddhas to stay*

By rejoicing at the merit of others, beseeching Dharma teaching, and requesting the Buddhas not to die –

དགེ་བ་ཅུང་ཟད་བདག་གིས་ཅི་བསགས་པ།

GE WA	CHUNG ZAD	DAG	GI	CHI	SAG PA
virtue	*small amount*	*me*	*by*	*whatever*	*collected*

Whatever small amount of virtue I have collected,

ཐམས་ཅད་བདག་གིས་བྱང་ཆུབ་ཕྱིར་བསྔོའོ།། །།

THAM CHE	DAG	GI	JANG CHUB	CHIR	NGO O
all	*me*	*by*	*enlightenment (for all beings)*	*for the sake of*	*dedicate*

I dedicate it all for the enlightenment of all beings.

By salutations, offerings, and confession, and by rejoicing at the merit of others, beseeching Dharma teaching, and requesting the Buddhas not to die – whatever small amount of virtue I have collected, I dedicate it all for the enlightenment of all beings.

འཇམ་དཔལ་དཔའ་བོས་ཇི་ལྟར་མཁྱེན་པ་དང་།

JAM PAL	PA WOE	JI TAR	KHYEN PA	DANG
Manjushri	*hero //by*	*like what*	*you know*	*and*

As much as is known by Manjushri the hero, and

ཀུན་ཏུ་བཟང་པོ་དེ་ཡང་དེ་བཞིན་ཏེ།

KUN TU ZANG PO	DE YANG	DE ZHIN	TE
Samantabhadra	*he also*	*like that*	*thus*

Is known by Samantabhadra,

དེ་དག་ཀུན་གྱི་རྗེས་སུ་བདག་སློབ་ཕྱིར།

DE DAG	**KUN**	**GYI**	**JE SU**	**DAG**	**LOB**	**CHIR**
that	*all*	*of*	*after*	*I*	*study and practice (present and future)*	*therefore*

I will follow the same in study and practice and

དགེ་བ་འདི་དག་ཐམས་ཅད་རབ་ཏུ་བསྔོ།། །།

GE WA	**DI DAG**	**THAM CHE**	**RAB TU**	**NGO**
virtue	*this*	*all (give all of it to others)*	*fully*	*dedicate*

Dedicate the virtue arising from this to all beings.

As much as is known by Manjushri the hero, and is known by Samantabhadra, I will follow the same in study and practice and dedicate the virtue arising from this to all beings.

སྤྱོད་འཇུག་ལེའུ་གཉིས་པ་ལས།

Honouring True Value
from
Chapter 2 of Entering the Path of Enlightenment

by
Shantideva

ACCUMULATING MERIT

རིན་ཆེན་སེམས་དེ་གཟུང་བར་བྱ་བའི་ཕྱིར།

RIN CHEN	**SEM**	**DE**	**ZUNG WAR**	**JA WAI**	**CHIR**
precious, jewel	*mind**	*that*	*grasp, not let it slip away*	*do*	*in order to*

*bodhicitta, mind focussed on enlightenment

In order to grasp this precious mind,

དེ་བཞིན་གཤེགས་པ་རྣམས་དང་དམ་པའི་ཆོས།

DE ZHIN SHEG PA	**NAM**	**DANG**	**DAM PAI**	**CHO**
buddha, tathagata, 'gone or come to thusness'	*plural*	*and*	*sacred, true*	*dharma*

To the Tathagatas and to the sacred Dharma,

དཀོན་མཆོག་དྲི་མ་མེད་དང་སངས་རྒྱས་སྲས།

KON CHOG	**DRI MA ME**	**DANG**	**SANG GYE SAE**
rare,best	*stainless*	*and*	*Buddha's sons, Bodhisattvas*

That stainless jewel, and to the offspring of the Buddha,

ཡོན་ཏན་རྒྱ་མཚོ་རྣམས་ལ་ལེགས་པར་མཆོད།

YON TEN	**GYA TSHO**	**NAM**	**LA**	**LEG PAR**	**CHOD**
good	*ocean*	*plural*	*to*	*nicely*	*offer*

Those oceans of good qualities, I sweetly offer:

In order to grasp this precious mind, to the Tathagatas and to the sacred Dharma that stainless jewel, and to the offspring of the Buddha those oceans of good qualities, I sweetly offer:

PRESENTING OFFERINGS

མེ་ཏོག་འབྲས་བུ་ཇི་སྙེད་ཡོད་པ་དང་།

ME TOG	DRAE BU	JI NYE YOE PA	DANG
flowers	*fruit*	*as many as I have and can be found in the world*	*and*

As many flowers and fruits as there are, and

སྨན་གྱི་རྣམ་པ་གང་དག་ཡོད་པ་དང་།

MEN	GYI	NAM PA	GANG DAG	YOE PA	DANG
medicines	*of*	*different types*	*whatever*	*there is, exists*	*and*

All the kinds of medicines that there are, and

འཇིག་རྟེན་རིན་ཆེན་ཇི་སྙེད་ཡོད་པ་དང་།

JIG TEN	RIN CHEN	JI NYE YOE PA	DANG
world	*jewels*	*as many as there are*	*and*

Whatever jewels there are in the world, and

ཆུ་གཙང་ཡིད་དུ་འོང་བ་ཅི་ཡོད་དང་།

CHU	TSANG	YID DU ONG WA	CHI YOD	DANG
water	*pure*	*beautiful*	*whatever there is*	*and*

Whatever pure and pleasing water there is; and

As many flowers and fruits as there are, and all the kinds of medicines that there are, and whatever jewels there are in the world, and whatever pure and pleasing water there is; and

རིན་ཆེན་རི་རབ་དང་ནི་དེ་བཞིན་དུ།

RIN CHEN	RI RAB	DANG NI	DE ZHIN DU
jewelled	*mountain*	*and*	*like that*

Jewelled mountains and similarly

ནགས་ཚལ་ས་ཕྱོགས་དབེན་ཞིང་ཉམས་དགའ་དང་།

NAG TSHAL	SA CHOG	WEN	ZHING	NYAM GA	DANG
forest	*place*	*quiet*	*place*	*happy feeling*	*and*

Forest groves, quiet and joyous, and

ལྗོན་ཤིང་མེ་ཏོག་རྒྱན་སྤྲས་སྤུད་པ་དང་།

JON SHING	ME TOG	GYAN TRAE	PUD PA	DANG
creeper	*flower*	*adorned with*	*decorated*	*and*

Creepers bedecked with adorning flowers, and

ཤིང་གང་འབྲས་བཟང་ཡལ་ག་དུད་པ་དང་།

SHING	GANG	DRAE	ZANG	YAL GA	DUD PA	DANG
trees	*many kinds*	*fruit*	*good*	*branches*	*bending*	*and*

Trees whose branches bow down with good fruit; and

Jewelled mountains and similarly forest groves, quiet and joyous, and creepers bedecked with adorning flowers, and trees whose branches bow down with good fruit; and

ལྷ་སོགས་འཇིག་རྟེན་ན་ཡང་དྲི་དང་ནི།

LHA	SOG	JIG TEN	NA YANG	DRI	DANG	NI
gods	*and so on*	*worlds*	*also*	*scent*	*and*	

Fragrances of the celestial and other realms, and

སྤོས་དང་དཔག་བསམ་ཤིང་དང་རིན་ཆེན་ཤིང་།

PO	DANG	PAG SAM SHING	DANG	RIN CHEN	SHING
incense	*and*	*wish-fulfilling trees*	*and*	*jewels*	*trees*

Incense, wish-fulfilling trees, and trees of jewels,

མ་རྨོས་འཁྲུངས་པའི་ལོ་ཏོག་རྣམ་པ་དང་།

MA MO	TRUNG PAI	LO TOG	NAM PA	DANG
without cultivation	*arising*	*harvest*	*kind*	*and*

Harvests appearing without having to be cultivated and

གཞན་ཡང་མཆོད་པར་འོས་པའི་རྒྱན་རྣམས་ནི།

ZHAN YANG	CHO PA	O PAI	GYEN	NAM	NI
other things also	*offering*	*worthy*	*ornament*	*plural*	

Everything else worthy of offering as ornaments; and

Fragrances of the celestial and other realms, and incense, wish-fulfilling trees, and trees of jewels, harvests appearing without cultivation and everything else worthy of offering as ornaments; and

མཚོ་དང་རྫིང་བུ་པདྨས་བརྒྱན་པ་དག།

TSHO	DANG	DZING BU	PAD MAE	GYEN PA DAG
lakes	*and*	*pond*	*lotus*	*adorned*

Lakes and ponds adorned with lotuses, and

ངང་པ་ཤིན་ཏུ་སྐད་སྙན་ཡིད་འོང་ལྡན།

NGANG PA	SHIN TU	KAE NYEN	YID ONG	DEN
ducks	*very*	*sweet sound*	*attractive*	*having*

The wonderfully pleasing cry of wild geese, and,

ནམ་མཁའ་རབ་འབྱམས་ཁམས་ཀྱིས་མཐས་གཏུགས་པ།

NAM KHA RAB JAM KHAM KYI THAE TUG PA
space infinite realm of reach the limit, touch the end of
Reaching to the very limit of the infinitely vast realm of the sky,

ཡོངས་སུ་བཟུང་བ་མེད་པ་དེ་དག་ཀུན།

YONG SU ZANG WA ME PA DE DAG KUN
completely owning without these all
All such gifts which belong to no one:

Lakes and ponds adorned with lotuses, and the wonderfully pleasing cry of wild geese, and all such gifts which belong to no one, reaching to the very limit of the infinitely vast realm of the sky:

REQUESTING ACCEPTANCE

བློ་ཡིས་བླངས་ནས་ཐུབ་པ་སྐྱེས་ཀྱི་མཆོག།

LO YI LANG NAE THUB PA KYE KYI CHO
mind by take up then buddha being of excellent
Imagining all these, I offer them to the Buddhas, the most excellent of beings,

སྲས་དང་བཅས་པ་རྣམས་ལ་ལེགས་འབུལ་ན།

SAE DANG CHE PA NAM LA LEG BUL NA
sons and those plural to goodly offer
Together with their offspring, the Bodhisattvas.

ཡོན་གནས་དམ་པ་ཐུགས་རྗེ་ཆེ་རྣམས་ཀྱིས།

YON NAE DAM PA THUG JE CHE NAM KYI
qualities place holy compassionate great plural by
May these compassionate ones, the excellent sites of good qualities,

བདག་ལ་བརྩེར་དགོངས་བདག་གི་འདི་དག་བཞེས།

DAG LA TSER GONG DAG GI DI DAG ZHE
me to compassion, kindness think of mine these please accept
Think kindly of me and accept my offerings.

Imagining all these, I offer them to the Buddhas, the most excellent of beings, together with their offspring, the Bodhisattvas. May these compassionate ones, the excellent sites of good qualities, think kindly of me and accept my offerings.

བདག་ནི་བསོད་ནམས་མི་ལྡན་བཀྲེན་ཆེན་ཏེ།

DAG NI SO NAM MI DEN TREN CHEN TE
I merit without, poor very thus
I am without merit and quite destitute, and

མཆོད་པའི་ནོར་གཞན་བདག་ལ་ཅང་མ་མཆིས།

CHOD PAI NOR ZHAN DAG LA CHANG MA CHI
offering wealth other I anything not have
Have no other wealth to offer.

དེས་ན་གཞན་དོན་དགོངས་པའི་མགོན་གྱིས་འདི།

DE NA ZHAN DON GONG PAI GON GYI DI
therefore other benefit consider benefactor by these
Therefore, benefactors, you who think of the welfare of others,

བདག་གི་དོན་སླད་ཉིད་ཀྱི་མཐུས་བཞེས་ཤིག།

DAG GI DON LAE NYI KYI THU ZHE SHIG
my benefit for the sake of power accept please!
(By the power of your wish to help me please accept this offering which you have no need of.)
Please accept these offerings for my sake.

I am without merit and quite destitute, and have no other wealth to offer. Therefore, benefactors, you who think of the welfare of others, please accept these offerings for my sake.

OFFERING ONESELF

རྒྱལ་དང་དེ་སྲས་རྣམས་ལ་བདག་གིས་ནི།

GYAL DANG DE SAE NAM LA DAG GI NI
buddhas, victors and their sons plural to me by
To the Victors and their offspring, I offer

བདག་གི་ལུས་ཀུན་གཏན་དུ་དབུལ་བར་བགྱི།

DAG GI LU KUN TEN DU BUL WAR GYI
my body all completely, forever I offer*
* my body in this life and in all my future lives
All my bodies, completely and forever.

སེམས་དཔའ་མཆོག་རྣམས་བདག་ནི་ཡོངས་བཞེས་ཤིག།

SEM PA CHOG NAM DAG NI YONG ZHE SHIG
heroic beings most excellent plural me fully, completely please accept
Most excellent heroic beings, please accept me fully!

གུས་པས་ཁྱེད་ཀྱི་འབངས་སུ་མཆི་བར་བགྱི།

GU PAE	**KHYE KYI**	**BANG**	**SU**	**CHI WAR GYI**
devotedly	*your*	*subject, servant*	*as*	*become*

I shall be your devoted servant.

To the Victors and their offspring, I offer all my bodies, completely and forever. Most excellent heroic beings, please accept me fully! I shall be your devoted servant.

BENEFITS OF THEIR CARE

བདག་ནི་ཁྱེད་ཀྱིས་ཡོངས་སུ་བཟུང་བས་ན།

DAG NI	**KHYE KYI**	**YONG SU**	**ZUNG**	**WAE NA**
me	*your*	*completely*	*hold*	*by*

Through being completely under your care,

སྲིད་ན་མི་འཇིགས་སེམས་ཅན་ཕན་པར་བགྱི།

SI	**NA**	**MI JIG**	**SEM CHEN**	**PHEN PAR**	**GYI**
samsara, becoming	*if*	*without fear*	*beings*	*benefit*	*do*

I become freed from fear of phenomenal existence and can act for the benefit of beings.

སྔོན་གྱི་སྡིག་ལས་ཡང་དག་འདའ་བགྱིད་ཅིང་།

NGON GYI	**DIG**	**LAE**	**YANG DAG**	**DA GYI CHING**
former	*sins*	*from*	*completely*	*passing beyond*

I turn away completely from my former unwholesome behaviour.

སྡིག་པ་གཞན་ཡང་སླན་ཆད་མི་བགྱིད་དོ།

DIG PA	**ZHAN YANG**	**LEN CHE**	**MI**	**GYI DO**
sins	*moreover*	*in future*	*not*	*doing*

Moreover in future I will not do anything unwholesome.

Through being completely under your care, I become freed from fear of phenomenal existence and can act for the benefit of beings. I turn away completely from my former unwholesome behaviour. Moreover in future I will not do anything unwholesome.

BATHING THEIR BODIES

ཁྲུས་ཀྱི་ཁང་པ་ཤིན་ཏུ་དྲི་ཞིམ་པ།

TRU	KYI	KHANG PA	SHIN TU	DRI	ZHIM PA
bathing	*of*	*house, building*	*very*	*smell*	*pleasing*

In exquisitely perfumed bath houses

ཤེལ་གྱི་ས་གཞི་གསལ་ཞིང་འཚེར་བ་བསྟར།

SHEL	GYI	SA ZHI	SAL ZHING	TSHER WA TAR
crystal	*of*	*floor*	*shining*	*brightly*

With brilliantly sparkling crystal floors and

རིན་ཆེན་འབར་བའི་ཀ་བ་ཡིད་འོང་ལྡན།

RIN CHEN	BAR WAI	KA WA	YID ONG	DEN
jewels	*blazing*	*pillars*	*beautiful*	*having, endowed with*

Enchanting pillars of glittering jewels and

མུ་ཏིག་འོད་ཆགས་བླ་རེ་བྲེས་པ་དེར།

MU TIG	OE CHAG	LA RE DRAE PA	DER
pearl	*bright*	*canopies*	*there*

Canopies of lustrous pearls,

In exquisitely perfumed bath houses with brilliantly sparkling crystal floors and enchanting pillars of glittering jewels and canopies of lustrous pearls,

དེ་བཞིན་གཤེགས་དང་དེ་ཡི་སྲས་རྣམས་ལ།

DE ZHIN SHEG	DANG	DE YI	SAE	NAM	LA
buddhas, tathagatas	*and*	*their*	*sons, bodhisattvas*	*plural*	*to*

Tathagatas and your offspring –

རིན་ཆེན་བུམ་པ་མང་པོ་སྤོས་ཀྱི་ཆུ།

RIN CHEN	BUM PA	MANG PO	POE KYI CHU
jewelled	*pot*	*many*	*scented water*

With many jewelled vases of scented water

ཡིད་འོང་ལེགས་པར་བཀང་བ་གླུ་དང་ནི།

YID ONG	LEG PAR	KANG WA	LU	DANG NI
beautiful	*goodly*	*full, bountiful*	*song*	*and*

That are beautiful and brimming

རོལ་མོར་བཅས་པ་དུ་མས་སྐུ་ཁྲུས་གསོལ།

ROL MOR	CHE PA	DU MAE	KU	TRU	SOL
music	*and so on*	*many*	*body*	*wash*	*I will do*

I will bathe your bodies to the accompaniment of song and music.

Tathagatas and your offspring – with many jewelled vases of scented water that are beautiful and brimming I will bathe your bodies to the accompaniment of song and music.

DRYING AND ADORNING THEIR BODIES

དེ་དག་སྐུ་ལ་མཚུངས་པ་མེད་པའི་གོས།

DE DAG	KU	LA	TSHUNG PA MED PAI	GO
their	*bodies*	*to*	*unequalled*	*cloths, towels*

I will dry your bodies with incomparable cloths

གཙང་ལ་དྲི་རབ་བསྒོས་པས་སྐུ་ཕྱིའོ།

TSANG	LA	DRI	RAB	GO PAE	KU	CHI O
pure	*and*	*perfumed*	*excellent*	*clothing*	*body*	*dry*

That are clean and exquisitely scented.

དེ་ནས་དེ་ལ་ཁ་དོག་ལེགས་བསྒྱུར་བའི།

DE NAE	DE LA	KHA DOG	LEG GYUR WAI
then	*to them*	*colours*	*suitable*

Then may I present you with suitably coloured

ན་བཟའ་ཤིན་ཏུ་དྲི་ཞིམ་དམ་པ་འབུལ།

NAB ZA	SHIN TU	DRI ZHIM	DAM PA	BUL
clothes	*very*	*sweet smelling*	*excellent*	*offer*

Superb and fragrant robes.

I will dry your bodies with incomparable cloths that are clean and exquisitely scented. Then may I present you with suitably coloured superb and fragrant robes.

ADORNING THE BODHISATTVAS

གོས་བཟང་སླབ་ལ་འཇམ་པ་སྣ་ཚོགས་དང་།

GO	ZANG	SAB	LA	JAM PA	NA TSHOG	DANG
clothes	*good*	*fine*	*to*	*soft*	*various*	*and*

With varied raiments, so soft and fine, and

རྒྱན་མཆོག་བརྒྱ་ཕྲག་དེ་དང་དེ་དག་གིས།

GYEN	CHOG	GYA TRAG	DE	DANG	DE DAG	GI
ornaments	*best*	*one hundred*	*that*	*and*	*these*	*by*

With a hundred excellent ornaments and still more,

འཕགས་པ་ཀུན་ཏུ་བཟང་དང་འཇམ་དབྱངས་དང་།

PHAG PA	KUN TU ZANG	DANG	JAM JANG	DANG
arya, pure	*Samantabhadra*	*and*	*Manjughosa*	*and*

I adorn the pure ones, Samantabhadra, Manjughosha,

འཇིག་རྟེན་དབང་ཕྱུག་སོགས་ལའང་བརྒྱན་པར་བགྱི།

JIG TEN WANG CHUG	SOG	LANG	GYEN PAR	GYI
Lokeshvara	*and so on*	*also*	*adorn*	*to do*

Avalokitesvara, and all the others.

With varied raiments, so soft and fine, and with a hundred excellent ornaments and still more, I adorn the pure ones, Samantabhadra, Manjughosha, Avalokitesvara, and all the others.

PERFUMING THEIR BODIES

སྟོང་གསུམ་ཀུན་ཏུ་དྲི་ངད་ལྡང་བ་ཡི།

TONG SUM	KUN TU	DRI NGED	DANG WA	YI
thousand million	*all*	*good smelling, perfume*	*pervade*	*of*

With fragrances which pervade the thousand million worlds

དྲི་མཆོག་རྣམས་ཀྱིས་ཐུབ་དབང་ཀུན་གྱི་སྐུ།

DRI	CHOG	NAM	KYI	THUB WANG	KUN	GYI	KU
perfumes	*best*	*all*	*by*	*sages*	*all*	*of*	*bodies*

I anoint the bodies of all the Buddhas with the most excellent of scents

གསེར་སྦྱངས་བཙོ་མ་ཇི་དོར་བྱས་པ་ལྟར།

SER	JANG	TSO MA	JI	DOR	JE PA	TAR
gold	*cleaned*	*refined*	*comparison*	*polishing*	*made*	*as*

So that, as with polishing pure refined gold,

འོད་ཆགས་འབར་བ་དེ་དག་བྱུགས་པར་བགྱི།

OE CHAG	BAR WA	DE DAG	JUG PAR	GYI
bright	*radiant*	*these*	*anoint*	*to do*

They blaze with radiant lustre.

With fragrances which pervade the thousand million worlds I anoint the bodies of all the Buddhas with the most excellent of scents so that, as with polishing pure refined gold, they blaze with radiant lustre.

OFFERING FLOWERS

ཐུབ་དབང་མཆོད་གནས་མཆོག་ལ་ཡིད་འོང་བའི།

THUB WANG	CHOD	NAE	CHOG	LA	YI ONG WAI
muni, Buddha	*offering*	*place*	*excellent*	*to*	*beautiful*

To the Buddhas, the most excellent sites of offering, I present

མེ་ཏོག་མནྡ་ར་དང་པདྨ་དང་།

ME TOG	MAN DA RA	DANG	PAD MA	DANG
flowers	*mandara, lily*	*and*	*lotus*	*and*

Beautiful flowers, mandara, lotus,

ཨུཏྤལ་ལ་སོགས་དྲི་ཞིམ་ཐམས་ཅད་དང་།

UT PAL LA	SOG	DRI ZHIM	THAM CHE	DANG
blue lotus	*and so on*	*rare fragrance*	*all*	*and*

Utpala and all the rest, each with rare fragrance and

ཕྲེང་བ་སྤེལ་ལེགས་ཡིད་འོང་རྣམས་ཀྱིས་མཆོད།

TRENG WA	PEL	LEG	YI ONG	NAM	KYI	CHO
garland	*arranged*	*well*	*beautifully*	*plural*	*with*	*offer*

Well arranged as attractive garlands.

To the Buddhas, the most excellent sites of offering, I present beautiful flowers, mandara, lotus, utpala and all the rest, each with rare fragrance and well arranged as attractive garlands.

OFFERING INCENSE AND FOOD

སྤོས་མཆོག་ཡིད་འཕྲོད་དྲི་ངད་ཁྱབ་པ་ཡི།

POE	CHOG	YID TRO	DRI NGAE	KHYAB PA YI
incense	*excellent*	*pleasing*	*subtle perfumes*	*pervasive*

Excellent incense with pervasive pleasing scent

བདུག་པའི་སྤྲིན་ཚོགས་རྣམས་ཀྱང་དེ་ལ་འབུལ།

DUG PAI	TRIN	TSHOG	NAM	KYANG	DE	LA	BUL
smoke	*clouds*	*hosts*	*all*	*also*	*these*	*to*	*offer*

Arising as great aromatic clouds I also offer to these Buddhas.

ཞལ་ཟས་བཟའ་བཏུང་སྣ་ཚོགས་བཅས་པ་ཡི།

ZHAL ZAE	**ZA**	**TUNG**	**NA TSHOG**	**CHE PA**	**YI**
food	*dry*	*liquid*	*different kinds*	*with*	*of*

With a diverse array of food and drink

ལྷ་བཤོས་རྣམས་ཀྱང་དེ་ལ་འབུལ་བར་བགྱི།

LHA	**SHO**	**NAM**	**KYANG**	**DE**	**LA**	**BUL WAR**	**GYI**
celestial	*food*	*plural*	*also*	*them*	*to*	*offer*	*to do*

I offer them celestial delicacies.

I also offer to these Buddhas excellent incense with pervasive pleasing scent arising as great aromatic clouds. With a diverse array of food and drink I offer them celestial delicacies.

OFFERING LAMPS AND BEAUTIFIED ENVIRONMENT

གསེར་གྱི་པདྨ་ཚར་དུ་དངར་བ་ཡི།

SER	**GYI**	**PAD MA**	**TSHAR**	**DU**	**NGAR WA**	**YI**
gold	*of*	*lotus*	*rows*	*in*	*arranged, put in*	*of*

On rows of golden lotuses

རིན་ཆེན་སྒྲོན་མེ་རྣམས་ཀྱང་དབུལ་བར་བགྱི།

RIN CHEN	**DRON ME**	**NAM**	**KYANG**	**BUL WAR**	**GYI**
jewelled	*lamps*	*plural*	*also*	*offer*	*do*

I offer jewelled lamps.

ས་གཞི་བསྟར་བ་སྤོས་ཀྱིས་བྱུགས་པ་དེར།

SA ZHI	**TAR WAR**	**POE**	**KYI**	**JUG PA**	**DER**
ground	*clean*	*perfume*	*with*	*anoint*	*there*

I clean the ground, sprinkle it with perfumed water and

མེ་ཏོག་ཡིད་འོང་སིལ་མ་དགྲམ་པར་བགྱི།

ME TOG	**YID ONG**	**SIL MA**	**DRAM WAR**	**GYI**
flowers	*pleasing*	*many small pieces*	*scatter*	*to do*

Scatter it with charming flower petals.

I offer jewelled lamps on rows of golden lotuses. I clean the ground, sprinkle it with perfumed water and scatter it with charming flower petals.

OFFERING PALACES

གཞལ་མེད་ཕོ་བྲང་བསྟོད་དབྱངས་ཡིད་འོང་ལྡན།

ZHAL ME	PHO DRANG	TOE	JANG	YID ONG	DEN
immeasurable	*palace*	*praise*	*melodies*	*enchanting*	*having, imbued with*

Vast palaces, filled with tender melodies of praise,

མུ་ཏིག་རིན་ཆེན་རྒྱན་འཕྱང་མཛེས་འབར་བ།

MU TIG	RIN CHEN	GYEN	CHANG	DZE	BAR WA
pearl	*jewels*	*ornaments*	*strung*	*beautiful*	*radiant*

Made bright and beautiful with strings of pearls and jewel ornaments,

དཔག་ཡས་ནམ་མཁའི་རྒྱན་གྱུར་དེ་དག་ཀྱང་།

PAG YAE	NAM KAI	GYEN	GYUR	DE DAG	KYANG
numberless	*sky's*	*ornaments*	*are*	*these*	*also*

Ornaments without number, enough to fill the sky, these also

ཐུགས་རྗེའི་རང་བཞིན་ཅན་ལ་དབུལ་བར་བགྱི།

THUG JEI	RANG ZHIN	CHEN	LA	BUL WA GYI
compassion	*nature*	*having*	*to*	*offer*

I offer to those whose nature is compassion.

Vast palaces, filled with tender melodies of praise, made bright and beautiful with strings of pearls and jewel ornaments, ornaments without number, enough to fill the sky, these I offer to those whose nature is compassion.

OFFERING PARASOLS

རིན་ཆེན་གདུགས་མཛེས་གསེར་གྱི་ཡུ་བ་ཅན།

RIN CHEN	DUG	DZE	SER GYI	YU WA	CHEN
jewelled	*parasols*	*beautiful*	*golden*	*handles*	*having*

Beautiful jewelled parasols with golden handles and

ཁོར་ཡུག་རྒྱན་གྱི་རྣམ་པར་ཡིད་འོང་བརྒྱན།

KHOR YUG	GYEN GYI NAM PAR	YID ONG	GYEN
edge	*ornamented*	*attractive*	*adorned*

Exquisite ornaments adorning the rims,

དབྱིབས་ལེགས་བལྟ་ན་སྡུག་པ་བསྒྲེང་བ་ཡང་།

YIB	LEG	TA	NA	DUG PA	DRENG WA	YANG
form	*nice*	*see*	*to*	*pleasant*	*hoisted, held up*	*also*
		(looks attractive)				

Their fine shapes so beautiful when held aloft –

རྟག་ཏུ་ཐུབ་དབང་རྣམས་ལ་དབུལ་བར་བགྱི།

TAG TU THUB WANG NAM LA BUL WA GYI
always sage, buddha plural to offer

Ceaselessly I offer them to the Buddhas.

To the Buddhas I ceaselessly offer beautiful jewelled parasols with golden handles and exquisite ornaments adorning the rims, their fine shapes so beautiful when held aloft. I offer them to the Buddhas.

OFFERING MUSIC

དེ་ལས་གཞན་ཡང་མཆོད་པའི་ཚོགས།

DE LAE ZHAN YANG CHOD PAI TSHOG
that than other also offering gathered

In addition may masses of offerings accompanied by

རོལ་མོ་དབྱངས་སྙན་ཡིད་འོང་ལྡན།

ROL MO JANG NYEN YID ONG DEN
music melodies sweet entrancing having

The music of sweet and entrancing melodies

སེམས་ཅན་སྡུག་བསྔལ་སིམ་བྱེད་པའི།

SEM CHEN DUG NGEL SIM JE PAI
beings sorrow alleviating
(In India the arrival of the monsoon clouds alleviates the suffering of the hot season.)

Alleviate the suffering of all sentient beings

སྤྲིན་རྣམས་སོ་སོར་གནས་གྱུར་ཅིག།

TRIN NAM SO SOR NAE GYUR CHIG
cloud plural each stay do

Like clouds in summer and remain wherever they are needed.

In addition may masses of offerings arise like summer clouds and, accompanied by the music of sweet and entrancing melodies, may they be present wherever they are needed to alleviate the sufferings of all sentient beings.

OFFERING TO THE SACRED SYMBOLS

དམ་ཆོས་དཀོན་མཆོག་ཐམས་ཅད་དང་།

DAM CHO KON CHOG THAM CHE DANG
sacred dharma jewel all and

Upon the jewel of the sacred Dharma, and

མཆོད་རྟེན་རྣམས་དང་སྐུ་གཟུགས་ལ།

CHO TEN NAM DANG KU ZUG LA
stupas plural and statues to
Upon stupas and statues,

རིན་ཆེན་མེ་ཏོག་ལ་སོགས་ཆར།

RIN CHEN ME TOG LA SOG CHAR
jewels flowers and so on fall
May jewels, flowers, and their like rain down

རྒྱུན་མི་ཆད་པར་འབབ་པར་ཤོག།

GYUN MI CHAD PAR BAB PAR SHOG
uninterrupted flow may it be
In an uninterrupted flow.

May jewels, flowers and their like rain down in an uninterrupted flow upon the jewel of the sacred Dharma, and on all stupas and statues.

OFFERING AS THE BODHISATTVAS DO

ཇི་ལྟར་འཇམ་དབྱངས་ལ་སོགས་པས།

JI TAR JAM YANG LA SOG PAE
just as Manjughosha and the others (especially Samantabhadra, with his method of multiplying)
Just as Manjughosha and the other Bodhisattvas

རྒྱལ་བ་རྣམས་ལ་མཆོད་མཛད་པ།

GYAL WA NAM LA CHO DZE PA
jinas , Buddha plural to make offerings
Made offerings to the Victors,

དེ་བཞིན་བདག་གིས་དེ་བཞིན་གཤེགས།

DE ZHIN DAG GI DE ZHIN SHEG
similarly me by Tathagatas
Similarly do I make offerings

མགོན་པོ་སྲས་དང་བཅས་རྣམས་མཆོད།

GON PO SAE DANG CHE NAM CHOD
benefactors offspring and so on plural offerings
To the Tathagatas, our benefactors, their offspring and all the rest.

As Manjughosha and the other Bodhisattvas made offerings to the Victors, similarly do I make offerings to the Tathagatas, our benefactors, their offspring and all the rest.

OFFERING PRAISE

ཡོན་ཏན་རྒྱ་མཚོ་རྣམས་ལ་བདག།

YON TEN GYAM TSO NAM LA DAG
good qualities ocean plural to I
To those oceans of good qualities,

བསྟོད་དབྱངས་ཡན་ལག་རྒྱ་མཚོས་བསྟོད།

TOD YANG YEN LAG GYAM TSOE TOD
praise melodies branches oceans praise
I offer praise, extolling them with oceans of diverse melodies.

བསྟོད་དབྱངས་སྙན་སྤྲིན་དེ་དག་ལ།

TOD YANG NYEN TRIN DE DAG LA
praise melodies sweet clouds these to
May clouds of sweet melodious praise

ངེས་པ་ཀུན་ཏུ་འབྱུང་གྱུར་ཅིག།

NGE WA KUN TU JUNG GYUR CHIG
certainly always arise may it be
Arise for them without fail.

To those oceans of good qualities, I offer praise, extolling them with oceans of diverse melodies. May clouds of sweet melodious praise arise for them without fail.

OBEISANCE TO THE THREE JEWELS

དུས་གསུམ་གཤེགས་པའི་སངས་རྒྱས་ཀུན།

DU SUM SHEG PAI SANG GYE KUN
three times coming and going buddhas all
To all the Buddhas in the three times who pass from samsara, and

ཆོས་དང་ཚོགས་ཀྱི་མཆོག་བཅས་ལ།

CHO DANG TSHOG KYI CHOG CHE LA
dharma and best assembly, sangha with to
To the Dharma and the Sangha, best of assemblies,

ཞིང་རྡུལ་ཀུན་གྱི་གྲངས་སྙེད་ཀྱི།

ZHING DUL KUN GYI DRANG NYED KYI
world dust all of number amount of
With bodies as numerous as the specks of dust in the universe

ལུས་བཏུད་པས་ནི་བདག་ཕྱག་འཚལ།

LU	**TU PAE**	**NI**	**DAG**	**CHAG TSAL**
body	*prostrations*		*I*	*make salutation*

I offer salutations, bowing with each one.

To all the Buddhas in the three times who pass from samsara and to the Dharma and to the Sangha, best of assemblies, with bodies as numerous as the specks of dust in the universe I offer salutations, bowing with each one.

OBEISANCE TO THE SACRED SITES AND TEACHERS

བྱང་ཆུབ་སེམས་ཀྱི་གཞི་རྣམས་དང་།

JANG CHUB SEM	**KYI**	**ZHI**	**NAM**	**DANG**
bodhicitta, mind enlightenment	*of*	*foundation**	*plural*	*and*

* The places, people, statues and so on that support one in developing bodhicitta.

To all that supports an Awakening Mind and

མཆོད་རྟེན་རྣམས་ལ་བདག་ཕྱག་འཚལ།

CHO TEN	**NAM**	**LA**	**DAG**	**CHAG TSAL**
stupas	*plural*	*to*	*I*	*make obeisance*

To the stupas I make obeisance.

མཁན་པོ་དེ་བཞིན་སློབ་དཔོན་དང་།

KHEN PO	**DE ZHIN**	**LOB PON**	**DANG**
abbots	*likewise*	*acharyas, scholars*	*and*

To the learned abbots and scholars and

བརྟུལ་ཞུགས་མཆོག་ལ་ཕྱག་འཚལ་ལོ།

TUL ZHUG	**CHOG**	**LA**	**CHAG TSHAL LO**
adepts	*supreme*	*to*	*make obeisance*

To the supreme adepts I make obeisance.

To all that supports an Awakening Mind and to the stupas I make obeisance. To the learned abbots and scholars and to the supreme adepts I make obeisance.

TAKING REFUGE IN THE THREE JEWELS

བྱང་ཆུབ་སྙིང་པོ་མཆིས་ཀྱི་བར།

JANG CHUB	**NYING POR**	**CHI**	**KYI BAR**
awakening	*essence*	*go*	*until*

Until I gain enlightenment

སངས་རྒྱས་རྣམས་ལ་སྐྱབས་སུ་མཆི།

SANG GYE NAM LA KYAB SU CHI
buddha plural to refuge for go
I go for refuge to the Buddhas.

ཆོས་དང་བྱང་ཆུབ་སེམས་དཔའ་ཡི།

CHO DANG JANG CHUB SEM PA YI
dharma and bodhisattvas of
In the same way, to the Dharma and

ཚོགས་ལའང་དེ་བཞིན་སྐྱབས་སུ་མཆི།

TSHOG LANG DE ZHIN KYAB SU CHI
sangha also similarly refuge for go
The Bodhisattva Sangha I go for refuge.

Until I gain enlightenment I go for refuge to the Buddhas. In the same way, to the Dharma and the Bodhisattva Sangha I go for refuge.

TAKING REFUGE IN THE BUDDHA

གཙོ་བོ་རྒྱལ་བ་འགྲོ་བའི་མགོན།

TSO WO GYAL WA DRO WAI GON
principal jinas, victors beings benefactors
To our leaders, the Victors, those benefactors of beings

འགྲོ་བ་སྐྱོབ་པའི་དོན་བརྩོན་པ།

DRO WA KYOB PAI DON TSON PA
beings protecting in order to striving
Who strive for the protection of beings and

སྟོབས་ཆེན་འཇིགས་པ་ཀུན་སེལ་ལ།

TOB CHEN JIG PA KUN SEL LA
great power fear all dispelling to
Dispel all fear with their great strength,

དེ་རིང་ཉིད་ནས་སྐྱབས་སུ་མཆི།

DE RING NYID NAE KYAB SU CHI
from today refuge for go
I go for refuge from this day onwards.

To our leaders, the Victors, those benefactors of beings who strive for the protection of beings and dispel all fear with their great strength, I go for refuge from this day onwards.

TAKING REFUGE IN THE DHARMA AND THE BODHISATTVA SANGHA

དེ་ཡིས་ཐུགས་སུ་ཆུད་པའི་ཆོས།

DE YI THUG SU CHUD PAI CHO
them by heart in impressed in dharma
To the Dharma all Buddhas keep in their hearts,

འཁོར་བའི་འཇིགས་པ་སེལ་བ་དང་།

KHOR WAI JIG PA SEL WA DANG
samsara fear dispel and
Dispelling the fears of samsara, and

བྱང་ཆུབ་སེམས་དཔའི་ཚོགས་ལ་ཡང་།

JANG CHUB SEM PAI TSHOG LA YANG
bodhisattva assembly, sangha to also
To the Sangha of Bodhisattvas

དེ་བཞིན་ཡང་དག་སྐྱབས་སུ་མཆི།

DE ZHIN YANG DAG KYAB SU CHI
similarly completely refuge for go
I likewise go for refuge without reservation.

All Buddhas keep in their hearts the Dharma that dispels all fear in samsara. To this and to the Sangha of Bodhisattvas I likewise go for refuge without reservation.

OFFERING ONE'S BODY

བདག་ནི་འཇིགས་པས་རྣམ་སྐྲག་ནས།

DAG NI JIG PAE NAM TRAG NAE
I fear terrified then
Trembling with fear at samsara

ཀུན་ཏུ་བཟང་ལ་བདག་ཉིད་དབུལ།

KUN TU ZANG LA DAG NYI BUL
Samantabhadra to myself offer
I give myself to Samantabhadra.

འཇམ་དཔལ་དབྱངས་ལའང་བདག་ཉིད་ཀྱིས།

JAM PAL JANG LANG DAG NYI KYI
Manjughosa also myself by
To Manjughosa, with my whole self

བདག་གི་ལུས་འདི་དབུལ་བར་བགྱི།

DAG GI LUE DI BUL WAR GYI
my body this give
I give this, my body.

Trembling with fear at samsara I give myself to Samantabhadra. To Manjughosa, with my whole self I give this, my body.

IMPLORING AVALOKITESVARA

ཐུགས་རྗེས་སྤྱོད་པ་མ་འཁྲུལ་བ།

THUG JE CHO PA MA TRUL WA
compassion conduct not confused
You whose compassionate conduct is never confused,

སྤྱན་རས་གཟིགས་མགོན་དེ་ལ་ཡང་།

CHEN RE ZIG GON DE LA YANG
Chenrezi benefactor him to also
Benefactor Avalokitesvara,

ཉམ་ཐག་ང་རོས་འོ་དོད་འབོད།

NYAM THAG NGA RO O DOD BOD
exhausted cry out lamentation
With a stricken cry I beg for help:

སྡིག་ལྡན་བདག་ལ་བསྐྱབ་ཏུ་གསོལ།

DIG DEN DAG LA KYAB TU SOL
sinful I to protect please
Please protect this sinner!

You whose compassionate conduct is never confused, benefactor Avalokitesvara, with a stricken cry I beg for help: please protect this sinner!

SEEKING HELP FROM THE BODHISATTVAS

འཕགས་པ་ནམ་མཁའི་སྙིང་པོ་དང་།

PHAG PA NAM KAI NYING PO DANG
Arya, Pure Akashagarbha and
To the Aryas Akashagarbha,

ས་ཡི་སྙིང་པོ་དག་དང་ནི།

SA YI NYING PO DAG DANG NI
Ksitigarbha the others and
Ksitigarbha, and the rest, and

ཐུགས་རྗེ་ཆེ་མགོན་ཐམས་ཅད་ལ།

THUG JE CHE GON THAM CHE LA
compassion great benefactors all to
To all the compassionate benefactors

སྐྱབས་འཚོལ་སྙིང་ནས་འོ་དོད་འབོད།

KYAB TSHOL NYING NAE O DOD BOD
protection looking for from the heart I cry out, lament
I cry to you from my heart, seeking protection.

To the Aryas Akasagarbha, Ksitigarbha, and the rest, and to all the compassionate benefactors, I cry from my heart, seeking your protection.

TAKING REFUGE IN VAJRAPANI

གང་ཞིག་མཐོང་ནས་གཤིན་རྗེ་ཡི།

GANG ZHIG THONG NAE SHIN JE YI
whoever sees then lord of death 's
Whichever of the malicious ones,

ཕོ་ཉ་ལ་སོགས་སྡང་བ་རྣམས།

PHO NYA LA SOG DANG WA NAM
messengers and so on malicious one plural
The messengers of the Lord of Death and all the rest, sees you

སྐྲག་ནས་ཕྱོགས་བཞིར་འབྱེད་བྱེད་པ།

TRAG NAE CHOG ZHIR JE JE PA
frightened four directions disperse, flee
They become fearful and disperse to the four directions:

རྡོ་རྗེ་ཅན་ལ་སྐྱབས་སུ་མཆི།

DOR JE CHEN LA KYAB SU CHI
Vajrapani to refuge for go
Vajrapani, I go to you for refuge.

When any of the malicious ones, the messengers and other attendants of the Lord of Death, see you they become fearful and disperse to the four directions: Vajrapani, I go to you for refuge.

FEELING REGRET AND SEEKING REFUGE

སྔོན་ཆད་ཁྱོད་ཀྱི་བཀའ་ལས་འདས།

NGON CHAD KHYOD KYI KA LAE DAE
formerly you of orders disobeyed, strayed
Previously I have strayed from your instructions

ད་ནི་འཇིགས་པ་ཆེར་མཐོང་ནས།

DA NI JIG PA CHER THONG NAE
now fear great see then
But now what I see brings great fear,

ཁྱོད་ལ་སྐྱབས་སུ་མཆི་ལགས་ཀྱིས།

KHYOD LA KYAB SU CHI LAG KYI
you to refuge for go truly by
So I truly go to you for refuge.

འཇིགས་པ་མྱུར་དུ་བསལ་དུ་གསོལ།

JIG PA NYUR DU SAL DU SOL
fear quickly remove please
Please quickly remove all my fears.

Previously I have strayed from your instructions but now what I see brings great fear, so I truly go to you for refuge. Please quickly remove all my fears.

CONFESSION

འདོད་ཆགས་ཞེ་སྡང་གཏི་མུག་དབང་གིས་ནི།

DOD CHAG ZHE DANG TI MUG WONG GI NI
desire anger dullness power by
Due to the power of desire, anger and opacity,

ལུས་དང་ངག་དང་དེ་བཞིན་ཡིད་ཀྱིས་ཀྱང་།

LU DANG NGAG DANG DE ZHIN YID KYI KYANG
body and speech and likewise mind by also
With my body, speech and mind

སྡིག་པ་བདག་གིས་བགྱིས་པ་ཅི་མཆིས་པ།

DIG PA DAG GI GYI PA CHI CHI PA
sin, unwholesome me by done whatever I did
I have been unwholesome. Whatever wrongs I have done

དེ་དག་ཐམས་ཅད་བདག་གིས་སོ་སོར་བཤགས། །

DE DAG THAM CHE DAG GI SO SOR SHAG
these all I by each confess and beg forgiveness
(I don't want to suffer the painful results of this bad karma)

I now confess each and every one of them and beg to be excused.

Due to the power of desire, anger and opacity with my body, speech and mind I have been unwholesome. Whatever wrongs I have done I now confess each and every one of them and beg to be excused.

Preparation for Taking the Bodhisattva Vow

OM SVASTI SIDDHAM

Indestructible Enlightenment.

བདག་སོགས་འགྲོ་བ་མ་གྱུར་ནམ་མཁའི་མཐའ་དང་

DAG SOG	DRO WA	MA	GYUR	NAM KAI	THA	DANG
we	*wanderers*	*mother*	*been*	*sky's*	*limit*	*and*

I and all beings, as many as would equal the extent of the sky,

མཉམ་པའི་སེམས་ཅན་ཐམས་ཅད་དུས་དེང་ནས་བཟུང་སྟེ་ཇི་སྲིད་

NYAM PAI	SEM CHEN	THAM CHE	DU	DENG	NAE ZUNG TE	JI SI
equalling	*sentient beings*	*all*	*time*	*now*	*from*	*as long as*

All of whom have been my own mother in my countless past lives,

བྱང་ཆུབ་སྙིང་པོ་ལ་མཆིས་ཀྱི་བར་དུ་

JANG CHUB	NYING PO	LA	CHI	KYI BAR DU
bodhi, awakening	*heart,*	*to*	*reach*	*until*

In all our future lives from this time on until enlightenment is attained

རྗེ་བཙུན་རྩ་བ་དང་བརྒྱུད་པར་བཅས་པའི་དཔལ་ལྡན་

JE TSUN	TSA WA	DANG	GYUD PAR	CHE PAI	PAL DEN
reverend	*root*	*and*	*lineage*	*together*	*glorious*

Go to refuge to our reverend root guru and

བླ་མ་དམ་པ་རྣམས་ལ་སྐྱབས་སུ་མཆིའོ།

LA MA	DAM PA	NAM	LA	KYAB	SU	CHI-O
gurus	*holy*	*all*	*to*	*refuge*	*go*	*for*

To the glorious holy gurus of the lineage.

ཡི་དམ་དཀྱིལ་འཁོར་གྱི་ལྷ་ཚོགས་རྣམས་ལ་སྐྱབས་སུ་མཆིའོ།

YI DAM	KYIL KHOR	GYI	LHA	TSHOG	NAM	LA	KYAB SU CHI-O
path deities	*mandala*	*of*	*god*	*host*	*all*	*to*	*go for refuge*

We go for refuge to the hosts of path deities in the mandalas.

རྫོགས་པའི་སངས་རྒྱས་བཅོམ་ལྡན་འདས་རྣམས་ལ་སྐྱབས་སུ་མཆིའོ།

DZOG PAI	**SANG GYE**	**CHOM DEN DAE**	**NAM**	**LA**	**KYAB SU CHI-O**
perfect	*buddha*	*bhagawan*	*plural*	*to*	*go for refuge*

We go for refuge to the perfect Bhagawan Buddha.

དམ་པའི་ཆོས་རྣམས་ལ་སྐྱབས་སུ་མཆིའོ།

DAM PAI	**CHO**	**NAM**	**LA**	**KYAB SU CHI-O**
excellent	*dharma*	*all*	*to*	*go for refuge*

We go for refuge to the most excellent Dharma.

འཕགས་པའི་དགེ་འདུན་རྣམས་ལ་སྐྱབས་སུ་མཆིའོ།

PHAG PAI	**GEN DUN**	**NAM**	**LA**	**KYAB SU CHI-O**
arya, pure	*sangha*	*all*	*to*	*go for refuge*

(consisting of the great bodhisattvas)

We go for refuge to the pure Sangha.

Indestructible Enlightenment. From this time on and in all our future lives until enlightenment is attained I and all beings, as many as would equal the extent of the sky, all of whom have been my own mother in my countless past lives, go for refuge to our reverend root guru and to the glorious holy gurus of the lineage. We go for refuge to the hosts of path deities in the mandalas. We go for refuge to the perfect Bhagawan Buddha. We go for refuge to the most excellent Dharma. We go for refuge to the pure Sangha.

[Recite this three times.]

སངས་རྒྱས་ཆོས་དང་ཚོགས་ཀྱི་མཆོག་རྣམས་ལ།

SANG GYE	**CHO**	**DANG**	**TSHOG**	**KYI**	**CHOG**	**NAM**	**LA**
Buddha	*Dharma*	*and*	*assembly (Sangha)*	*of*	*best*	*plural*	*to*

To the Buddha, Dharma and the best Assembly

བྱང་ཆུབ་བར་དུ་བདག་ནི་སྐྱབས་སུ་མཆི།

JANG CHUB	**BAR DU**	**DAG NI**	**KYAB SU CHI**
bodhi, awakening	*until*	*I*	*go for refuge*

I go for refuge until enlightenment.

བདག་གི་སྦྱིན་སོགས་བགྱིས་པའི་བསོད་ནམས་ཀྱིས།

DAG GI	**JIN**	**SOG**	**GYI PAI**	**SO NAM**	**KYI**
my	*generosity*	*and so on**	*done*	*merit*	*by*

*moral discipline, patience, diligence, meditative stability and discerning wisdom

By the merit gained from generosity and the other transcendent qualities

འགྲོ་ལ་ཕན་ཕྱིར་སངས་རྒྱས་འགྲུབ་པར་ཤོག།

DRO LA PHEN CHIR SANG GYE DRUB PAR SHOG
wanderers for benefit for the sake of buddhahood achieve will

May I gain Buddhahood in order to benefit all those wandering in samsara.

To the Buddha, Dharma and the best Assembly I go for refuge until enlightenment. By the merit arising from generosity and the other transcendent qualities I will gain Buddhahood in order to benefit all those wandering in samsara.

འགྲོ་རྣམས་བསྒྲལ་འདོད་བསམ་པ་ཡིས།

DRO NAM DRAL DOD SAM PA YI
wanderers plural carry across wish intention by

With the desire and intention to take all beings out of samsara,

སངས་རྒྱས་ཆོས་དང་དགེ་འདུན་ལ།

SANG GYE CHO DANG GEN DUN LA
Buddha Dharma and Sangha to

To the Buddha, Dharma and Sangha

བྱང་ཆུབ་སྙིང་པོ་མཆིས་ཀྱི་བར།

JANG CHUB NYING PO CHI KYI BAR
awakening heart reach of until

Until full enlightenment is gained

རྟག་པར་བདག་ནི་སྐྱབས་སུ་མཆི།

TAG PAR DAG NI KYAB SU CHI
continuously I go for refuge

I go for refuge ceaselessly.

With the desire and intention to take all beings out of samsara, until full enlightenment is gained I ceaselessly go to the Buddha, Dharma and Sangha for refuge.

ཤེས་རབ་སྙིང་རྗེ་དང་ལྡན་པའི།

SHE RAB NYING JE DANG DEN PAI
discerning wisdom kindness having

With wisdom and kindness imbuing

བརྩོན་པས་སེམས་ཅན་དོན་དུ་བདག།

TSON PAE SEM CHEN DON DU DAG
with diligence sentient beings for the sake of I

My diligence, working for the sake of beings

སངས་རྒྱས་དྲུང་དུ་གནས་བཅའ་ནས།

SANG GYE DRUNG DU NAE CHA NE
Buddha in front of stay then*
*as did the Bodhisattva Samantabhadra
I will stay close to countless Buddhas and

རྫོགས་པའི་བྱང་ཆུབ་སེམས་བསྐྱེད་དོ།

DZOG PAI JANG CHUB SEM KYED DO
complete awakening intention, mind develop
Develop completely enlightened mind.

Working for the sake of beings, with discerning wisdom and kindness imbuing my diligence, I will stay close to countless Buddhas and develop completely enlightened mind.

སེམས་ཅན་ཐམས་ཅད་བདེ་བ་དང་

SEM CHEN THAM CHE DE WA DANG
sentient beings all happiness and
May all sentient beings have happiness

བདེ་བའི་རྒྱུ་དང་ལྡན་པར་གྱུར་ཅིག།

DE WAI GYU DANG DEN PAR GYUR CHIG
happiness cause and have may this come to be
And the cause of happiness.

སེམས་ཅན་ཐམས་ཅད་སྡུག་བསྔལ་དང་

SEM CHEN THAM CHE DUG NGAL DANG
sentient beings all suffering and
May all sentient beings be freed from suffering

སྡུག་བསྔལ་གྱི་རྒྱུ་དང་བྲལ་བར་གྱུར་ཅིག།

DUG NGAL GYI GYU DANG DRAL WAR GYUR CHIG
suffering of cause and separate, free of may this come to be
And the cause of suffering.

སེམས་ཅན་ཐམས་ཅད་སྡུག་བསྔལ་མེད་པའི་

SEM CHEN THAM CHE DUG NGAL MED PAI
sentient beings all suffering free of
May all sentient beings never be separated from

བདེ་བ་དང་མི་བྲལ་བར་གྱུར་ཅིག།

DE WA DANG MI DRAL WAR GYUR CHIG
happiness and not separate may this come to be
The happiness that is free of suffering.

སེམས་ཅན་ཐམས་ཅད་ཉེ་རིང་ཆགས་སྡང་དང་

SEM CHEN	**THAM CHE**	**NYE**	**RING**	**CHAG**	**DANG**	**DANG**
sentient beings	*all*	*near*	*far*	*desire*	*anger*	*and*

May all sentient beings abide in equanimity free from cherishing friends and relatives

བྲལ་བའི་བཏང་སྙོམས་ལ་གནས་པར་གྱུར་ཅིག།

DRAL WAI	**TANG NYOM**	**LA**	**NAE PAR**	**GYUR CHIG**
free of	*equanimity*	*with*	*abide*	*may this come to be*

And being dismissive of strangers and enemies.

May all sentient beings have happiness and the cause of happiness. May all sentient beings be freed from suffering and the cause of suffering. May all sentient beings never be separated from the happiness that is free of suffering. May all sentient beings abide in equanimity free from cherishing friends and relatives and being dismissive of strangers and enemies.

ཐམས་ཅད་དུ་ཡངས་ས་གཞི་དག།

THAM CHE DU	**YANG**	**SA ZHI**	**DAG**
everywhere	*wide*	*foundation*	*all*

The vast foundation is completely

གསེག་མ་ལ་སོགས་མེད་པ་དང་།

SEG MA	**LA SOG**	**ME PA**	**DANG**
pebbles	*and so on*	*without*	*and*

Free from small stones and other such irritants.

ལག་མཐིལ་ལྟར་མཉམ་བཻ་ཌཱུརྱའི།

LAG	**THIL**	**TAR**	**NYAM**	**BE DUR YAI**
hand	*palm*	*like*	*like*	*beduria stone*

Made from beduria it is smooth and flat like the palm of the hand, and

རང་བཞིན་བཟང་པོར་གནས་གྱུར་ཅིག།

RANG ZHIN	**ZANG POR**	**NAE**	**GYUR CHIG**
naturally	*good**	*place*	*has become*

* It is a nice place to invite the Buddha to.

Is a truly pleasant environment.

The vast foundation is completely free from small stones and such irritants. Made from beduria it is smooth and flat like the palm of the hand, and is a truly pleasant environment.

མ་ལུས་སེམས་ཅན་ཀུན་གྱི་མགོན་གྱུར་ཅིང་།

MA LU	**SEM CHEN**	**KUN**	**GYI**	**GON**	**GYUR CHING**
without exception	*sentient beings*	*all*	*of*	*protector*	*is*

You are the benefactor of all beings without exception,

བདུད་སྡེ་དཔུང་བཅས་མི་བཟད་འཇོམས་མཛད་ལྷ།

DUD	**DE**	**PUNG**	**CHE**	**MI ZAD**	**JOM DZAE**	**LHA**
demon	*type*	*group*	*with*	*irresistible, dangerous*	*defeat*	*god*

The god who defeats the very dangerous hosts of demons, and

དངོས་རྣམས་མ་ལུས་ཇི་བཞིན་མཁྱེན་གྱུར་པའི།

NGO NAM	**MA LU**	**JI ZHIN**	**KYHEN**	**GYUR PAI**
everything	*without exception*	*as it is*	*know*	*does*

Who knows all things without exception just as they are.

བཅོམ་ལྡན་འཁོར་བཅས་གནས་འདིར་གཤེགས་སུ་གསོལ།

CHOM DEN	**KHOR**	**CHE**	**NAE**	**DIR**	**SHEG**	**SU SOL**
bhagawan	*entourage*	*with*	*place*	*here*	*complete*	*please*

Bhagawan Buddha, please come here with your entourage.

Bhagawan Buddha, you are the benefactor of all beings without exception, the god who defeats the very dangerous hosts of demons. You know all things without exception just as they are. Please come here with your entourage.

བཅོམ་ལྡན་བསྐལ་པ་གྲངས་མེད་དུ་མ་རུ།

CHOM DEN	**KAL PA**	**DRANG MED**	**DU MA**	**RU**
bhagawan	*aeon*	*innumerable*	*many*	*in*

Bhagawan Buddha, for innumerable aeons

འགྲོ་ལ་བརྩེ་ཕྱིར་ཐུགས་རྒྱུད་རྣམ་སྦྱངས་ཤིང་།

DRO	**LA**	**TSE**	**CHIR**	**THUG GYUD**	**NAM**	**JANG SHING**
wanderers	*to*	*care, love*	*in order to*	*character, heart*	*fully*	*purifying*

You purified your character in order to care for wandering beings and

སྨོན་ལམ་རྒྱ་ཆེར་དགོངས་པ་ཡོངས་རྫོགས་པའི།

MON LAM	**GYA CHER**	**GONG PA**	**YONG DZOG PAI**
aspiration	*vast*	*intention, attention*	*complete*

You completed the intention of your vast aspiration.

ཁྱོད་བཞེད་འགྲོ་དོན་མཛད་དུས་འདི་ལགས་ན།

KHYO	ZHE	DRO	DON	DZED	DU	DI	LAG	NA
you	*wish*	*wanderers*	*benefit*	*do*	*time*	*this*	*doing*	*if, when*

Now, as you wish to benefit beings,

དེ་ཕྱིར་ཆོས་དབྱིངས་ཕོ་བྲང་ལྷུན་གྲུབ་ནས།

DE CHIR	CHO YING	PHO DRANG	LHUN DRUB	NAE
therefore	*dharmadhatu, all-encompassing space*	*mandala palace*	*effortlessly arising*	*from*

Effortlessly arising from the palace of all-encompassing space,

རྫུ་འཕྲུལ་བྱིན་རླབས་སྣ་ཚོགས་སྟོན་མཛད་ཅིང་།

DZU TRUL	JIN LAB	NA TSHOG	TON	DZED CHING
magical, miracle	*blessing*	*various*	*show*	*doing*

Displaying the blessing of diverse miracles,

མཐའ་ཡས་སེམས་ཅན་ཚོགས་རྣམས་བསྒྲལ་བའི་ཕྱིར།

THA YAE	SEM CHEN	TSHOG NAM	DRAL WAI	CHIR
limitless	*sentient beings*	*host*	*take across, liberate*	*in order to*

In order to take limitless sentient beings out of samsara,

ཡོངས་དག་འཁོར་དང་བཅས་ཏེ་གཤེགས་སུ་གསོལ།

YONG DAG	KHOR	DANG CHE TE	SHEG	SU SOL
entire	*retinue*	*together with*	*come*	*please*

Please come here with your entire retinue.

Bhagawan Buddha, for innumerable aeons you purified your character in order to care for wandering beings and you completed the intention of your vast aspiration. Now, as you wish to benefit beings, please effortlessly arise from the palace of all-encompassing space and, displaying the blessing of diverse miracles, please come here with your entire retinue in order to take limitless sentient beings out of samsara.

ཆོས་རྣམས་ཀུན་གྱི་དབང་ཕྱུག་གཙོ།

CHO NAM	KUN	GYI	WANG CHUG	TSO
dharmas	*all*	*of*	*powerful*	*chief*

(Buddha Shakyamuni)

Mighty lord of all dharmas,

བཙོ་མ་གསེར་གྱི་མདོག་འདྲ་ཞིང་།

TSO MA	SER GYI	DOG	DRA ZHING
refined	*golden*	*colour*	*like*

Your colour of refined gold

ཉི་མ་ལས་ལྷག་གཟི་བརྗིད་ཆེ།

NYI MA	**LAE**	**LHAG**	**ZI JID**	**CHE**
sun	*than*	*better*	*splendid*	*great*

Is more splendid than the sun.

དད་པས་སྤྱན་ནི་དྲང་བར་བགྱི།

DE PAE	**CHEN NI**	**DRANG WAR**	**GYI**
with faith	*eye*	*draw, invite*	*do*

With faith we invite you here.

Mighty lord of all dharmas, your colour of refined gold is more splendid than the sun. With faith we invite you here.

ཞི་ཞིང་ཐུགས་རྗེ་ཆེ་ལྡན་པ།

ZHI ZHING	**THUG JE**	**CHE**	**DEN PA**
pacifying	*kindness*	*great*	*having*

Your great kindness brings peace,

དུལ་ཞིང་བསམ་གཏན་ས་ལ་བཞུགས།

DUL ZHING	**SAM TEN**	**SA**	**LA**	**ZHUG**
controlled	*mental stability*	*level**	*on*	*establish*

*up to and including the fifth way

You the disciplined ones who stay on the stages of calm stability.

ཆོས་དང་ཡེ་ཤེས་ཆགས་བྲལ་བ།

CHO	**DANG**	**YE SHE**	**CHAG**	**DRAL WA**
dharma (Dharmakaya)	*and*	*original knowing*	*desire*	*free of*

With dharma and original knowing free from desire,

ཀུན་ཏུ་མི་ཟད་ནུས་པར་ལྡན།

KUN TU	**MI ZAD**	**NU PAR**	**DEN**
always	*never exhausted*	*power**	*have*

*i.e. the power to help others

Your power is never exhausted.

ཚུར་སྤྱོན་ཚུར་སྤྱོན་ཞི་དག་ལ།

TSHUR	**CHON**	**TSHUR**	**CHON**	**ZHI DAG**	**LA**
here	*come*	*here*	*come*	*peaceful ones*	

Peaceful ones, please come, please come!

Disciplined ones who stay on the stages of calm stability, your great kindness brings peace. With dharma and original knowing free from desire, your power is never exhausted. Peaceful ones, please come, please come!

ཐུབ་པའི་སྐྱེས་མཆོག་ཐམས་ཅད་མཁྱེན།

THUB PAI KYE	**CHOG**	**THAM CHE**	**KHYEN**
sages	*supreme*	*all*	*knowing*

Omniscient One, supreme among sages,

ཤིན་ཏུ་ལེགས་བྱས་གཟུགས་བརྙན་འདིར།

SHIN TU	**LEG**	**CHE**	**ZUG**	**NYEN**	**DIR**
very	*good*	*made*	*form*	*image*	*here*

Show your handsome, perfectly formed body here.

དད་པས་སྤྱན་ནི་དྲང་བར་བགྱི།

DE PAE	**CHEN NI DRANG WAR**	**GYI**
with faith	*invite, beckon*	*do*

With faith we invite you to come and show

གཤེགས་འབྱོན་སྐྱེ་འགྲིབ་མེད་པའི་སྐུ།

SHEG	**JON**	**KYE**	**DRIB**	**ME PAI**	**KU**
coming	*going*	*birth*	*death*	*without*	*body*

Your body free of coming and going, birth and death.

འཇིག་རྟེན་སྨོན་བཞིན་ཡོད་པ་དག།

JIG TEN	**MON**	**ZHIN**	**YOD PA**	**DAG**
world	*aspire, wish*	*according to*	*have*	*all*

In accordance with the wishes of all beings in this world,

དཀར་པོ་འཆར་བའི་ཚུལ་བཞིན་དུ།

KAR PO	**CHAR WAI**	**TSHUL**	**ZHIN DU**
white	*rising*	*manner*	*similar*

Like the rising moon,

འཇིག་རྟེན་སྐྱོབ་ཕྱིར་གཤེགས་སུ་གསོལ།

JIG TEN	**KYOB**	**CHIR**	**SHEG SU**	**SOL**
world	*protect*	*in order to*	*come*	*please*

Please come here in order to protect the world.

Omniscient One, supreme among sages, please show your handsome, perfectly formed body here. With faith we invite you to come and show your body free of coming and going, birth and death. In accordance with the wishes of all beings in this world, like the rising moon, please come here in order to protect the world.

འཕགས་ཡུལ་ཡངས་པ་ཅན་གྱི་གྲོང་ཁྱེར་ནས།

PHAG YUL	**YANG PA CHEN**	**GYI**	**DRONG KHYER**	**NAE**
pure country	*Vaishali*	*of*	*city*	*from*

From the city of Vaishali in the pure land of India,

བདེ་བར་གཤེགས་པ་ཤཱཀྱ་སེང་གེ་ནི།

DE WAR SHEG PA	**SHAK KYA**	**SENG GE**	**NI**
Sugata. Happily Gone	*Shakya's*	*lion (Buddha)*	*emphasis*

Happily Gone Lion of the Shakyas,

སུམ་ཁྲི་དྲུག་སྟོང་འཁོར་དང་ལྷན་ཅིག་ཏུ།

SUM	**TRI**	**DRUG**	**TONG**	**KHOR**	**DANG LEN CHIG TU**
three	*ten thousand*	*six*	*thousand*	*retinue**	*together with*

*of Bodhisattvas

Together with your retinue of thirty-six thousand,

སྤྱན་འདྲེན་མཆོད་པའི་གནས་འདིར་གཤེགས་སུ་གསོལ།

CHEN DRENG	**CHO PAI**	**NAE**	**DIR**	**SHEG SU**	**SOL**
invite	*offering*	*place*	*here*	*come*	*please*

We invite you to come here to this place of offerings.

From the city of Vaishali in the pure land of India, Happily Gone Lion of the Shakyas together with your retinue of thirty-six thousand, we invite you to come here to this place of offerings.

བཅོམ་ལྡན་འདིར་ནི་བྱོན་པ་ལེགས།

CHOM DEN	**DIR NI**	**JON PA**	**LEG**
Bhagawan	*here*	*come*	*good, happy*

We are happy that Bhagawan Buddha has come here,

བདག་ཅག་བསོད་ནམས་སྐལ་པར་ལྡན།

DAG CHE	**SO NAM**	**KAL PAR**	**DEN**
we	*merit*	*fortunate*	*having*

We fortunate people who have merit enough to experience this.

ཇི་སྲིད་མཆོད་པ་བདག་འབུལ་ན།

JI SI	**CHO PA**	**DAG**	**BUL**	**NA**
for as much as	*offering*	*we*	*present*	*if*

For the duration of our offerings to you,

འདི་སྲིད་བཅོམ་ལྡན་བཞུགས་སུ་གསོལ།

DI SI	**CHOM DEN**	**SHUG SU**	**SOL**
this much	*Bhagawan*	*stay, sit*	*please*

Bhagawan, we request you to stay.

We are happy that Bhagawan Buddha has come here, we fortunate people who have merit enough to experience this. Bhagawan, we request you to stay while we make these offerings to you.

རིན་ཆེན་དུ་མ་ལས་གྲུབ་སེང་གེའི་ཁྲི།

RIN CHEN	**DU MA**	**LAE**	**DRUB**	**SENG GEI**	**TRI**
jewels	*many*	*from*	*made*	*lion*	*throne*

This lion throne made of many jewels is

ཡིད་འཕྲོག་སྣ་ཚོགས་གོས་ཀྱིས་བཀབ་པའི་སྟེང་།

YID	**TROG**	**NA TSHOG**	**GO**	**KYI**	**KAB PAI**	**TENG**
mind	*pleasing, captivating*	*various*	*clothes, robes*	*by*	*cover*	*on top of*

Adorned with a variety of pleasing brocades

པདྨ་ཉི་ཟླ་འོད་འབར་གདན་འབུལ་ན།

PAD MA	**NYI**	**DA**	**OD BAR**	**DEN**	**BUL**	**NA**
lotus	*sun*	*moon*	*shining*	*cushion*	*present*	*when*

On top of which are shining cushions of lotus, sun and moon. We offer this to you, so

བརྩེ་བས་དགོངས་ཏེ་ཅི་བདེར་བཞུགས་སུ་གསོལ།

TSE WAE	**GONG**	**TE**	**CHI DER**	**ZHUG SU**	**SOL**
kind	*think of us*	*then*	*happily*	*rest, stay*	*please*

Please think of us kindly and remain here happily.

This lion throne made of many jewels is adorned with a variety of pleasing brocades on top of which are shining cushions of lotus, sun and moon. We offer this to you, so please think of us kindly and remain here happily.

འདིར་ནི་གཟུགས་དང་ལྷན་ཅིག་ཏུ།

DIR NI	**ZUG**	**DANG**	**LEN CHIG TU**
here	*body*	*and*	*together*

(i.e. please come with a body that we can see)

Coming here in bodily form

འགྲོ་བའི་དོན་དུ་བཞུགས་ནས་ཀྱང་།

DRO WAI	**DON DU**	**ZHUG**	**NAE**	**KYANG**
wanderers	*for the sake of*	*stay, sit*	*then*	*also*

Please stay in order to benefit all beings. Moreover

ནད་མེད་ཚེ་དང་དབང་ཕྱུག་དང་།

NAD MED TSHE DANG WANG CHUG DANG
sickness without life and wealth and power and

Please grant us wealth, lives free of sickness and

མཆོག་རྣམས་ལེགས་པར་སྩོལ་དུ་གསོལ།

CHOG NAM LEG PAR TSAL DU SOL
everything excellent well, pleasing bestow on us please

Generously bestow on us all that is best.

Coming here in bodily form please stay in order to benefit all beings. Moreover please grant us wealth, lives free of sickness and generously bestow on us all that is best.

ཁྲུས་ཀྱི་ཁང་པ་ཤིན་ཏུ་དྲི་ཞིམ་པ།

TRU KYI KHANG PA SHIN TU DRI ZHIM PA
bathing of house very small pleasing

In exquisitely perfumed bath houses

ཤེལ་གྱི་ས་གཞི་གསལ་ཞིང་འཚེར་བ་བསྟར།

SHEL GYI SA ZHI SA ZHING TSHER WA TAR
crystal of floor shining brightening

With brilliantly sparkling crystal floors,

རིན་ཆེན་འབར་བའི་ཀ་བ་ཡིད་འོང་ལྡན།

RIN CHEN BAR WAI KA WA YID ONG DEN
jewel blazing pillars beautiful having, endowed with

Enchanting pillars of glittering jewels and

མུ་ཏིག་འོད་ཆགས་བླ་བྲེ་བྲེས་པ་དེར།

MU TIG OE CHAG LA DRE DRE PA DER
pearl bright canopies spreading there

Spreading canopies of lustrous pearls,

དེ་བཞིན་གཤེགས་པ་རྣམས་དང་དེ་སྲས་ལ།

DE ZHIN SHEG PA NAM DANG DE SAE LA
Tathagata, Buddha all and their sons, bodhisattvas to

Tathagatas and your offspring,

རིན་ཆེན་བུམ་པ་མང་པོ་སྤོས་ཀྱི་ཆུས།

RIN CHEN BUM PA MANG PO POE KYI CHU
jewelled pot many scented water

With many jewelled pots of scented water

ཡིད་འོང་ལེགས་པར་བཀང་བ་གླུ་དང་ནི།

YID ONG LEG PAR KANG WA LU DANG NI
beautiful well filled song and
That are beautiful and brimming,

རོལ་མོར་བཅས་པ་དུ་མས་སྐུ་ཁྲུས་གསོལ།

ROL MOR CHE PA DU MAE KU TRU SOL
music and so on with many body bathe I will do
We will bathe your bodies to the accompaniment of music and song.

Tathagatas and your offspring, in exquisitely perfumed bath houses with brilliantly sparkling crystal floors, enchanting pillars of glittering jewels and spreading canopies of lustrous pearls, with many jewelled pots of scented water that are beautiful and brimming, we will bathe your bodies to the accompaniment of music and song.

ཇི་ལྟར་བལྟམས་པ་ཙམ་གྱིས་ནི།

JI TAR TAM PA TSAM GYI NI
just as birth as done
Just as at birth

ལྷ་རྣམས་ཀྱིས་ནི་ཁྲུས་གསོལ་ལྟར།

LHA NAM KYI NI TRU SOL TAR
gods all by bathe as
Gods are bathed by the gods

ལྷ་ཡི་ཆུ་ནི་དག་པ་ཡིས།

LHA YI CHU NI DAG PA YI
gods of water pure with
With the pure water of the gods,

དེ་བཞིན་བདག་གིས་སྐུ་ཁྲུས་གསོལ།

DE ZHIN DAG GI KU TRU SOL
similarly me by body bathe
We will likewise bathe your bodies.

Just as at birth gods are bathed by the gods with the pure water of the gods, we will similarly bathe your bodies.

རྒྱལ་བའི་སྐུ་གསུང་ཐུགས་ལ་ཉོན་མོངས་མི་མངའ་ཡང་།

GYAL WAI KU SUNG THUG LA NYON MONG MI NGA YANG
Jinas' Body Speech Mind to afflictions not have yet*
*of stupidity, anger, desire, etc.
Although the Buddhas' Body, Voice and Mind are free from the afflictions,

སེམས་ཅན་ལུས་ངག་ཡིད་གསུམ་དྲི་མ་སྦྱང་སླད་དུ།

SEM CHEN	LU	NGAG	YID	SUM	DRI MA	CHANG	LAE DU
sentient beings	*body*	*speech*	*mind*	*three*	*impurities*	*cleanse*	*in order to*

For the sake of cleansing the impurities of body, voice and mind of all beings

རྒྱལ་བའི་སྐུ་གསུང་ཐུགས་ལ་ཁྲུས་ཆབ་འདི་གསོལ་བས།

GYAL WAI	KU	SUNG	THUG	LA	TRU	CHAB	DI	SOL WAE
Jinas', Victors'	*Body*	*Speech*	*Mind*	*to*	*washing*	*water*	*this*	*by offering*

We offer this bathing water to the Victors' Body, Voice and Mind so that

སེམས་ཅན་ལུས་ངག་ཡིད་གསུམ་སྒྲིབ་པ་དག་གྱུར་ཅིག།

SEM CHEN	LU	NGAG	YID	SUM	DRIB PA	DAG	GYUR CHIG
sentient beings	*body*	*speech*	*mind*	*three*	*impurities, obscurations*	*pure*	*must become*

The obscurations of body, voice and mind of all beings will be purified.

Although the Buddhas' Body, Voice and Mind are free from the afflictions, for the sake of cleansing the impurities of body, voice and mind of all beings we offer this bathing water to the Victors' Body, Voice and Mind so that the obscurations of body, voice and mind of all beings will be purified.

འདི་ནི་ཁྲུས་མཆོག་དཔལ་དང་ལྡན།

DI NI	TRU	CHOG	PAL DANG DEN
this	*bath*	*excellent*	*splendid*

This excellent and splendid bath has

ཐུགས་རྗེའི་ཆུ་ནི་བླ་ན་མེད།

THUG JEI	CHU NI	LA NA MED
kindness	*water*	*unsurpassed*

The unsurpassed water of kindness,

བྱིན་རླབས་ཡེ་ཤེས་ཆུ་ཡིས་ནི།

JIN LAB	YE SHE	CHU	YI NI
blessing	*original knowing*	*water*	*by*

The blessing water of original knowing.

ཅི་འདོད་དངོས་གྲུབ་རྩལ་དུ་གསོལ།

CHI	DOD	NGO DRUB	TSAL DU	SOL
whatever	*desired*	*attainment*	*bestow*	*we request*

By offering you this may we be granted whatever attainments we wish.

This excellent and splendid bath has the unsurpassed water of kindness, the blessing water of original knowing. By offering this to you may we be granted whatever attainments we wish.

དེ་དག་སྐུ་ལ་མཚུངས་པ་མེད་པའི་གོས།

DE DAG KU LA TSHUNG PA MED PAI GOE
their body to equal without cloths, towels
We apply matchless towels to your bodies, and

གཙང་ལ་དྲི་རབ་བགོས་པས་སྐུ་ཕྱིའོ།

TSANG LA DRI RAB GOE PAE KU CHI-O
pure and perfumed excellent clothing body surface, cover
Wrap them with these clean and fine smelling cloths.

དེ་ནས་དེ་ལ་ཁ་དོག་ལེགས་བསྒྱུར་བའི།

DE NAE DE LA KHA DOG LEG GYUR WAI
then them to colour suitable
Then we present you with charmingly coloured

ན་བཟའ་ཞིན་ཏུ་དྲི་ཞིམ་དམ་པ་འབུལ།

NAB ZA ZHIN TU DRI ZHIM DAM PA BUL
clothes very scent pleasing excellent present
Superb robes most exquisitely perfumed.

We apply matchless towels to your bodies, and wrap them with these clean and fine smelling cloths. Then we present you with charmingly coloured superb robes most exquisitely perfumed.

གོས་བཟང་སྲབ་ལ་འཇམ་པ་སྣ་ཚོགས་དང་།

GOE ZANG SAB LA ZAM PA NA TSHOG DANG
clothes good fine to soft various and
With varied raiments, so soft and fine, and

རྒྱན་མཆོག་བརྒྱ་ཕྲག་དེ་དང་དེ་དག་གིས།

GYEN CHOG GYA TRAG DE DANG DE DAG GI
ornaments excellent one hundred these and these by
With a hundred excellent ornaments and still more,

འཕགས་པ་ཀུན་བཟང་དང་འཇམ་དབྱངས་དང་།

PHAG PA KUN ZANG DANG JAM YANG DANG
arya, pure Samantabhadra and Manjughosa and
We adorn the bodhisattvas, Samantabhadra, Manjughosa,

འཇིག་རྟེན་དབང་ཕྱུག་སོགས་ལའང་བརྒྱན་པར་བགྱི།

JIG TEN WANG CHUG SOG LANG GYEN PAR GYI
Lokeshvara, Avalokiteshvara and so on also adorn do

Avalokiteshvara, and all the others.

With varied raiments, so soft and fine, and with a hundred excellent ornaments and still more, we adorn the bodhisattvas, Samantabhadra, Manjughosa, Avalokiteshvara, and all the others.

སྲབ་འཇམ་ཡངས་པ་ལྷ་ཡི་གོས།

SAB JAM YANG PA LHA YI GOE
fine soft generous gods' clothes

Divine clothes, fine, soft and generous,

མི་བསྐྱོད་རྡོ་རྗེའི་སྐུ་བརྙེས་ལ།

MI KYOD DOR JEI KU NYE LA
unshakeable vajra, indestructible body have to*
*(i.e. the dharmakaya)

To your indestructible body

མི་ཕྱེད་དད་པས་བདག་འབུལ་ན།

MI CHE DAE PAE DAG BUL NA
undiminished faith I, we present if, then

We offer with total devotion –

བདག་ཀྱང་རྡོ་རྗེའི་སྐུ་ཐོབ་ཤོག།

DAG KYANG DOR JEI KU THOB SHOG
I, we also Vajra Body get must, may

By this may we also gain the indestructible body.

With total devotion we offer divine clothes, fine, soft and generous, to your indestructible body. Through this may we also gain the indestructible body.

སྣ་ཚོགས་དབང་པོའི་གཞུ་ལྟར་རབ་བཀྲ་ཞིང་།

NA TSHOG WANG POI ZHU TAR RAB TRA ZHING
various rainbow as excellent variegated

As wonderfully variegated as multiple rainbows,

གང་ལ་རེག་ན་བདེ་བའི་རྒྱུ་གྱུར་པ།

GANG LA REG NA DE WAI GYU GYUR PA
whoever, wherever to touch if happiness cause becomes

Bringing happiness wherever they touch,

གོས་བཟང་རིན་ཆེན་བདག་བློ་སྦྱང་ཕྱིར་འབུལ།

GOE	ZANG	RIN CHEN	DAG	LO	JANG	CHIR	BUL
clothing	*good*	*jewelled*	*I, we*	*mind, intellect*	*purify*	*in order to*	*offer*

This fine jewelled clothing we offer in order to purify our minds –

བཟོད་པ་དམ་པའི་གོས་ཀྱིས་བརྒྱན་པར་ཤོག།

ZOD PA	DAM PAI	GOE	KYI	GYEN PAR	SHOG
patience	*best*	*clothing*	*by*	*adorned*	*may*

May we be adorned with the supreme clothing of patience.

This fine jewelled clothing which brings happiness to all who touch it is as wonderfully varied as diverse rainbows. We offer this in order to purify our minds, may we be adorned with the supreme clothing of patience.

ས་གཞི་སྤོས་ཀྱིས་བྱུགས་ཤིང་མེ་ཏོག་བཀྲམ།

SA ZHI	POE	KYI	JUG SHING	ME TOG	TRAM
foundation	*perfume*	*by*	*anointing*	*flowers*	*scatter*

We anoint the foundation of the universe with perfume and scatter it with flowers.

རི་རབ་གླིང་བཞི་ཉི་ཟླས་བརྒྱན་པ་འདི།

RI RAB	LING	ZHI	NYI	DAE	GYEN PA	DI
Mt Meru	*continents*	*four*	*sun*	*moon*	*adorned*	*this*

Adorning it with Mt. Meru, the four continents, and the sun and moon

སངས་རྒྱས་ཞིང་དུ་དམིགས་ཏེ་ཕུལ་བ་ཡིས།

SANG GYE	ZHING	DU	MIG TE	PHUL WA	YI
Buddha	*realm*	*as*	*imagine*	*offer*	*by*

We imagine the Buddha's realm and offer it there

འགྲོ་ཀུན་རྣམ་དག་ཞིང་དུ་སྤྱོད་པར་ཤོག།

DRO	KUN	NAM DAG	ZHING	DU	CHO PAR	SHOG
wanderers	*all*	*completely pure*	*realm*	*in, as*	*enjoy*	*may*

So that all beings may enjoy the very pure realm.

We anoint the foundation of the universe with perfume and scatter it with flowers. Adorning it with Mt. Meru, the four continents, and the sun and moon we imagine the Buddha's realm and offer it there so that all beings may enjoy the very pure realm.

མཉེས་ཕྱིར་མཎྜལ་བཟང་པོ་འདི་ཕུལ་བས།

NYE	**CHIR**	**MAN DAL**	**ZANG PO**	**DI**	**PUL WAE**
please, gladden	*in order to*	*mandala*	*excellent*	*this*	*by offering*

By offering this excellent mandala in order to bring joy,

བྱང་ཆུབ་ལམ་ལ་བར་ཆད་མི་འབྱུང་ཞིང་།

JANG CHUB	**LAM**	**LA**	**BAR CHE**	**MI**	**JUNG ZHING**
bodhi, awakening	*path*	*on*	*obstacles*	*not*	*arising*

With no obstacles arising on the path to awakening,

དུས་གསུམ་རྒྱལ་བའི་དགོངས་པ་རྟོགས་པ་དང་།

DU	**SUM**	**GYAL WAI**	**GONG PA**	**TOG PA**	**DANG**
times	*three*	*Buddhas'*	*mind, intention*	*awaken to*	*and*

(past, present, and future)

May we awaken to the clarity of all the Buddhas of the three times, and,

སྲིད་པར་མི་འཁྲུལ་ཞི་བར་མི་གནས་པར།

SID PAR	**MI**	**THRUL**	**ZHI WAR**	**MI**	**NAE PAR**
samsara	*not*	*bewildered*	**tranquillity*	*not*	*remain*

*the arahats' stage of peace and non-disturbance

Without being confused by samsara and without resting in tranquillity,

ནམ་མཁའ་དང་མཉམ་པའི་འགྲོ་རྣམས་སྒྲོལ་བར་ཤོག། །

NAM KHA	**DANG**	**NYAM PAI**	**DRO**	**NAM**	**DROL WAR**	**SHOG**
sky	*and*	*equal*	*wanderers*	*all*	*liberate*	*may*

May we liberate all beings filling the infinite sky.

We offer this excellent mandala in order to bring joy to the Buddhas. Due to this may no obstacles arise on the path to awakening. May we awaken to the clarity of all the Buddhas of the three times. May we liberate all beings as many as would fill the sky so that they are neither bewildered in samsara nor becalmed in nirvana.

Taking the Bodhisattva Vow
The Main Practice

Salutation

མགོན་པོ་ཐུགས་རྗེ་ཆེ་ལྡན་པ།

GON PO	THUG JE	CHE	DEN PA
protector, benefactor	*compassion*	*great*	*having*

Our most compassionate benefactor,

ཐམས་ཅད་མཁྱེན་པའི་སྟོན་པ་པོ།

THAM CHE	KHYEN PAI	TON PA PO
all	*knowing*	*teacher*

Omniscient teacher and

བསོད་ནམས་ཡོན་ཏན་རྒྱ་མཚོའི་ཞིང་།

SO NAM	YON TEN	GYAM TSHO	SHING
merit	*good qualities*	*ocean*	

Ocean of good qualities and merit,

དེ་བཞིན་གཤེགས་ལ་ཕྱག་འཚལ་ལོ།

DE ZHIN SHEG	LA	CHAG TSHAL LO
Tathagata, Buddha Thus Gone	*to*	*we offer salutation*

Thus Gone, we bow to you.

Our most compassionate benefactor, omniscient teacher and ocean of good qualities and merit, Thus Gone, we bow to you.

དག་པ་འདོད་ཆགས་བྲལ་བའི་རྒྱུ།

DAG PA	DOD CHAG	DRAL WAI	GYU
pure	*desire*	*free from*	*cause*

The cause that is pure and free from desire,

དགེ་བས་ངན་སོང་ལས་སྒྲོལ་ཞིང་།

GE WAE	NGEN	SONG	LAE	DROL ZHING
virtue	**woe*	*gone*	*from*	*freeing, liberating*

*hells, preta, animal

With virtue that liberates the lower realms,

གཅིག་ཏུ་དོན་དམ་མཆོག་གྱུར་པ།

CHIG TU DON DAM CHOG GYUR PA
only one absolute value supreme it is

Is the sole supreme absolute value.

ཞི་གྱུར་ཆོས་ལ་ཕྱག་འཚལ་ལོ།

ZHI GYUR CHO LA CHAG TSHAL LO
pacifying, calming dharma to salutation

To the Dharma, bringer of peace, we bow.

The cause that is pure and free from desire, with virtue that liberates the lower realms, is the sole supreme absolute value. To the Dharma, bringer of peace, we bow.

གྲོལ་ནས་གྲོལ་བའི་ལམ་ཡང་སྟོན།

DROL NAE DROL WAI LAM YANG TON
liberation then liberation's path also showing

Gaining liberation you show the path to liberation

བསླབ་པ་དག་ལ་རབ་ཏུ་གུས།

LAB PA DAG LA RAB TU GU
training pure to full reverence*
*in moral conduct, meditation and wisdom

With deep reverence for the pure training.

ཞིང་གི་དམ་པ་ཡོན་ཏན་ལྡན།

ZHING GI DAM PA YON TEN DEN
realms of excellent good qualities having

Holy fields of good qualities,

དགེ་འདུན་ལ་ཡང་ཕྱག་འཚལ་ལོ།

GEN DUN LA YANG CHAG TSHAL LO
sangha to also offer salutation

Sangha we bow to you.

Gaining liberation you show the path to liberation with deep reverence for the pure training. Holy fields of good qualities, Sangha we bow to you.

སྟོན་པ་བླ་མེད་སངས་རྒྱས་རིན་པོ་ཆེ།

TON PA LA ME SANG GYE RIN PO CHE
teacher unsurpassed Buddha precious

Precious Buddha, our unexcelled teacher,

སྐྱོབ་པ་བླ་མེད་དམ་ཆོས་རིན་པོ་ཆེ།
KYOB PA LA ME DAM CHO RIN PO CHE
protection unexcelled holy dharma precious
Precious holy Dharma, our unexcelled protection,

འདྲེན་པ་བླ་མེད་དགེ་འདུན་རིན་པོ་ཆེ།
DREN PA LA ME GEN DUN RIN PO CHE
guide, leader unexcelled sangha precious
Precious Sangha, our unexcelled guides,

བླ་མེད་དཀོན་མཆོག་གསུམ་ལ་ཕྱག་འཚལ་ལོ།
LA ME KON CHOG SUM LA CHAG TSHAL LO
unexcelled rare and precious three to salutation, obeisance, prostration
(these Three Jewels)
Unexcelled Three Jewels, we bow to you.

Precious Buddha, our unexcelled teacher, Precious holy Dharma, our unexcelled protection, Precious Sangha, our unexcelled guides, Unexcelled Three Jewels, we bow to you.

འཕགས་པ་ཐོགས་མེད་ལས་བརྒྱུད་པའི་རྒྱ་ཆེན་སྤྱོད་པའི་བླ་བརྒྱུད་ནི།

The Lineage of the Gurus of Arya Asanga's Vast Bodhisattva Conduct Lineage

མཉམ་མེད་ཐུབ་པའི་དབང་པོ་བཅོམ་ལྡན་འདས།

NYAM MED THUB PAI WANG PO JOM DEN DAE

equal not sage powerful bhagawan, liberated*

*This prayer lists the unbroken lineage of preceptors who have received, maintained and transmitted the bodhisattva vow in the line of Arya Asanga.

Unequalled powerful sage, Bhagawan Shakyamuni,

རྒྱལ་ཚབ་བྱམས་པ་འཕགས་པ་ཐོགས་མེད་ཞབས།

GYAL TSAB JAM PA PAG PA TOG ME ZHAB

jina, victor representative Maitreya arya, pure unimpeded, Asanga feet (honorific)

Buddha's representative Maitreya and Arya Asanga,

སློབ་དཔོན་དབྱིག་གཉེན་འཕགས་པ་རྣམ་གྲོལ་སྡེ།

LO PON JIG NYEN PHAG PA NAM DROL TE

scholar Vasubandhu arya Vimuktisen thus

Acharya Vasubandhu and Arya Vimuktisen,

གསོལ་བ་འདེབས་སོ་དོན་གཉིས་མཐར་ཕྱིན་ཤོག།

SOL WA DEB SO DON NYI THAR CHIN SHOG

prayer make benefit two fulful must

We pray to you that enlightenment will be gained by all beings and ourselves.

Unequalled powerful sage, Bhagawan Shakyamuni, Buddha's representative Maitreya and Arya Asanga, Acharya Vasubandhu and Arya Vimuktisen, we pray to you that enlightenment will be gained by all beings and ourselves.

གྲོལ་དང་མཆོག་དང་དུལ་བའི་སྡེ་རྣམ་གསུམ།

DROL DANG CHOG DANG DUL WAI DE NAM SUM

liberation and supreme and discipline these groups three

The three lineages of Drol, Chog and Dulwa,

རྣམ་པར་སྣང་མཛད་སེང་གེ་བཟང་པོའི་ཞབས།

NAM PAR NANG DZE SENG GE ZANG POI ZHAB
Vairocana lion good feet (honorific)
Nampar Nangdze and Senge Zangpo,

སངས་རྒྱས་ཡེ་ཤེས་ཡོན་ཏན་བཤེས་གཉེན་ལ།

SANG GYE YE SHE YON TEN SHE NYEN LA
Buddha original knowing qualities friend to
Sangye Yeshe and Yonten Shenyen,

གསོལ་བ་འདེབས་སོ་དོན་གཉིས་མཐར་ཕྱིན་ཤོག།

SOL WA DEB SO DON NYI THAR CHIN SHOG
prayer make benefit two fulful must
We pray to you that enlightenment will be gained by all beings and ourselves.

The three lineages of Drol, Chog and Dulwa, Nampar Nangdze and Senge Zangpo, Sangye Yeshe and Yonten Shenyen, we pray to you that enlightenment will be gained by all beings and ourselves.

རིན་ཆེན་རི་བོ་ཟླ་བཟང་འབུམ་གསུམ་པ།

RIN CHEN RI WO DA ZANG BUM SUM PA
Rinchen Riwo and Dazang Bumsumpa,

རྔོག་ལོ་ཆེན་པོ་འབྲེ་སྟོན་ཤེས་རབ་འབར།

NGOG LO CHEN PO DRE TON SHE RAB BAR
Ngoglo Chenpo and Treton Sherab Bar,

བྱང་ཆུབ་ཡེ་ཤེས་ཁུ་གཞོན་བརྩོན་འགྲུས་ལ།

JANG CHUB YE SHE KHU ZHON TSON DRU LA
Jangchub Yeshe and Khuzhon Tsondru,

གསོལ་བ་འདེབས་སོ་དོན་གཉིས་མཐར་ཕྱིན་ཤོག།

SOL WA DEB SO DON NYI THAR CHIN SHOG
We pray to you that enlightenment will be gained by all beings and ourselves.

Rinchen Riwo and Dazang Bumsumpa, Ngoglo Chenpo and Treton Sherab Bar, Jangchub Yeshe and Khuzhon Tsondru, we pray to you that enlightenment will be gained by all beings and ourselves.

དཀར་ཆུང་རིང་མོ་ཞང་ཡེ་ཆེན་པོ་དང་།

KAR CHUNG RING MO ZHANG YE CHEN PO DANG

Karchung Ringmo and Zhangye Chenpo,

གཉལ་ཞིག་འཇམ་དཔལ་རྡོ་རྗེ་རྒྱ་འཆིང་རུས།

NYAL ZHIG JAM PAL DOR JE GYA CHING RU

Nyalzhig Jampal and Dorje Gyaching Ru,

ཆུ་མིག་སེང་གེ་དཔལ་དང་ལྷོ་བྲག་པར།

CHU MI SENG GE PAL DANG LHO DRAG PAR

Chumig Senge Pal and Lhodragpa,

གསོལ་བ་འདེབས་སོ་དོན་གཉིས་མཐར་ཕྱིན་ཤོག།

SOL WA DEB SO DON NYI THAR CHIN SHOG

We pray to you that enlightenment will be gained by all beings and ourselves.

Karchung Ringmo and Zhangye Chenpo, Nyalzhig Jampal and Dorje Gyaching Ru, Chumig Senge Pal and Lhodragpa, we pray to you that enlightenment will be gained by all beings and ourselves.

བཙན་དགོན་པ་དང་ཆོས་དཔལ་རྒྱ་མཚོ་དང་།

TSEN GON WA DANG CHO PAL GYAM TSHO DANG

Tsen Gonwa and Chopal Gyamsto,

དྲི་མེད་འོད་ཟེར་ཁྱབ་བརྡལ་ལྷུན་གྲུབ་དང་།

DRI MED OD ZER KHYAB DAL LHUN DRUB DANG

Drime Ozer and Khyabdal Lhundrub,

གྲགས་པ་འོད་ཟེར་སངས་རྒྱས་དབོན་པོ་ལ།

DRAG PA OD ZER SANG GYE ON PO LA

Dragpa Ozer and Sangye Onpo,

གསོལ་བ་འདེབས་སོ་དོན་གཉིས་མཐར་ཕྱིན་ཤོག།

SOL WA DEB SO DON NYI THAR CHIN SHOG

We pray to you that enlightenment will be gained by all beings and ourselves.

Tsen Gonwa and Chopal Gyamsto, Drime Ozer and Khyabdal Lhundrub, Dragpa Ozer and Sangye Onpa, we pray to you that enlightenment will be gained by all beings and ourselves.

ཟླ་བ་གྲགས་པ་ཀུན་བཟང་རྡོ་རྗེ་དང་།

DA WA DRAG PA KUN ZANG DOR JE DANG

Dawa Dragpa and Kunzang Dorje,

ཀུན་དགའ་རྒྱལ་མཚན་སྣ་ཚོགས་རང་གྲོལ་ཞབས།

KUN GA GYAL TSEN NA TSHOG RANG DROL ZHAB

Kunga Gyaltsen and Natshog Rangdrol,

བསྟན་འཛིན་གྲགས་པ་མདོ་སྔགས་བསྟན་འཛིན་ལ།

TEN DZIN DRAG PA DO NGAG TEN DZIN LA

Tendzin Dragpa and Dongag Tendzin,

གསོལ་བ་འདེབས་སོ་དོན་གཉིས་མཐར་ཕྱིན་ཤོག།

SOL WA DEB SO DON NYI THAR CHIN SHOG

We pray to you that enlightenment will be gained by all beings and ourselves.

Dawa Dragpa and Kunzang Dorje, Kunga Gyaltsen and Natshog Rangdrol, Tendzin Dragpa and Dongag Tendzin, we pray to you that enlightenment will be gained by all beings and ourselves.

འཕྲིན་ལས་ལྷུན་གྲུབ་པདྨ་འཕྲིན་ལས་ཞབས།

TRIN LAE LHUN DRUB PE MA TRIN LAE ZHAB

Trinlae Lhundrub and Pema Trinlae,

པདྨ་དབང་རྒྱལ་པདྨ་དབང་ཕྱུག་དང་།

PE MA WANG GYAL PE MA WANG CHUG DANG

Pema Wangyal and Pema Wangchug,

ངག་དབང་འཕྲིན་ལས་ཁམས་གསུམ་ཟིལ་གནོན་ལ།

NGA WANG TRIN LAE KHAM SUM ZIL NON LA

Ngawang Trinlae and Khamsum Zilnon,

གསོལ་བ་འདེབས་སོ་དོན་གཉིས་མཐར་ཕྱིན་ཤོག།

SOL WA DEB SO DON NYI THAR CHIN SHOG

We pray to you that enlightenment will be gained by all beings and ourselves.

Trinlae Lhundrub and Pema Trinlae, Pema Wangyal, and Pema Wangchug, Ngawang Trinlae and Khamsum Zilnon, we pray to you that enlightenment will be gained by all beings and ourselves.

ནམ་མཁའ་ཀློང་ཡངས་བདུད་འདུལ་རྡོ་རྗེ་དང་།

NAM KHA LONG YANG DU DUL DOR JE DANG

Namkha Longyang and Dudul Dorje,

རྒྱལ་བའི་མྱུ་གུ་མཉམ་ཉིད་རྡོ་རྗེ་ཞབས།

GYAL WAI NYU GU NYAM NYID DOR JE ZHAB

Gyalwai Nyugu and Nyamnyid Dorje,

ཐུབ་བསྟན་མདོ་སྔགས་བསྟན་པའི་ཉི་མ་དང་།

THUB TEN DO NGAG TEN PAI NYI MA DANG

Thubten Dongag Tenpai Nyima,

ཚུལ་ཁྲིམས་བཟང་པོ་འཆི་མེད་རིག་འཛིན་བར།

TSHUL TRIM ZANG PO CHI MED RIG DZIN BAR

Tshultrim Zangpo and Chimed Rigdzin,

གསོལ་བ་འདེབས་སོ་དོན་གཉིས་མཐར་ཕྱིན་ཤོག།

SOL WA DEB SO DON NYI THAR CHIN SHOG

We pray to you that enlightenment will be gained by all beings and ourselves.

Namkha Longyang and Dudul Dorje, Gyalwai Nyugu and Nyamnyid Dorje, Thubten Dongag Tenpai Nyima, Tshultrim Zangpo and Chimed Rigdzin, we pray to you that enlightenment will be gained by all beings and ourselves.

སློབ་དཔོན་ཀླུ་སྒྲུབ་ལུགས་ཀྱི་ཟབ་མོ་དབུ་མ་དང་འབྲེལ་བའི་བླ་བརྒྱུད་ནི།
The Lineage of Gurus in Acharya Nagarjuna's System of the Profound Madhyamika Middle Way

བསྟན་པའི་བདག་པོ་སངས་རྒྱས་བཅོམ་ལྡན་འདས།

TEN PAI DAG PO SANG GYE CHOM DEN DAE
doctrine master buddha bhagawan, enlightened
Master of the Doctrine, Bhagawan Buddha Shakyamuni,

འཕགས་པ་འཇམ་དཔལ་སློབ་དཔོན་ཀླུ་སྒྲུབ་ཞབས།

PHAG PA JAM PAL LO PON LU DRUB ZHAB
arya, pure Manjushri acharya, scholar Nagarjuna feet (honorific)
Arya Manjushri and Acharya Nagarjuna,

རྒྱལ་སྲས་ཞི་བ་ལྷ་དང་འཕགས་པ་ལྷ།

GYAL SAE ZHI WA LHA DANG PHAG PA LHA
victor's son Shantideva and Aryadeva
Bodhisattva Santideva and Aryadeva,

སངས་རྒྱས་བསྐྱངས་དང་ཟླ་བ་གྲགས་པ་ལ།

SANG GYE KYANG DANG DA WA DRAG PA LA
Buddha cherished and moon fame to
Buddhapalita and Chandrakirti,

གསོལ་བ་འདེབས་སོ་མཐའ་བྲལ་དོན་རྟོགས་ཤོག།

SOL WA DEB SO THA DRAL DON TOG SHOG
prayer make sunyata, emptiness awaken to must
We pray to you that we may awaken to infinite presence.

Master of the Doctrine, Bhagawan Buddha Shakyamuni, Arya Manjushri and Acharya Nagarjuna, Bodhisattva Santideva and Aryadeva, Buddhapalita and Chandrakirti, we pray to you that we may awaken to infinite presence.

རིག་པའི་ཁུ་བྱུག་ཀུ་སི་ལི་ཆེ་ཆུང་།

RIG PAI KHU JUG KU SI LI CHE CHUNG
Rigpai Khujug and Kusili Chechung,

ཡེ་ཤེས་བྱེད་པ་བྱང་སེམས་ཟླ་བ་རྒྱལ།

YE SHE JE PA JANG SEM DA WA GYAL

Yeshe Jepa and Jangsem Dawagyal,

གྲོ་ལུང་པ་དང་སྤྱི་བོར་ལྷས་པ་ལ།

DRO LUNG PA DANG CHI WOR LHAE PA LA

Drolungpa and Chiwor Lhaepa,

གསོལ་བ་འདེབས་སོ་མཐའ་བྲལ་དོན་རྟོགས་ཤོག།

SOL WA DEB SO THAR DRAL DON TOG SHOG

We pray to you that we may awaken to infinite presence.

Rigpai Khujug and Kusili Chechung, Yeshe Jepa and Jangsem Dawagyal, Drolungpa and Chiwor Lhaepa, we pray to you that we may awaken to infinite presence.

མ་སྟོན་ཤཱཀ་སེང་མཆིམས་སྟོན་ནམ་མཁའ་གྲགས།

MA TON SHAK SENG CHIM TON NAM KHA DRAG

Maton Shakseng and Chimton Namkha Drag,

སྨོན་ལམ་ཚུལ་ཁྲིམས་བྱང་སེམས་གྲུབ་པ་དང་།

MON LAM TSHUL TRIM JANG SEM DRUB PA DANG

Monlam Tsultrim and Jangsem Drubpa,

གཞོན་ནུ་རྡོ་རྗེ་དྲི་མེད་འོད་ཟེར་ལ།

ZHON NU DOR JE DRI MED O ZER LA

Zhonu Dorje and Drime Ozer,

གསོལ་བ་འདེབས་སོ་མཐའ་བྲལ་དོན་རྟོགས་ཤོག།

SOL WA DEB SO THA DRAL DON TOG SHOG

We pray to you that we may awaken to infinite presence.

Maton Shakseng and Chimton Namkha Drag, Monlam Tsultrim and Jangsem Drubpa, Zhonu Dorje and Drime Özer, we pray to you that we may awaken to infinite presence.

ཁྱབ་བརྡལ་ལྷུན་གྲུབ་གྲགས་པ་འོད་ཟེར་དང་།

KHYAB DAL LHUN DRUB DRAG PA O ZER DANG

Kyabdal Lhundrub and Dragpa Ozer,

སངས་རྒྱས་དབོན་པོ་ཟླ་བ་གྲགས་པ་དང་།

SANG GYE ON PO DA WA DRAG PA DANG

Sangye Onpo and Dawa Dragpa,

ཀུན་བཟང་རྡོ་རྗེ་ཀུན་དགའ་རྒྱལ་མཚན་ལ།

KUN ZANG DOR JE KUN GA GYAL TSHEN LA

Kunzang Dorje and Kunga Gyalsten,

གསོལ་བ་འདེབས་སོ་མཐའ་བྲལ་དོན་རྟོགས་ཤོག།

SOL WA DEB SO THA DRAL DON TOG SHOG

We pray to you that we may awaken to infinite presence.

Khabdal Lhundrub and Dragpa Ozer, Sangye Onpo and Dawa Dragpa, Kunzang Dorje and Kunga Gyaltsen, we pray to you that we may awaken to infinite presence.

སྣ་ཚོགས་རང་གྲོལ་བསྟན་འཛིན་གྲགས་པ་དང་།

NA TSHOG RANG DROL TEN DZIN DRAG PA DANG

Natshog Rangdrol and Tendzin Dragpa,

མདོ་སྔགས་བསྟན་འཛིན་འཕྲིན་ལས་ལྷུན་གྲུབ་ཞབས།

DO NGAG TEN DZIN TRIN LAE LHUN DRUB ZHAB

Dongag Tendzin and Trinlae Lhundrub,

པདྨ་འཕྲིན་ལས་པདྨ་དབང་རྒྱལ་ལ།

PE MA TRIN LAE PE MA WANG GYAL LA

Pema Trinlae and Pema Wangyal,

གསོལ་བ་འདེབས་སོ་མཐའ་བྲལ་དོན་རྟོགས་ཤོག།

SOL WA DEB SO THA DRAL DON TOG SHOG

We pray to you that we may awaken to infinite presence.

Natshog Rangdrol and Tendzin Dragpa, Dongag Tendzin and Trinale Lhundrub, Pema Trinlae and Pema Wangyal, we pray to you that we may awaken to infinite presence.

པདྨ་དབང་ཕྱུག་ངག་དབང་འཕྲིན་ལས་དང་།

PE MA WANG CHUG NGA WANG TRIN LAE DANG

Pema Wangchug and Ngawang Trinlae,

ཁམས་གསུམ་ཟིལ་གནོན་ནམ་མཁའ་ཀློང་ཡངས་ཞབས།

KHAM SUM ZIL NON NAM KHA LONG YANG ZHAB

Khamsum Zilnon and Namkha Longyang,

བདུད་འདུལ་རྡོར་རྗེ་རྒྱལ་བའི་མྱུ་གུ་ལ།

DUN DUL DOR JE GYAL WAI NYU GU LA

Dudul Dorje and Gyalwai Nyugu,

གསོལ་བ་འདེབས་སོ་མཐའ་བྲལ་དོན་རྟོགས་ཤོག།

SOL WA DEB SO THA DRAL DON TOG SHOG

We pray to you that we may awaken to infinite presence.

Pema Wangchug and Ngawang Trinlae, Khamsum Zilnon and Namkha Longyang, Dudul Dorje and Gyalwai Nyugu, we pray to you that we may awaken to infinite presence.

དམ་པ་དེ་དག་ཀུན་གྱིས་རྗེས་བཟུང་ཞིང་།

DAM PA	**DE DAG**	**KUN**	**GYI**	**JE ZUNG ZHING**
holy ones	*these*	*all*	*by*	*following after*

Following all these holy ones are

ངུར་སྨིག་འཛིན་པ་བརྟུལ་ཞུགས་དམ་པ་ཡིས།

NGUR MIG	**DZIN PA**	**TUL ZHUG**	**DAM PA**	**YI**
red	*wearing*	*bhikshu mode*	*holy, excellent*	*by*

The holy Bhikhus dressed in red,

རྒྱལ་བསྟན་ཉིན་མོར་བྱེད་པའི་ལྷག་བསམ་ཅན།

GYAL TEN	**NYIN MOR**	**JE PAI**	**LHAG**	**SAM**	**CHEN**
Jina's doctrines	*as sun*	*doing*	*excellent*	*thoughts*	*one who has*

Whose excellent thoughts raise the sun of the Victor's Doctrines,

མཉམ་ཉིད་རྡོ་རྗེ་ཤཱི་ལ་བྷ་དྲ་ལམ།

NYAM NYI DOR JE SHI LA BHA DRA LAM

Nyamnyid Dorje, and Shila Bhadra also known as

ཚུལ་ཁྲིམས་བཟང་པོ་འཆི་མེད་རིག་འཛིན་བར།

TSHUL TRIM ZANG PO CHI MED RIG DZIN BAR

Tsultrim Zangpo, and the yogi Chimed Rigdzin,

གསོལ་བ་འདེབས་སོ་མཐའ་བྲལ་དོན་རྟོགས་ཤོག།

SOL WA DEB SO THA DRAL DON TOG SHOG

We pray to you that we may awaken to infinite presence.

Following all these holy ones, the holy Bhikshus dressed in red, whose excellent thoughts raise the sun of the Victor's Doctrines, Nyamnyid Dorje, and Shila Bhadra also known as Tsultrim Zangpo, and the yogi Chimed Rigdzin, we pray to you that we may awaken to infinite presence.

Lineage Prayer for the Bodhisattva Vow

བསྐལ་བཟང་འགྲོ་བའི་སྒྲོན་མེ་ཟས་གཙང་སྲས༔

KAL	**ZANG**	**DRO WAI**	**DRON ME**	**ZAE**	**TSANG**	**SAE**
kalpa, aeon	*good*	*sentient beings*	*lamp**	*food*	*pure*	*son*

* the father of Buddha Sakyamuni

Buddha Shakyamuni, the lamp for beings in this good aeon,

རྒྱལ་སྲས་འཇམ་པའི་དབྱངས་དང་ཀླུ་སྒྲུབ་ཞབས༔

GYAL	**SAE**	**JAM PAI JANG**	**DANG**	**LU DRUB**	**ZHAB**
victor's bodhisattvas	*son*	*Manjughosa*	*and*	*Nagarjuna*	*feet (honorfic)*

The Bodhisattva Manjughosa and Nagarjuna,

ཞི་བ་ལྷ་སོགས་ཟབ་མོ་ལྟ་བའི་ལུགས༔

ZHI WA LHA	**SOG**	**ZAB MO**	**TA WAI**	**LUG**
Santideva	*and so on*	*profound (emptiness)*	*view*	*style, way*

Santideva and the others, to you who revealed the method of the profound view,

དབུ་མའི་སྲོལ་འབྱེད་རྣམས་ལ་གསོལ་བ་འདེབས༔

U MAI	**SOL**	**JE**	**NAM**	**LA**	**SOL WA DEB**
Madhyamika Middle Way	*practice, way*	*open*	*plural*	*to*	*pray*

The practice of Madhyamika, we pray.

Buddha Shakyamuni, the lamp for beings in this good aeon, the Bodhisattva Manjughosa and Nagarjuna, Santideva and the others, we pray to you who opened the path of the profound view, the practice of Madhyamika.

རྒྱལ་ཚབ་བྱམས་མགོན་འཕགས་པ་ཐོགས་མེད་དང༔

GYAL	**TSHAB**	**JAM GON**	**PHAG PA**	**THOG ME**	**DANG**
Victor, Buddha	*representative*	*Maitreyanatha*	*arya, pure*	*unobstructed Asanga*	*and*

Maitreyanatha, the representative of the Buddha, along with Arya Asanga,

དབྱིག་གཉེན་ལ་སོགས་རྒྱ་ཆེན་སྤྱོད་པའི་ལུགས༔

JIG NYEN	**LA SOG**	**GYA CHEN**	**CHOD PAI**	**LUG**
Vasubandha	*and so on*	*vast*	*conduct*	*style, way*

Vasubandhu and the others – you established the way of vast conduct,

སེམས་ཙམ་སྲོལ་འཛིན་ཐེག་ཆེན་ཐུན་མོང་གི༔

SEM TSAM	**SOL**	**DZIN**	**THEG CHEN**	**THUN MONG**	**GI**
mind only Yogacara	*practice, way*	*hold, keep*	*Mahayana*	*ordinary, not tantra*	*of*

The practice of Mind Only in the ordinary Mahayana,

བརྒྱུད་པའི་བླ་མ་རྣམས་ལ་གསོལ་བ་འདེབས༔

GYUD PAI	**LA MA**	**NAM**	**LA**	**SOL WA DEB**
lineage	*lamas*	*plural*	*to*	*pray*

We pray to the Gurus of this lineage.

Maitreyanatha, the representative of the Buddha, along with Arya Asanga, Vasubandhu and the others – you established the way of vast conduct. We pray to the Gurus of this lineage of the practice of Mind Only in the ordinary Mahayana.

ཐུན་མོང་མ་ཡིན་རྒྱུད་སྡེའི་སྲོལ་འཛིན་པ༔

THUN MONG	**MA YIN**	**GYUD**	**DEI**	**SOL**	**DZIN PA**
ordinary	*not*	*tantra*	*class, section*	*way, system*	*holding*

The holders of the system of the special Tantric series,

དཔལ་ལྡན་བི་རུ་པ་དང་ན་རོ་པ༔

PAL DEN	**BI RU PA**	**DANG**	**NA RO PA**
glorious	*Birupa*	*and*	*Naropa*

Glorious Birupa and Naropa,

མཉམ་མེད་ཨ་ཏི་ཤ་སོགས་ཉམས་ལེན་གྱི༔

NYAM ME	**A TI SHA**	**SOG**	**NYAM**	**LEN**	**GYI**
unequalled	*Atisha*	*and so on*	*tantric*	*practice*	*of*

Unequalled Atisha and the others in the sadhana practice

བྱིན་རླབས་བརྒྱུད་པ་རྣམས་ལ་གསོལ་བ་འདེབས༔

JIN LAB	**GYUD PA**	**NAM**	**LA**	**SOL WA DEB**
blessing	*lineage*	*plural*	*to*	*pray*

Blessing lineage – we pray to you.

The holders of the system of the special Tantric series, glorious Birupa and Naropa, unequalled Atisha and the others in the sadhana practice blessing lineage – we pray to you.

དབུ་སེམས་སྔགས་ཀྱི་ལམ་སྟེ་ལུགས་གསུམ་གྱི༔

U SEM NGAG KYI LAM TE LUG SUM GYI

Madhyamika Yogacara Tantra of path these ways three of

The lineages of these three styles, the paths of Madhyamika, Yogacara and Tantra,

བརྒྱུད་པའི་ཆུ་བོ་གཅིག་འདྲེས་སྲོལ་འཛིན་པ༔

GYUD PAI CHU WO CHIG DRE SOL DZIN PA

lineages' stream one mix path did

Were merged into one stream

སེམས་དཔའ་ཆེན་པོ་དཀོན་མཆོག་དཔལ་འབྱོར་ཞབས༔

SEM PA CHEN PO KON CHOG PAL JOR ZHAB

heroic being great Konchog Paljor (his name) feet

By the heroic being, Konchog Paljor.

པདྨ་ཕྲིན་ལས་རྣམས་ལ་གསོལ་བ་འདེབས༔

PE MA TRIN LAE NAM LA SOL WA DEB

Padma Trinlae (his name) plural to we pray

We pray to you and to all the lineage gurus down to Padma Trinlae.

The lineages of these three styles, the paths of Madhyamika, Yogacara and Tantra, were merged into one stream by the heroic being, Konchog Paljor. We pray to you and to all the lineage gurus down to Padma Trinlae.

ངེས་དོན་བསྟན་པ་སྤེལ་མཛད་རིག་འཛིན་མཆོག༔

NGE DON TEN PA PEL DZED RIG DZIN CHOG

certain (how the mind is) meaning doctrine spread vidyadhara, adept supreme

The most excellent Vidyadhara who spreads the doctrine of definitive truth,

ཀུན་བཟང་རྒྱ་མཚོ་རིགས་ཀུན་འདུས་པའི་གཙོ༔

KUN ZANG GYAM TSO RIG KUN DUE PAI TSO

all good ocean (his name, Kunzang Gyamtso) kulas, buddha families all encompassing chief

Kunzang Gyamtso, the leader encompassing all the buddha families, and

པདྨའི་ཐུགས་སྤྲུལ་འགྲོ་རྣམས་སྨིན་གྲོལ་བཀོད༔

PE MAI THUG TRUL DRO NAM MIN DROL KO

Padmasambhava's mind apparition beings all ripen, empowerment) liberate (teaching) does, establishes

Padmasambhava's mind apparition, ripening and liberating all beings,

རྡོ་རྗེ་ཐོགས་མེད་ཞབས་ལ་གསོལ་བ་འདེབས༔

DOR JE THOG ME ZHAB LA SOL WA DEB
vajra, indestructible (his name, Dorje Thogme) unimpeded feet at pray

Dorje Thogme – at your feet we pray.

The most excellent Vidyadhara who spreads the doctrine of definitive truth, Kunzang Gyamtso, the leader encompassing all the buddha families, and Padmasambhava's mind apparition, ripening and liberating all beings, Dorje Thogme – at your feet we pray.

བསམ་བཞིན་རྡོ་རྗེ་འཛིན་པའི་རོལ་གར་ཅན༔

SAM ZHIN DOR JE DZIN PA ROL GAR CHEN
wish according to vajra, emptiness holding drama, free play being, having

Manifesting free play displaying the wishfulfilling Vajra

འཕྲིན་ལས་སྒྲུབ་པའི་དབང་ཕྱུག་རྨད་བྱུང་བ༔

TRIN LAE DRUB PAI WANG CHUG ME JUNG WA
activity accomplish powerful amazing, wonderful

You have the marvellous power of accomplishing all necessary activities,

ཧེ་རུ་ཀ་དཔལ་པདྨ་བཤེས་གཉེན་ཞབས༔

HE RU KA PAL PAD MA SHE NYEN ZHAB
fierce liberation glorious lotus friend, guide (his name, Padma Shenyen) feet

Glorious Heruka, Padma Shenyen,

འགྱུར་མེད་ལྷུན་གྲུབ་རྡོ་རྗེར་གསོལ་བ་འདེབས༔

GYUR ME LHUN DRUB DOR JER SOL WA DEB
unchanging spontaneous vajra (his name, Gyurme Lhundrub Dorje) pray

To you and to Gyurme Lhundrub Dorje we pray.

Manifesting free play displaying the wishfulfilling Vajra you have the marvellous power of accomplishing all necessary activities, Glorious Heruka, Padma Shenyen, to you and to Gyurme Lhundrub Dorje we pray.

རྒྱལ་དབང་པདྨའི་ལུང་འཛིན་ཐུགས་སྲས་མཆོག༔

GYAL WANG PAD MAI LUNG ZIN THUG SAE CHOG
jina, victor, Buddha powerful Padmasambhava teaching transmission keeps heart son supreme

The supreme heart son maintaining the teaching of Padmasambhava, our powerful Buddha, and

རྡོ་རྗེ་འཆང་དངོས་ནམ་མཁའ་ཀློང་ཡངས་དང༔

DOR JE CHANG	NGO	NAM KHA	LONG YANG	DANG
Vajradhara, full enlightenment	*actual*	*sky*	*vast*	*and*
		(his name, Namkha Longyang)		

The actual primordial Buddha, Namkha Longyang, and

རིགས་ཀུན་ཁྱབ་བདག་པདྨ་དབང་རྒྱལ་སྡེ༔

RIG	KUN	KHYAB DAG	PAD MA	WANG GYAL DE
buddha families	*all*	*pervading master*	*lotus*	*powerful Buddha*
			(his name, Padma Wangyal De)	

The pervading master of all the families, Padma Wangyal De, and

སྒྲུབ་རིགས་འཇིགས་མེད་རྒྱལ་བའི་མྱུ་གུའི་ཞབས༔

DRUB	RIG	JIG ME	GYAL WAI	NYU GU	ZHAB
practice, accomplishment	*family*	*fearless*	*Buddha's*	*shoot*	*feet (honorific)*
		(his name, Jigme Gyalwai Nyugu)			

Jigme Gyalwai Nyugu of the family of accomplishment, and

ཚུལ་ཁྲིམས་བཟང་པོ་འཆི་མེད་རིག་འཛིན་བར།

TSHUL TRIM ZANG PO CHI MED RIG DZIN BAR

Tsultrim Zangpo and Chimed Rigdzin,

རྩ་བའི་བླ་མའི་ཞབས་ལ་གསོལ་བ་འདེབས༔

TSA WAI	LA MA	ZHAB	LA	SOL WA DEB
root	*guru*	*feet*	*at*	*pray*

To you and to my root Guru we pray.

The supreme heart son maintaining the teaching of Padmasambhava, our powerful Buddha, and the actual primordial Buddha, Namkha Longyang, and the pervading master of all the families, Padma Wangyal De, and Jigme Gyalwai Nyugu of the family of accomplishment, and Tsultrim Zangpo and Chimed Rigdzin – to you and to my root Guru we pray.

སྨོན་འཇུག་བྱང་སེམས་སྡོམ་པ་ཆོག་བཞིན༔

MON	JUG	JANG SEM	DOM PA	CHO GA	ZHIN
aspiration, intention	*actual practice*	*bodhisattva*	*vows*	*ritual*	*accordingly properly*

With the ritual of the Bodhisattva Vows of Aspiration and Engagement

ལེགས་ནོས་སློབ་པ་ལམ་གྱི་གནས་སྐབས་སུ༔

LEG	NO	LOB PA	LAM	GYI	NAE KAB SU
well	*receive*	*learning*	*path*	*of*	*occasion, during*

Fully obtained, during the paths of learning*

(*Relative Truth Bodhicitta is the practice in the 1st and 2nd of the 5 Ways. It is a constructed product of thought dependent on identifying real beings with real problems. Absolute Truth Bodhicitta starts to develop on entering the 3rd Way and is intrinsic spontaneous compassion arising effortlessly whenever and wherever needed. It is fulfilled on completion of the 5th Way where it is non-dual with emptiness.)

ཀུན་རྫོབ་དོན་དམ་བྱང་ཆུབ་སེམས་བསྒོམས་མཐུས༔

KUN DZOB	DON DAM	JANG CHUB SEM	GOM	THU
relative	*absolute*	*bodhicitta, mind of awakening*	*meditation, practice*	*by the power of*

We will practise Relative and Absolute Bodhicitta.

འགྲོ་བའི་དོན་དུ་སངས་རྒྱས་ཐོབ་པར་ཤོག༔

DRO WAI	DON	DU	SANG GYE	THOB PAR	SHOG
sentient beings	*benefit*	*for*	*buddhahood, enlightenment*	*obtain*	*may we*

Then, by the power of this, may we gain Buddhahood for the sake of all beings.

With the ritual of the Bodhisattva Vows of Aspiration and Engagement fully obtained, during the paths of learning we will practise Relative and Absolute Bodhicitta. Then, by the power of this, may we gain Buddhahood for the sake of all beings.

བྱང་སྡོམ་བརྒྱུད་པའི་རིམ་པ་སྟེ་གཉིས་པ།

This concludes the Bodhisattva Vow lineage in the second stage of vows. Honoring the Three Jewels as the basis for Pratimoksha Vows came first, and now the Tantric Vow lineage comes third.

བྱིན་རླབས་ཉེ་བརྒྱུད་སྔགས་ཀྱི་བརྒྱུད་པ་ནི།
The Short Blessing Lineage of the Tantric Lineage

རིགས་ཀུན་ཁྱབ་བདག་བཅོམ་ལྡན་རྣམ་སྣང་མཛད།

RIG	KUN	KHYAB	DAG	CHOM DEN	NAM NANG DZE
buddha families	*all*	*pervade*	*lord*	*Bhagawan, enlightened*	*Vairocana*

Pervading master of all the families, Bhagawan Vairocana,

བསྟན་པའི་བདག་པོ་མཉམ་མེད་ཐུབ་པའི་དབང་།

TEN PAI	DAG PO	NYAM ME	THUB PAI	WANG
doctrine	*chief, master*	*unequalled*	*mighty*	*powerful*

Master of the Doctrine, unequalled Shakyamuni,

ལྷ་དབང་བརྒྱ་བྱིན་དགྲ་བཅོམ་ཀུན་དགའ་བོར།

LHA	WANG	GYA JIN	DRA	JOM	KUN	GA WOR
god	*powerful*	*Indra*	*enemy*	*defeat*	*all*	*joyful*
			(arhat	*)*	*(Ananda*	*)*

Indra, King of the Gods, and the arhat Ananda,

གསོལ་བ་འདེབས་སོ་དོན་གཉིས་ལྷུན་འགྲུབ་ཤོག།

SOL WA DEB SO	DON	NYI	LHUN DRUB	SHOG
pray	*benefit*	*two*	*arise effortlessly*	*may*

We pray to you that our own and others' welfare be effortlessly accomplished.

Pervading master of all the families, Bhagawan Vairocana, Master of the Doctrine, unequalled Shakyamuni, Indra, King of the Gods, and the arhat Ananda, we pray to you that our own and others' welfare be effortlessly accomplished

སློབ་དཔོན་ཀླུ་སྒྲུབ་ཤཱཀྱ་སེང་གེ་ཞབས།

LOB PON	LU DRUB	SHA KYA	SENG GE	ZHAB
acharya, scholar	*Nagarjuna*	**Shakya clan*	*lion*	*feet*

* here this indicates Padmasambhava, the 'Second Buddha'

Acharya Nargajuna, and Shakya Senge,

སྣ་ནམ་རྡོ་རྗེ་བདུད་འཇོམས་རྗེ་འབངས་བཅས།

NA NAM DOR JE DUD JOM	**JE**	**BANG**	**CHE**
one of the five intimate disciples of Padmasambhava	*this refers to King Trisong Deutsen*	*this refers to the remaining 23 disciples*	*with*

Nanam Dorje Dujom, King Trisong Deutsen and the rest of the twenty-five disciples, and

རིག་འཛིན་ཆེན་པོ་དངོས་གྲུབ་རྒྱལ་མཚན་ལ།

RIG DZIN	**CHEN PO**	**NGO DRUB GYAL TSHEN**
vidyadhara	*great*	*Ngodrub Gyaltsen (his name)*

The great Vidyadhara, Ngodrub Gyaltsen,

གསོལ་བ་འདེབས་སོ་དོན་གཉིས་ལྷུན་འགྲུབ་ཤོག།

SOL WA DEB SO	**DON**	**NYI**	**LHUN DRUB**	**SHOG**
pray	*benefit*	*two*	*arise effortlessly*	*may*

We pray to you that our own and others' welfare be effortlessly accomplished.

Acharya Nagarjuna and Shakya Senge, Nanam Dorje Dujom, King Trisong Deutsan and the rest of the twenty-five disciples, and the great Vidyadhara Ngodrub Gyaltsen – to you we pray to you that our own and others' welfare be effortlessly accomplished.

རྣམ་རྒྱལ་མགོན་པོ་སྔགས་འཆང་རྡོ་རྗེ་དཔལ།

NAM GYAL GON PO NGAG CHANG DOR JE PAL

Namgyal Gonpo and Ngagchang Dorje Pal,

རྡོ་རྗེ་མགོན་པོ་བྱམས་པ་བཤེས་གཉེན་དང་།

DOR JE GON PO JAM PA SHE NYEN DANG

Dorje Gonpo and Jampa Shenyen,

ངག་དབང་གྲགས་པ་སངས་རྒྱས་དཔལ་བཟང་ལ།

NGA WANG DRAG PA SANG GYE PAL ZANG LA

Ngawang Dragpa and Sangye Palzang,

གསོལ་བ་འདེབས་སོ་དོན་གཉིས་ལྷུན་འགྲུབ་ཤོག།

SOL WA DEB SO	**DON**	**NYI**	**LHUN DRUB**	**SHOG**
pray	*benefit*	*two*	*arise effortlessly*	*may*

We pray to you that our own and others' welfare be effortlessly accomplished.

Namgyal Gonpo and Ngachang Dorje Pal, Dorje Gonpo and Jampa Shenyen, Ngawang Dragpa and Sangye Palzang, we pray to you that our own and others' welfare be effortlessly accomplished.

ཀུན་དགའ་དོན་གྲུབ་ཀུན་དགའ་ལྷུན་གྲུབ་ཞབས།

KUN GA DON DROB KUN GA LHUN DRUB ZHAB

Kunga Dondrub and Kunga Lhundrub,

ཤཱཀྱ་བཟང་པོ་པདྨ་དབང་གི་རྒྱལ།

SHA KYA ZANG PO PE MA WANG GI GYAL

Shakya Zangpo and Pema Wangi Gyal,

ལེགས་ལྡན་རྡོ་རྗེ་བཀྲ་ཤིས་སྟོབས་རྒྱལ་ལ།

LEG DEN DOR JE TRA SHI TOB GYAL LA

Legden Dorje and Tashi Tobgyal,

གསོལ་བ་འདེབས་སོ་དོན་གཉིས་ལྷུན་འགྲུབ་ཤོག།

SOL WA DEB SO DON NYI LHUN DRUB SHOG

We pray to you that our own and others' welfare be effortlessly accomplished.

Kunga Dondrub and Kunga Lhundrub, Shakya Zangpo and Pema Wangi Gyal, Legden Dorje and Tashi Tobgyal, we pray to you that our own and others' welfare be effortlessly accomplished.

ངག་གི་དབང་པོ་བསྟན་འཛིན་ནོར་བུ་དང་།

NGA GI WANG PO TEN DZIN NOR BU DANG

Ngagi Wangpo and Tendzin Norbu,

ཆོས་དབྱིངས་རང་གྲོལ་དྲག་རྩལ་རྡོ་རྗེ་ཞབས།

CHO YING RANG DROL DRAG TSAL DOR JE

Choying Rangdrol and Dragtsal Dorje,

པདྨ་འཕྲིན་ལས་སྐལ་བཟང་པདྨ་དབང་།

PE MA TRIN LAE KAL ZANG PE MA WANG

Peme Trinlae and Kalzang Pemawang,

གསོལ་བ་འདེབས་སོ་དོན་གཉིས་ལྷུན་འགྲུབ་ཤོག།

SOL WA DEB SO DON NYI LHUN DRUB SHOG

We pray to you that our own and others' welfare be effortlessly accomplished.

Ngagi Wangpo and Tendzin Norbu, Choying Rangdrol and Dragtsal Dorje, Pema Trinlae and Kalzang Pemawang, we pray to you that our own and others' welfare be effortlessly accomplished.

པདྨ་བཤེས་གཉེན་ཁམས་གསུམ་ཟིལ་གནོན་ཞབས།
PAD MA SHE NYEN KHAM SUM ZIL NON ZHAB
Padma Shenyen and Khasum Zilnon,

འཇིགས་མེད་དཔའ་བོ་ནམ་མཁའ་ཀློང་ཡངས་དང་།
JIG ME PA WO NAM KHA LONG YANG DANG
Jigme Pawo and Namkha Longyang,

པདྨ་དབང་རྒྱལ་བདུད་འདུལ་རྡོ་རྗེ་ལ།
PAD MA WANG GYAL DU DUL DOR JE
Padma Wangyal and Dudul Dorje,

གསོལ་བ་འདེབས་སོ་དོན་གཉིས་ལྷུན་གྲུབ་ཤོག།
SOL WA DEB SO DON NYI LHUN DRUB SOG
We pray to you that our own and others' welfare be effortlessly accomplished.

Padma Sheyen and Khamsum Zilnon, Jigme Pawo and Namkha Longyang, Padma Wangyal and Dudul Dorje, we pray to you that our own and others' welfare be effortlessly accomplished.

རྒྱལ་བའི་མྱུ་གུ་མཉམ་ཉིད་རྡོ་རྗེ་དང་།
GYAL WAI NYU GU NYAM NYI DOR JE DANG
Gyalwai Nyugu and Nyamnyi Dorje,

ཐུབ་བསྟན་མདོ་སྔགས་བསྟན་པའི་ཉི་མ་དང་།
THUB TEN DO NGAG TEN PAI NI MA DANG
Thubten Dongag and Tenpai Nyima,

ཚུལ་ཁྲིམས་བཟང་པོ་འཆི་མེད་རིག་འཛིན་བར།
TSHUL TRIM ZANG PO CHI MED RIG DZIN BAR
Tsultrim Zangpo and Chimed Rigdzin,

གསོལ་བ་འདེབས་སོ་དོན་གཉིས་ལྷུན་གྲུབ་ཤོག།
SOL WA DEB SO DON NYI LHUN DRUB SHOG
We pray to you that our own and others' welfare be effortlessly accomplished.

Gyalwai Nyugu and Nyamnyi Dorje, Thubten Dongag and Tenpai Nyima, Tsultrim Zangpo and Chimed Rigdzin, we pray to you that our own and others' welfare be effortlessly accomplished.

Directing the Benefit of the Lineage Prayers

འདི་ལྟར་གསོལ་བ་བཏབ་པའི་བྱིན་རླབས་ཀྱིས།

DI TAR SOL WA TAB PAI JIN LAB KYI
this like praying blessing by
By the blessing of having prayed in this way,

རྒྱ་ཆེན་སྤྱོད་པའི་རིང་ལུགས་མཐར་ཕྱིན་ཅིང་།

GYA CHEN CHOD PAI RING LUG THAR CHIN CHING
vast great conduct, activity tradition completing
(Yogachara)
Completing the practice path of the vast Bodhisattva Conduct,

ཟབ་མོ་དབུ་མའི་ལྟ་བའི་དོན་རྟོགས་ནས།

ZAB MO U MAI TA WAI DON TOG NAE
profound Madhyamika view meaning awaken to then
May we awaken to the meaning of the Profound Middle Way. Then

མཐའ་བྲལ་འོད་གསལ་གཉུག་མའི་རང་ངོ་རུ།

THA DRAL OE SAL NYUG MAI RANG NGO RU
limit free of light clear original own face, essence as, to
(The inseparability of emptiness and awareness which is the essenceof all beings.)
To the boundless clear light of the original intrinsic essence

མཁའ་མཉམ་འགྲོ་བ་མ་ལུས་འདྲེན་པར་ཤོག།

KHA NYAM DRO WA MA LU DREN PAR SHOG
sky equal sentient beings without exception lead may
May we lead all beings without exception, equal in extent to the sky.

By the blessing of having prayed in this way, completing the practice path of the vast Bodhisattva Conduct of the Buddha Dharma, may we awaken to the meaning of the Profound Middle Way. Then may we lead all beings without exception, equal in extent to the sky, to the boundless clear light of the original intrinsic essence.

བྱམས་དང་སྙིང་རྗེའི་ལྷ་ལམ་ཡངས་པ་ལ།

JAM DANG NYING JEI LHA LAM YANG PA LA
love and kindness gods path vast in
The vast sky of love and kindness is

ཐོས་བསམ་སྒོམ་པ་ནམ་མཁའི་ནོར་བུ་གང་།

THO	SAM	GOM PA	NAM KAI	NOR BU	GANG
study	*reflection*	*meditation*	*sky's*	*jewel*	*filled*
			(the sun	*)*	

Filled with the sun of study, reflection and meditation.

རྨད་བྱུང་འོད་ཀྱི་གཏེར་ཆེན་བླ་མེད་ཀྱིས།

MAE JUNG	OD	KYI	TER	CHEN	LA MED	KYI
marvellous	*light*	*of*	*treasure*	*great*	*unsurpassed*	*by*

By the marvellous light of this unsurpassed great treasure

སྔ་འགྱུར་བསྟན་པའི་པད་ཚལ་བཞད་པར་མཛོད།

NGA	GYUR	TEN PAI	PAD	TSAL	ZHAD PAR	DZOD
early	*translation*	*doctrines*	*lotus*	*grove*	*blossom*	*treasury*
(Nyingma	*)*					

May the lotus garden of the Nyingma Doctrines be a treasury of blossom.

The vast sky of love and kindness is fully illuminated by the sun of study, reflection and meditation. By the marvellous light of this unsurpassed great treasure may the lotus garden of the Nyingma Doctrines be a treasury of blossom.

སླུ་མེད་དཀོན་མཆོག་རྒྱ་མཚོའི་བདེན་པ་དང་།

LU ME	KON CHOG	GYAM TSOI	DEN PA	DANG
unfailing	*jewels*	*ocean*	*truth*	*and*
undeceptive	*(Buddha, Dharma, Sangha)*			

By the truth of the ocean of the unfailing Jewels, and

རབ་འབྱམས་རྒྱལ་བ་རྒྱ་མཚོའི་ཐུགས་རྗེ་དང་།

RAB JAM	GYAL WA	GYAM TSHOI	THUG JE	DANG
vast	*jinas, victors*	*ocean*	*kindness*	*and*

By the kindness of the ocean of the omnipresent Buddhas, and

མཐུ་ལྡན་ཆོས་སྲུང་རྒྱ་མཚོའི་ནུས་མཐུ་ཡིས།

THU DEN	CHO	SUNG	GYAM TSHOI	NU	THU	YI
strength	*dharma*	*protectors*	*ocean*	*force*	*strength*	*by*

By the forceful strength of the ocean of strong Dharma Protectors,

འདུས་སྡེ་བསྐལ་པ་རྒྱ་མཚོར་བརྟན་གྱུར་ཅིག།

DU DE	KAL PA	GYAM TSOR	TEN	GYUR CHIG
sangha, assembly	*aeon*	*ocean*	*steady,*	*be*
of practitioners			*remain*	

May the Sangha remain for an ocean of aeons.

By the truth of the ocean of the unfailing Jewels, and by the kindness of the ocean of the omnipresent Buddhas, and by the forceful strength of the ocean of strong Dharma Protectors, may the Sangha remain for an ocean of aeons.

རྒྱལ་བསྟན་སྤྱི་དང་རྡོ་རྗེ་ཐེག་པ་ཡི།

GYAL	**TEN**	**CHI**	**DANG**	**DOR JE**	**THEG PA**	**YI**
Buddha, victor	*doctrine*	*general*	*and*	*vajra, indestructible*	*yana, vehicle (tantra)*	*of*

The general doctrines of the Buddha and those of the Vajrayana

བསྟན་པ་འཛིན་སྐྱོང་སྤེལ་ལ་བླ་མེད་པ།

TEN PA	**DZIN**	**KYONG**	**PEL**	**LA**	**LA ME PA**
doctrine	*held*	*protected*	*spread, developed*	*as*	*unsurpassed*

Are held, protected and developed in unsurpassed fashion

གུ་རུ་པདྨའི་ཨེ་ཝཾ་ལྕོག་སྒར་པའི།

GU RU PAD MAI	**E VAM**	**CHO**	**GAR PAI**
Padmasambhava's	*wisdom and kindness*	*cloth*	*tent's*

(the head monastery in Tibet of the Changter Lineage)

At the monastery of Guru Padmai Ewam Chogar.

བསྟན་པ་མཐའ་གྲུར་ཁྱབ་པའི་བཀྲ་ཤིས་ཤོག།

TEN PA	**THA GRUR**	**KHYAB PAI**	**TA SHI**	**SHOG**
doctrines	*spacious*	*pervade*	*happiness*	*may*

May these doctrines spread everywhere bringing happiness to all!

The general doctrines of the Buddha and those of the Vajrayana are held, protected and developed in unsurpassed fashion at the monastery of Guru Padmai Evam Chogar. May these doctrines spread everywhere bringing happiness to all!

Taking Refuge

སངས་རྒྱས་དང་བྱང་ཆུབ་སེམས་དཔའ་ཐམས་ཅད་བདག་ལ་དགོངས་སུ་གསོལ།

SANG GYE DANG JANG CHUB SEM PA THAM CHE DAG LA GONG SU SOL

buddhas and bodhisattvas all me to please listen, please pay heed

All Buddhas and Bodhisattvas please listen to me!

སློབ་དཔོན་བདག་ལ་དགོངས་སུ་གསོལ།

LOB PON DAG LA GONG SU SOL

teacher me to please listen

Teacher please listen to me!

བདག་མིང་(………)འདི་ཞེས་བགྱི་བ་དུས་འདི་ནས་བཟུང་ནས་

DAG MING DI ZHE GYI WA DU DI NAE ZUNG NAE

I name this called now, this time from future lives

From this time on, I (say own name), in all my future lives,

ཇི་སྲིད་བྱང་ཆུབ་སྙིང་པོ་ལ་མཆིས་ཀྱི་བར་དུ།

JI SI JANG CHUB NYING PO LA CHI KYI BAR DU

as long as enlightenment heart essence to come, get until

In as many lives as it takes to reach full enlightenment,

རྐང་གཉིས་རྣམས་ཀྱི་མཆོག་སངས་རྒྱས་ལ་སྐྱབས་སུ་མཆིའོ།

KANG NYI NAM KYI CHOG SANG GYE LA KYAB SU CHIO

legs two (humans) (plural) of, among best, supreme buddha to I go for refuge

Go for refuge to the Buddha, supreme among humans,

འདོད་ཆགས་དང་བྲལ་བ་རྣམས་ཀྱི་མཆོག་

DOD CHAG DANG DRAL WA NAM KYI CHOG

desire free from (plural) of best

Go for refuge to the Dharma,

ཆོས་ལ་སྐྱབས་སུ་མཆིའོ།

CHO LA KYAB SU CHIO

dharma to I go for refuge*

(*Dharma is the original unchanging, sole truth of emptiness – it is self-existing and desires and requires nothing)

The best of all paths, free from desire,

ཚོགས་རྣམས་ཀྱི་མཆོག་དགེ་འདུན་ལ་སྐྱབས་སུ་མཆིའོ།

TSHOG NAM	**KYI**	**CHOG**	**GEN DUN**	**LA**	**KYAB SU CHIO**
assemblies	*of*	*best*	*sangha**	*to*	*I go for refuge*

(*the sangha here means the Bodhisattva Sangha, who have 7th Stage 4th Way or at least 1st Stage 3rd Way. They must 1) have highest Dharma knowledge, 2) be worthy of respect on account of their own good qualities, not because of money, social position or worldly power, 3) always speak and act peacefully.)

Go for refuge to the Sangha, the best of assemblies.

All Buddhas and Bodhisattvas please listen to me! Teacher, please listen to me! From this time on in all my future lives, in as many as it takes to reach full enlightenment, I (…say own name…), go for refuge to the Buddha, supreme among humans, go for refuge to the Dharma, the best of all paths, free from desire, go for refuge to the Sangha, the best of assemblies.

ཕྱོགས་བཅུའི་སངས་རྒྱས་བྱང་ཆུབ་སེམས་དཔའ་དང༔

CHOG	**CHUI**	**SANG GYE**	**JANG CHUB SEM PA**	**DANG**
directions	*ten*	*buddhas*	*bodhisattvas*	*and*

Buddhas and Bodhisattvas of the ten directions,

བླ་མ་ཡི་དམ་མཁའ་འགྲོ་དགོངས་སུ་གསོལ༔

LA MA	**YI DAM**	**KHAN DRO**	**GONG SU SOL**
gurus	*path deities*	*dakinis*	*please hear me*

Gurus, Path Deities and Dakinis, please hear me!

དེང་ནས་བཟུང་སྟེ་བྱང་ཆུབ་མ་ཐོབ་བར༔

DENG	**NAE**	**ZUNG TE**	**JANG CHUB**	**MA THOB**	**BAR**
today	*from*	*lives I will have*	*enlightenment*	*not get*	*until*

From today, in all my lives for as long as enlightenment is not gained,

རྐང་གཉིས་གཙོ་བོ་སངས་རྒྱས་བཅོམ་ལྡན་འདས༔

KANG	**NYI**	**TSO WO**	**SANG GYE**	**CHOM**	**DEN**	**DAE**
legs	*two*	*principle, chief*	*buddha*	*defeated all sin*	*having all good qualities*	*going from samsara*
				(	*Bhagawan*	*)*

To Bhagawan Buddha, the chief of all humans,

ཞི་བ་ཆགས་བྲལ་བདེན་གཉིས་དམ་པའི་ཆོས༔

ZHI WA	**CHAG DRAL**	**DEN NYI**	**DAM PAI**	**CHO**
peaceful	*free of desire*	*two truths (relative and absolute)*	*holy*	*dharma*

To the holy Dharma of relative and absolute truth, peaceful and free of desire,

ཚོགས་མཆོག་འཕགས་པའི་དགེ་འདུན་ཐམས་ཅད་ལ༔

TSHOG	**CHO**	**PHAG PAI**	**GEN DUN**	**THAM CHE**	**LA**
assembly, society	*best*	*arya, noble (great Bodhisattvas)*	*sangha*	*all*	*to*

To all the Sangha of great Bodhisattvas, the best assembly,

བདག་ནི་ཉེ་བར་གུས་པས་སྐྱབས་སུ་མཆི༔

DAG NI	**NYE WAR**	**GUE PAE**	**KYAB SU CHI**
I	*intimate, genuine*	*devotion*	*go for refuge*

I go for refuge with genuine devotion.

Buddhas and Bodhisattvas of the ten directions, Gurus, Path Deities and Dakinis, please hear me! From today, in all my lives for as long as enlightenment is not gained, to Bhagawan Buddha, the chief of all humans, to the holy Dharma of relative and absolute truth, peaceful and free of desire, to all the Sangha of great Bodhisattvas, the best assembly, I go for refuge with genuine devotion.

ཞེས་ལན་གསུམ༔ [Say this three times]

མི་དགེ་བཅུ་སྤང་གི་སྡོམ་པ་བཟུང་བ་ནི༔

[Holding to the firm intention to abandon the ten unvirtuous actions listed below, recite as follows:]

སྐྱབས་གནས་བསླུ་མེད་དཀོན་མཆོག་རྣམ་པ་གསུམ༔

KYAB NAE	**LU MED**	**KON CHOG**	**NAM PA**	**SUM**
refuge place	*unfailing, not cheating*	*jewels (Buddha, Dharma, Sangha)*	*kinds*	*three*

I pray that my unfailing refuge, the Three Jewels

དེང་འདིར་བདག་ལ་ཉེ་བར་དགོངས་སུ་གསོལ༔

DENG	**DIR**	**DAG**	**LA**	**NYE WAR**	**GONG**	**SU SOL**
today	*here*	*me*	*to*	*truly*	*consider*	*please*

Will be attentive to me here and now.

I pray that my unfailing refuge, the Three Jewels will be attentive to me here and now.

འཕགས་པ་དཀོན་མཆོག་གསུམ་གྱི་སྤྱན་སྔ་རུ༔

PHAG PA	**KON CHOG**	**SUM**	**GYI**	**CHEN NGA**	**RU**
arya, noble	*jewels*	*three*	*of*	*in front*	*to*

Before the noble Three Jewels,

བདག་གི་ལུས་ངག་ཡིད་གསུམ་དད་པ་ཡིས༔

DAG GI	LU	NGAG	YI	SUM	DAE PA	YI
my	*body*	*speech*	*mind*	*three*	*faith*	*by*

With sincere faith and my entire body, speech and mind,

གཞན་ལ་གནོད་པ་སྤངས་ལ་དགེ་བ་བསྒྲུབ༔

ZHEN	LA	NOE PA	PANG	LA	GE WA	DRUB
others	*to*	*harm, trouble*	*give up*	*then*	*virtue*	*practice*

I abandon harming others and will now practise only virtue.

Before the noble Three Jewels with sincere faith and my body, speech and mind, I abandon harming others and will now practise only virtue.

སྲོག་གཅོད་མ་སྦྱིན་ལེན་དང་ལོག་པར་གཡེམ༔

SOG CHO	MA JIN LEN	DANG	LOG PAR YEM
killing	*taking what is not given, stealing*	*and*	*immoderate sexual activity*

Killing, taking what is not given and immoderate sexual activity –

ལུས་ཀྱི་མི་དགེ་གསུམ་པོ་རབ་སྤངས་ནས༔

LU	KYI	MI GE	SUM PO	RAB	PANG	NAE
body	*of*	*sins, unvirtue*	*three*	*fully*	*abandon*	*then*

These three sins of the body I completely renounce and

དགེ་བའི་ལས་གསུམ་བསྒྲུབ་པར་དམ་བཅའ་འོ༔

GE WAI	LAE	SUM	DRUB PAR	DAM CHA O
virtuous	*action*	*three*	*practice*	*I vow, firmly decide*

(i.e. saving beings from death, giving whatever one has to help others, and keeping within the bounds of morality)

Firmly decide and promise to practise the three virtuous activities of the body.

Killing, taking what is not given and immoderate sexual activity – these three sins of the body I completely give up and firmly decide and promise to practise the three virtuous activities of the body

རྫུན་དང་ཕྲ་མ་ཚིག་རྩུབ་ངག་འཁྱལ་སྟེ༔

DZUN	DANG	TRA MA	TSHIG TSUB	NGAG KHYAL	TE
lies	*and*	*calumny, back biting*	*rough speech*	*idle, worthless talk*	*these*

Lying, calumny, rough speech and worthless, idle talk –

ངག་གི་མི་དགེ་བཞི་པོ་རབ་སྤངས་ནས༔

NGAG GI MI GE ZHI PO RAB PANG NAE
speech of sins, unvirtues four completely abandon then

These four sins of speech I completely renounce and

དགེ་བའི་ལས་བཞི་བསྒྲུབ་པར་དམ་བཅའ་འོ༔

GE WAI LAE ZHI DRUB PAR DAM CHA O
virtuous actions four practice firmly decide to

(speaking only the pure truth, reconciling those who are quarrelling, speaking sweetly and calmly, and saying mantras and reading holy books)

Firmly decide and promise to practise the four virtuous activities of speech.

Lying, calumny, rough speech and worthless idle talk – these four sins of speech I completely renounce and firmly decide and promise to practise the four virtuous activities of speech.

བརྣབ་སེམས་གནོད་སེམས་ལོག་པར་ལྟ་བ་སོགས༔

NAB SEM NOD SEM LOG PAR TA WA SOG
covetousness malice, ill-will wrong views (plural)

Covetousness, malice and wrong views –

ཡིད་ཀྱི་མི་དགེ་གསུམ་པོ་རབ་སྤངས་ནས༔

YI KYI MI GE SUM PO RAB PANG NAE
mind of sins,unvirtue three completely give up then

These three sins of the mind I completely renounce and

དགེ་བའི་ལས་གསུམ་བསྒྲུབ་པར་དམ་བཅའ་འོ༔

GE WAI LAE SUM DRUB PAR DAM CHA O
virtuous actions three practise firmly decide to

(i.e. knowing one's own wealth to be sufficient and being free of need for more, concerning oneself with the welfare of others, and having faith in karma and the Three Jewels).

Firmly decide and promise to practise the three virtuous activities of mind.

Covetousness, malice and wrong views – these three sins of the mind I completely renounce and firmly decide and promise to practise the three virtuous activities of mind.

Taking the Bodhisattva Vows

སློབ་དཔོན་དགོངས་སུ་གསོལ།

LO PON — *teacher, officiator*
GONG SU SOL — *please hear me*

Teacher, please hear me!

ཇི་ལྟར་སྔོན་གྱི་དེ་བཞིན་གཤེགས་པ་དགྲ་བཅོམ་པ།

JI TAR — *just as*
NGON GYI — *the previous*
DE ZHIN SHEG PA — *tathagata, buddha*
DRA — **enemy*
CHOM PA — *defeater, (arhat)*

* this refers not to the hinayana arhat but is a title of Buddha as one who has overcome the afflictions and their subtle traces

Just as in previous times the Tathagatas, Arhats,

ཡང་དག་པར་རྫོགས་པའི་སངས་རྒྱས་བཅོམ་ལྡན་འདས་རྣམས་དང་།

YANG DAG PAR — *supreme*
DZOG PAI — *completely*
SANG GYE — *buddha*
CHOM DEN DAE — *bhagawan (title of buddha)*
NAM — *(plural)*
DANG — *and*

Supreme and complete Bhagawan Buddhas, and

ས་ཆེན་པོ་ལ་རབ་ཏུ་བཞུགས་པའི་བྱང་ཆུབ་སེམས་དཔའ་རྣམས་ཀྱིས།

SA — *stages**
CHEN PO — *great*
LA — *on*
RAB TU ZHUG PAI — *firmly staying*
JANG CHUB SEM PA — *bodhisattvas*
NAM — *(plural)*
KYI — *by*

*the ten stages of the Bodhisattva path to enlightenment.

The Bodhisattvas firmly staying on the great Stages,

དང་པོ་བླ་ན་མེད་པ་ཡང་དག་པར་རྫོགས་པའི

DANG PO — *at first, when beginning their careers*
LA NA ME PA — *unsurpassed, unexcelled*
YANG DAG PAR — *supreme*
DZOG PAI — *complete*

When they first began their careers, gave rise to the altruistic intention to gain the unexcelled supreme and complete

བྱང་ཆུབ་ཆེན་པོར་ཐུགས་བསྐྱེད་པ་དེ་བཞིན་དུ།

JANG CHUB — *enlightenment*
CHEN POR — *great*
THUG KYE PA — *raised the altruistic intention to awaken*
DE ZHIN DU — *like that, similarly*

Great enlightenment,

བདག་མིང་(………)འདི་ཞེས་བགྱི་བ་ཡང་།

DAG	**MING**	**DI ZHE**	**GYI WA**	**YANG**
I	*name*	*so-called*	*do*	*also*

Now, in the same way, I, (…say one's own name…), also

སློབ་དཔོན་གྱིས་བླ་ན་མེད་པ་ཡང་དག་པར་རྫོགས་པའི

LO PON	**GYI**	**LA NA ME PA**	**YANG DAG PAR**	**DZOG PAI**
teacher	*from**	*unsurpassed*	*supreme*	*complete*

*I request the teacher to awaken and develop this wish in me. The wish to benefit all beings by leading them to enlightenment is inherent in our inherent Buddha potential, but it needs to be awakened and developed.

Request from the teacher

བྱང་ཆུབ་ཆེན་པོར་སེམས་བསྐྱེད་པར་མཛད་དུ་གསོལ།

JANG CHUB CHEN POR	**SEM KYE PAR**	**DZO DU SOL**
great enlightenment	*intention, give rise to*	*request*

The raising of the altruistic intention to gain the unsurpassed, supreme and complete great enlightenment.

Teacher, please hear me! Just as in previous times the Tathagatas, Arhats, supreme and complete Bhagawan Buddhas and the Bodhisattvas firmly staying on the great Stages, when they first began their careers, gave rise to the altruistic intention to gain the unexcelled supreme and complete great enlightenment, now, in the same way, I [...say one's own name...] also request from the teacher the raising of the altruistic intention to gain the unsurpassed supreme and complete great enlightenment.

ཕན་པར་བསམས་པ་ཙམ་གྱིས་ཀྱང་།

PHEN PAR	**SAM PA**	**TSAM**	**GYI**	**KYANG**
helpful, beneficial for others, good	*thought*	*just, only*	*by*	*even*

When merely the thought of helping others

སངས་རྒྱས་མཆོད་ལས་ཁྱད་འཕགས་ན།

SANG GYE	**CHOD**	**LAE**	**KHYED**	**PHAG**	**NA**
buddha	*offer worship*	*than (comparative)*	*special*	*noble,*	*if, therefore*

Is more excellent than the worship of the Buddhas,

སེམས་ཅན་མ་ལུས་ཐམས་ཅད་ཀྱི།

SEM CHEN	**MA LU**	**THAM CHE**	**KYI**
beings, all those in samsara	*without exception*	*all*	*of*

It is unnecessary even to mention the greatness of striving

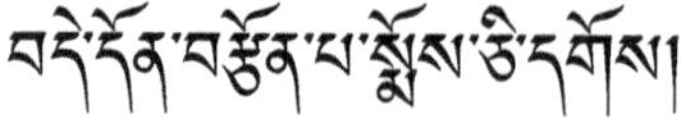

DE	**DON**	**TSON PA**	**MOE CHI GOE**
happiness	*benefit, advantage*	*strongly, diligenty, energetically*	*it is not necessary even to say*

For the happiness and welfare of all beings without exception.

When merely the thought of helping others is more excellent than the worship of the Buddhas, it is unnecessary even to mention the greatness of striving for the happiness and welfare of all beings without exception.

སྨོན་པ་སེམས་བསྐྱེད་ནི༔
Developing the Bodhicitta of Aspiration

བསླུ་མེད་དཀོན་མཆོག་གསུམ་པོ་དགོངས་སུ་གསོལ༔

LU ME	**KON CHOG**	**SUM PO**	**GONG SU SOL**
unfailing	*jewels*	*three*	*please hear me*
(Buddha, Dharma, Sangha)			

Unfailing Three Jewels please pay heed to me.

བདག་མིང་(.........)ཞེས་བགྱི་བས༔

DAG	**MING**	**ZHE GYI WAE**
I	*name*	*thus called by*

I, (...say one's own name...),

འདི་ནས་བཟུང་སྟེ་བྱང་ཆུབ་མ་ཐོབ་བར༔

DI	**NAE**	**ZUNG TE**	**JANG CHUB**	**MA**	**THOB**	**BAR**
now	*from*	*future life*	*enlightenment*	*not*	*gained*	*while, until*

From now on in all my lives until enlightenment is gained,

བདག་གི་མར་གྱུར་འགྲོ་བ་སེམས་ཅན་ལ༔

DAG GI	**MAR GYUR**	**DRO WA**	**SEM CHEN**	**LA**
my	*who have been my mother*	*going in samsara*	*being*	*to*

Towards the beings who move in samsara, all of whom have been my own mother in my countless past lives,

མ་དང་བུ་ཡི་འདུ་ཤེས་རབ་བསྐྱེད་ནས༔

MA	**DANG**	**BU YI**	**DU SHE**	**RAB**	**KYE**	**NAE**
mother	*and*	*child of*	*knowledge, thinking*	*fully*	*develop*	*then*

Will fully develop the attitude of a mother to her children.

སེམས་ཅན་མ་སྒྲོལ་བ་རྣམས་བསྒྲོལ་བ་དང༔

SEM CHEN	**MA DRAL WA NAM**	**DRAL WA DANG**
beings	*who have not been taken out of samsara*	*take out*

Then all those beings who have not yet come out of samsara I will take out, and

མ་གྲོལ་བ་རྣམས་དགྲོལ་བར་བྱ་བ་དང༔

MA	DROL WA	NAM	DROL WAR	JA WA	DANG
not	*freed*	*all (those)*	*free*	*do*	*and*

I will liberate all those who are not free, and

དབུགས་མ་དབྱུང་བ་དག་ནི་དབུགས་དབྱུང་ཕྱིར༔

WUG MA JUNG WA DAG NI	WUG JUNG	CHIR
those who are without hope and confidence	*inspiring, give breath to*	*in order to*

I will inspire and help all those who are without hope and confidence.

སྨོན་པ་བྱང་ཆུབ་མཆོག་ཏུ་སེམས་བསྐྱེད་དོ༔

MON PA	JANG CHUB	CHOG	TU	SEM	KYE DO
aspiration	*enlightenment*	*best*	*to*	*intention*	*raise up, develop*

In order to do this, I give rise to the altruistic aspiration towards the most excellent Enlightenment.

Unfailing Three Jewels, please pay heed to me! From now on in all my lives until enlightenment is gained, I, (…say one's own name …), will fully develop the attitude of a mother to her children towards the beings who move in samsara, all of whom have been my own mother in my countless past lives. Then I will bring out all those beings who have not yet come out of samsara, and I will liberate all those who are not free, and I will inspire and help all those who are without hope and confidence. In order to do this I give rise to the altruistic aspiration towards the most excellent Enlightenment.

ཕྱོགས་བཅུ་ན་བཞུགས་པའི་སངས་རྒྱས་དང་།

CHOG	CHU	NA	ZHUG PAI	SANG GYE	DANG
direction	*ten*	*in*	*staying*	*buddhas*	*and*

All Buddhas and Bodhisattvas staying in the ten directions –

བྱང་ཆུབ་སེམས་དཔའ་ཐམས་ཅད་བདག་ལ་དགོངས་སུ་གསོལ།

JANG CHUB SEM PA	THAM CHE	DAG	LA	GONG	SU SOL
bodhisattvas	*all*	*me*	*to*	*pay heed*	*I pray*

Please pay heed to me.

སློབ་དཔོན་བདག་ལ་དགོངས་སུ་གསོལ།

LO PON	DAG	LA	GONG	SU SOL
teacher	*me*	*to*	*pay heed*	*please*

Teacher, please pay heed to me.

All Buddhas and Bodhisattvas staying in the ten directions, please pay heed to me. Teacher, please pay heed to me.

བདག་མིང་(………)འདི་ཞེས་བགྱི་བ་བདག་གི་སྐྱེ་བ་གཞན་དག་ཏུ་

DAG MING	**DI ZHE**	**GYI WA**	**DAG GI**	**KYE WA**	**ZHAN DAG**	**TU**
my name	*(own name)*	*done*	*my*	*lives*	*others*	*in*

In all my previous lives, I, (…say one's own name…),

སྦྱིན་པ་ལས་བྱུང་བ་དང་།

JIN PA	**LAE**	**JUNG WA**	**DANG**
generosity	*from*	*arising*	*and*

By generosity,

ཚུལ་ཁྲིམས་ལས་བྱུང་བ་དང་།

TSHUL THRIM	**LAE**	**JUNG WA**	**DANG**
morality	*from*	*arising*	*and*

By morality, and

བསྒོམ་པ་ལས་བྱུང་བའི་དགེ་བའི་རྩ་བ་བགྱིས་པ་དང་།

GOM PA	**LAE**	**JUNG WAI**	**GE WAI**	**TSA WAI**	**GYI PA**	**DANG**
meditation	*from*	*arising*	*virtuous*	*root (merit)*	*made, done*	*and*

By meditation have generated merit and also

གཞན་ལ་བགྱིད་དུ་སྩལ་བ་དང་།

ZHEN	**LA**	**GYID DU**	**TSAL WA**	**DANG**
others	*to*	*doing*	*encourage*	*and*

By encouraging others to practise virtue, and

གཞན་གྱིས་བགྱིས་པ་ལ་རྗེས་སུ་ཡི་རངས་པ་དེས།

ZHEN	**GYI**	**GYI PA**	**LA**	**JE SU**	**YI RANG PA**	**DE**
others	*by*	*deed*	*to*	*sympathetic*	*rejoice*	*by*

By rejoicing in the virtue done by others. I will now make use of all this merit.

ཇི་ལྟར་སྔོན་གྱི་དེ་བཞིན་གཤེགས་པ་དགྲ་བཅོམ་པ་ཡང་དག་པ་

JI TAR	**NGON GYI**	**DE ZHIN SHEG PA**	**DRA CHOM PA**	**YANG DAG PA**
just as	*previous*	*tathagatas*	*arhats (all buddhas, not hinayana stage)*	*supreme*

Just as the earlier Tathagatas, Arhats, supreme and

རྫོགས་པའི་སངས་རྒྱས་བཅོམ་ལྡན་འདས་རྣམས་དང་།

DZOG PAI	**SANG GYE**	**CHOM DEN DAE**	**NAM**	**DANG**
complete	*buddha*	*bhagawan*	*(plural)*	*and*

Complete Bhagawan Buddhas and

ས་ཆེན་པོ་ལ་རབ་ཏུ་བཞུགས་པའི་བྱང་ཆུབ་སེམས་དཔའ་

SA	**CHEN PO**	**LA**	**RAB TU**	**ZHUG PAI**	**JANG CHUB SEM PA**
**stages*	*great*	*on*	*firmly*	*staying*	*bodhisattvas*

* Above the 7th of the 10 Budhisattva stages

The Bodhisattvas and Mahasattvas firmly staying on the

སེམས་དཔའ་ཆེན་པོ་རྣམས་ཀྱིས།

SEM PA CHEN PO	**NAM**	**KYI**
mahasattvas, great heroes	*(plural)*	*by*

Great Stages, did,

དང་པོ་བླ་ན་མེད་པ་ཡང་དག་པ་རྫོགས་པའི་

DANG PO	**LA NA ME PA**	**YANG DAG PA**	**DZOG PAI**
at first	*unsurpassed*	*supreme*	*complete*

At the beginning of their spiritual careers,

བྱང་ཆུབ་ཆེན་པོ་ཐུགས་བསྐྱེད་པ་དེ་བཞིན་དུ།

JANG CHUB	**CHEN PO**	**THUG**	**KYE PA**	**DE ZHIN DU**
enlightenment	*great*	*mind, intention*	*develop*	*similar*

Raise the altruistic intention to gain the unsurpassed, supreme and complete, great enlightenment,

བདག་མིང་(.........)འདི་ཞེས་བགྱི་བས་ཀྱང་།

DAG	**MING**	**DI ZHE**	**GYI WAE**	**KYANG**
I	*name*	*(own name)*	*done by me*	*also*

So in the same way, I (…say own name...)

དུས་འདི་ནས་བཟུང་སྟེ།

DUE DI	**NAE**	**ZUNG TE**
now	*from*	*in all future lives*

Also, from this time on in all my lives

ཇི་སྲིད་བྱང་ཆུབ་སྙིང་པོ་ལ་མཆིས་ཀྱི་བར་དུ།

JI SI	**JANG CHUB**	**NYING PO**	**LA**	**CHI KYI**	**BAR DU**
for as long as	*enlightenment*	*heart*	*to*	*get*	*until*

(Using all my virtue gathered in the three times I will fulfil these vows, putting the enlightenment of others before mine.)

Until enlightenment is gained by all beings

སེམས་ཅན་མ་བསྒྲལ་བ་རྣམས་བསྒྲལ་བ་དང་།

SEM CHEN	**MA DRAL WA NAM**	**DRAL WA**	**DANG**
beings	*those who are not yet out of samsara*	*take out*	*and*

Will take out all those beings who have not yet come out of samsara, and

མ་གྲོལ་བ་རྣམས་དགྲོལ་བ་དང་།

MA DROL WA NAM DROL WA DANG
those who are not free *free* *and*
I will free all those who are not yet freed, and

དབུགས་མ་དབྱུང་རྣམས་དབུགས་དབྱུང་བ་དང་།

WUG MA JUNG NAM WUG JUNG WA DANG
breath, inspiration *not* *breathe* *those* *inspiration* *breathe* *and*
I will give hope and confidence to those in whom inspiration is lacking, and

ཡོངས་སུ་མྱ་ངན་ལས་མ་འདས་པ་རྣམས།

YONG SU NYA NGEN LAE MA DAE PA NAM
completely *suffering* *from* *not* *free* *those*
All those who have not completely gone from suffering,

མྱ་ངན་ལས་འདས་བའི་སླད་དུ།

NYA NGEN LAE DAE WAI LAE DU
suffering *from* *go* *in order to*
(gain enlightenment)
I will cause to pass from suffering – and in order to do this

བླ་ན་མེད་པ་ཡང་དག་པར་རྫོགས་པའི་

LA ME PA YANG DAG PAR DZOG PAI
unsurpassed *supreme* *and* *complete*
I raise the altruistic intention

བྱང་ཆུབ་ཆེན་པོར་སེམས་བསྐྱེད་པར་བགྱིའོ།

JANG CHUB CHEN POR SEM KYE PAR GYIO
great enlightenment *raise*
To gain the supreme and complete great enlightenment.

In all my previous lives, I, (…say one's own name…), by generosity, by morality, and by meditation have generated merit and also by encouraging others to practise virtue, and by rejoicing in the virtue done by others. I will now make use of all this merit. Just as the earlier Tathagatas, Arhats, supreme and complete Bhagawan Buddhas and the Bodhisattvas and Mahasattvas firmly staying on the Great Stages, did, at the beginning of their spiritual careers, raise the altruistic intention to gain the unsurpassed, supreme and complete, great enlightenment, so in the same way, from this time on in all my lives until enlightenment is gained by all beings, I (…say own name...) also, will bring out all those beings who have not yet come out of samsara, and I will free all those who are not yet freed, and I will give hope and confidence to those in whom inspiration is lacking, and I will cause to pass from suffering all those who have not completely gone from suffering. In order to do this I raise the altruistic intention to gain the supreme and complete great enlightenment.

གོང་གི་ཚིག་རྣམས་བསྟན་འགྱུར་ནང་གི་ཚིག་ཡིན་ལ་ཁ་གསལ་བའི་ཕྱིར་འདི་ལྟར་འཚང་མ་རྒྱ་བ་རྣམས་འཚང་རྒྱ་ནས། ཞི་བ་བྱང་ཆུབ་ཆེན་པོའི་གོ་འཕང་ཐོབ་པའི་སླད་དུ། ཞེས་པའི་དོན་ནོ།

[The above words are from the Tangyur collection and they make clear that the meaning of the words we recite is "for the sake of enlightening the unenlightened and gaining the stage of the great peaceful awakening."]

འཇུག་པ་སེམས་བསྐྱེད་ནི།
Bodhicitta of Engagement in Actual Practice

དངོས་གཞི་ནི། Main Practice

སློབ་མས་སྡོམ་པ་ལེན་པའི་སེམས་བསྐྱེད་ལ། [The disciple who wishes to take the vow committing them to the actual practice of enacting bodhicitta should engage as follows:]

སློབ་དཔོན་གྱིས་རིགས་ཀྱི་བུ་མིང་(………)འདི་ཞེས་བྱ་བ་ཁྱོད།

LO PON	**GYI**	**RIG**	**KYI**	**BU**	**MING**	**DI**	**ZHE JA WA**	**KHYO**
teacher	*by*	*family*	*of*	*child*	*name [disciples name]*	*this*	*called*	*you*

The teacher says, "Good person called [...disciple's name...] do you wish to receive

བྱང་ཆུབ་སེམས་དཔའ་མིང་(………)འདི་ཞེས་བྱ་བ་ལས།

JANG CHUB SEM PA	**MING**	**DI**	**ZHE JA WA**	**LAE**
bodhisattva	*name [teacher's name]*	*this*	*called*	*from*

From this Bodhisattva called [...teacher's name...],

འདས་པའི་བྱང་ཆུབ་སེམས་དཔའ་ཐམས་ཅད་ཀྱི་

DAE PAI	**JANG CHUB SEM PA**	**THAM CHE**	**KYI**
previous	*bodhisattvas*	*all*	*of*

The vows of the training of all the

བསླབ་པའི་གཞི་གང་དག་དང་།

LAB PAI	**ZHI**	**GANG DAG**	**DANG**
trainings	*foundations, vows*	*whatever*	*and*

Bodhisattvas of the past and

ཚུལ་ཁྲིམས་གང་དག་དང་།

TSHUL RIM	**GANG DAG**	**DANG**
morality practices	*whatever*	*and*

All their moral disciplines, and

མ་འོངས་པའི་བྱང་ཆུབ་སེམས་དཔའ་ཐམས་ཅད་ཀྱི་

MA ONG PAI	**JANG CHUB SEM PA**	**THAM CHE**	**KYI**
future	*bodhisattvas*	*all*	*of*

The vows of the training of all the

བསླབ་པའི་གཞི་གང་དག་དང་།

LAB PAI	**ZHI**	**GANG DAG**	**DANG**
training	*foundation, vows*	*whatever*	*and*

Bodhisattvas of the future and

ཚུལ་ཁྲིམས་གང་དག་དང་།

TSHUL TRIM	**GANG DAG**	**DANG**
morality, practices	*whatever*	*and*

All their moral disciplines and

ད་ལྟ་ཕྱོགས་བཅུའི་འཇིག་རྟེན་གྱི་ཁམས་ན་བཞུགས་པའི་

DA TA	**CHOG**	**CHU**	**JIG TEN**	**GYI**	**KHAM**	**NA**	**ZHUG PAI**
now	*directions*	*ten*	*the world*	*of*	*realms*	*in*	*staying*

The vows of the training of

བྱང་ཆུབ་སེམས་དཔའ་ཐམས་ཅད་ཀྱི་བསླབ་པའི་གཞི་གང་དག་དང་།

JANG CHUB SEM PA	**THAM CHE**	**KYI**	**LAB PAI**	**ZHI**	**GANG DAG**	**DANG**
bodhisattva	*all*	*of*	*training*	*vows*	*whatever*	*and*

All the Bodhisattvas who reside now in all the realms in the ten directions of the world and

ཚུལ་ཁྲིམས་གང་དག་ལ།

TSHUL TRIM	**GANG DAG**	**LA**
practices	*whatever*	*to*

All their moral disciplines,

འདས་པའི་བྱང་ཆུབ་སེམས་དཔའ་ཐམས་ཅད་ཀྱིས་

DAE PAI	**JANG CHUB SEM PA**	**THAM CHE**	**KYI**
previous, past	*bodhisattvas*	*all*	*by*

All that was trained in by all the previous

བསླབས་པར་གྱུར་པ་དང་།

LAB PAR	**GYUR PA**	**DANG**
training in, practised	*did*	*and*

Bodhisattvas, and

མ་འོངས་པའི་བྱང་ཆུབ་སེམས་དཔའ་ཐམས་ཅད་སློབ་པར་འགྱུར་པ་དང་།

MA ONG PAI JANG CHUB PA THAM CHE LOB PAR GYUR PA DANG
future bodhisattva all study will and

All that will be trained in by all the future Bodhisattvas, and

ད་ལྟ་ཕྱོགས་བཅུའི་འཇིག་རྟེན་གྱི་ཁམས་ཐམས་ཅད་ན་བཞུགས་པའི་

DA TA CHOG CHUI JIG TEN GYI KHAM THAM CHE NA ZHUG PAI
present ten directions the worlds of realms all in staying

All that are being trained in by all the Bodhisattvas

བྱང་ཆུབ་སེམས་དཔའ་ཐམས་ཅད་ཀྱི་བསླབ་པའི་གཞི་ཐམས་ཅད་དང་།

JANG CHUB SEM PA THAM CHE KYI LAB PAI ZHI THAM CHE DANG
bodhisattvas all of training basis all and

Staying at present in the realms in the ten directions of the world,

བྱང་ཆུབ་སེམས་དཔའི་ཚུལ་ཁྲིམས་ཐམས་ཅད་

JANG CHUB SEM PAI TSUL TRIM THAM CHE
bodhisattva moral all

All the moral practices of the Bodhisattvas,

དེར་སྡོམ་པའི་ཚུལ་ཁྲིམས་དང་།

DER DOM PAI TSHUL TRIM DANG
their vows morality and

Their moral practices of vows,

དགེ་བའི་ཆོས་སྡུད་པའི་ཚུལ་ཁྲིམས་དང་།

GE WAI CHO DUD PAI TSUL TRIM DANG
virtuous dharma collect morality and

Their moral practices of accumulating virtuous Dharmas, and

སེམས་ཅན་གྱི་དོན་བྱ་བའི་ཚུལ་ཁྲིམས་ལེན་པར་འདོད་དམ།

SEM CHEN GYI DON JA WAI TSUL TRIM LEN PAR DO DAM
beings of benefit doing morality adopt, receive wish to or not?

Their moral practices of benefitting beings – do you wish to receive this?

The teacher says, "Good person called [disciple's name] do you wish to receive from this Bodhisattva called [teacher's name] the vows of the training of all the Bodhisattvas of the past and all their moral disciplines, and the vows of the training of all the Bodhisattvas of the future and all their moral disciplines, and the vows of the training of all the Bodhisattvas who currently reside in all the realms in the ten direc-

tions of the world and all their moral disciplines, all that was trained in by all the previous Bodhisattvas, and all that will be trained in by all the future Bodhisattvas, and all that are being trained in by all the Bodhisattvas currently residing in the realms in the ten directions of the world, all the moral practices of the Bodhisattvas, their moral practices of vows, their moral practices of accumulating virtuous Dharmas, and their moral practices of benefitting beings? Do you wish to receive this?

ཞེས་ལན་གསུམ་དྲིས་ལ། [The disciple is asked this three times]

སློབ་མས་འཚལ་ལགས། ཞེས་ལན་གསུམ་བརྗོད་དོ།། [The disciple who wishes to receive them replies "Yes, I do" three times]

བསླུ་མེད་དཀོན་མཆོག་གསུམ་པོ་དགོངས་སུ་གསོལ༔

LU ME KON CHOG SUM PO GONG SU SOL
unfailing jewels three please pay heed to me
Unfailing Three Jewels, please pay heed to me.

བདག་མིང་(………)ཞེས་བགྱི་བས༔

DAG MING *.............* ZHE GYI WAE
my name so called
I, (say one's own name),

རྫོགས་པའི་སངས་རྒྱས་བྱང་ཆུབ་སེམས་དཔའ་དང༔

DZOG PAI SANG GYE JANG CHUB SEM PA DANG
complete buddhas bodhisattvas and
As all the perfect Buddhas, Bodhisattvas,

སྔོན་གྱི་འདས་པའི་རྒྱལ་བ་ཐམས་ཅད་ཀྱང༔

NGON GYI DAE PAI GYAL WA THAM CHE KYANG
previously gone (from samsara) jinas, Buddhas all also
And previously passed beyond Victors

སྡོམ་པ་ལ་ནི་རབ་ཏུ་གནས་པ་ལྟར༔

DOM PA LA NI RAB TU NAE PA TAR
vows to/with firmly, steadily staying as, like that
Stay firmly in their vows, in the same way

དེང་ནས་བཟུང་སྟེ་འཁོར་བ་མ་སྟོངས་བར༔

DENG	**NAE**	**ZUNG TE**	**KHOR WA**	**MA**	**TONG**	**BAR**
today	*from*	*future lives*	*samsara*	*not*	*emptied*	*until, for as long as*

From today on in all my lives for as long as samsara is not emptied,

མ་ལུས་འགྲོ་བ་སྒྲོལ་བའི་དོན་གྱི་ཕྱིར༔

MA LU	**DRO WA**	**DROL WAI**	**DON GYI**	**CHIR**
without exception	*beings*	*liberate*	*benefit*	*in order to*

In order to benefit absolutely all beings by liberating them

བླ་མེད་འཇུག་པའི་བྱང་ཆུབ་སེམས་བསྐྱེད་ནས༔

LA ME	**JUG PAI**	**JANG CHUB SEM**	**KYE**	**NAE**
unsurpassed	*engaging in actual practice*	*bodhicitta*	*raise*	*then, and*

I will raise the unsurpassed bodhicitta of engagement and

ཕ་རོལ་ཕྱིན་པ་དྲུག་ལ་བསླབ་པར་བགྱི༔

PHA ROL CHIN PA	**DRUG**	**LA**	**LAB PAR**	**GYI**
*paramitas**	*six*	*in*	*training*	*do*

*generosity, morality, patience, diligence, meditation and true discernment

Will train in the practice of the six paramitas.

Unfailing Three Jewels, please pay heed to me! Just as all the perfect Buddhas, Bodhisattvas, and previously passed beyond Victors stay firmly in their vows, in the same way I, (say one's own name), from today on in all my lives for as long as samsara is not emptied, for the sake of benefitting all beings by liberating them, I will raise the unsurpassed bodhicitta of engagement and will train in the practice of the six paramitas.

སེམས་ཅན་མ་ལུས་སྒྲོལ་ཕྱིར་བརྩོན་འགྲུས་བསྐྱེད༔

SEM CHEN	**MA LU**	**DROL**	**CHIR**	**TSON DRU**	**KYE**
beings	*without exception*	*liberate*	*in order to*	*diligence*	*develop*

Developing diligence in order to liberate all beings without exception,

ཚུལ་ཁྲིམས་རྣམ་པ་གསུམ་ཡང་བསྲུང་བར་བགྱི༔

TSHUL TRIM	**NAM PA**	**SUM**	**YANG**	**SUNG WAR**	**GYI**
morality	*kinds*	*three*	*also*	*protect*	*do*

(of vows, of virtuous Dharmas, and of doing benefit for others)

I will maintain the three kinds of morality.

བདག་གིས་བྱང་ཆུབ་མཆོག་ཏུ་སེམས་བསྐྱེད་ནས༔

DAG	GI	JANG CHUB	CHOG	TU	SEM KYE	NAE
me	*by*	*enlightenment*	*best*	*to*	*bodhicitta*	*then*

In myself I raise the altruistic intention to gain the most excellent enlightenment.

ཁམས་གསུམ་འཁོར་བའི་སེམས་ཅན་མ་ལུས་ཀུན༔

KHAM	SUM	KHOR WAI	SEM CHEN	MU LU	KUN
world	*three*	*samsara*	*beings*	*without exception*	*all*

(the three worlds of desire, form, formless)

Then all beings without exception in the three worlds of samsara

མ་བསྒྲལ་བསྒྲལ་དང་མ་གྲོལ་དགྲོལ་བར་བྱ༔

MA	DRAL	DRAL	DANG	MA	DROL	DROL WAR	JA
not	*taken out*	*taken out*	*and*	*not*	*freed*	*free*	*do*

Who have not yet come out, I will take out and who have not been freed, I will free.

དབུགས་མ་དབྱུང་བ་དག་ཀྱང་དབུགས་དབྱུང་ནས༔

UG MA JUNG WA	DAG	KYANG	UG JUNG	NAE
without hope and confidence	*I*	*also*	*will inspire*	*then*

Those who are without hope and confidence I will help and encourage, and

བླ་མེད་མྱ་ངན་འདས་པའི་ས་ལ་འགོད༔

LA ME	NYA NGAN DAE PAI	SA	LA	GOD
unsurpassed	*nirvana, freedom from all sorrows*	*stage*	*in*	*put*

I will establish all beings on the stage of unsurpassed nirvana.

Developing diligence in order to liberate all beings without exception, I will maintain the three kinds of morality. In myself I raise the altruistic intention to gain the most excellent enlightenment. Then all beings without exception who have not yet come out of the three worlds of samsara, I will take out and who have not been freed, I will free. Those who are without hope and confidence I will help and encourage, and I will establish all beings on the stage of unsurpassed nirvana.

དོན་དམ་སེམས་བསྐྱེད་ནི༔
Developing the Absolute Bodhicitta

བསླུ་མེད་དཀོན་མཆོག་གསུམ་པོ་དགོངས་སུ་གསོལ༔

LU ME KON CHOG SUM PO GONG SU SOL

unfailing jewel three hear me please

Unfailing Three Jewels, please pay heed to me!

བདག་དང་མཁའ་ཁྱབ་མཐའ་ཡས་སེམས་ཅན་ཀུན༔

DAG DANG KHA KHYAB THA YE SEM CHEN KUN

I and sky pervading limitless beings all

I and all limitless sentient beings filling the sky,

ཡེ་ནས་སངས་རྒྱས་རང་བཞིན་ཡིན་པ་ལ༔

YE NAE SANG GYE RANG ZHIN YIN PA LA

beginning from buddha inherent, essence have, are hence
(primordially)

Are, from the very beginning, essentially Buddha.

དེ་ལྟར་ཡིན་པར་ཤེས་པའི་བདག་ཉིད་ཀྱིས༔

DE TAR YIN PAR SHE PAI DAG NYID KYI

like that is know presence, truth with, having
(free of the reified duality of subject and object)

The full presence of knowing that this is how we are

མཐའ་བྲལ་བྱང་ཆུབ་མཆོག་ཏུ་སེམས་བསྐྱེད་དོ༔

THA DRAL JANG CHUB CHOG TU SEM KYE DO

limitless (sunyata) enlightenment best to bodhicitta give rise to

Reveals the mind as limitless perfect awakening.

Unfailing Three Jewels, please pay heed to me! I and all limitless sentient beings filling the sky, are, from the very beginning, essentially Buddha. The full presence of knowing that this is how we are reveals the mind as limitless perfect awakening.

དབང་རྟུལ་ལ་བསླབ་བྱ་གཅིག་ཏུ་བསྡུག་པ་ནི།
Instruction in the Unified Teaching for Simple People

རྒྱལ་པོ་ལ་གདམས་པའི་མདོ་ལས།
From the Raja Upadesa Sutra

རྒྱལ་པོ་ཆེན་པོ། ཁྱོད་ནི་འདི་ལྟར་བྱ་བ་མང་བ།

GYAL PO CHEN PO	KHYO NI	DI TAR	JA WA	MANG WA
great king	*you*	*like this*	*doing action*	*many*

Great King, you have many works to do yourself

བྱེད་པ་མང་བ་སྟེ། ཐམས་ཅད་ཀྱིས་ཐམས་ཅད་དུ་

JE PA	MANG WA	TE	THAM CHE	KYI	THAM CHE	DU
actor	*many*	*thus*	*all*	*by*	*all*	*to*

And many orders to give to others. You are so busy that you have

སྦྱིན་པ་ནས་ཤེས་རབ་ཀྱི་ཕ་རོལ་དུ་ཕྱིན་པའི་

JIN PA	NAE	SHE RAB	KYI	PHA ROL DU CHIN PAI
giving, generosity	*from*	*wisdom, true discernment*	*of*	*paramitas, transcendent qualities*

No time to practise the full training, from generosity to wisdom,

བར་ལ་བསླབ་པར་མི་ནུས་ཀྱི།

BAR	LA	LAB PAR	MI NU KYI
up to	*in*	*train*	*not strongly*

Of all six paramitas.

དེ་བས་ན་རྒྱལ་པོ་ཆེན་པོ་ཁྱོད་ཡང་

DE WAE	NA	GYAL PO	CHEN PO	KHYO	YANG
therefore	*if*	*king*	*great*	*you*	*also*

Therefore, Great King,

དག་པར་རྫོགས་པའི་བྱང་ཆུབ་ལ་འདུན་པ་དང་། དད་པ་དང་།

DAG PAR	DZOG PAI	JANG CHUB	LA	DUN PA	DANG	DAE PA	DANG
supreme	*complete*	*enlightenment*	*to*	*wish, longing*	*and*	*faith*	*and*

Towards supreme and complete enlightenment, with longing, faith and

དོན་དུ་གཉེར་བའི་སྨོན་པ་དང་གསུམ།

DON DU	**NYER WAI**	**MON PA**	**DANG**	**SUM**
for the sake of	*caring for*	*aspiration*	*and*	*three*

Tender aspiration,

འགྲོ་ཡང་རུང་། འདུག་ཀྱང་རུང་། ཉལ་ཡང་རུང་།

DRO	**YANG RUNG**	**DUG**	**KYANG RUNG**	**NYAL**	**YANG RUN**
going	*also*	*staying*	*also*	*sleeping*	*also*

Whether going or staying, sleeping

སད་ཀྱང་རུང་། ཟ་ཡང་རུང་། བཏུང་ཡང་རུང་།

SAE	**KYANG RUNG**	**ZA**	**YANG RUNG**	**TUNG**	**YANG RUNG**
waking	*also*	*eating*	*also*	*drinking*	*also*

Or waking, eating or drinking,

རྟག་པར་རྒྱུན་དུ་དྲན་པས་ཡིད་ལ་བཟུང་སྟེ་སྒོམས་ཤིག།

TAG PAR	**GYUN DU**	**DREN PAE**	**YID LA ZUNG**	**TE GOM SHIG**
always	*continuously*	*recollection*	*hold in mind*	*meditate in that way*

You must always continuously maintain recollection and keep this as your meditation.

Great King, you have many works to do yourself and many orders to give to others. You are so busy that you have no time to practise the full training of all six paramitas from generosity to wisdom. Therefore, great King, whether going or staying, sleeping or waking, eating, or drinking you must always continuously maintain recollection of supreme and complete enlightenment, with longing, faith and tender aspiration. This is your meditation.

གཞན་གྱི་དགེ་བ་ལ་རྗེས་སུ་ཡི་རང་བར་གྱིས་ཤིག།

ZHEN	**GYI**	**GE WA**	**LA**	**JE SU YI RANG WAR**	**GYI**	**SHIG**
other	*of*	*virtue*	*in*	*rejoice*	*do*	*must*

Rejoice in the virtue done by others,

རྗེས་སུ་ཡི་རང་ནས་ཀྱང་སངས་རྒྱས་དང་བྱང་ཆུབ་སེམས་དཔའ་

JE SU YI RANG	**NAE**	**KYANG**	**SANG GYE**	**DANG**	**JANG CHUB SEM PA**
rejoicing in their virtues	*then*	*also*	*buddha*	*and*	*bodhisattvas*

And make an offering of that sympathetic rejoicing

དང་ཉན་ཐོས་དང་རང་སངས་རྒྱས་ཐམས་ཅད་ལ་ཕུལ་ཅིག།

DANG	**NYEN THO**	**DANG**	**RANG SANG GYE**	**THAM CHE**	**LA**	**PHUL**	**CHIG**
and	*listeners*	*and*	*isolating buddhas*	*all*	*to*	*offer*	*do*

To all the Buddhas, Bodhisattvas, Listeners, and Isolating Buddhas.

ཕུལ་ནས་སེམས་ཅན་ཐམས་ཅད་དང་ཐུན་མོང་དུ་གྱིས་ཤིག།

PHUL NAE SEM CHEN THAM CHE DANG THUN MONG DU GYI SHIG

offer then beings all and sharing do

Make offerings to them, and share the virtue with all beings.

དེ་ནས་སེམས་ཅན་ཐམས་ཅད་ཀྱིས་སངས་རྒྱས་ཀྱི་ཆོས་ཡོངས་སུ་

DE NAE SEM CHEN THAM CHE KYI SANG GYE KYI CHO YONG SU

then beings all by buddhas of dharma fully

Then dedicate the merit so that all beings may become fully complete

རྫོགས་པར་འགྱུར་བར་ཉིན་གཅིག་བཞིན་དུ་

DZOG PAR GYUR WAR NYIN CHIG ZHIN DU

complete become, get day one as

Within the dharma of the Buddha in just one day

བླ་ན་མེད་པའི་བྱང་ཆུབ་ཏུ་བསྔོས་ཤིག།

LA NA ME PAI JANG CHUB TU NGO SHIG

unsurpassed enlightenment dedicate

And thus gain unsurpassed enlightenment.

Rejoice in the virtue done by others, and make an offering of that sympathetic rejoicing to all the Buddhas, Bodhisattvas, Listeners, and Isolating Buddhas. Make offerings to them, and share the virtue with all beings. Then dedicate the merit so that all beings may become fully complete within the dharma of the Buddha in just one day and thus gain unsurpassed enlightenment.

རྒྱལ་པོ་ཆེན་པོ། དེ་ལྟར་ན་རྒྱལ་སྲིད་ཀྱང་བྱེད་ལ།

GYAL PO CHEN PO DE TAR NA GYAL SI KYANG JE LA

great king like that if kingdom also do to

Great King, if you act in this way you will be able

རྒྱལ་པོའི་བྱ་བ་ཡང་ཉམས་པར་མི་འགྱུར་ལ།

GYAL POI JA WA YANG NYAM PAR MI GYUR LA

king's activity also not deteriorate, not diminish

To rule without any decline in the kingdom, and

བྱང་ཆུབ་ཀྱི་ཚོགས་ཀྱང་ཡོངས་སུ་རྫོགས་པར་འགྱུར་རོ།

JANG CHUB KYI TSHOG KYANG YONG SU DZOG PAR GYUR RO

enlightenment of accumulations also fully complete come

You and your subjects will all fully complete the accumulations of merit and wisdom necessary for gaining enlightenment.

Great King, if you act in this way you will be able to rule without any decline in the kingdom and you and your subjects will all fully complete the accumulations of merit and wisdom necessary for gaining enlightenment.

This ends the Sutra extract.

ཇི་ལྟར་སྔོན་གྱི་བདེ་གཤེགས་ཀྱིས།

JI TAR	**NGON GYI**	**DE SHEG**	**KYI**
in the same manner	*former, previous*	*sugatas, buddhas, Happily Gone*	*by*

Just as the earlier Buddhas

བྱང་ཆུབ་ཐུགས་ནི་བསྐྱེད་པ་དང་།

JANG CHUB	**THUG NI**	**KYE PA**	**DANG**
enlightenment	*mind, heart*	*raised and developed*	*and*

Developed in their hearts the intention to gain enlightenment for the sake of others,

བྱང་ཆུབ་སེམས་དཔའི་བསླབ་པ་ལ།

JANG CHUB SEM PAI	**LAB PA**	**LA**
bodhisattvas'	*training*	*to, of*

And pursued the training of the Bodhisattvas,

དེ་དག་རིམ་བཞིན་གནས་པ་ལྟར།

DE DAG	**RIM**	**ZHIN**	**NAE PA**	**TAR**
these	*stages*	*gradually*	*stayed*	*like, as*

Progressing through the stages of the path,

བདག་ཀྱང་འགྲོ་ལ་ཕན་དོན་དུ།

DAG	**KYANG**	**DRO**	**LA**	**PHEN**	**DON DU**
I	*also*	*beings*	*to, for*	*benefit*	*in order to*

I also, in order to bring benefit to beings,

བྱང་ཆུབ་སེམས་ནི་བསྐྱེད་བགྱི་ཞིང་།

JANG CHUB SEM	**NI**	**KYE GYI ZHING**
intention to gain enlightenment for others	*this*	*raising and developing*

Raise and develop the intention to gain enlightenment for others,

དེ་བཞིན་དུ་ནི་བསླབ་པ་ལ།

DE ZHIN DU	**NI**	**LAB PA**	**LA**
similarly	*this*	*training*	*to*

And like the Buddhas will follow this training,

རིམ་པ་བཞིན་དུ་བསླབ་པར་བགྱི།

RIM PA ZHIN DU LAB PAR GYI
stages as, gradually train will

Practising each of its stages.

Just as the earlier Buddhas developed in their hearts the intention to gain enlightenment for the sake of others and pursued the training of the bodhisattvas, progressing through the stages of the path, I also in order to bring benefit to beings, raise and develop the altruistic intention towards enlightenment and like the Buddhas will follow this training, practising each of its stages.

དེང་དུས་བདག་ཚེ་འབྲས་བུ་ཡོད།

DENG DU DAG TSHE DRAE BU YO
this time I life fruit have

Now, at this time, my life is fruitful.

མི་ཡི་སྲིད་པ་ལེགས་པར་ཐོབ།

MI YI SID PA LEG PAR THOB
human existence well, full got

I have truly attained human existence.

དེ་རིང་སངས་རྒྱས་རིགས་སུ་སྐྱེས།

DE RING SANG GYE RIG SU KYE
today buddhas family in born

Today I am born in the Buddha's family,

སངས་རྒྱས་སྲས་སུ་ད་གྱུར་ཏོ།

SANG GYE SAE SU DA GYUR TO
buddha son as now become

I have become a child of the Buddhas, a bodhisattva.

Now, at this time, my life is fruitful. I have truly attained human existence. Today I am born in the Buddha's family. I have become a child of the Buddhas, a bodhisattva.

ད་ནི་བདག་གིས་ཅི་ནས་ཀྱང་།

DE NI DAG GI CHI NAE KYANG
now me by whatever also

From now on I must only

རིགས་དང་མཐུན་པའི་ལས་བརྩམས་ཏེ།

RIG	DANG	THUN PAI	LAE	TSAM TE
Buddha family	*and*	*harmonious*	*action, behaviour*	*practice*

Practice activity which is in harmony with my new family, so that

སྐྱོན་མེད་བཙུན་པའི་རིགས་འདི་ལ།

KYON ME	TSUN PAI	RIG	DI	LA
faultless	*reverend*	*family*	*this*	*to*

This faultless, reverend family

རྙོག་པར་མི་འགྱུར་དེ་ལྟར་བྱ།

NYOG PAR	MI	GYUR	DE TAR	JA
spoiled, make trouble for	*not*	*become*	*like that*	*do*

Does not become spoiled by my actions.

From now on I must only practice activity which is in harmony with my new family so that this faultless, reverend family does not become spoiled by my actions.

བདག་གིས་དེ་རིང་སྐྱོབ་པ་ཐམས་ཅད་ཀྱི།

DAG	GI	DE RING	KYOB PA	THAM CHE	KYI
me	*by*	*today*	*buddhas, protectors*	*all*	*of*

I, today, before all the Buddhas,

སྤྱན་སྔར་འགྲོ་ལ་བདེ་གཤེགས་ཉིད་དང་ནི།

CHEN NGAR	DRO	LA	DE SHEG NYID	DANG NI
before	*beings*	*to*	*buddhahood*	*and*

Invite all beings to be my guests

བར་དུ་དེ་ལ་མགྲོན་དུ་བོས་ཟིན་གྱི།

BAR DU	DE	LA	DRON	DU	BOE	ZIN	GYI
until	*that*	*to*	**guest*	*as*	*call, invite*	*do*	*of*

*(I will take care of them)

Until they reach Buddhahood.

ལྷ་དང་ལྷ་མིན་ལ་སོགས་དགའ་བར་བྱོས།

LHA	DANG	LHA MIN	SOG	GA WAR	JO
gods	*and*	*asuras*	*and so on*	*happy*	*be*

Therefore may the gods, demi-gods and all beings be happy!

Today, before all the Buddhas I invite all beings to be my guests until they reach Buddhood. Therefore may the gods, asuras and all beings be happy!

བྱང་ཆུབ་སེམས་མཆོག་རིན་པོ་ཆེ།

JANG CHUB SEM	CHOG	RIN PO CHE
bodhicitta, mind of enlightenment	*excellent supreme*	*precious*

This precious, excellent altruistic intention towards enlightenment,

མ་སྐྱེས་པ་རྣམས་སྐྱེས་གྱུར་ཅིག།

MA KYE PA NAM	KYE	GYUR CHIG
those in whom it has not arisen	*arise*	*may it*

May it arise in those in whom it has not yet arisen.

སྐྱེས་པ་ཉམས་པ་མེད་པ་ཡང་།

KYE PA	NYAM PA ME PA	YANG
for those in whom it has arisen	*not deteriorate*	*also*

For those in whom it has arisen may it not deteriorate, and

གོང་ནས་གོང་དུ་འཕེལ་བར་ཤོག།

GONG NAE GONG DU	PHEL WAR	SHOG
more and more	*increase*	*may it, it must*

May it increase ever more!

This precious, excellent altruistic intention towards enlightenment, may it arise in those in whom it has not yet arisen. May it not deteriorate in those in whom it has arisen. May it increase ever more.

བྱང་ཆུབ་སེམས་དང་མི་འབྲལ་ཞིང་།

JANG CHUB SEM	DANG	MI DRAL ZHING
bodhicitta, altruistic intention towards enlightenment	*and*	*never being separated from*

Never being separated from the altruistic intention towards enlightenment,

བྱང་ཆུབ་སྤྱོད་ལ་གཞོལ་བ་དང་།

JANG CHUB	CHO	LA	ZHOL WA	DANG
bodhisattva	*conduct*	*in*	*fixed in, absorbed in*	*and*

And staying true to the conduct of a bodhisattva,

སངས་རྒྱས་རྣམས་ཀྱིས་ཡོངས་བཟུང་ནས།

SANG GYE	**NAM**	**KYI**	**YONG**	**ZUNG**	**NAE**
buddha	*(plural)*	*by*	*totally, fully*	*hold*	*then*

May I be completely held by the Buddhas and

བདུད་ཀྱི་ལས་རྣམས་སྤོང་བར་ཤོག།

DUD	**KYI**	**LAE**	**NAM**	**PONG WAR**	**SHOG**
*maras, demons**	*of*	*karmic activity*	*(plural)*	*abandon*	*may*

*who obstruct the path to enlightenment

May I abandon all karmic activities arising due to the obstructing demons.

Never being separated from the altruistic intention towards enlightenment, and staying true to the conduct of a bodhisattva, may I be completely held by all the Buddhas. May I abandon all karmic activities arising due to the obstructing demons.

སྐྱིད་ན་བདེ་བ་ཚོགས་སུ་བསྔོ།

KYI	**NA**	**DE WA**	**TSHOG**	**SU**	**NGO**
happy, gladness	*if*	*happiness*	*all*	*to*	*dedicate*

Whenever I am glad, I will dedicate that joy to the happiness of all beings –

ཕན་བདེས་ནམ་མཁའ་གང་བར་ཤོག།

PHEN DE	**NAM KHA**	**GANG WAR**	**SHOG**
benefit and happiness, with well-being	*sky*	*become full, so much**	*may it*

*i.e. enough to satisfy all beings

May their happiness be enough to fill the sky!

སྡུག་ན་ཀུན་གྱི་སྡུག་བསྔལ་ཁུར།

DUG	**NA**	**KUN GYI**	**DUG NGAL**	**KHUR**
trouble, sorrow	*if*	*all beings*	*suffering*	*I take that burden*

Whenever I get trouble I will take the suffering of all beings as my own burden –

སྡུག་བསྔལ་རྒྱ་མཚོ་སྐེམས་པར་ཤོག།

DUG NGA	**GYAM TSHO**	**KEM PAR**	**SHOG**
sorrows	*oceans*	*thin, dried up*	*may it become*

May the oceans of suffering become dry!

Whenever I am glad I will dedicate that joy to the happiness of all beings – may their happiness fill the sky! Whenever I get trouble I will take the suffering of all beings as my own burden – may the oceans of suffering become dry!

བདག་གི་དགེ་བའི་ལས་རྣམས་འདི་དག་གིས།

DAG GI	**GE WAI**	**LAE**	**NAM**	**DI DAG**	**GI**
my	*virtuous*	*actions*	*(plural)*	*these*	*by*

May all my virtuous actions

འཇིག་རྟེན་དུ་ནི་མྱུར་དུ་འཚང་རྒྱ་ཤོག།

JIG TEN	**DU**	**NI**	**NYUR DU**	**TSHANG GYA**	**SHOG**
world	*in*	*emphasis*	*quickly*	*get enlightenment*	*must gain*

Quickly bring all beings in the world to enlightenment.

འགྲོ་ལ་ཕན་ཕྱིར་ཆོས་རྣམས་སྟོན་བགྱིད་ཅིང་།

DRO	**LA**	**PHEN**	**CHIR**	**CHO NAM**	**TON**	**GYI CHING**
beings	*for*	*to help*	*in order to*	*dharma*	*teaching*	*do*

In order to benefit beings I will teach the Dharma and

སེམས་ཅན་སྡུག་བསྔལ་མང་པོས་གཟིར་ལས་སྒྲོལ།། ༎

SEM CHEN	**DUG NGAL**	**MANG POE**	**ZIR**	**LAE DROL**
beings	*sorrows*	*many*	*pressed down*	*free from*

Thus free all beings from the many sorrows that oppress them.

May all my virtuous actions quickly bring all beings in the world to enlightenment. In order to benefit beings I will teach the Dharma and thus free all beings from the many sorrows that oppress them.

ཤཱ་ཀྱའི་རྒྱལ་པོ་ཁྱོད་སྐུ་ཅི་འདྲ་དང་།

SHA KYAI	**GYAL PO**	**KHYOD**	**KU**	**CHI DRA**	**DANG**
Shakya	*king*	*you*	*body*	*like what, similar to what*	*and*

Buddha Shakyamuni, similar to you in body

འཁོར་དང་སྐུ་ཚེའི་ཚད་དང་ཞིང་ཁམས་དང་།

KHOR	**DANG**	**KU TSHEI**	**TSHE**	**ZHING KHAM**	**DANG**
retinue	*and*	*lifespan*	*amount*	*realm*	*and*

In retinue, lifespan and realm, and

ཁྱོད་ཀྱི་མཚན་མཆོག་བཟང་པོ་ཅི་འདྲ་བ།

KHYO KYI	**TSEN**	**CHOG**	**ZANG PO**	**CHI DRA WA**
your	*signs,*	*supreme*	*good*	*similar to what*

Similar to your supreme and excellent qualitites,

དེ་འདྲ་ཁོ་ནར་བདག་སོགས་འགྱུར་བར་ཤོག།

DE DRA	KHO NAR	DAG SOG	GYUR WAR SHOG
like that	*truly*	*we*	*may we become*

May we truly become like that!

Buddha Shakyamuni, may we become like you in body, in retinue, lifespan and realm, and like you in your supreme and excellent distinguishing features. May we truly become like you!

ཁྱེད་ལ་བསྟོད་ཅིང་གསོལ་བ་བཏབ་པའི་མཐུས།

KHYE	LA	TO CHING	SOL WA TAB PAI	THU
you	*to*	*praising*	*praying*	*by power of*

By the power of praising you in prayer,

བདག་སོགས་གང་དུ་གནས་པའི་ས་ཕྱོགས་སུ།

DAG SOG	GANG DU	NAE PAI	SA CHOG	SU
we	*wherever*	*staying*	*places*	*in*

May all of us, wherever we stay,

ནད་དང་དབུལ་ཕོངས་འཐབ་རྩོད་ཞི་བ་དང་།

NAE	DANG	UL PHONG	THAB TSO	SHI WA	DANG
sickness	*and*	*poverty*	*disputes*	*pacify, clear away*	*and*

Have our sickness, poverty and disputes removed, and

ཆོས་དང་བཀྲ་ཤིས་འཕེལ་བར་མཛད་དུ་གསོལ།

CHO	DANG	TRA SHI	PHEL WAR	DZE DU SOL
dharma	*and*	*good fortune*	*increase*	*please do*

May Dharma and felicity thrive and spread.

By the power of praising you in prayer, may we all, wherever we abide, have our sickness, poverty and disputes removed, and may the Dharma and felicity thrive and spread.

སྟོན་པ་འཇིག་རྟེན་ཁམས་སུ་བྱོན་པ་དང་།

TON PA	JIG TEN	KHAM	SU	JON PA	DANG
teacher	*world*	*realm*	*to*	*came*	*and*

Buddha, our teacher, came to this world realm, and

བསྟན་པ་ཉི་འོད་བཞིན་དུ་གསལ་བ་དང་།

TEN PA	NYI	OD	ZHIN DU	SAL WA	DANG
doctrine	*sun's*	*light*	*similar*	*made clear*	*and*

Gave the doctrine which illuminates like the light of the sun.

བསྟན་འཛིན་ཕོ་ནུ་བཞིན་དུ་མཐུན་པ་ཡིས།

TEN DZIN	**PHO DU**	**ZHIN DU**	**THUN PA**	**YI**
doctrine holders	*warm relationship like brother and sister*	*like*	*harmony*	*by*

With the doctrine holders like harmonious siblings

བསྟན་པ་ཡུན་རིང་གནས་པའི་བཀྲ་ཤིས་ཤོག། །།

TEN PA	**YUN RING**	**NAE PAI**	**TRA SHI**	**SHOG**
doctrine	*long time*	*remaining, staying*	*prosperity, happiness*	*may it be so*

May there be the good fortune of the long duration of the Dharma.

Buddha, our teacher, came to this world realm and gave the doctrine which illuminates like the light of the sun. With the doctrine holders like harmonious siblings, may there be the good fortune of the long duration of the Dharma.

Compiled by Chimed Rigdzin Rinpoche.

Honouring the Buddha's Speech
The Heart Sutra

༄༅། གུ་རུ་དེ་ཝ་ཌཱ་ཀི་ནི༔

GURU	**DE VA**	**DAK KI NI**
spiritual	*god*	*dakini, goddess master*

Guru, Deva, Dakini;

བླ་མ་ཡི་དམ་མཁའ་འགྲོ་གསུམ་ལ་སྐྱབས་སུ་མཆི༔

LA MA	**YI DAM**	**KHAN DRO**	**SUM**	**LA**	**KYAB**	**SU**	**CHI**
guru	*meditation deity*	*dakini*	*three*	*to*	*refuge, protection*	*for*	*go (make salutation)*

Spiritual Master, meditation deities and dakinis – to these three we go to refuge.

སངས་རྒྱས་ཆོས་དང་དགེ་འདུན་གསུམ་ལ་སྐྱབས་སུ་མཆི༔

SANG GYE	**CHO**	**DANG**	**GEN DUN**	**SUM**	**LA**	**KYAB**	**SU**	**CHI**
buddha	*dharma*	*and*	*sangha*	*three*	*to*	*refuge*	*for*	*go*

Buddha, Dharma and Sangha – to these three we go for refuge.

ཡེ་ཤེས་ལྷ་དང་དམ་ཚིག་ལྷ་ལ་སྐྱབས་སུ་མཆི༔

YE SHE	**LHA**	**DANG**	**DAM TSHIG**	**LHA**	**LA**	**KYAB**	**SU**	**CHI**
original knowing	*god*	*and*	*samaya, obligation*	*god*	*to*	*refuge*	*for*	*go*

Original knowing deities and commitment deities – to you we go to refuge.

ཆོས་སྐུ་ལོངས་སྐུ་སྤྲུལ་སྐུ་གསུམ་ལ་སྐྱབས་སུ་མཆི༔

CHO KU	**LONG SU**	**TRUL KU**	**SUM**	**LA**	**KYAB**	**SU**	**CHI**
dharmakaya, intrinsic mode	*sambhogakaya, radiant mode*	*nirmanakaya, participative mode*	*three*	*to*	*refuge*	*for*	*go*

Dharmakaya, Sambhogakaya, Nirmanakaya – to these three we go for refuge.

Guru, Deva, Dakini; Spiritual Master, meditation deities and dakinis – to you we go for refuge. Buddha, Dharma and Sangha – to you we go for refuge. Original knowing deities and commitment deities – to you we go for refuge. Intrinsic mode, radiant mode, participative mode – to you we go for refuge.

བདག་དང་དྲིན་ཅན་ཕ་མས་གཙོ་བྱས་སེམས་ཅན་རྣམས༔

DA	**DANG**	**DRIN CHEN**	**PA**	**MAE**	**TSO JAE**	**SEM CHEN NAM**
I	*and*	*kind, helpful*	*father*	*mother*	*chiefly*	*sentient beings*

I and all sentient being, and in particular my very kind parents,

ཡེ་ནས་སངས་རྒྱས་ཡིན་པ་ཉིད་ལ་དེར་ཤེས་ཀྱི༔

YE NAE	**SANG GYE**	**YIN PA**	**NYID**	**LA**	**DER**	**SHE**	**KYI**
from the very beginning	*buddha*	*are*	*truly*	*to*	*to that*	*know*	*of*

Have been buddhas from the very beginning. The knowledge of this

བྱང་ཆུབ་མཆོག་ཏུ་རྒྱ་ཆེན་སེམས་ནི་བསྐྱེད་པར་བགྱི༔

JANG CHUB	**CHOG**	**TU**	**GYA CHEN**	**SEM NI**	**KYE PA**	**GYI**
bodhi, enlightenment	*excellent*	*as*	*very large*	*mind, attitude*	*develop*	*do*

Is perfect awakening and so towards this we arouse a vast intention.

I and all sentient beings, and in particular my very kind parents, have been buddhas from the very beginning. The knowledge of this is perfect awakening and so towards this we arouse a vast intention.

ཨོཾ་སྭ་བྷཱ་ཝ་ཤུདྡྷཿ སརྦ་དྷརྨཱ

OM	**SWA BHA VA**	**SHUD DHA**	**SAR WA**	**DHAR MA**
five wisdoms	*nature*	*pure*	*all*	*phenomena*

Om. Pure nature. All phenomena have very pure nature.

སྭ་བྷཱ་ཝ་བི་ཤུདྡྷོ་ཨ་ཧཾ༔

SWA BHA VA	**BI SHUD DHO**	**A HAM**
nature	*very pure*	*I, myself*

This is my nature.

ཕྱི་ནང་སྣོད་བཅུད་སྟོང་པ་ཉིད་གྱུར་དེ་ཡི་ངང༔

CHI	**NANG**	**NOD**	**CHUD**	**TONG PA NYID**	**GYUR**	**DE YI NGANG**
outer	*inner*	*container, universe*	*contents, all beings*	*sunyata, emptiness*	*are, become*	*that's state*

In the state where everything outer and inner, the universe and all beings, is emptiness,

ཨོཾ་མ་ཎི་པདྨེ་ཧཱུྃ་ཞེས་བརྗོད་པའི་མཐུས༔

OM MA NI PAD ME HUNG	**ZHE**	**JO PAI**	**THU**
the mantra of Chenrezi	*thus*	*reciting*	*by power of*

By the power of saying "Om Mani Padme Hung",

གཉིས་སུ་མེད་དང་གཉིས་མེད་ལ་གནས་སྐད་ཅིག་གིས༔

NYI SU ME DANG NYI ME LA NAE KAE CHIG GI

two as not and two not as stay an instant by

Abiding in non-separation and non-duality, in an instant,

དྲི་མེད་པདྨ་ཉི་ཟླ་བརྩེགས་པའི་གདན་སྟེང་དུ༔

DRI ME PAD MA NYI DA TSEG PAI DAN TENG DU

stainless lotus sun moon built up cushion on top of

On top of cushions built up of a stainless lotus, sun and moon,

རང་ཉིད་འཕགས་པ་སྤྱན་རས་གཟིགས་དབང་སྐུ་མདོག་དཀར༔

RANG NYID PHAG PA CHEN RAE ZI WONG KU DO KAR

myself arya Avalokitesvara body colour white

I appear as noble Chenrezi. My body is white,

ཕྱག་གཡས་ཤེལ་དཀར་ཕྲེང་བ་གཡོན་པས་ཨུཏྤལ་བསྣམས༔

CHAG YAE SHEL KAR TRENG WA YON PAE UT PAL NAM

hand right crystal white mala, rosary left lotus hold

With my right hand holding a rosary of white crystal, and a lotus in my left.

རིན་ཆེན་རྒྱན་དང་སྐུ་སྨད་དར་གྱི་འཁོར་གསུམ་ཁེབས༔

RIN CHEN GYAN DANG KU MAE DAR GYI KHOR SUM KHEB

jewel ornaments and body lower silk of fully cover

I am adorned with jewels and the lower part of my body is draped with silk.

Om. Pure nature. All phenomena have very pure nature. This is my nature.

In the state where everything outer and inner, the universe and all beings, is emptiness, by the power of saying "Om Mani Padma Hung", abiding in non-separation and non-duality, in an instant, on top of cushions built up of a stainless lotus, sun and moon, I appear as noble Chenrezi. My body is white, with my right hand holding a rosary of white crystal, and lotus in my left. I am adorned with jewels and the lower part of my body is draped with silk.

ཐུགས་ཀའི་ཧཱུྃ་ལས་འོད་ཟེར་སྤྲོ་བསྡུའི་སྦྱོར་བ་ཡིས༔

THU KAI HUNG LAE O ZER TRO DUI JOR WA YI

heart letter from light rays radiate gather join by

From a letter Hung in my heart, rays of light radiate out and gather back merging in the Hung.

འཕགས་པ་མཆོད་དང་སེམས་ཅན་ཀུན་གྱི་དོན་བྱེད་གྱུར༔

PHA PA	**CHO**	**DANG**	**SEM CHEN**	**KUN**	**GYI**	**DON**	**JE**	**GYUR**
arya, noble	*offering*	*and*	*sentient*	*all*	*of*	*benefit, welfare*	*doing*	*become**

*Firstly the rays of light travel upwards as offerings to all Buddhas and Bodhisattvas, becoming whatever pleasing things are desired. Then the light returns to the letter with the blessings of the holy ones. Then again light radiates out, this time going down and touching all the beings in the six realms purifying their sins.

By means of this, offerings are made to the noble ones and benefit for all beings is performed.

བདག་མདུན་རྩ་བ་སྲ་འཏན་བྱང་ཆུབ་དཔག་བསམ་ཤིང༔

DA	**DUN**	**TSA WA**	**SA TEN**	**JANG CHU**	**PA SAM**	**SHING**
myself	*before*	*root*	*strong, steady*	*bodhi*	*wishing*	*tree*

In front of me is the firmly rooted Bodhi wishing tree

ཡལ་ག་ལོ་མ་མེ་ཏོག་འབྲས་བུ་ཕུན་ཚོགས་དཔལ༔

YAL GA	**LO MA**	**ME TO**	**DRAE BU**	**PHUN TSHO**	**PAL**
branch	*leaf*	*flower*	*fruit*	*very good*	*splendid*

With branches, leaves, flowers and fruit, all excellent and splendid.

From a letter Hung in my heart, rays of light radiate out and gather back merging in the Hung. By means of this, offerings are made to the noble ones and benefit for all beings is performed. In front of me is the firmly rooted Bodhi wishing tree with branches, leaves, flowers and fruit, all excellent and splendid.

གཏེར་ཆེན་བུམ་པས་ཀུན་ནས་ཡོངས་གང་མཆོད་པའི་སྤྲིན༔

TER	**CHEN**	**BUM PAE**	**KUN NAE**	**YONG**	**GANG**	**CHO PAI**	**TRIN**
treasure	*great*	*pot*	*always*	*fully*	*filled*	*offering*	*cloud*

Like the pot of great treasure the tree is always full of clouds of offerings.

དེ་དབུས་སེང་ཁྲི་པདྨ་ཉི་ཟླའི་གདན་གྱི་སྟེང༔

DE	**WU**	**SENG**	**TRI**	**PA MA**	**NYI**	**DAI**	**DAN**	**GYI TENG**
that	*centre*	*lion*	*throne*	*lotus*	*sun*	*moon*	*cushions*	*on top of*

In its centre upon a lion throne on top of cushions of lotus, sun and moon,

འཇའ་འོད་ཁ་དོག་སྣ་ལྔ་ཀུན་ཏུ་འཁྲིགས་པའི་ཀློང༔

JA	**OD**	**KHA DO**	**NA NGA**	**KUN**	**TU**	**TRI PAI**	**LONG**
rainbow	*light,rays*	*colours*	*five kinds**	*all*	*is*	*moving, shimmering*	*depth*

* white, red, blue, yellow, green

Within a shimmering mass of rainbow light rays of the five colours,

མཉམ་མེད་ཐུབ་པའི་དབང་པོ་ཤཱཀྱ་སེང་གེ་ཉིད༔

NYAM ME	**THUB PAI**	**WONG PO**	**SHA KYA SENG GE NYID**
unequalled	*Muni, sage (title of Buddha)*	*Indra, lord*	*Buddha Shakyamuni*

Is the unequalled lord of sages, Shakya Senge.

Like the pot of great treasure the tree is always full of clouds of offerings. In its centre upon a lion throne on top of cushions of lotus, sun and moon, within a shimmering mass of rainbow light rays of the five colours, is the unequalled lord of sages, Shakya Senge.

སྐུ་མདོག་སེར་པོ་འཛམ་བུ་ཆུ་བོའི་གསེར་མདངས་ལྡན༔

KU	**DO**	**SER PO**	**DZAM BU CHU WOI SER**	**DANG DAN**
body	*colour*	*yellow, golden*	*orange coloured gold hue*	*has*

His body is yellow with the hue of orange-coloured gold.

ཕྱག་གཉིས་གཡས་པས་ས་གནོན་གཡོན་པས་མཉམ་བཞག་སྟེང༔

CHA	**NYI**	**YAE**	**PAE**	**SA**	**NON**	**YON**	**PAE**	**NYAM ZHA**	**TENG**
hands	*two*	*right*	*by*	*earth*	*touch, press down*	*left*	*by*	*in meditation resting in lap*	*on top of*

He has two hands, the right one touching the earth, the left rests in his lap

བཻ་ཌཱུར་ཡ་ཡི་ལྷུང་བཟེད་བདུད་རྩིས་བཀང་བ་བསྣམས༔

BE DUR YA	**YI**	**LHUNG ZE**	**DU TSI**	**KANG WA**	**NAM**
lapislazuli	*of*	*monk's begging bowl*	*amrita, liberating elixir*	*full*	*holding*

Holding a lapislazuli monk's bowl of full of amrita.

His body is yellow with the hue of orange-coloured gold. He has two hands, the right one touch-ing the earth, the left rests in his lap holding a lapislazuli monk's bowl of full of amrita.

དབུ་ལ་གཙུག་ཏོར་ཕྱག་ཞབས་འཁོར་ལོས་མཚན་པ་སོགས༔

WU	**LA**	**TSUG TOR**	**CHA**	**ZHA**	**KHOR LOE**	**TSHAN PA SO**
head	*on*	*usnisha,dome-like protuberance*	*hands*	*feet*	*wheel*	*signed,marked and*

His head rises in a dome, his hands and feet are adorned with the shapes of wheels, and he shows

མཚན་མཆོག་བཟང་པོ་སོ་གཉིས་དཔེ་བྱད་བརྒྱད་བཅུས་སྤྲས༔

TSHAN	CHO	ZANG PO	SO NYI	PE JE	GYA CHUE	TRAE
marks	*excellent*	*good*	*thirty-two*	*minor*	*eighty*	*adorned with*

All the other excellent thirty-two major and eighty minor signs of a Budhha's body

སྐུ་ལ་ཆོས་གོས་རྣམས་གསུམ་གསོལ་ཞིང་རི་དབང་ལྟར༔

KU	LA	CHO	GO	NAM SUM	SOL ZHING	RI WONG	TAR
body	*on*	*dharma*	*cloth*	*kinds three*	*wearing*	*Mt. Meru*	*as*

He wears the three Dharma robes on his body, and like Mt. Meru

ལྷང་ངེ་ལྷན་ནེ་ལྷམ་མེར་བརྗིད་པའི་ཉམས་དང་བཅས༔

LANG NGE	LHAN NE	LHAM MER	JI PAI NYAM	DANG CHE
powerful	*steadfast, calm and peaceful*	*magnificent*	*great personality*	*with*

He is powerful, steadfast and magnificently impressive.

His head rises in a dome, his hands and feet are adorned with the shapes of wheels, and he shows all the other excellent thirty-two major and eighty minor signs of a Buddha's body. He wears the three Dharma robes on his body, and like Mt. Meru he is powerful, steadfast and magnificently impressive.

འཛུམ་པའི་ཞལ་རས་བརྩེ་བའི་སྤྱན་གྱིས་ཀུན་ལ་གཟིགས༔

DZUM PAI	ZHAL RAE	TSE WAI	CHEN	GYI	KUN	LA	ZI
smiling	*face*	*compassionate*	*eye*	*by,with*	*all*	*to*	*looks*

His face is smiling and his compassionate eyes look on all beings.

གཡས་སུ་པདྨའི་གདན་ལ་སྤྱན་རས་གཟིགས་དབང་སོགས༔

YAE SU	PA MAI	DAN	LA	CHEN RAE ZI WONG	SOG
at his right	*lotus*	*cushion*	*on*	*Avalokitesvara*	*etc.*

To his right, upon a lotus cushion, are Avalokitesvara and the other

ལོངས་སྐུའི་ཆས་འཛིན་བྱང་ཆུབ་སེམས་དཔའ་རྣམས་དང་ནི༔

LONG KUI	CHAE	DZIN	JANG CHUB SEM PA NAM	DANG NI
sambhogakaya	*dress*	*wearing*	*bodhisattvas*	

Bodhisattvas wearing sambhogakaya dress.

གཡོན་དུ་གདིང་བའི་སྟེང་དུ་ཤཱ་རི་བུ་ལ་སོགས༔

YON DU	DING WAI	TENG DU	SHA RI BU	LA SOG
left	*monk's cushion*	*on top of*	*Shariputra*	*and so on*

To his left, upon monks' cushions, are Shariputra and the other

བྱང་ཆུབ་སེམས་དཔའ་འདུལ་འཛིན་འཕགས་པ་རྣམས་ཀྱིས་བསྐོར༔

JANG CHUB SEM PA	**DUL**	**DZIN**	**PHAG PA NAM**	**KYI**	**KOR**
bodhisattva	*morality (in bhikshus form)*	*holy*	*aryas (bodhisattvas)*	*by*	*surrounded*

Bodhisattvas appearing in the form of monks, and thus he is surrounded by the noble ones.

His face is smiling and his compassionate eyes look on all beings. To his right, upon lotus cushions, are Avalokitesvara and the other bodhisattvas wearing sambhogakaya dress. To his left, upon monks' cushions, are Shariputra and the other bodhisattvas appearing in the form of monks, and thus he is surrounded by the noble ones.

རྒྱབ་ཏུ་ཉན་ཐོས་དང་ནི་རང་སངས་རྒྱས་ཀྱི་ཚོགས༔

GYAB	**TU**	**NYAN THOE**	**DANG NI**	**RANG SANG GYE**	**KYI**	**TSHO**
back	*at*	*sravakas, listeners*	*and*	*pratyekabuddhas, non-teaching buddhas*	*of*	*groups*

At his back are the hosts of listeners and non-teaching buddhas

གུས་པས་ལུས་བཏུད་མཐུ་ལྡན་ཕྱག་ན་རྡོ་རྗེ་མདུན༔

GUE PAE	**LU**	**TU**	**THU DEN**	**CHA NA DOR JE**	**DUN**
respect, faith	*body*	*bow*	*powerful*	*Vajrapani*	*in front*

Bowing their bodies in respect. The powerful Vajrapani is at the front.

སྟེང་ཕྱོགས་ཤིང་གི་རྩེ་མོར་དེ་བཞིན་གཤེགས་མང་པོ༔

TENG	**CHO**	**SHING**	**GI**	**TSE MOR**	**DE ZHIN SHE**	**MANG PO**
upper	*direction*	*tree*	*of*	*top point*	*tathagatas, buddha*	*many*

In the upper direction at the top of the tree are many tathagatas.

གཞན་ཡང་ཡལ་ག་ལ་གནས་ལྷ་ཡི་བུ་བུ་མོ༔

ZHAN YANG	**YUL GA**	**LA**	**NAE**	**LHA YI**	**BU**	**BU MO**
moreover	*branch*	*on*	*staying*	*gods*	*sons*	*daughters*

Many gods and goddesses are on the branches

མང་པོས་བསྐོར་ཞིང་མེ་ཏོག་ལ་སོགས་མཆོད་པར་འབུལ༔

MANG POE	**KHOR ZHING**	**ME TO**	**LA SO**	**CHO PAR**	**BUL**
many by	*surrounded*	*flowers*	*and so on*	*offerings*	*make*

Surrounding the Buddha and they offer him flowers and all that is beautiful.

At his back are the hosts of listeners and non-teaching buddhas, bowing their bodies in respect. The powerful Vajrapani is at the front. In the upper direction at the top of the tree are many tathagatas. Many gods

and goddesses are on the branches surrounding the Buddha and they offer him flowers and all that is beautiful.

གཙོ་བོས་གསུངས་རྣམས་ཇི་ལྟར་སེམས་པའི་སྒྲ་ཆེན་སྒྲོགས༔

TSO WOE	SUNG NAM	JI TAR	SEM PAI	DRA	CHEN	DRO
chief (Buddha)	*speech*	*as is suitable*	*mind*	*sound*	*great*	*proclaims*

With a powerful voice the Buddha proclaims whatever words are suitable for their minds.

དགའ་མགུའི་ཚུལ་གྱིས་འཁོར་རྣམས་རྗེས་སུ་ཡི་རང་བསྟོད༔

GA GUI	TSHUL	GYI	KHOR NAM	JE SU YI RANG	TO
very happy	*method, system*	*by*	*circle, retinue*	*rejoice at his virtues*	*praise his qualities*

His entire entourage happily rejoice at this and praise him.

སྟེང་འོག་རྐན་གཉིས་རྔ་བོ་ཆེ་ལས་གསུང་རབ་རྣམས༔

TENG	OG	KAN	NYI	NGA WO CHE	LAE	SUNG	RAB NAM
above	*below*	*palate*	*both*	*great drum*	*from*	*speech*	*excellent*

From the great drum of his upper and lower palates,

ལྕེ་ཡི་དབྱུ་གུས་བསྐུལ་ཞིང་ཆོས་སྒྲས་ཡོངས་གང་གྱུར༔

CHE	YI	JU GUE	KUL ZHING	CHO	DRA	YONG	GANG	GYUR
tongue	*of*	*drumstick*	*invoking*	*dharma*	*sound*	*fully*	*fill*	*is*

Excellent speech is invoked by the drumstick of his tongue, filling all the worlds with the sound of Dharma.

With a powerful voice the Buddha proclaims whatever words are suitable for their minds. His entire entourage happily rejoice at this and praise him. From the great drum of his upper and lower palates, excellent speech is invoked by the drumstick of his tongue, filling all the worlds with the sound of Dharma.

སྨྲ་བསམ་བརྗོད་མེད་ཤེས་རབ་ཕ་རོལ་ཕྱིན།

MA	SAM	JO	ME	SHE RAB	PHA ROL	CHIN
speech	*thought*	*expression*	*without*	*prajna, wise discerning**	*further side*	*gone*

*transcendent, beyond dualism

Transcendental wise discerning beyond speech, thought or expression

མ་སྐྱེས་མི་འགག་ནམ་མཁའི་ངོ་བོ་ཉིད།

MA	KYE	MI	GAG	NAM KAI	NGO WO	NYI
not	*born*	*not*	*stopping*	*sky's (sunyata)*	*real nature*	*itself*

Is unbegun and unstopped, like the actuality of the sky.

སོ་སོ་རང་རིག་ཡེ་ཤེས་སྤྱོད་ཡུལ་བ།

SO SO	**RANG RIG**	**YE SHE**	**CHOD**	**YUL WA**
each thing	*swavidya, own natural awareness*	*jnana,* original knowing*	*activity*	*sphere*

* by means of this primordial knowing she knows all things just as they are in sunyata

This is the sphere of activity of original knowing revealing each appearance just as it is.

དུས་གསུམ་རྒྱལ་བའི་ཡུམ་ལ་ཕྱག་འཚལ་ལོ།། །།

DU	**SUM**	**GYAL WAI**	**YUM**	**LA**	**CHAG TSHAL LO**
times	*three **	*jinas, buddhas*	*Mother #*	*to*	*salutation*

* past, present, future, i.e, all

there is no buddhahood without awakening to emptiness

We make salutation to the Mother of all the Buddhas of the three times.

Transcendental wise discerning beyond speech, thought or expression is unbegun and unstopped, like the actuality of the sky. This is the sphere of activity of original knowing revealing each appearance just as it is. We make salutation to the Mother of all the Buddhas of the three times.

The Heart of Perfect Liberating Transcendental Wise Discerning

རྒྱ་གར་སྐད་དུ།

GYA GAR	**KAE**	**DU**
India (Sanskrit)	*language*	*in*

In the language of India:

བྷ་ག་ཝ་ཏི་པྲཛྙཱ་པཱ་ར་མི་ཏཱ་ཧྲི་ད་ཡ།

BHA GA WA TI	**PRAJ NYA**	**PA RA MI TA**	**HRI DA YA**
perfect, victorious and liberated	*highest knowledge*	*gone beyond, transcendent*	*heart, essence*

Bhagawatiprajnaparamitahridaya.

བོད་སྐད་དུ།

BO	**KAE**	**DU**
Tibet	*language*	*in*

In the language of Tibet:

བཅོམ་ལྡན་འདས་མ་ཤེས་རབ་ཀྱི་ཕ་རོལ་

CHOM	**DAN**	**DAE**	**MA**	**SHE RAB**	**KYI**	**PHA ROL**
victorious over sin and ignorance	*possessing good qualities*	*going from samsara*	*(female ending)*	*finest knowing, wise discerning*	*of*	*far side*

ཏུ་ཕྱིན་པའི་སྙིང་པོ།

TU	**CHIN PAI**	**NYING PO**
to	*gone*	*heart, essence (of the Prajnaparamita teaching)*

bChom-lDan-'Das-Ma Shes-Rab-Kyi Pha-Rol-Tu Phyin-Pa'i sNying-Po.

བམ་པོ་གཅིག་གོ།

BAM PO	**CHI GO**
bundle of papers, volumes	*only one*

Forming just one bundle of paper.

In the language of India: Bhagawatiprajnaparamitahridaya. In the language of Tibet: bChom lDan-'Das-Ma Shes-Rab-Kyi Pha-Rol-Tu Phyin-Pa'i sNying-Po. Forming just one bundle of paper.

འདི་སྐད་བདག་གིས་ཐོས་པ་དུས་གཅིག་ན།

DI KAE	**DA**	**GI**	**THO PA**	**DU**	**CHI**	**NA**
this language, speech	*I*	*by*	*heard*	*time*	*once*	*at*

Thus have I heard: at one time

བཅོམ་ལྡན་འདས་རྒྱལ་པོའི་ཁབ་བྱ་རྒོད་ཕུང་པོའི་རི་ལ་

CHOM DAN DAE	**GYAL POI KHAB**	**JA GO**	**PHUNG POI**	**RI**	**LA**
Bhagawan, Buddha Shakyamuni	*Rajagriha in Bihar state, India*	*vulture*	*heap, peak*	*hill*	*at*

Bhagawan was staying at the Vulture Peak hill at Rajagriha

དགེ་སློང་གི་དགེ་འདུན་ཆེན་པོ་དང་།

GE LONG	**GI**	**GEN DUN**	**CHEN PO**	**DANG**
bhikshu, fully ordained monks	*of*	*sangha (hinayana bhikshus)*	*great **	*and*

* The use of 'great' means that at least one thousand were present

Together with a great assembly of the sangha of ordained monks

བྱང་ཆུབ་སེམས་དཔའི་དགེ་འདུན་ཆེན་པོ་དང་ཐབས་ཅིག་ཏུ་བཞུགས་ཏེ།

JANG CHUB SEM PAI	**GEN DUN**	**CHEN PO**	**DANG**	**THAB CHIG TU**	**ZHU**	**TE**
bodhisattva (bodhisattvas but in bhikshu robes)	*sangha*	*great*	*and*	*together*	*sat*	*thus*

And bodhisattvas.

Thus I have heard: at one time Bhagawan was staying at the Vulture Peak hill at Rajagriha together with a great assembly of the sangha of ordained monks and bodhisattvas.

དེའི་ཚེ་བཅོམ་ལྡན་འདས་ཟབ་མོ་སྣང་བ་ཞེས་བྱ་བའི་

DEI	**TSHE**	**CHOM DAN DAE**	**ZAB MO**	**NANG WA**	**ZHE JA WAI**
that	*time*	*Bhagawan, Buddha Shakyamuni*	*profound*	*illumination*	*known as*

At that time Bhagawan was resting evenly in the absorbed contemplation known as *"Profound Illumination"*

ཆོས་ཀྱི་རྣམ་གྲངས་ཀྱི་ཏིང་ངེ་འཛིན་

CHO	**KYI**	**NAM DRANG**	**KYI**	**TING NGE DZIN**
dharmas, phenomena	*of*	*examine, look at the details*	*of*	*samadhi, absorbed contemplation*

ལ་སྙོམས་པར་ཞུགས་སོ།

LA	**NYOM PAR**	**ZHU SO**
in	*maintaining*	*equalness*

(meditation on emptiness free of discursiveness)

Which discerns the nature of phenomena.

At that time Bhagawan was resting evenly in the absorbed contemplation known as "Profound Illumination" which discerns the nature of phenomena.

ཡང་དེའི་ཚེ་བྱང་ཆུབ་སེམས་དཔའ་ཆེན་པོ་འཕགས་པ་

YANG	**DEI**	**TSHE**	**JANG CHUB SEM PA**	**CHEN PO**	**PHAG PA**
also	*that*	*time*	*bodhisattva*	*great*	*arya, noble*

At that time the great bodhisattva

སྤྱན་རས་གཟིགས་དབང་ཕྱུག་ཤེས་རབ་ཀྱི་ཕ་རོལ་ཏུ་ཕྱིན་པ་

CHEN RE ZI	**WONG CHU**	**SHE RAB**	**KYI**	**PHA ROL**	**TU**	**CHIN PA**
Avalokitesvara	*powerful*	*prajna, wise*	*of*	*far side*	*to*	*gone*
discerning						

Arya Avalokitesvara was clearly observing

ཟབ་མོའི་སྤྱོད་པ་ཉིད་ལ་རྣམ་པར་བལྟ་ཞིང་

ZAB MOI	**CHO PA NYI**	**LA**	**NAM PAR**	**TA ZHING**
deep	*practicing*	*in, with*	*fully, well*	*looking*

Within the profound practice of transcendental wise discerning.

ཕུང་པོ་ལྔ་པོ་དེ་དག་ལ་ཡང་རང་བཞིན་གྱིས་

PHUNG PO	**NGA PO**	**DE DA**	**LA**	**YANG**	**RANG ZHIN**	**GYI**
skandhas,	*five**	*these*	*to*	*also*	*naturally,*	*by*
composition					*inherent*	

* form, feeling, perception, formation, consciousness

Through this he truly saw

སྟོང་པར་རྣམ་པར་བལྟའོ།

TONG PAR	**NAM PAR**	**TA O**
empty, without	*fully, well*	*saw*
inherent existence		

The natural emptiness of the five factors of composition.

At that time the great bodhisattva Arya Avalokitesvara was clearly observing within the profound practice of transcendental wise discerning. Through this he truly saw the inherent emptiness of the five factors of composition.

དེ་ནས་སངས་རྒྱས་ཀྱི་མཐུས་ཚེ་དང་ལྡན་པ་ཤ་རིའི་བུས་

DE NAE	**SANG GYE**	**KYI**	**THU**	**TSHE DANG DEN PA**	**SHA RI BUE**
then	*Buddha*	*of*	*by that*	*ayushman, title of respect*	*Shariputra, by*
	(Shakyamuni)		*power*		

Then, through the power of the Buddha, the venerable Shariputra

བྱང་ཆུབ་སེམས་དཔའ་སེམས་དཔའ་ཆེན་པོ་འཕགས་པ་

JANG CHU SEM PA	**SEM PA CHEN PO**	**PHAG PA**
bodhisattva	*mahasattva, great being*	*arya, noble*

Spoke as follows to the bodhisattva-mahasattva

སྤྱན་རས་གཟིགས་དབང་ཕྱུག་ལ་འདི་སྐད་ཅེས་སྨྲས་སོ།

CHEN RE ZI WONG CHU	**LA**	**DI**	**KAE CHE**	**MA SO**
Avalokitesvara	*to*	*this*	*speech*	*said*

Arya Avalokitesvara:

རིགས་ཀྱི་བུ་གང་ལ་ལ་ཤེས་རབ་ཀྱི་ཕ་རོལ་ཏུ་ཕྱིན་པ་

RIG KYI BU	**GANG LA LA**	**SHE RAB KYI PHA ROL TU CHIN PA**
kulaputra, son of a good family	*someone, whoever, whichever of them*	*prajnaparamita, transcendental wise discerning*

"In what manner should they train,

ཟབ་མོའི་སྤྱོད་པ་སྤྱད་པར་འདོད་པ་དེས་

ZAB MOI	**CHO PA**	**CHAE PAR**	**DO PA**	**DE**
deep	*conduct, way, mode*	*practice, meditate*	*like, desire to do*	*by them*

Those of good family who wish to follow the profound practice

ཇི་ལྟར་བསླབ་པར་བྱ། དེ་སྐད་ཅེས་སྨྲས་པ་དང་།

JI TAR	**LA PAR**	**JA**	**DE**	**KAE CHE**	**MAE PA**	**DANG**
in what way, how	*train, practice*	*do*	*that*	*speech*	*said*	*and*

Of transcendental wise discerning?" Thus he spoke.

Then, through the power of the Buddha, the venerable Shariputra spoke as follows to the bodhisattva-mahasattva Arya Avalokitesvara: "In what manner should they train, those of good family who wish to follow the profound practice of transcendental wise discerning?" Thus he spoke.

བྱང་ཆུབ་སེམས་དཔའ་སེམས་དཔའ་ཆེན་པོ་

JANG CHU SEM PA	**SEM PA CHEN PO**
bodhisattva	*mahasattva*

Bodhisattva-mahasattva

འཕགས་པ་སྤྱན་རས་གཟིགས་དབང་ཕྱུག་གིས་

PHAG PA	**CHEN RE ZI WONG CHU**	**GI**
arya	*Avalokitesvara*	*by*

Arya Avalokitesvara

ཚེ་དང་ལྡན་པ་ཤཱ་རི་དྭ་ཏིའི་བུ་ལ་འདི་སྐད་ཅེས་སྨྲས་སོ།

TSHE DANG DAN PA	**SHA RI DVA TAI BU**	**LA**	**DI**	**KAE CHE**	**MA SO**
ayushman, venerable	*Shariputra*	*to*	*this*	*speech*	*said*

Made this reply to the venerable Shariputra:

ཤཱ་རིའི་བུ་རིགས་ཀྱི་བུ་འམ། རིགས་ཀྱི་བུ་མོ་གང་ལ་ལ་

SHA RI BU	**RIG KYI BU**	**AM**	**RIG KYI BU MO**	**GANG**	**LA LA**
Shariputra	*kulaputra, son of a good family*	*or*	*kulaputri, daughter of a good family*	*whoever*	*to each of them*

(i.e. a suitable disciple)

"Shariputra, whichever of those sons or daughters of a good family

ཤེས་རབ་ཀྱི་ཕ་རོལ་ཏུ་ཕྱིན་པ་ཟབ་མོའི་སྤྱོད་པ་

SHE RAB KYI PHA ROL TU CHIN PA	**ZAB MOI**	**CHO PA**
transcendental wise discerning	*deep*	*practice, way*

Wish to follow the profound practice of transcendental wise discerning

སྤྱད་པར་འདོད་པ་དེས་འདི་ལྟར་རྣམ་པར་བལྟ་བར་བྱ་སྟེ།

CHAD PAR	**DO PA**	**DE**	**DI TAR**	**NAM PAR**	**TA WAR**	**JA**	**TE**
practice	*like to*	*by them*	*like this*	*fully, well*	*looking*	*do*	*this*

Should look thoroughly in the manner I will describe

ཕུང་པོ་ལྔ་པོ་དེ་དག་ཀྱང་རང་བཞིན་གྱིས་

PHUNG PO	**NGA PO**	**DE DAG**	**KYANG**	**RANG ZHIN GYI**
skandhas, heaps	*five* *	*these*	*also*	*naturally, inherently*

* form, feeling, perception, formation, consciousness

And thus clearly see that the five factors of composition

སྟོང་པར་རྣམ་པར་ཡང་དག་པར་རྗེས་སུ་བལྟའོ།

TONG PAR	**NAM PAR**	**YANG DAG PAR**	**JE SU**	**TA O**
empty, non-substantial	*fully*	*purely*	*at, after*	*look, see*

Are intrinsically empty of inherent existence."

Bodhisattva-mahasattva Arya Avalokitesvara made this reply to the venerable Shariputra: "Shariputra, whichever of those sons or daughters of a good family wish to follow the profound practice of transcendental wise discerning should look thoroughly in the manner I will describe and thus clearly see that the five factors of composition are intrinsically empty of inherent existence."

གཟུགས་སྟོང་པའོ། སྟོང་པ་ཉིད་གཟུགས་སོ།

ZUG	**TONG PA O**	**TONG PA NYI**	**ZUG SO**
form	*empty, sunyata*	*sunyata, emptiness*	*form*

"Form is empty. Emptiness is form.

གཟུགས་ལས་སྟོང་པ་ཉིད་གཞན་མ་ཡིན།

ZUG	**LAE**	**TONG PA NYI**	**ZHAN**	**MA**	**YIN**
form	*from*	*sunyata, emptiness*	*other*	*not*	*is*

Emptiness is not other than form.

སྟོང་པ་ཉིད་ལས་ཀྱང་གཟུགས་གཞན་མ་ཡིན་ནོ།

TONG PA NYI	**LAE**	**KYANG**	**ZUG**	**ZHAN**	**MA**	**YIN NO**
sunyata, emptiness	*from*	*also*	*form*	*other*	*not*	*is*

Form is not other than emptiness.

དེ་བཞིན་དུ་ཚོར་བ་དང་། འདུ་ཤེས་དང་།

DE ZHIN DU	**TSHOR WA**	**DANG**	**DU SHE**	**DANG**
similarly, in that way	*feeling*	*and*	*perception, identification*	*and*

In the same way, feeling, perception,

འདུ་བྱེད་དང་། རྣམ་པར་ཤེས་པ་རྣམས་སྟོང་པའོ།

DU JE	**DANG**	**NAM PAR SHE PA**	**NAM**	**TONG PA O**
associating and constructing	*and*	*consciousness*	*all*	*empty*

Formation and consciousness are all empty."

"Form is empty. Emptiness is form. Emptiness is not other than form. Form is not other than emptiness. In the same way, feeling, perception, formation and consciousness are all empty."

ཤཱ་རིའི་བུ། དེ་ལྟར་ཆོས་ཐམས་ཅད་སྟོང་པ་ཉིད་དེ།

SHA RI BU	**DE TAR**	**CHO**	**THAM CHE**	**TONG PA NYI**	**DE**
Shariputra	*in that way*	*dharmas*	*all*	*sunyata*	*that*

"Thus Shariputra, in this way all phenomena are themselves emptiness.

མཚན་ཉིད་མེད་པ། མ་སྐྱེས་པ། མ་འགགས་པ།

TSHAN NYI	**ME PA**	**MA KYE PA**	**MA GAG PA**
*characteristic**	*without*	*unborn*	*unstopped*

*their actuality cannot be perceived through reliance on signs

They are free of signs and identification. They are unbegun and unstopped,

དྲི་མ་མེད་པ། དྲི་མ་དང་བྲལ་བ། མེད་པ།

DRI MA	ME PA	DRI MA	DANG DRAL WA	ME PA
stain	*without*	*stain*	*free from*	*without*

Without stain and without freedom from stains,

བྲི་བ་མེད་པ། གང་བ་མེད་པའོ།

DRI WA	ME PA	GANG WA	ME PA O
decline, diminish	*without*	*full, complete, increase*	*without*

And are without decrease or increase."

"Thus, Shariputra, in that way all phenomena are themselves emptiness. They are free of signs and identification. They are unbegan and unstopped, without stain and without freedom from stains, and are without decrease or increase."

ཤཱ་རིའི་བུ། དེ་ལྟ་བས་ན་སྟོང་པ་ཉིད་ལ་གཟུགས་མེད།

SHA RI BU	DE TAR WAE NA	TONG PA NYI	LA	ZUG	ME
Shariputra	*in that way, therefore*	*sunyata, emptiness*	*to, in*	*form*	*without*

Therefore, Shariputra, emptiness is without form,

ཚོར་བ་མེད། འདུ་ཤེས་མེད།

TSHOR WA	ME	DU SHE	ME
feeling	*without*	*perception*	*without*

Without feeling, without perception,

འདུ་བྱེད་རྣམས་མེད། རྣམ་པར་ཤེས་པ་མེད།

DU JE NAM	ME	NAM PAR SHE PA	ME
formation	*without*	*consciousness*	*without*

Without formation and without consciousness;

མིག་མེད། རྣ་བ་མེད། སྣ་མེད། ལྕེ་མེད།

MIG	ME	NA WA	ME	NA	ME	CHE	ME
eye	*without*	*ear*	*without*	*nose*	*without*	*tongue*	*without*

Without eye, without ear, without nose, without tongue,

ལུས་མེད། ཡིད་མེད། གཟུགས་མེད། སྒྲ་མེད།

LUE	ME	YI	ME	ZUG	ME	DRA	ME
body	*without*	*mentation*	*without*	*form*	*without*	*sound*	*without*

Without body, without mentation; without form, without sound,

དྲི་མེད། རོ་མེད། རེག་བྱ་མེད། ཆོས་མེད་དོ།

DRI	ME	RO	ME	REG JA	ME	CHO	ME DO
smell objects	*without*	*taste*	*without*	*tangible*	*without*	*phenomena*	*without*

Without smell, without taste, without sensation, and without objects of mentation.

མིག་གི་ཁམས་མེད་པ་ནས་ཡིད་ཀྱི་ཁམས་མེད།

MIG	GI	KHAM	ME PA	NE	YI	KYI	KHAM	ME
eye	*of*	*sphere of operation*	*without*	*from, up until*	*mentation*	*of*	*sphere of operation*	*without*

(i.e. all 18 dhatus of six organs, six objects and six consciousnesses)

Emptiness is without the domain of vision and without the domain of the other senses up to and including the domain of mentation.

ཡིད་ཀྱི་རྣམ་པར་ཤེས་པའི་ཁམས་ཀྱི་བར་དུ་མེད་དོ།

YID	KYI	NAM PAR SHE PAI	KHAM	KYI	BAR DU	ME DO
mind, mentation	*of*	*vijnana, consciousness*	*sphere of operation*	*of*	*until*	*without*

(i.e. none of the possibilities of existence are inherently real)

And emptiness is without all the domains of consciousness up to and including mentation consciousness.

"Therefore, Shariputra, emptiness is without form, without feeling, without perception, without formation and without consciousness; without eye, without ear, without nose, without tongue, without body, without mentation; without form, without sound, without smell, without taste, without sensation, and without objects of mentation. Emptiness is without the domain of vision and without the domain of the other senses up to and including the domain of mentation. And emptiness is without all the domains of consciousness up to and including mentation consciousness.

མ་རིག་པ་མེད། མ་རིག་པ་ཟད་པ་མེད་པ་

MA RIG PA	ME	MA RIG PA	ZAE PA	ME PA
ignorance	*without*	*ignorance*	*finish*	*without*

Emptiness is free of ignorance, and of the extinction of ignorance

ནས་རྒ་ཤི་མེད།

NAE	GA	SHI	ME
from	*old age*	*death*	*without*

And of all twelve factors of dependent co-arising up until old age and death

རྒ་ཤི་ཟད་པའི་བར་དུའང་མེད་དོ།

GA SHI ZAE PAI BAR DU ANG ME DO

old age death finish until also without*

*Thus all the following twelve links of dependent conditioned existence are empty:1 ignorance; 2 formation; 3 consciousness; 4 name and form; 5 the six sense organs; 6 contact; 7 feelings; 8 craving or hankering after; 9 sensual enthrallment; 10 procreation; 11 birth; 12 old age and death

And the extinction of old age and death.

དེ་བཞིན་དུ་སྡུག་བསྔལ་བ་དང་། ཀུན་འབྱུང་བ་དང་།

DE ZHIN DU DU NGAL WA DANG KUN JUNG WA DANG

in this way suffering and the cause of suffering and

Similarly, emptiness is free of suffering, its cause,

འགོག་པ་དང་། ལམ་མེད།

GO PA DANG LAM ME

*the cessation of suffering and path from suffering without**

* Thus the four noble truths are shown to be within emptiness

Its cessation and the path that leads to the cessation of suffering.

ཡེ་ཤེས་མེད། ཐོབ་པ་མེད། མ་ཐོབ་པའང་མེད་དོ།

YE SHE ME THO PA ME MA THO PA ANG ME DO

original knowing without attainment without non-attainment also without

Emptiness is free of intrinsic original knowing and is free of attainment and also of non-attainment.

"Emptiness is free of ignorance, and of the extinction of ignorance and of all twelve factors of dependent co-arising up until old age and death and the extinction of old age and death. Similarly, emptiness is free of suffering, its cause, its cessation and the path that leads to the cessation of suffering. Emptiness is free of intrinsic original knowing and is free of attainment and also of non-attainment."

ཤཱ་རིའི་བུ། དེ་ལྟ་བས་ན་བྱང་ཆུབ་སེམས་དཔའ་རྣམས་

SHA RI BU DE TAR WAE NA JANG CHUB SEM PA NAM

Shariputra therefore bodhisattvas

Therefore Shariputra,

ཐོབ་པ་མེད་པའི་ཕྱིར།

THO PA ME PAI CHIR

attainment without for that reason*

*nothing inherently substantial that can be gained

Because there is nothing to be gained, bodhisattvas

ཤེས་རབ་ཀྱི་ཕ་རོལ་ཏུ་ཕྱིན་པ་ལ་བརྟེན་ཅིང་གནས་ཏེ།

SHE RAB KYI PHA ROL TU CHIN PA LA TEN CHING NAE TE
prajna paramita, transcendental wise discerning on relying, using stay thus
Rely on transcendental wise discerning and, dwelling

སེམས་ལ་སྒྲིབ་པ་མེད་པས་སྐྲག་པ་མེད་དེ།

SEM LA DRI PA ME PAE TRAG PA ME DE
mind to obscuration, covering without/therefore fear without
With minds free of obscuration, are without fear.

ཕྱིན་ཅི་ལོག་ལས་ཤིན་ཏུ་འདས་ནས་

CHIN CHI LO LAE SHIN TU DAE NE
deception, falsity from completely pass then
Having passed completely from the domain of deception

མྱ་ངན་ལས་འདས་པར་མཐར་ཕྱིན་ཏོ།

NYA NGAN LAE DAE PAR THAR CHIN TO
nirvana, beyond sorrow /to, in finish, fulfil
They attain the full release of nirvana.

"Therefore Shariputra, because there is nothing to be gained, bodhisattvas rely on transcendental wise discerning and, dwelling with minds free of obscuration, are without fear. Having passed completely from the domain of deception they attain the full release of nirvana.

དུས་གསུམ་དུ་རྣམ་པར་བཞུགས་པའི་སངས་རྒྱས་ཐམས་ཅད་ཀྱང་

DU SUM DU NAM PA ZHU PAI SANG GYE THAM CHE KYANG
three times (past (present, future) in well staying buddhas all also
All the buddhas abiding in the three times also

ཤེས་རབ་ཀྱི་ཕ་རོལ་ཏུ་ཕྱིན་པ་ལ་བརྟེན་ནས་

SHE RAB KYI PHA ROL TU CHIN PA LA TEN NAE
transcendental wise discerning on relying then
Rely on transcendental wise discerning and thus,

བླ་ན་མེད་པ་ཡང་དག་པར་རྫོགས་པའི་བྱང་ཆུབ་

LA NA ME PA YANG DA PAR DZO PAI JANG CHUB
unexcelled (mahayana) very pure, perfect complete bodhi, enlightenment
With unexcelled, perfect awakening,

ཏུ་མངོན་པར་རྫོགས་པར་སངས་རྒྱས་སོ།

TU	**NGON PAR**	**DZO PAR**	**SANG GYE SO**
with	*manifest*	*complete*	*buddhahood*

Are completely enlightened buddhas.

All buddhas abiding in the three times also rely on transcendental wise discerning and thus, with unexcelled, perfect awakening, are completely enlightened buddhas.

དེ་ལྟ་བས་ན་ཤེས་རབ་ཀྱི་ཕ་རོལ་ཏུ་ཕྱིན་པའི་སྔགས།

DE TA WAE NA	**SHE RAB KYI PHA ROL TU CHIN PAI**	**NGA**
therefore	*transcendental wise discerning*	*mantra, that which protects the mind*

Due to this being so there is the mantra of transcendental wise discerning,

རིག་པ་ཆེན་པོའི་སྔགས། བླ་ན་མེད་པའི་སྔགས།

RIG PA	**CHEN POI**	**NGA**	**LA NA ME PAI**	**NGA**
vidya, awareness	*great*	*mantra*	*unsurpassed*	*mantra*

The mantra of great awareness, the unsurpassed mantra.

མི་མཉམ་པ་དང་མཉམ་པར་བྱེད་པའི་སྔགས།

MI NYAM PA	**DANG**	**NYAM PAR**	**JED PAI**	**NGA**
not equal	*and*	*equal, even*	*doing, making*	*mantra*

This is the mantra which balances the unbalanced.

སྡུག་བསྔལ་ཐམས་ཅད་རབ་ཏུ་ཞི་བར་བྱེད་པའི་སྔགས།

DU NGAL	**THAM CHE**	**RAB TU**	**ZHI WAR**	**JE PAI**	**NGA**
suffering	*all*	*fully*	*pacify*	*doing*	*mantra*

This is the mantra which completely pacifies all suffering.

མི་རྫུན་པས་ན་བདེན་པར་ཤེས་པར་བྱ་སྟེ།

MI	**DZUN PAE NA**	**DEN PAR**	**SHE PAR**	**JA**	**TE**
not	*lying/therefore*	*true*	*know*	*do*	*thus*

This is not deception so you can come to know that it is true.

Due to this being so there is the mantra of transcendental wise discerning, the mantra of great awareness, the unsurpassed mantra. This is the mantra which balances the unbalanced. This is the mantra which completely purifies all suffering. This is not deception so you can come to know that it is true.

ཤེས་རབ་ཀྱི་ཕ་རོལ་ཏུ་ཕྱིན་པའི་སྔགས་སྨྲས་པ།

SHE RAB KYI PHA ROL TU CHIN PAI	NGA	MAE PA
prajnaparamita, transcendental wise discerning	*mantra*	*say*

Recite the mantra of transcendental wise discerning:

ཏ་དྱ་ཐཱ། ག་ཏེ་ག་ཏེ་པཱ་ར་ག་ཏེ་

TA DYA THA	GA TE	GA TE	PA RA GA TE
thus it is like this	*gone*	*gone*	*gone beyond*

In this way, gone, gone, gone beyond,

པཱ་ར་སཾ་ག་ཏེ་བོ་དྷི་སྭཱ་ཧཱ།།

PA RA SAM GA TE	BO DHI	SVA HA
completely gone beyond (never come back)	*awakened, enlightened*	*so it is*

Fully gone beyond. Awakened – as it is!

ཤཱ་རིའི་བུ་བྱང་ཆུབ་སེམས་དཔའ་སེམས་དཔའ་ཆེན་པོས་དེ་ལྟར་

SHA RI BU	JANG CHUB SEM PA	SEM PA CHEN POE		DE TAR
Shariputra	*bodhisattva, enlightened being*	*mahasattva great being*	*/by*	*like that*

Shariputra, in this way a bodhisattva-mahasattva

ཤེས་རབ་ཀྱི་ཕ་རོལ་ཏུ་ཕྱིན་པ་ཟབ་མོ་ལ་བསླབ་པར་བྱའོ།

SHE RAB KYI PHA ROL TU CHIN PA	ZAB MO	LA	LA PAR	JA O
transcendental wise discerning	*deep*	*to, in*	*train,*	*do practice*

Should train in profound transcendental wise discerning.

Recite the mantra of transcendental wise discerning:'In this way, gone, gone, gone beyond, fully gone beyond. Awakened – as it is!' Shariputra, in this way a bodhisattva-mahasattva should train in profound transcendental wise discerning."

དེ་ནས་བཅོམ་ལྡན་འདས་ཏིང་ངེ་འཛིན་དེ་ལས་བཞེངས་ཏེ་

DE NAE	CHOM DEN DAE	TING NGE DZIN	DE	LAE	ZHENG	TE
then	*bhagawan (Shakyamuni)*	*samadhi, absorbed contemplation*	*that*	*from*	*arise*	*thus*

Then Bhagawan arose from his absorbed contemplation

བྱང་ཆུབ་སེམས་དཔའ་སེམས་དཔའ་ཆེན་པོ་

JANG CHU SEM PA	SEM PA CHEN PO
bodhisattva	*mahasattva*

And praised the bodhisattva-mahasattva

འཕགས་པ་སྤྱན་རས་གཟིགས་དབང་ཕྱུག་ལ་

PHAG PA	CHEN RE ZI WONG CHU	LA
arya, noble	*Avalokitesvara*	*to*

Arya Avalokitesvara

ལེགས་སོ་ཞེས་བྱ་བ་བྱིན་ནས།

LEG SO	ZHE JA WA	JIN	NAE
good, well	*thus*	*is*	*then*

Saying,

ལེགས་སོ་ལེགས་སོ། རིགས་ཀྱི་བུ། དེ་དེ་བཞིན་ནོ།

LEG SO	LEG SO	RIG	KYI	BU	DE	DE ZHIN NO
yes, very good	*yes, very good*	*family*	*of*	*son*	*that*	*like that*

"Very good. Very good. Son of a good family, it is like that.

དེ་དེ་བཞིན་ཏེ། ཇི་ལྟར་ཁྱོད་ཀྱིས་བསྟན་པ་བཞིན་དུ་

DE	DE ZHIN	TE	JI TAR	KHYO	KYI	TAN PA	ZHIN DU
that	*like that*	*thus*	*like what*	*you*	*by*	*shown*	*like that*

It is like that, and so just as you have shown it

ཤེས་རབ་ཀྱི་ཕ་རོལ་ཏུ་ཕྱིན་པ་ཟབ་མོ་ལ་སྤྱོད་པར་བྱ་སྟེ།

SHE RAB KYI PHA ROL TU CHIN PA	ZAB MO	LA	CHA PAR	JA TE
transcendental wise discerning	*deep*	*to*	*practice*	*do this*

Profound transcendental wise discerning is to be practised.

དེ་བཞིན་གཤེགས་པ་རྣམས་ཀྱང་རྗེས་སུ་ཡི་རང་ངོ།

DE ZHIN SHEG PA NAM	KYANG	JE SU YI RANG NGO
*tathagatas,**	*also*	*are happy at this*

*those who have gone this way, buddhas.

All the Tathagatas will rejoice at this."

Then Bhagawan arose from his absorbed contemplation and praised the bodhisattva-mahasattva Arya Avalokitesvara, saying: "Very good. Very good. Son of a good family, it is like that. It is like that, and so profound transcendental wise discerning is to be practised just as you have shown it. All the Tathagatas will rejoice at this."

བཅོམ་ལྡན་འདས་ཀྱིས་དེ་སྐད་ཅེས་བཀའ་སྩལ་ནས།

CHOM DEN DAE	KYI	DE KAE CHE	KA TSAL	NAE
bhagawan (Shakyamuni)	*by*	*like that*	*spoke*	*then*

Bhagawan spoke thus, and then

ཚེ་དང་ལྡན་པ་ཤཱ་རི་དྭ་ཏིའི་བུ་དང་།

TSHE DANG DAN PA	**SHA RI DVA TI BU**	**DANG**
ayushman, venerable	*Shariputra*	*and*

The venerable Shariputra and

བྱང་ཆུབ་སེམས་དཔའ་སྤྱན་རས་གཟིགས་དབང་ཕྱུག་དང་།

JANG CHU SEM PA	**CHEN RE ZI WONG CHU**	**DANG**
bodhisattva	*Avalokitesvara*	*and*

The bodhisattva Avalokitesvara and

ཐམས་ཅད་དང་ལྡན་པའི་འཁོར་དེ་དག་དང་།

THAM CHE	**DANG DAN PAI**	**KHOR**	**DE DA**	**DANG**
all	*together*	*circle, entourage*	*these*	*and*

All of their retinues, and all

ལྷ་དང་། མི་དང་། ལྷ་མ་ཡིན་དང་།

LHA	**DANG**	**MI**	**DANG**	**LHA MA YIN**	**DANG**
gods	*and*	*men*	*and*	*asuras*	*and*

The gods, men, jealous gods,

དྲི་ཟར་བཅས་པའི་འཇིག་རྟེན་ཡི་རངས་ཏེ།

DRI ZAR	**CHE PAI**	**JIG TEN**	**YI RANG TE**
gandharvas, local spirits	*and so on*	*world*	*rejoice*

Local spirits and so on of the world rejoiced and

བཅོམ་ལྡན་འདས་ཀྱིས་གསུངས་པ་ལ་མངོན་པར་བསྟོད་དོ།།

CHOM DAN DAE	**KYI**	**SUNG PA**	**LA**	**NGON PAR**	**TOE DO**
Bhagawan	*by*	*speech*	*to*	*manifestly*	*praised*

Sincerely praised the speech of Bhagawan Buddha.

Bhagawan spoke thus, and then the venerable Shariputra and the bodhisattva Avalokitesvara and all of their retinues, and all the gods, men, jealous gods, local spirits and so on of the world rejoiced and sincerely praised the speech of Bhagawan Buddha.

འཕགས་པ་ཤེས་རབ་ཀྱི་ཕ་རོལ་ཏུ་ཕྱིན་པའི་སྙིང་པོ་རྫོགས་སོ།། །།

This concludes *The Heart of Perfect Liberating Transcendental Wise Discerning.*

ན་མོ། བླ་མ་ལ་ཕྱག་འཚལ་ལོ།

NA MO	LA MA	LA	CHA TSHAL LO
obeisance	*guru*	*to*	*salutation*

Namo. Salutation to the Guru.

སངས་རྒྱས་ལ་ཕྱག་འཚལ་ལོ།

SANG GYE	LA	CHA TSHAL LO
buddha	*to*	*salutation*

Salutation to the Buddha.

ཆོས་ལ་ཕྱག་འཚལ་ལོ།

CHO	LA	CHA TSHAL LO
dharma	*to*	*salutation*

Salutation to the Dharma.

དགེ་འདུན་ལ་ཕྱག་འཚལ་ལོ།

GEN DUN	LA	CHA TSHAL LO
sangha	*to*	*salutation*

Salutation to the Sangha.

ཡུམ་ཆེན་མོ་ཤེས་རབ་ཀྱི་ཕ་རོལ་ཏུ་ཕྱིན་མ་ལ་

YUM CHEN MO	SHE RAB KYI PHA ROL TU CHIN MA	LA
Great Mother (sunyata as Mother of all the Buddhas)	*transcendental wise discerning (conceived of as a goddess)*	*with*

Salutation to the Great Mother Transcendental Wise Discerning and

སྲས་ཕྱོགས་བཅུའི་སངས་རྒྱས་ཀྱི་འཁོར་གྱིས་

SAE	CHO CHUI	SANG GYE	KYI	KHOR	GYI
sons	*ten directions*	*buddhas*	*of*	*retinue*	*by (i.e. everywhere)*

To her surrounding circle of sons,

བསྐོར་བ་དང་བཅས་པ་ལ་ཕྱག་འཚལ་ལོ།

KOR WA	DANG CHE WA	LA	CHA TSHAL LO
surrounded	*together*	*to*	*salutation*

The Buddhas of the ten directions.

ཁྱེད་རྣམས་ལ་ཕྱག་འཚལ་བའི་མཐུ་དང་ནུས་པ་ལ་བརྟེན་ནས།

KHYE NAM	LA	CHA TSHAL WAI	THU	DANG	NU PA	LA TE NAE
you	*to*	*salutation's*	*effective power*	*and*	*power, force*	*in consequence of, depending on*

By the force and effective power of making salutation to you

བདག་གི་བདེན་པའི་ཚིག་འདི་འགྲུབ་པར་གྱུར་ཅིག།

DA GI	DEN PAI	TSHIG	DI	DRU PAR	GYUR CHI
my	*true*	*words*	*this*	*accomplished, come to pass*	*must be*

These true words of mine must be fulfilled.

Namo. Salutation to the guru. Salutation to the Buddha. Salutation to the Dharma. Salutation to the Sangha. Salutation to the Great Mother Transcendental Wise Discerning and to her surrounding circle of sons, the Buddhas of the ten directions. By the force and effective power of making salutation to you, these true words of mine must be fulfilled.

སྔོན་ལྷའི་དབང་པོ་བརྒྱ་བྱིན་གྱིས་ཤེས་རབ་ཀྱི་ཕ་རོལ་ཏུ་ཕྱིན་པའི་

NGON	LHAI WONG PO	GYA JIN	GYI	SHE RAB KYI PHA ROL TU CHIN PAI
formerly	*Devindra (the king of the gods)*	*Shakra*	*by*	*transcendental wise discerning*

In former times Lhawong Gyajin

དོན་ཟབ་མོ་ཡིད་ལ་བསམ་ཞིང་

DON	ZAB MO	YI	LA	SAM ZHING
meaning	*deep*	*mind, mentation*	*in, with*	*thinking*

Contemplated the deep meaning of transcendental wise discerning.

ཚིག་ཟབ་མོ་ཁ་ཏོན་དུ་བྱས་པ་ལ་བརྟེན་ནས་

TSHI	ZAB MO	KHA TON DU	JAE PA	LA TEN NAE
words	*deep*	*reading*	*do*	*on the basis of, in consequence of*

He read its profound words and thus

བདུད་སྡིག་ཅན་ཕྱིར་བཟློག་པ་དེ་བཞིན་དུ།

DU	DI CHAN	CHIR DO PA	DE ZHIN DU
mara,	*sinful*	*repel, repulse*	*like that, accordingly demon*

Was able to repulse all corrupting demonic tendencies.

བདག་གིས་ཀྱང་ཤེས་རབ་ཀྱི་ཕ་རོལ་ཏུ་ཕྱིན་པའི་

DA	GI	KYANG	SHE RAB KYI PA ROL TU CHIN PAI
me	*by*	*also*	*transcendental wise discerning*

Similarly, we also contemplate the profound meaning

དོན་ཟབ་མོ་ཡིད་ལ་བསམས་ཤིང་།

DON	ZAB MO	YI	LA	SAM ZHING
meaning mentation	*deep*	*mind,*	*in, with*	*thinking*

Of transcendental wise discerning and

ཚིག་ཟབ་མོ་ཁ་ཏོན་དུ་བྱས་པ་ལ་བརྟེན་ནས་

TSHI	**ZAB MO**	**KHA TON**	**DU JAE PA**	**LA TEN NAE**
words	*deep*	*read*	*doing*	*in consequence*

Read these profound words, and due to this

བདག་ཅག་དཔོན་སློབ་ཡོན་མཆོད་འཁོར་

DA CHA	**PON**	**LOB**	**YON**	**CHO**	**KHOR**
we	*guru*	*disciple*	*sponsors*	*sponsored*	*circle*

We gurus, disciples, sponsors, beneficiaries and all these connected with us

དང་བཅས་པ་ཐམས་ཅད་ཀྱི་འགལ་རྐྱེན་བར་ཆད་

DANG CHE PA	**THAM CHE**	**KYI**	**GAL KYEN**	**BAR CHAE**
together	*all*	*of*	*difficulties, troubles*	*interruptions, obstacles*

Must have all our troubles, obstacles and

མི་མཐུན་པའི་ཕྱོགས་ཐམས་ཅད་ཕྱིར་བཟློག་པར་གྱུར་ཅིག།

MI THUN PAI	**CHO**	**THAM CHE**	**CHIR DO PAR**	**GYUR CHI**
unhelpful, inharmonious	*side*	*all*	*repelled, repulsed*	*must be!*

Difficulties completely repelled!

མེད་པར་གྱུར་ཅིག། ཞི་བར་གྱུར་ཅིག།

ME PAR	**GYUR CHI**	**ZHI WAR**	**GYUR CHI**
without	*must be!*	*pacified*	*must be!*

We must be without them! They must be pacified!

In former times Lhawong Gyajin contemplated the deep meaning of transcendental wise discerning. He read its profound words and thus was able to repulse all corrupting demonic tendencies. Similarly, we also contemplate the profound meaning of transcendental wise discerning and read these profound words, and due to this we gurus, disciples, sponsors, beneficiaries and all those we connected with us must have all our troubles, obstacles and difficulties completely repelled! We must be without them! They must be pacified!

གང་གི་རྟེན་ཅིང་འབྲེལ་བར་འབྱུང་།

GANG	**GI**	**TEN CHING**	**DREL WAR**	**JUNG**
which	*of*	*dependent*	*connected*	*arise*

Whatever arises in dependent co-origination

འགགས་པ་མེད་པ་སྐྱེ་མེད་པ།

GAG PA	**ME PA**	**KYE**	**ME PA**
stopping,	*without*	*birth, beginning*	*without interruption*

Is without stopping and without starting,

ཆད་པ་མེད་པ་རྟག་མེད་པ།

CHA PA	**ME PA**	**TAG**	**ME PA**
nihilism, non-continuity	*without*	*permanence*	*without*

Without annihilation and without permanence,

འོང་བ་མེད་པ་འགྲོ་མེད་པ།

ONG WA	**ME PA**	**DRO**	**ME PA**
coming	*without*	*going*	*without*

Without coming and without going,

ཐ་དད་དོན་མིན་དོན་གཅིག་མིན།

THA DA	**DON**	**MIN**	**DON**	**CHI**	**MIN**
different, separate	*meaning*	*without*	*meaning*	*only one*	*without*

Without diverse meanings and without just one meaning –

སྤྲོས་པ་ཉེར་ཞི་ཞི་བསྟན་པ།

TRO PA	**NYER ZHI**	**ZHI**	**TAN PA**
concepts	*fully pacified*	*peaceful*	*doctrines*

Thus all conceptual constructs are fully pacified. To the peaceful doctrines,

རྫོགས་པའི་སངས་རྒྱས་སྨྲ་རྣམས་ཀྱི།

DZO PAI	**SANG GYE**	**MA NAM**	**KYI**
perfect	*buddha*	*speech*	*of*

The excellent teachings of the speech of the perfect Buddha,

དམ་པ་དེ་ལ་ཕྱག་འཚལ་ལོ།།

DAM PA	**DE**	**LA**	**CHA TSHAL LO**
excellent,	*that*	*to*	*salutation holy*

We pay homage.

Whatever arises in dependent co-origination is without stopping and without starting, without annihilation and without permanence, without coming and without going, without diverse meanings and without just one meaning – thus all conceptual constructs are fully pacified. To the peaceful doctrines, the excellent teachings of the speech of the perfect Buddha we pay homage.

ཐབས་དང་སྐྱབས་དང་དག་པ་དང་།

THAB DANG KYAB DANG DA PA DANG
method and save and pure and

Method, protection, purity and

ཐེག་ཆེན་ངེས་པར་འབྱུང་བ་དང་།

THEG CHEN NGE PAR JUNG WA DANG
mahayana decline (one's practice becomes hinayana) and

Mahayana practice in decline, and

སེམས་ཅན་རྣམས་ནི་རབ་བསླུ་བའི།

SEM CHEN NAM NI RAB LU WAI
sentient beings fully deceiving, cheating

The work of mara who deceives sentient beings –

བདུད་ཀྱི་ལས་ཀྱང་སྤོང་བར་ཤོག ། །།

DU KYI LAE KYANG PONG WAR SHO
mara, demon of work also abandon, drive away must be

All these troubles must be repelled.

Method, protection, purity and mahayana practice in decline, and the work of mara who deceives sentient beings – all these troubles must be repelled.

རྫོགས་པའི་བྱང་ཆུབ་བསྒྲུབ་པ་ལ།

DZO PAI JANG CHUB DRU PA LA
complete bodhi, enlightenment practice to

For those practicing to gain complete enlightenment,

ཕྱི་དང་ནང་གི་འཚེ་བ་ཡི།

CHI DANG NANG GI TSHE WA YI
outer and inner of troubles of

All outer and inner troubles

བར་དུ་གཅོད་པ་ཐམས་ཅད་ཀུན།

BAR DU CHO PA THAM CHE KUN
interruptions, obstacles all all

Which create obstacles

ཉེ་བར་ཞི་བར་མཛད་དུ་གསོལ།། །།

NYE WAR ZHI WAR DZA DU SOL
fully pacify do please

Must be fully pacified!

For those practicing to gain complete enlightenment, all outer and inner troubles which create obstacles must be fully pacified!

འདི་ཡང་བོད་རྒྱ་ལ་ལོའི་ས་རྟ་ལོར་འཕགས་ཡུལ་འཁོར་གདོང་བླ་བྲང་ནང་རྒྱལ་བའི་བཀའ་འགྱུར་ཆེན་མོ་རྟེན་གཙོར་གསར་ཞེངས་སྐབས་བོད་ཟླ་དྲུག་པ་ཆུ་སྟོད་ཟླ་བའི་ཆོས་བཞིའི་ཉིན་སྟོན་ཡུལ་ཝཱ་རཱ་ཎ་སིར་དྲང་སྲོང་ལྷུང་བ་རི་དྭགས་ཀྱི་ནགས་སུ་འཁོར་ལྔ་སྡེ་བཟང་པོ་ལ་བཀའ་དང་པོ་བདེན་པ་བཞིའི་ཆོས་ཀྱི་འཁོར་ལོ་བསྐོར་བའི་ཉིན་གྱི་དུས་དྲན་སྲུང་ཆེད་མར་མེའི་ཕྲེང་བ་བརྒྱ་ཕྲག་འགའ་ཞིག་འབུལ་སྐབས་འདོན་དགོས་རྒྱུའི་ཆེད། བྱང་བདག་བཀྲ་ཤིས་སྟོབས་རྒྱལ་དབང་པོའི་སྡེའི་གསུང་ལ་ཁ་བསྒྱུར་བྱས་ནས་འཁོར་གདོང་གཏེར་སྤྲུལ་འཆི་མེད་རིག་འཛིན་གྱིས་སྐད་གསུམ་ཤན་སྦྱར་བྱས་པའོ།། །།

This ceremony of homage to the Buddha's speech, including the Heart Sutra, was translated for the occasion of the installation of the bKa'-'Gyur, the Tibetan Tripitaka, in the 'Khor- gDong bLa-Brang in India. This ceremony was performed on the 8th of August, 1978, the 4th day of the Tibetan sixth month of the 2904th year from the date of the first turning of the wheel of the Dharma according to the Tibetan tradition, and the 2522nd year of the Buddhist Era according to the Theravada tradition. This day is important as the Buddha's speech day, being the day on which Buddha Shakyamumi first taught the Dharma of the Four Noble Truths to the first five disciples including Aniruddha at Sarnath. Khordong Tertrul Chimed Rigdzin united these three texts on the basis of the words of Jangdag Trashi Tobgyal Wangpoi De.

Translated by C.R. Lama and James Low in 1978
Revised translation by James Low August 2013

༄༅། གངས་ཅན་བསྟན་པའི་སྲོལ་འབྱེད་ཆེན་པོ་ཉེར་ལྔ་ལ་གསོལ་འདེབས་དད་པའི་མེ་ཏོག་ཅེས་བྱ་བ་བཞུགས་སོ།

The Flower of Faith
being
The Prayer to the Twenty-Five Great Ones Who Established the Dharma Systems of Tibet

རྩ་གསུམ་ཀུན་འདུས་སློབ་དཔོན་པདྨ་འབྱུང་།

TSA SUM	**KUN**	**DU**	**LOB PON**	**PE MA JUNG**
*three roots**	*all*	*encompassing*	*acharya, teacher*	*Padmasambhava*

**guru, deva, dakini*

Acharya Padmasambhava who encompasses the three roots,

མཁན་ཆེན་ཞི་འཚོ་ཆོས་རྒྱལ་ཁྲི་སྲོང་ཞབས།

KHAN	**CHEN**	**ZHI TSHO**	**CHO GYAL**	**TRI SONG**	**ZHAB**
scholar, abbot	*great*	*Shantarakshita*	*dharmaraja**	*Trisong Deutsan*	*feet*

*A king who supports and rules according to the Dharma

The great scholar Shantarakshita, Dharma-king Trisong Deutsan,

གནུབ་ཆེན་སངས་རྒྱས་ཉང་སྟོན་ཉི་མ་འོད།

NUB CHEN SANG GYE	**NYANG TON NYI MA OE**
(disciple of Padmasambhava)	*(the great gTer-sTon)*

Nubchen Sangye Yeshe and Nyangton Nyima Ozer –

བཀའ་གཏེར་ཤིང་རྟ་ལྔ་ལ་གསོལ་བ་འདེབས།

KA	**TER**	**SHING TA**	**NGA**	**LA**	**SOL WA DEB**
kama, spoken doctrines	*terma, treasure doctrines*	*great scholars who made easily available*	*five*	*to*	*pray*

We pray to the five great chariots of the spoken and treasure doctrines.

Acharya Padmasambhava who encompasses the three roots, the great scholar Shantarakshita, Dharma-king Trisong Deutsan, Nubchen Sangye Yeshe and Nyangton Nyima Özer – we pray to the five great chariots of the spoken and treasure doctrines.

རྡོར་རྗེ་འཆང་དངོས་བླ་ཆེན་སྙིང་པོའི་ཞབས།

DOR JE CHANG	**NGO**	**LA**	**CHEN**	**NYING POI**	**ZHAB**
vajradhara, primordial buddha	*actual*	*guru*	*great*	*Sa-Chen Kun-dGa' sNying-Po*	*feet (honorific)*

The actual Vajradhara, great guru Kunga Nyingpo,

བསོད་ནམས་ཙེ་མོ་གྲགས་པ་རྒྱལ་མཚན་དང་།

SO NAM TSE MO DRAG PA GYAL TSHAN DANG
(name) (name) and

Sonam Tsemo, Dragpa Gyaltshan,

ས་སྐྱ་པཎ་ཆེན་འཕགས་པ་རིན་པོ་ཆེ།

SA KYA PAN CHEN PHAG PA RIN PO CHE
(name) (name)

Sakya Panchen and Phagpa Rinpoche –

རྗེ་བཙུན་གོང་མ་ལྔ་ལ་གསོལ་བ་འདེབས།

JE TSUN GONG MA NGA LA SOL WA DEB
reverend, saintly upper, early five (founders of the Sakyapa school) to pray

We pray to these five founding saints.

The actual Vajradhara, great guru Kunga Nyingpo, Sonam Tsemo, Dragpa Gyaltshan, Sakya Panchen and Phagpa Rinpoche – we pray to the five founding saints.

དགྱེས་མཛད་རྡོ་རྗེ་མར་སྟོན་བློ་གྲོས་ཞབས།

GYE DZAE DOR JE MAR TON LO DRO ZHAB
Hevajra (marpa practised Hevajra) (Marpa) feet

Marpa Chokyi Lodro who practised Hevajra,

མི་ལ་རས་ཆེན་མཉམ་མེད་སྒམ་པོ་པ།

MI LA RE CHEN NYAM MED GAM PO PA
Milarepa unequalled Gampopa

Milarepa and the unequalled Gampopa,

དུས་གསུམ་མཁྱེན་པ་འགྲོ་མགོན་བསོད་ནམས་གྲགས།

DU SUM KHYEN PA DRO GON SO NAM DRAG
(first Karmapa) (name)

Dusum Khyenpa, and Drogon Sonam Drag –

བཀའ་བརྒྱུད་གོང་མ་ལྔ་ལ་གསོལ་བ་འདེབས།

KA GYU GONG MA NGA LA SOL WA DEB
kadgyupa upper five to pray

We pray to the five founders of the Kagyupa lineage.

Marpa Chokyi Lodro who practised Hevajra, Milarepa and the unequalled Gampopa, Dusum Khyenpa, and Drogon Sonam Drag – we pray to the five founders of the Kagyupa lineage.

འོད་དཔག་མེད་མགོན་དཔལ་ལྡན་མར་མེ་མཛད།

OE PA ME GON PAL DEN MAR ME DZAE
Amitabha benefactor Dipamkara Srijnana, Atisha

Sri Dipamkara, the actual presence of the benefactor Amitabha,

རྒྱལ་བའི་འབྱུང་གནས་སྤྱན་ལྔ་ཚུལ་ཁྲིམས་འབར།

GYAL WAI JUNG NAE CHEN NGA TSHUL TRIM BAR
(Dromton) (name)

Gyalwai Jungnae, Chenga Tshultrim Bar,

རིན་ཆེན་གསལ་དང་གཞོན་ནུ་རྒྱལ་མཚན་ཞབས།

RIN CHEN SAL DANG ZHON NU GYAL TSHAN ZHAB
(name) and (name) feet

Rinchen Sal and Zhonu Gyaltshan –

བཀའ་གདམས་བཤེས་གཉེན་ལྔ་ལ་གསོལ་བ་འདེབས།

KA DAM SHE NYEN NGA LA SOL WA DEB
Kadampa kalyanmitra, spiritual friends five to pray

We pray to the five Kadampa spiritual friends.

Sri Dipamkara, the actual presence of the benefactor Amitabha, Gyalwai Jungnae, Chenga Tshultrim Bar, Rinchen Sal and Zhonu Gyaltshan – we pray to the five Kadampa spiritual friends.

བརྟེན་པའི་འཁོར་ལོ་རྗེ་བཙུན་ཙོང་ཁ་པ།

TEN PAI KHOR LO JE TSUN TSONG KA PA
(title of Manjushri's wife) saintly (name)

Jetsun Tsong Khapa, befriended by Tenpai Khorlo,

རྒྱལ་ཚབ་ཆོས་རྗེ་མཁས་གྲུབ་དགེ་ལེགས་དཔལ།

GYAL TSHAB CHO JE KHAE DRUB GE LEG PAL
(Dharma Rinchen) (name)

Gyaltshab Choje, Khaedrub Geleg Palzang,

དགེ་འདུན་གྲུབ་པ་པཎ་ཆེན་ཆོས་ཀྱི་རྒྱལ།

GEN DUN DRUB PA PAN CHEN CHO KYI GYAL
(name) (name)

Gendun Drubpa and Panchen Chokyi Gyal –

འཇམ་མགོན་ཡབ་སྲས་ལྔ་ལ་གསོལ་བ་འདེབས།

JAM GON	**YAB**	**SAE**	**NGA**	**LA**	**SOL WA DEB**
Manjushri	*father,guru*	*son*	*five*	*to*	*pray*
	(the five who established the Gelug)				

We pray to Manjushri the father and his five sons.

Jetsun Tsong Khapa befriended by Tenpai Khorlo, Gyaltshab Choje, Khaedrub Geleg Pazang, Gendun Drubpa and Panchen Chokyi Gyal – we pray to Manjushri the father and his five sons.

དེ་ལྟར་གསོལ་བ་བཏབ་པའི་བྱིན་རླབས་ཀྱིས།

DE TAR	**SOL WA TAB PAI**	**JIN LAB**	**KYI**
in that way	*praying*	*blessing*	*by*

By the blessing of having prayed in this way,

བདག་སོགས་ཚེ་རིང་ནད་མེད་ཆོས་བཞིན་སྤྱོད།

DAG SOG	**TSHE RING**	**NAE ME**	**CHO**	**ZHIN**	**CHOE**
we (I and all sentient beings)	*long life*	*free of sickness*	*dharma according to*	*as,*	*practise, act behave*

May we have long lives free of sickness and always act in harmony with the Dharma.

ཡོངས་འཛིན་བཤེས་གཉེན་མཆོག་གིས་རྗེས་བཟུང་ནས།

YONG DZIN	**SHE NYEN**	**CHOG**	**GI**	**JE ZUNG**	**NAE**
great scholars and teachers	*spiritual friends*	*most excellent*	*by*	*held, taken care of*	*then*

Being fostered by the most excellent gurus and spiritual friends,

མྱུར་དུ་བྱང་ཆུབ་གོ་འཕང་ཐོབ་པར་ཤོག།

NYUR DU	**JANG CHUB**	**GO PANG**	**THOB PAR**	**SHO**
quickly	*bodhi, enlightenment*	*stage, rank*	*get*	*must*

May we quickly gain the stage of enlightenment.

By the blessing of having prayed in this way, may we have long lives free of sickness and always act in harmony with the Dharma. Being fostered by the most excellent gurus and spiritual friends, may we quickly gain the stage of enlightenment.

རིས་མེད་ ཐུབ་བསྟན་འཛིན་ པའི་དམ་པ་རྣམས།

RI ME	**THUB TAN**	**DZIN PAI**	**DAM PA NAM**
impartial, without bias among sects	*buddha's doctrines*	*holding, keeping*	*holy ones*

May the holy ones who maintain the Buddha's doctrines without bias

བསྐལ་བརྒྱར་ཞབས་བརྟན་འཕྲིན་ལས་ཕྱོགས་བཅུར་འཕེལ།

KAL	GYAR	ZHAB TAN	TRIN LAE	CHOG	CHUR	PHEL
kalpas, aeons	*in a hundred*	*remain, stay and keep healthy*	*deeds*	*directions*	*ten*	*spread*

Remain for a hundred aeons and spread their activity in the ten directions.

དགེ་འདུན་སྡེ་དང་བཤད་སྒྲུབ་བསྟན་པ་རྒྱས།

GEN DUN	DE	DANG	SHAE	DRUB	TAN PA	GYE
sangha	*groups*	*and*	*explain*	*practice*	*doctrines*	*spread, increase*

May these sangha groups and their doctrines of explanation and practice increase and

ས་གསུམ་བཀྲ་ཤིས་སྣང་བས་ཁྱབ་གྱུར་ཅིག།

SA	SUM	TRA SHI	NANG WAE	KHYAB	GYUR CHIG
*levels, worlds**	*three*	*good luck*	*appearances, light*	*fill*	*become*

* gods, men, naga, i.e. above, on and below the earth

May the three worlds be filled with all that is auspicious.

May the holy ones who maintain the Buddha's doctrines without bias remain for a hundred aeons and spread their activity in the ten directions. May these groups and their doctrines of explanation and practice increase, and may the three worlds be filled with all that is auspicious.

ཅེས་རྨི་ལམ་གྱི་སྣང་ཚུལ་ཅུང་ཟད་ཅིག་ལ་བརྟེན་ནས་ཐུབ་བསྟན་རིས་སུ་མ་ཆད་པ་ལ་གུས་པའི་བྱ་བྲལ་མ་མཉྫུ་གྷོ་ཥས་བྲིས་པ་དགེ།

On the basis of a slight idea that appeared in a dream, I, Bya-Bral Manjughosha (Mipham Rinpoche), wrote this with impartial devotion towards all the Buddha's Doctrines.

༄༅།། སློབ་དཔོན་པདྨས་མཛད་པའི་སྨོན་ལམ་ཕྱོགས་བཅུ་དུས་བཞི་བཞུགས།། །།

The Ten Directions and The Four Times

A Prayer of Aspiration

by

Padma Sambhava

ན་མོ་གུ་རུ༔ སྤྲེལ་ལོ་སྤྲེལ་ཟླ་ར་བའི་ཚེས་བཅུ་ལ༔ བསམ་ཡས་བར་ཁང་གཡུ་ཞལ་ཅན་དུ་རྡོ་རྗེ་དབྱིངས་ཀྱི་དཀྱིལ་འཁོར་ཞལ་ཕྱེས་ཚེ་ཨོ་རྒྱན་གྱིས་སྨོན་ལམ་འདི་གསུངས་པས་རྗེ་འབངས་ཐམས་ཅད་ཀྱིས་ཐུགས་དམ་ནར་མར་མཛོད༔ ཕྱི་རབས་རྣམས་ཀྱིས་འདི་ལ་ཐུགས་དམ་རྩེ་གཅིག་ཏུ་མཛོད༔

Salutation to the Guru. On the tenth day of the monkey month in the monkey year, in the green-floored middle story of Samye monastery when the Vajradhatu mandala was meditated on and revealed by Padma Sambhava, he spoke this prayer of aspiration (for the benefit of beings) and said that the king and all his subjects (King Trisong Deutsan and the rest of the twenty-five inner disciples) should practise it with vigour. Those who come in future times must also always practise it one-pointedly.

ཕྱོགས་བཅུ་དུས་བཞིའི་རྒྱལ་བ་སྲས་དང་བཅས༔

CHOG	**CHU**	**DU**	**ZHI**	**GYAL WA**	**SAE**	**DANG CHE**
directions	*ten**	*times*	*four#*	*Buddhas*	*Bodhisattvas*	*with*

*4 cardinals, 4 intermediate and up and down - i.e. everywhere

past, present, future and time beyond time

Buddhas and Bodhisattvas of the ten directions and the four times, with

བླ་མ་ཡི་དམ་མཁའ་འགྲོ་ཆོས་སྐྱོང་ཚོགས༔

LA MA	**YI DAM**	**KHA DRO**	**CHO KYONG**	**TSOG**
gurus	*path deities*	*dakinis*	*dharma protectors*	*hosts*

The hosts of gurus, path deities, dakinis and dharma protectors,

མ་ལུས་ཞིང་གི་རྡུལ་སྙེད་གཤེགས་སུ་གསོལ༔

MA LUS	ZHING	GI	DUL	NYE	SHEG SU SOL
without exception, everybody	*realm, the universe*	*of*	*dust*	*as much as there is*	*come please*

All without exception, as numerous as the particles of dust in the universe—please come here!

Buddhas and Bodhisattva of the ten directions and the four times, with the hosts of gurus, path deities, dakinis and dharma protectors, all without exception, as numerous as the particles of dust in the universe – please come here!

མདུན་གྱི་ནམ་མཁར་པད་ཟླའི་གདན་ལ་བཞུགས༔

DUN GYI	NAM KHAR	PAE	DAI	DEN	LA	ZHU
in front	*sky*	*lotus*	*moon*	*seat, cushion*	*on*	*sit*

Please sit in the sky before me upon cushions of sun and moon.

ལུས་ངག་ཡིད་གསུམ་གུས་པས་ཕྱག་འཚལ་ལོ༔

LU	NGAG	YID	SUM	GUE	PAE	CHAG TSHAL LO
body	*speech*	*mind*	*three*	*devotion*	*by, with*	*make salutation, obeisance, prostration*

With body, speech and mind I devotedly make obeisance, and

ཕྱི་ནང་གསང་བ་དེ་བཞིན་ཉིད་ཀྱིས་མཆོད༔

CHI	NANG	SANG WA	DE ZHIN NYID	KYI	CHOE
outer (the universe)	*inner (my friends, possessions etc.)*	*secret (my own body)*	*tathata, the direct thusness of actuality*	*by*	*offer*

Make the outer, inner and secret offerings within the presence of openness.

རྟེན་མཆོག་བདེ་གཤེགས་རྣམས་ཀྱི་སྤྱན་སྔ་རུ༔

TEN CHOG	DE SHEG NAM	KYI	CHEN NGA RU
great ones	*Sugatas, Buddhas*	*of*	*before*

Before the great ones, the Sugatas,

སྔོན་གྱི་སྡིག་པའི་ཚོགས་ལ་བདག་གནོང་ཞིང༔

NGON GYI	DIG PAI	TSHOG	LA	DAG	NONG ZHING
former	*harmful errors*	*accumulation*	*to*	*I*	*shame and sadness*

I feel shame and sorrow at the harmful errors I have accumulated in the past.

ད་ལྟའི་མི་དགེ་འགྱོད་པས་རབ་ཏུ་བཤགས༔

DAN TAI	**MI GE**	**GYOE PAE**	**RAB TU**	**SHAG**
present	*unvirtue*	*regret, with repentance*	*fully, greatly*	*confess and beg to be excused*

With regret I truly confess and beg forgiveness for my present unvirtues, and

ཕྱིན་ཆད་དེ་ལས་ལྡོག་ཕྱིར་བདག་གིས་བསྡམ༔

CHIN CHAE	**DE**	**LAE**	**DOG CHIR**	**DAG**	**GI**	**DAM**
in future	*these harmful errors*	*from*	*give up, turn from and not do again*	*I, me*	*by*	*promise, firmly decide*

I promise that in future I will abandon these ways.

བསོད་ནམས་དགེ་ཚོགས་ཀུན་ལ་ཡི་རང་ངོ༔

SO NAM	**GE**	**TSHOG**	**KUN**	**LA**	**YI RANG NGO**
merit	*virtue*	*accumulation*	*all*	*to, with*	*sympathetically rejoice*
(all the good deeds of others)					

I rejoice at the merit and virtue accumulated by all beings.

རྒྱལ་བའི་ཚོགས་རྣམས་མྱ་ངན་མི་འདའ་བར༔

GYAL WAI	**TSHOG NAM**	**NYA NGAN**	**MI**	**DA WAR**
Jinas	*hosts*	*nirvana*	*not*	*pass into, get*
(all gurus etc.)		*(not die)*		

I request the hosts of enlightened ones not to pass into nirvana but

སྡེ་སྣོད་གསུམ་དང་བླ་མེད་ཆོས་འཁོར་བསྐོར༔

DE NOE	**SUM**	**DANG**	**LA ME**	**CHO KHOR**	**KOR**
pitaka, baskets	*three*	*and*	*unsurpassed*	*dharmachakra*	*turn*
(vinaya, sutra, abhidharma)			*(mahayana)*	*(teach the dharma)*	

To teach the foundational and mahayana doctrines.

དགེ་ཚོགས་མ་ལུས་འགྲོ་བའི་རྒྱུད་ལ་བསྔོ༔

GE TSHOG	**MA LU**	**DRO WAI**	**GYUD**	**LA NGO**
*virtues**	*without exception*	*beings, those moving in samsara*	*minds, continuity*	*to give, dedicate*

*especially those coming from this prayer

All virtues without exception I dedicate to the mind-streams of all beings –

འགྲོ་རྣམས་བླ་མེད་ཐར་པའི་སར་ཕྱིན་ཤོག༔

DRO NAM	**LA ME**	**THAR PAI**	**SAR**	**CHIN**	**SHOG**
beings	*unsurpassed*	*liberation*	*stage, rank*	*get*	*they must*
	(the mahayana nirvana which does not rest anywhere)				

They all must gain the stage of unsurpassed liberation.

Please sit in the sky before me upon cushions of sun and moon. With body, speech and mind I devotedly make obeisance, and make the outer, inner and secret offerings within the presence of openness. Before the great ones, the Sugatas, I feel shame and sorrow at the harmful errors I have accumulated in the past. With regret I truly confess and beg forgiveness for my present unvirtues, and I promise that in future I will abandon these ways.

I rejoice at the merit and virtue accumulated by all beings. I request the hosts of enlightened ones not to pass into nirvana but to teach the foundational and mahayana doctrines. All virtues without exception I dedicate to the mind-streams of all beings – they must gain the stage of unsurpassed liberation.

སངས་རྒྱས་སྲས་བཅས་བདག་ལ་དགོངས་སུ་གསོལ༔

SANG GYE	**SAE**	**CHE**	**DAG**	**LA**	**GONG SU SOL**
Buddhas	*Bodhisattvas*	*with, etc*	*me*	*to*	*listen, pay heed*

Buddhas, Bodhisattvas, please listen to me!

བདག་གིས་བརྩམས་པའི་སྨོན་ལམ་རབ་བཟང་འདི༔

DAG	**GI**	**TSAM PAI**	**MON LAM**	**RAB ZANG**	**DI**
me, Padma Sambhava	*by*	*writing*	*prayer of aspiration*	*very good*	*this*

(we also follow him by reciting this and using it as a basis for our study)

By making this very good prayer of aspiration,

རྒྱལ་བ་ཀུན་ཏུ་བཟང་དང་དེ་སྲས་དང༔

GYAL WA	**KUN TU ZANG**	**DANG**	**DE SAE**	**DANG**
Jina, Buddha	*Samantabhadra*	*and*	*Bodhisattvas*	*and*

May a knowledge similar to that of the Victor, of Samantabhadra and the Bodhisattvas and of

འཕགས་པ་འཇམ་དཔལ་དབྱངས་ཀྱིས་མཁྱེན་པ་ལྟར༔

PHAG PA	**JAM PAL YANG**	**KYI**	**KHYEN PA**	**TAR**
arya, noble	*Manjughosha*	*by*	*known, knowledge*	*like, that, similar to*

Arya Manjugosha

དེ་དག་ཀུན་གྱི་རྗེས་སུ་བདག་སློབ་ཤོག༔

DE DAG	**KUN**	**GYI**	**JE SU**	**DAG**	**LOB**	**SHO**
that	*all*	*of*	*following after*	*I*	*study*	*will!*

Be gained by me through study and practice.

Buddhas, Bodhisattvas, please listen to me! By making this very good prayer of aspiration, may knowledge similar to that of the Victor, of Samantabhadra and the Bodhisattvas and of Arya Manjugosha be gained by me through study and practice.

བསྟན་པའི་དཔལ་གྱུར་བླ་མ་རིན་ཆེན་རྣམས༔

TEN PAI	**PAL**	**GYUR**	**LA MA**	**RIN CHEN**	**NAM**
Buddha's doctrines	*glory, excellence*	*is*	*guru*	*precious*	*(pl.)*

The precious gurus who are the glory of the doctrine,

ནམ་མཁའ་བཞིན་དུ་ཀུན་ལ་ཁྱབ་པར་ཤོག༔

NAM KHA	**ZHIN DU**	**KUN**	**LA**	**KHYAB PAR SHOG**
sky	*like*	*all*	*to*	*pervade! spread!*

May they spread everywhere like the sky.

ཉི་ཟླ་བཞིན་དུ་ཀུན་ལ་གསལ་བར་ཤོག༔

NYI	**DA**	**ZHIN DU**	**KUN**	**LA**	**SAL WAR**	**SHOG**
sun	*moon*	*like, similar to*	*all*	*to*	*clear, shining**	*must be!*

*shining with clear understanding of the dharma

May they illuminate in all places like the sun and moon.

རི་བོ་བཞིན་དུ་རྟག་ཏུ་བརྟན་པར་ཤོག༔

RI WO	**ZHIN DU**	**TAG TU**	**TEN PAR**	**SHOG**
Mt Meru	*like*	*always*	*firm, steady**	*must be!*

*steady with clear understanding of the dharma

May they always be firm and steady like Mt. Meru.

May the precious gurus who are the glory of the doctrine spread everywhere like the sky. May they illuminate in all places like the sun and moon. May they always be firm and steady like Mt. Meru.

བསྟན་པའི་གཞི་མ་དགེ་འདུན་རིན་པོ་ཆེ༔

TEN PAI	**ZHI MA**	**GEN DUN**	**RIN PO CHE**
doctrines'	*ground, foundation (they maintain the direct understanding of the dharma)*	*sangha, assembly of those that practise virtue*	*precious*

May the precious sangha who are the foundation of the doctrine

ཐུགས་མཐུན་ཁྲིམས་གཙང་བསླབ་གསུམ་གྱིས་ཕྱུག་ཤོག༔

THUG	**THUN**	**TRIM**	**TSANG**	**LAB SUM**	**GYI**	**CHUG SHOG**
minds	*harmonious*	*morality,ethical practice*	*pure*	*three studies (morality, contemplation, wisdom)*	*by*	*become rich*

Have harmonious minds and pure morality and be rich in the three studies.

བསྟན་པའི་སྙིང་པོ་གསང་སྔགས་སྒྲུབ་པའི་སྡེ༔

TEN PAI	**NYING PO**	**SANG NGAG**	**DRUB PAI**	**DE**
doctrines'	*essence*	*vajrayana, tantra*	*practising*	*group, people*

May those who practise the essence of the doctrine, the vajrayana,

དམ་ཚིག་ལྡན་ཞིང་བསྐྱེད་རྫོགས་མཐར་ཕྱིན་ཤོག༔

DAM TSHIG	**DEN ZHING**	**KYE**	**DZOG**	**THAR CHIN**	**SHO**
vows, promises, firm intent	*having*	*developing system*	*perfecting, system*	*fulfill, complete*	*they must!*

Have pure vows and complete the developing and perfecting systems.

May the precious sangha who are the foundation of the doctrine have harmonious minds and pure morality and be rich in the three studies. May those who practise the essence of the doctrine, the vajrayana, have pure vows and complete the developing and perfecting systems.

བསྟན་པའི་སྦྱིན་བདག་ཆོས་སྐྱོང་རྒྱལ་པོ་ཡང༔

TEN PAI	**JIN DAG**	**CHO KYONG**	**GYAL PO**	**YANG**
doctrines'	*sponsors, patrons*	*dharma helping, protecting*	*king*	*also*

Also for the patron of the doctrine, the king who helps the dharma,

ཆབ་སྲིད་རྒྱས་ཤིང་བསྟན་ལ་སྨན་པར་ཤོག༔

CHAB SI	**GYAE SHING**	**TEN**	**LA**	**MEN PAR**	**SHOG**
rule, administration	*spreading*	*doctrine*	*to*	*medicine*	*do!*
		(i.e. be helpful for it)			

May his administration spread and be like a medicine for the doctrine.

བསྟན་པའི་ཞབས་འདེགས་རྒྱལ་རིགས་བློན་པོ་ཡང༔

TEN PAI	**ZHAB DEG**	**GYAL RIG**	**LON PO**	**YANG**
doctrines'	*protect*	*king's family*	*ministers*	*also*

For the king's family and ministers who protect the doctrines

བློ་གྲོས་རབ་འཕེལ་རྩལ་དང་ལྡན་པར་ཤོག༔

LO DRO	**RAB**	**PHEL**	**TSAL**	**DANG DEN PAR**	**SHOG**
intellect	*greatly*	*increase*	*powerful*	*become*	*must be!*

With their intellects greatly increasing, may they become powerful.

Also for the patron of the doctrine, the king who helps the dharma, may his administration spread and be like a medicine for the doctrine. For the king's family and ministers who protect the doctrines, with their intellects greatly increasing, may they become powerful.

བསྟན་པའི་གསོས་བྱེད་ཁྱིམ་བདག་འབྱོར་ལྡན་རྣམས༔

TEN PAI	**SOE JE**	**CHIM DAG**	**JOR DEN NAM**
doctrines'	*who is offering, sponsor*	*householder*	*rich people*

For those who are sponsors of the doctrine, the householders and rich people,

ལོངས་སྤྱོད་ལྡན་ཞིང་ཉེར་འཚེ་མེད་པར་ཤོག༔

LONG CHOE	**DEN ZHING**	**NYER TSHE**	**ME PAR**	**SHO**
wealth	*having*	*troubles, difficulties*	*without*	*must be!*

May they have wealth and be free of troubles.

བསྟན་ལ་དད་པའི་ཡངས་པའི་རྒྱལ་ཁམས་ཀུན༔

TEN	**LA**	**DAE PAI**	**YANG PAI**	**GYAL KHAM**	**KUN**
doctrine	*to*	*faith*	*vast*	*kingdom's people (everyone)*	*all*

For all beings everywhere who have faith in the dharma,

བདེ་སྐྱིད་ལྡན་ཞིང་བར་ཆད་ཞི་བར་ཤོག༔

DE KYI	**DEN ZHING**	**BAR CHAD**	**ZHI WAR**	**SHO**
happiness	*having*	*obstacles, obstructions*	*pacified*	*must be!*

May they have happiness and the cessation of all obstacles.

For those who are sponsors of the doctrine, the householders and rich people, may they have wealth and be free of troubles. For all beings everywhere who have faith in the dharma, may they have happiness and the cessation of all obstacles.

ལམ་ལ་གནས་པའི་རྣལ་འབྱོར་བདག་ཉིད་ཀྱང༔

LAM	**LA**	**NAE PAI**	**NAL JOR**	**DAG NYID**	**KYANG**
path	*on*	*staying*	*yogi, strong practitioner*	*I*	*also*
(i.e. do practice)					

Also for me, the yogi abiding on the path,

དམ་ཚིག་མི་ཉམས་བསམ་པ་འགྲུབ་པར་ཤོག༔

DAM TSIG	**MI NYAM**	**SAM PA**	**DRUB PAR**	**SHO**
vows	*not lose*	*thoughts, wishes*	*accomplished*	*must be*

With my vows not being lost, all my wishes must be accomplished.

བདག་ལ་བཟང་ངན་ལས་ཀྱིས་འབྲེལ་གྱུར་གང༔

DAG	**LA**	**ZANG**	**NGAN**	**LAE**	**KYI**	**TREL GYUR**	**GANG**
me	*to*	*good*	*bad*	*actions, karma*	*by*	*connection*	*whatever*
(whether they have helped me or harmed me)							

All beings who are connected with me, whether by good or by bad actions,

གནས་སྐབས་མཐར་ཐུག་རྒྱལ་བས་རྗེས་འཛིན་ཤོག༔

NAE KAB	**THAR THUG**	**GYAL WAE**	**JE DZIN**	**SHO**
temporary	*ultimately*	*Buddhas, gurus*	*hold*	*they must*
	(till the attainment of the stage of Dorje Chang)			

Must be held by the Buddhas both at the present time and until the ultimate attainment.

འགྲོ་རྣམས་བླ་མེད་ཐེག་པའི་སྒོར་ཞུགས་ནས༔

DRO NAM	LA ME	THEG PAI	GOR	ZHUG	NAE
beings, those wandering in samsara	*unsurpassed*	*yana, vehicle*	*door*	*enter*	*then*
	(annuttara, vajrayana and atiyoga)				

May all beings enter the door of the unsurpassed vehicle, and then

ཀུན་བཟང་རྒྱལ་སྲིད་ཆེན་པོ་ཐོབ་པར་ཤོག༔ ༎

KUN ZANG	GYAL SI	CHEN PO	THOB PAR	SHO
Samantabhadra, dharmakaya	*kingdom (dharmadhatu)*	*great*	*get*	*must*

Gain the vast kingdom of Kuntuzangpo.

Also for me, the yogi abiding on the path, with my vows not being lost, all my wishes must be accomplished. All beings who are connected with me, whether by good or by bad actions, must be held by the Buddhas both at the present time and until the ultimate attainment. May all beings enter the door of the unsurpassed vehicle, and then gain the vast kingdom of Kuntuzangpo.

དེ་ལྟར་གྱི་སྨོན་ལམ་དུས་དྲུག་ཏུ་བརྩོན་པར་བྱ༔ ས་མ་ཡ་རྒྱ༔ ལྷ་སྲས་མུ་རུབ་རྣམ་འཕྲུལ་གཏེར་ཆེན་མཆོག་གྱུར་བདེ་ཆེན་གླིང་པས་གནས་མཆོག་སེང་ཆེན་གནམ་བྲག་གི་གཡས་ཟུར་བྲག་རི་རིན་ཆེན་བརྩེགས་པའི་གོང་མོ་འགོ་མ་ནས་ཁྲོམ་གཏེར་དུ་སྤྱན་དྲངས་པའི་བཻ་རོའི་སྐུ་ཆོས་དང་ཤོག་དོས་མཚོ་རྒྱལ་ཕྱག་བྲིས་བོད་ཡིག་བཤུར་མ་ལས། དེ་འཕྲལ་ཉིད་དུ་པདྨ་གར་དབང་བློ་གྲོས་མཐའ་ཡས་ཀྱིས་དག་པར་བཤུས་པ་དགེ་ལེགས་འཕེལ།། ༎

Diligently practice this prayer of aspiration during the six periods of the day and night. Vows. Seal.

The incarnation of King Trisong Deutsan's son, Murub Tsanpo, the great Terton Chogyur Dechen Lingpa, at the great holy place of Sengchen Namdrag from the right side of the rock hill called Rinchen Tsegpai Gongmo Ogma for the welfare of beings (took out the treasure).

There was some cloth from Vairocana (the translator), some silk paper upon which Yeshe Tsogyal had written in the handwriting script.

He gave it immediately to Padma Garwang Lodro Thayae who made a correct copy. May virtue spread.

DEWACHEN

ཀྱི་སྒྲུབ་འགྲོ་བ་ཀུན་གྲོལ་གྱི་སྨོན་ལམ་ཆ་ལག་བདེ་བ་ཅན་གྱི་ཞིང་ཁམས་ཀྱི་བཀོད་པའི་ཡོན་ཏན་མ་ཞེས་བྱ་བ་བཞུགས༔

The Aspiration that Brings Birth in Dewachen

བཅོམ་ལྡན་ཤཱཀྱའི་རྒྱལ་པོའི་ཞིང་འདི་ནས༔

CHOM DE SHA KYAI GYAL POI ZHING DI NE
Bhagawan Shakyamuni realm this from
From this realm of Bhagawan Shakyamuni,

ནུབ་ཕྱོགས་གང་གའི་ཀླུང་གི་བྱེ་མ་སྙེད༔

NUB CHOG GANG GAI LUNG GI JE MA NYED
west direction Ganges river of sand as much as
Travelling in the western direction across lands as numerous as the sands of the Ganges

རྫོགས་སངས་རྒྱས་ཀྱི་ཞིང་ཁམས་བདེ་བ་ཅན༔

DZOG SANG GYE KYI ZHING KHAM DE WA CHEN
complete, perfect buddha (Amitabha) of realm, sphere happy great
Lies Dewachen, the realm of the Perfect Buddha.

ཁྲག་ཁྲིག་ཕྲག་བརྒྱ་འདས་པའི་ཕ་རོལ་ན༔

TRAG TRIG TRAG GYA DAE PAI PHA ROL NA
a hundred thousand million passed other side, go beyond there
Inconceivably far away

ཞིང་ཁམས་སྐྱོན་མེད་རྣམ་དག་བདེ་བ་ཅན༔

ZHING KHAM KYON ME NAM DAG DE WA CHEN
realm free of fault very pure Sukhavati
Is this realm free of faults, the very pure Dewachen.

From this realm of Bhagawan Shakyamuni, travelling in the western direction across lands as numerous as the sands of the Ganges lies Dewachen, the realm of the Perfect Buddha. Dewachen, this very pure realm free of faults is so very, very far away.

ས་གཞི་ཐམས་ཅད་རིན་ཆེན་རང་བཞིན་ཏེ༔

SA ZHI THAM CHE RIN CHEN RANG ZHIN TE
foundation, ground all jewels nature then, thus
The ground is made entirely of jewels and, being

ལག་མཐིལ་ལྟར་མཉམ་ཅོང་རོང་མེད་པའི་གནས༔

LAG THIL	**TAR**	**NYAM**	**CHONG RONG**	**ME PEI**	**NAE**
palm of the hand	*like*	*flat, equal*	*difficult places, peaks and gorges*	*without*	*place*

Flat like the palm of the hand, it presents no difficulties.

མེ་ཏོག་པདྨའི་ཚོགས་ཀྱིས་རབ་བརྒྱན་ཞིང༔

ME TOG	**PAD MAI**	**TSHOG**	**KYI**	**RAB**	**GYEN ZHING**
flowers	*lotus*	*hosts*	*by*	*well, fully*	*adorning*

Well adorned with myriad flowers and lotuses,

ལྟ་བས་མི་ངོམ་མཛེས་ཤིང་ཡིད་དུ་འོང༔

TA WAE	**MI**	**NGOM**	**DZE SHING**	**YID DU ONG**
by looking	*not*	*tired*	*beautiful*	*attractive*

It is endlessly fascinating, beautiful and attractive.

The ground is made entirely of jewels and, being flat like the palm of the hand, it presents no difficulties. Well adorned with myriad flowers and lotuses, it is endlessly fascinating, beautiful and attractive.

ཞིང་མཆོག་དེ་ན་ལྷ་མིའི་སྟོན་པ་ནི༔

ZHING	**CHOG**	**DE**	**NA**	**LHA**	**MI**	**TON PA**	**NI**
realm	*supreme*	*that*	*in*	*gods*	*men*	*teacher*	

In this most excellent realm, the teacher of gods and men,

སྐུ་ཚེ་དཔག་མེད་རྫོགས་པའི་སངས་རྒྱས་བཞུགས༔

KU	**TSHE PAG ME**	**DZOG PAI**	**SANG GYE**	**ZHUG**
body	*Amitayus (limitless life)*	*complete*	*Buddha*	*sitting*

The perfect Buddha Amitayus resides.

ཉོན་མོངས་སྤངས་ཤིང་སྨོན་ལམ་དག་པའི་གནས༔

NYON MONG	**PANG SHING**	**MON LAM**	**DAG PAI**	**NAE**
*afflictions, kleshas**	*abandoning*	*prayer of aspiration*	*pure*	*place*

*stupidity, anger, desire and so on

Abandoning all afflictions, in this place arising from pure aspiration

བདག་དང་འགྲོ་ཀུན་ཞིང་དེར་སྐྱེ་འགྱུར་ཤོག༔

DAG	**DANG**	**DRO**	**KUN**	**ZHING**	**DER**	**KYE**	**GYUR SHOG**
I	*and*	*beings*	*all*	*realm*	*there*	*born*	*may*

May I and all sentient beings be born there.

In this most excellent realm, resides the perfect Buddha, Amitayus, the teacher of gods and men. Giving up all our afflictions, may I and all sentient beings be born in this realm of pure aspiration.

དག་གསལ་སྲ་བའི་ཞིང་ཁམས་བདེ་བ་ཅན༔

DAG	**SAL**	**SA WAI**	**ZHING KHAM**	**DE WA CHEN**
pure	*clear*	*firm, solid*	*realm*	*Sukhavati*

In the realm of Dewachen, pure, clear and stable,

རྒྱལ་བའི་རྣམ་འཕྲུལ་སྙན་པའི་སྒྲ་དབྱངས་འབྱིན༔

GYAL WAI	**NAM TRUL**	**NYEN PAI**	**DRA**	**YANG**	**JIN**
Jina, Victor, Buddha	*phantom, magical appearance*	*sweet*	*sound*	*melody*	*appears, comes out*

Sweet melodies arise as magical emanations of the Victors.

འཚོ་བའི་ཡོ་བྱད་ཇི་ལྟར་བསམས་པ་བཞིན༔

TSHO WAI	**YO JAD**	**JI TAR**	**SAM PA**	**ZHIN**
life's	*necessary articles*	*whatever they are*	*wish*	*according to*

All life's requirements, whatever is wished for,

འབད་རྩོལ་མེད་པར་ལེགས་པར་འབྱུང་བའི་གནས༔

BAE	**TSOL**	**ME PAR**	**LEG PAR**	**JUNG WAI**	**NAE**
effort	*striving*	*without*	*well, good*	*arising*	*place*

Arise easily there, without effort or striving.

In the realm of Dewachen, so pure and clear and stable, sweet melodies arise as magical emanations of the Victors. All life's requirements, whatever is wished for, arise easily there, without effort or striving.

ཞིང་མཆོག་དེ་ན་སེམས་ཅན་ངན་སོང་དང༔

ZHING	**CHOG**	**DE**	**NA**	**SEM CHEN**	**NGEN SONG**	**DANG**
realm	*most excellent*	*that*	*in*	*sentient beings*	**states of woe*	*and*

*hell, insatiable ghosts, animals

In this most excellent realm sentient beings

ལྷ་མ་ཡིན་དང་གཤིན་རྗེའི་མིང་ཡང་མེད༔

LHA MA YIN	**DANG**	**SHIN JEI**	**MING**	**YANG**	**ME**
jealous gods, asuras	*and*	*lord of death*	*name*	*also*	*without*

(there are no bad things to disturb the mind)

Never even hear the words 'states of woe', 'jealous gods' or 'the lord of death'.

དེ་ན་ཕལ་པའི་བུད་མེད་ཡོད་མ་ཡིན༔

DE	**NA**	**PHEL PAI**	**BUE ME**	**YOE MA YIN**
that	*in*	*ordinary*	*women*	*are not*

Because no one has a female body in Dewachen

མངལ་ན་གནས་པའང་ཡོད་པ་མ་ཡིན་ནོ༔

NGEL	**NA**	**NAE**	**PANG**	**YOE PA**	**MA YIN NO**
womb	*in*	*staying*	*also*	*exists*	*is not*

No one is born there from a womb.

In this most excellent realm sentient beings never even hear the words 'states of woe', 'jealous gods' or 'the lord of death'. Because no one has a female body in Dewachen no one is born there from a womb.

རིན་ཆེན་རྣམས་ཀྱི་མེ་ཏོག་པདྨ་ལས༔

RIN CHEN	**NAM**	**KYI**	**ME TOG**	**PAE MA**	**LAE**
jewels	*(plural)*	*of*	*flower*	*lotus*	*from*

Appearing from a lotus flower made of jewels

བརྫུས་ཏེ་སྐྱེས་པའི་རང་བཞིན་ཤ་སྟག་གོ༔

DZU	**TE**	**KYE PAI**	**RANG ZHIN**	**SHA TAG GO**
miraculous, magical	*thus*	*birth*	*way*	*only, simply*

Is the magical way of birth for all there.

མི་དགེ་སྤངས་ཤིང་སྨོན་ལམ་དག་པའི་གནས༔

MI GE	**PANG SHING**	**MON LAM**	**DAG PAI**	**NAE**
unvirtue, sin	*abandoning*	*aspiration*	*pure*	*place*

On entering this land arising from pure aspiration all unvirtue is discarded.

བདག་དང་འགྲོ་ཀུན་ཞིང་དེར་སྐྱེ་འགྱུར་ཤོག༔

DAG	**DANG**	**DRO**	**KUN**	**ZHING**	**DER**	**KYE**	**GYUR SHOG**
I	*and*	*sentient beings*	*all*	*realm*	*there*	*born*	*must be*

May I and all sentient beings be born in this realm.

The only mode of birth to be found there is magical appearance on a lotus made of jewels. On entering this land arising from pure aspiration all unvirtue is discarded. May I and all sentient beings be born in this realm.

རྣམ་དག་འོད་གསལ་ཞིང་ཁམས་བདེ་བ་ཅན༔

NAM DAG	**OE SEL**	**ZHING KHAM**	**DE WA CHEN**
very pure	*clear light*	*realm*	*Sukhavati, Happy*

Dewachen is the realm of completely pure light.

ཞིང་དེར་སྐྱེས་པའི་སེམས་ཅན་ཐམས་ཅད་ལ༔

ZHING	**DER**	**KYE PAI**	**SEM CHEN**	**THAM CHE**	**LA**
realm	*there*	*born*	*sentient beings*	*all*	*to*

All sentient beings born in this realm

ན་ཚ་ལ་སོགས་སྡུག་བསྔལ་གཏན་མི་འབྱུང༔

NA TSHA	**LA SOG**	**DUG NGEL**	**TEN**	**MI**	**JUNG**
fever	*and so on*	*sufferings*	*really*	*not*	*arise*

Will never experience fever or other sufferings.

ཞིང་དེར་སྐྱེས་ནས་ངན་སོང་འབྱུང་མི་སྲིད༔

ZHING	**DER**	**KYE**	**NE**	**NGEN SONG**	**JUNG**	**MI**	**SI**
realm	*there*	*born*	*then*	*states of woe, the three lower realms*	*arising, coming*	*not*	*possible*

Having been born there it is not possible to fall into the states of woe, nor

མི་ཁོམ་གནས་སུ་སྐྱེ་བ་མི་སྲིད་དོ༔

MI KHOM	**NAE**	**SU**	**KYE WA**	**MI**	**SI DO**
difficult	*places*	*in*	*born*	*not*	*possible*

(places without opportunity for practising Dharma)

Is it possible to be born where there are difficulties.

Dewachen is the realm of completely pure light. All sentient beings born in this realm will never experience fever or other sufferings. Having been born there one cannot fall into the states of woe or be born where there are obstacles.

ཞིང་དེར་སྐྱེས་པའི་བྱང་ཆུབ་སེམས་དཔའ་རྣམས༔

ZHING	**DER**	**KYE PAI**	**JANG CHUB SEM PA NAM**
realm	*there*	*born*	*Bodhisattvas (i.e. all those born in Dewachen)*

The Bodhisattvas who are born in this realm

ཚེ་ལོ་དཔག་ཏུ་མེད་པ་སྐུ་བཞུགས་ནས༔

TSHE LO	**PAG TU ME PA**	**KU**	**ZHUG**	**NAE**
lifespan years	*immeasurable*	*body*	*stay*	*then*

Remain in one body for lives of immeasurable duration.

སྐྱེ་བ་དུ་མར་བྱང་སེམས་སར་གནས་ཏེ༔

KYE WA	**DU MAR**	**JANG SEM**	**SAR**	**NAE TE**
lives	*many*	*bodhisattva*	*stages, bhumis*	*stay*

Then for many lives they stay on the bodhisattva stages, and

སྤྱོད་པ་རླབས་ཆེན་མཛད་བཞེད་མ་གཏོགས་པ༔

CHOD PA	**LAB CHEN**	**DZE**	**ZHED**	**MA TOG PA**
deeds, activities (for others)	*great wave*	*doing*	*wish, desire*	*only**

*The great Bodhisattvas in Dewachen can enter Buddhahood whenever they wish, having fully completed the path. They act as compassionate Bodhisattvas until the time is appropriate for them to enter Buddhahood and further act for the welfare of all.

Their only wish is to make a great wave of beneficial activity and then,

སྐྱེ་བ་གཅིག་རྗེས་རྫོགས་སངས་རྒྱས་གྱུར་ཅིང༔

KYE WA	**CHIG**	**JE**	**DZOG**	**SANG GYE**	**GYUR CHING**
birth	*one*	*after*	*complete*	*buddhahood*	*coming, getting*

After one final birth, to gain complete Buddhahood.

ཚོགས་གཉིས་རབ་རྫོགས་སྨོན་ལམ་དག་པའི་ཞིང༔

TSHOG	**NYI RAB**	**DZOG**	**MON LAM**	**DAG PAI**	**ZHING**
accumulations (merit and wisdom)	*two fully*	*complete*	*aspiration*	*pure*	*realm*

In this realm of pure aspiration the two accumulations are fully completed.

བདག་དང་འགྲོ་ཀུན་ཞིང་དེར་སྐྱེ་འགྱུར་ཤོག༔

DAG	**DANG**	**DRO**	**KUN**	**ZHING**	**DER**	**KYE**	**GYUR SHOG**
I	*and*	*beings*	*all*	*realm*	*there*	*born*	*must be!*

May I and all sentient beings be born in this realm!

The Bodhisattvas who are born in this realm remain in one body for lives of immeasurable duration. For many such lives they stay on the bodhisattva stages and their only wish is to make a great wave of beneficial activity and then, after one final birth, to gain complete Buddhahood. In this realm of pure aspiration the two accumulations are fully completed. May I and all sentient beings be born in this realm!

ཐུབ་པས་བསྔགས་པའི་ཞིང་ཁམས་བདེ་བ་ཅན༔

THUB PAE	**NGAG PAI**	**ZHING KHAM**	**DE WA CHEN**
Muni, Buddha, by	*praised*	*realm*	*Sukhavati*

The realm of Dewachen has been praised by the Buddhas.

དང་བ་ཅན་གྱི་རིན་ཆེན་ཕོ་བྲང་ན༔

DANG WA CHEN	**GYI**	**RIN CHEN**	**PHO DRANG**	**NA**
pure, clear	*of*	*jewel*	*palace*	*in*

In the palace of pure, clear jewels

སྐུ་ཚེ་དཔག་མེད་རྫོགས་པའི་སངས་རྒྱས་བཞུགས༔

KU TSHE	**PAG ME**	**DZOG PAI**	**SANG GYE**	**ZHUG**
lifespan	*immeasurable*	*complete*	*buddha*	*stays*

(Tsepagme – immeasurable life)

Resides the perfect Buddha Tsepagme.

ཚེ་དཔག་མེད་མགོན་གཡས་ན་སྤྱན་རས་གཟིགས༔

TSHE PAG ME	**GON**	**YAE**	**NA**	**CHEN RAE ZIG**
Amitayus, Amitabha	*protector, benefactor*	*right*	*on*	*Avalokitesvara*

To the right of the benefactor Tsepagme is Chenrezi

བྱམས་དང་སྙིང་རྗེས་འགྲོ་བ་ཀུན་ལ་གཟིགས༔

JAM	**DANG**	**NYING JE**	**DRO WA**	**KUN**	**LA**	**ZIG**
love	*and*	*compassion*	*sentient beings*	*all*	*to*	*looking (and helping)*

Who looks on all beings with love and compassion.

The realm of Dewachen has been praised by the Budhas. In the palace of pure clear jewels resides the perfect Buddha Tsepagme. To the right of the benefactor Tsepagme is Chenrezi who looks on all beings with love and compassion.

མགོན་པོའི་གཡོན་ན་བྱང་སེམས་མཐུ་ཆེན་ཐོབ༔

GON POI	**YON**	**NA**	**JANG SEM**	**THU CHEN THOB**
Protector (Amitayus)	*left*	*on*	*bodhisattva*	*Vajrapani*

On the left of the benefactor is the Bodhisattva Vajrapani

དྲི་མེད་བསྟན་པ་རྒྱས་པའི་ཕྲིན་ལས་མཛད༔

DRI MED	**TEN PA**	**GYE PAI**	**TRIN LAE**	**DZAE**
stainless	*doctrine*	*spreading*	*activity*	*doing*

Who performs the activity of spreading the stainless doctrine.

རྒྱལ་བའི་འཁོར་གཞན་ཡོན་ཏན་ཕུན་ཚོགས་ཤིང༔

GYAL WAI	**KHOR**	**ZHEN**	**YON TEN**	**PHUN TSHOG SHING**
Jina's, Victor's	*circle*	*other*	*good qualities*	*fully developed, everything is good*

The rest of the Victor's entourage have all good qualities fully developed, and

ཡེ་ཤེས་ཆེར་རྒྱས་བསམ་གྱིས་མི་ཁྱབ་བཞུགས༔

YE SHE	CHER	GYE	SAM	GYI	MI	KHYAB	ZHUG
original knowing	*great*	*spreading*	*mind*	*by*	*not*	*encompass*	*staying*

Reside radiating inconceivable great original knowing.

On the left of the benefactor is the Bodhisattva Vajrapani who performs the activity of spreading the stainless doctrine. The rest of the Victor's entourage have all good qualities fully developed. They reside spreading inconceivable great original knowing.

བདག་ནི་ནམ་ཞིག་འཆི་བའི་དུས་བྱུང་ཚེ༔

DAG NI	NAM ZHIG	CHI WAI	DU	JUNG	TSHE
I (and all beings)	*when*	*die*	*time*	*coming*	*time, then*

When the time of our death arrives,

གནས་ངན་རྣམས་སུ་ནམ་ཡང་མི་གོལ་བར༔

NAE	NGEN NAM	SU	NAM YANG	MI	GOL WAR
places	*bad*	*in*	*never*	*not*	*go astray*

May we not stray into bad places.

ལྷ་མཆོག་ཁྱེད་ཀྱི་ཞལ་མཐོང་མདུན་བསུས་ནས༔

LHA	CHOG	KHYE KYI	ZHAL	THONG	DUN	SUE	NE
God (Amitayus)	*most excellent*	*your*	*face*	*see*	*before*	*meet*	*then*

Most excellent deity, may we come before you and see your face.

བདེ་བ་ཅན་གྱི་ཞིང་དེར་སྐྱེ་བར་ཤོག༔

DE WA CHEN	GYI	ZHING	DER	KYE WAR	SHOG
Sukhavati	*of*	*realm*	*there*	*born, in*	*must be!*

We must be born there, in the realm of Dewachen.

When the time of our death arrives, may we not stray into bad places. Most excellent deity, may we come before you and see your face. We must be born there, in the realm of Dewachen.

པདྨ་ལས་འཁྲུངས་དམ་ཆོས་ཉན་གྱུར་ཞིང༔

PAE MA	LAE	TRUNG	DAM	CHO	NYEN GYUR ZHING
lotus	*from*	*born*	*holy*	*dharma*	*hearing*

Born from a lotus and hearing the holy Dharma,

རྒྱལ་བས་ལུང་བསྟན་མངོན་ཤེས་རྫུ་འཕྲུལ་ཐོབ༔

GYAL WAE	LUNG TEN	NGON SHE	DZE TRUL	THOB
Jina, Victor, by (Amitayus)	*prediction**	*super-knowledge power*	*miracle*	*get*

*about my future dharma path and Buddhahood

May we receive predictions from the Victor and gain foreknowledge and other miraculous powers.

སེམས་ཅན་ཐམས་ཅད་ཞིང་མཆོག་དམ་པ་དེར༔

SEM CHEN	THAM CHE	ZHING	CHOG	DAM PA	DER
sentient beings	*all*	*realm*	*most excellent*	*holy*	*there*

To that most excellent holy realm, may all sentient beings

བདག་གིས་འདྲེན་པའི་རྟེན་འབྲེལ་སྒྲིག་པར་ཤོག༔

DAG	GI	DREN PAI	TEN DREL	DRIG PAR	SHOG
me	*by*	*guide*	*connection**	*arrange*	*must be*

*may I be able to, may I have the chance to

Have the connection with me that lets me lead them there.

Born from a lotus and hearing the holy Dharma, may we receive predictions from the Victor and gain foreknowledge and other miraculous powers. May all sentient beings have the connection with me that lets me lead them there, to that most excellent holy realm.

དེ་ལྟར་བདག་གི་སྨོན་ལམ་བཟང་པོ་འདི༔

DE TAR	DAG GI	MON LAM	ZANG PO	DI
like	*my*	*aspiration*	*good*	*this*

This is my pure aspiration.

བླ་མ་མཆོག་དང་མགོན་པོ་སྤྱན་རས་གཟིགས༔

LA MA	CHOG	DANG	GON PO	CHEN RE ZI
guru	*most excellent*	*and*	*protector*	*Avalokiteshvara*

May the most excellent gurus, and the benefactor Chenrezi, with

འཁོར་བཅས་ལ་སོགས་རྒྱལ་དང་རྒྱལ་བ་ཡི༔

KHOR CHE	LA SOG	GYAL	DANG	GYAL WA	YI
with retinue, circle	*and so on*	*Jina, Victor Amitayus*	*and*	*Jina*	*of*

All their retinue, and the Victor and his excellent disciples

སྲས་མཆོག་རྣམས་ཀྱིས་འགྲུབ་པར་མཛད་དུ་གསོལ༔

SAE	CHOG	NAM	KYI	DRUB PAR	DZE DU	SOL
disciples (bodhisattvas)	*most excellent*	*plural*	*by*	*fulfil*	*do*	*please*

Cause it to be fulfilled.

This is my pure aspiration. May the most excellent gurus and the benefactor Chenrezi along with all their retinues and the Victor and his excellent disciples cause it to be fulfilled.

ནུབ་ཟངས་མཛོད་དུ་མར་པོ་ནུས་སྤྲུལ་སྐུ་རིག་འཛིན་ཆེན་པོས་(རིག་འཛིན་རྒོད་ལྡེམ་)གཏེར་ནས་སྤྱན་དྲངས་པའོ།

[From the western red copper treasury the incarnation Rigdzin Chenpo (Rig-Dzin-rGod-lDem) revealed this from the hidden treasure. It is part of the aspirations belonging to the outer sadhana of Chenrezi.]

པདྨ་འདམ་གྱིས་མ་གོས་ལྟར།

PAE MA	**DAM**	**GYI**	**MA**	**GOE**	**TAR**
lotus	*mud*	*by*	*not*	*touched, affected*	*as*

As the lotus is not tainted by mud,

སྲིད་གསུམ་དྲི་མས་མ་གོས་པའི།

SI	**SUM**	**DRI MAE**	**MA**	**GOE PAI**
worlds (of samsara)	*three*	*stains, by impurities*	*not*	*affected*

Without being tainted by the impurities of the three worlds,

སྲིད་པའི་པདྨོ་ལས་བྱུང་བའི།

SI PAI	**PAD MO**	**LAE**	**JUNG WAI**
becoming	*lotus*	*from*	*coming out*

Appearing from the lotus of becoming,

བདེ་བ་ཅན་དུ་སྐྱེ་བར་ཤོག།

DE WA CHEN	**DU**	**KYE WAR**	**SHOG**
Sukhavati	*in*	*born*	*must be*

May we be born in Dewachen.

As the lotus is not tainted by mud, may we be born in Dewachen appearing from a lotus untainted by the impurities of the three worlds.

འདི་ནས་ཉིང་མཚམས་སྦྱར་མ་ཐག།

DI NAE	**NYING TSHAM JAR**	**MA THAG**
here (in this world)	*taking rebirth, leaving this world*	*immediately*

Immediately on leaving this world,

དག་པའི་ཞིང་ཁམས་བདེ་བ་ཅན།

DAG PAI	**ZHING KHAM**	**DE WA CHEN**
pure	*realm*	*Sukhavati*

In the pure realm of Dewachen

པདྨའི་སྙིང་པོའི་ཟེའུ་འབྲུ་ལ།

PAE MAI	**NYING POI**	**ZEU DRU**	**LA**
lotus	*centre, heart*	*stamen*	*on*

Upon the stamen in the heart of the lotus,

བརྫུས་ཏེ་སྐྱེ་བ་ལེན་པར་ཤོག།

DZU TE	**KYE WA**	**LEN PAR**	**SHOG**
miraculous	*birth*	*take*	*may we*

May we take miraculous birth.

Immediately on leaving this world may we take miraculous birth in the pure realm of Dewachen upon the stamen in the heart of a lotus.

མི་གཙང་ལུས་འདི་བོར་བར་གྱུར་མ་ཐག།

MI TSANG	**LU**	**DI**	**BOR WAR**	**GYUR**	**MA THAG**
impure	*body*	*this*	*give up*	*comes*	*immediately*

Immediately on discarding this impure body,

བདེ་བ་ཅན་དུ་བརྫུས་ཏེ་སྐྱེ་བར་ཤོག།

DE WA CHEN	**DU**	**DZU TE**	**KYE WAR**	**SHOG**
Sukhavati	*in*	*miraculous*	*birth*	*must get*

We must take miraculous birth in Dewachen!

སྐྱེས་མ་ཐག་ཏུ་ས་བཅུ་རབ་བགྲོད་ནས།

KYE MA	**THAG TU**	**SA CHU**	**RAB**	**DRO**	**NAE**
birth	*immediately*	*ten stages to enlightenment*	*full*	*go up, traverse*	*then*

Immediately at birth we must ascend the ten stages and then

སྤྲུལ་པས་ཕྱོགས་བཅུར་གཞན་དོན་བྱེད་པར་ཤོག།

TRUL PAE	**CHOG CHUR**	**ZHEN**	**DON**	**JE PAR**	**SHOG**
incarnation, by emanation	*ten directions, everywhere*	*others*	*benefit, welfare*	*act for, do*	*must*

Act for the benefit of others by sending emanations in all directions.

Immediately on abandoning this impure body we must take miraculous birth in Dewachen. Immediately at birth we must ascend the ten stages and act for the benefit of others by sending emanations in all directions.

༄༅།། བདེ་བ་ཅན་དུ་སྐྱེ་བ་འཛིན་པའི་ཆོག་མདོར་བསྡུས་པ་ཞིང་མཆོག་བསྒྲོད་པའི་བདེ་ལམ་ཞེས་བྱ་བ་བཞུགས།།

A Swift Path to Cross Easily to the Excellent Realm

being

A Brief Ritual for Being Born in Dewachen

ན་མོ་གུ་རུ། བདེ་ཆེན་ཞིང་ཆོག་མདོར་བསྡུས་བྱེད་ན། བདེ་བར་གཤེགས་པའི་སྐུ་བརྙན་དང་
འོད་མདོའི་གླེགས་བམ་སོགས་རྟེན་གསུམ་གྱི་མདུན། འབྱོར་བ་དང་བ་སྦྱན་པའི་བཀོད་པ་གང་
འབྱོར་བཤམས། སྐྱབས་སེམས་ནི།

Salutation to the Guru. When performing the brief ritual of the realm of Great Happiness, in front of the three symbolic representations consisting of a statue or painting of the Thus Gone (Amitabha), the bound volume of the Amitabha Sutra and a stupa, display whatever offerings you can afford.

Firstly perform taking refuge and the development of enlightened mind.

REFUGE

སངས་རྒྱས་ཆོས་དང་ཚོགས་ཀྱི་མཆོག་རྣམས་ལ།

SANG GYE	**CHO**	**DANG**	**TSHOG**	**KYI**	**CHOG**	**NAM**	**LA**
Buddha	*dharma*	*and*	*assembly, sangha*	*of*	*excellent, best*	*(plural)*	*to*

To Buddha, Dharma and the best Assembly

བྱང་ཆུབ་བར་དུ་བདག་ནི་སྐྱབས་སུ་མཆི།

JANG CHUB	**BAR DU**	**DAG**	**NI**	**KYAB SU CHI**
bodhi, enlightenment	*until*	*I (and all beings)*	*(emphasis)*	*go for refuge,*

We go for refuge until enlightenment is gained.

བདག་གི་སྦྱིན་སོགས་བགྱིས་པའི་བསོད་ནམས་ཀྱིས།

DAG GI	**JIN**	**SOG**	**GYI PAI**	**SO NAM**	**KYI**
my	*giving, generosity*	*and so on.**	*done*	*merit*	*by*

*i.e. the other paramitas and bodhisattva practices

By the merit of having practised generosity and so on

འགྲོ་ལ་ཕན་ཕྱིར་སངས་རྒྱས་འགྲུབ་པར་ཤོག།

DRO	**LA**	**PHAN**	**CHIR**	**SANG GYE**	**DRUB PAR**	**SHOG**
beings, those moving in samsara	*to*	*benefit, help*	*in order to*	*buddhahood*	*accomplish, gain*	*may I, I must*

May we gain buddhahood in order to benefit all beings.

To the Buddha, Dharma and the best Assembly, we go for refuge until enlightenment is gained. By the merit of having practised generosity and so on, may we gain buddhahood in order to benefit all beings.

DEVELOPMENT OF BODHICITTA

སེམས་ཅན་ཐམས་ཅད་བདེ་བ་དང་

SEM CHEN	**THAM CHE**	**DE WA**	**DANG**
sentient	*all*	*happiness*	*and*

May all sentient beings have happiness

བདེ་བའི་རྒྱུ་དང་ལྡན་པར་གྱུར་ཅིག།

DE WEI	**GYU**	**DANG**	**DEN PAR**	**GYUR CHIG**
happiness of	*cause*	*and*	*with*	*may*

And the cause of happiness.

སྡུག་བསྔལ་དང་སྡུག་བསྔལ་གྱི་རྒྱུ་དང་བྲལ་བར་གྱུར་ཅིག།

DUN NGEL	DANG	DUN NGEL	GYI	GYU	DANG	DREL BAR	GYUR CHIG
suffering	*and*	*suffering*	*of*	*cause*	*and*	*separate,*	*they must be free from*

May they be free of sorrow and the cause of sorrow.

སྡུག་བསྔལ་མེད་པའི་བདེ་བ་དང་མི་བྲལ་བར་གྱུར་ཅིག༔

DUN NGEL	ME PAI	DE WA	DANG	MI	DREL WAR	GYUR CHIG
suffering	*free of*	*happiness*	*and*	*not*	*separate*	*they must*

May they never be separated from happiness free of sorrow.

ཉེ་རིང་ཆགས་སྡང་གཉིས་དང་བྲལ་བའི་

NYE	RING	CHAG	DANG	NYI	DANG	DREL WAI
near (friends, relatives)	*far (enemies, strangers)*	*desire, attachment*	*anger, dislike*	*both*	*and*	*free from*

May they abide in the equanimity free of both desire for friends and relatives

བཏང་སྙོམས་ལ་གནས་པར་གྱུར་ཅིག༔

TANG NYOM	LA	NAE PAR	GYUR CHIG
equanimity, impartiality	*in*	*stay*	*they must*

And enmity towards enemies and strangers.

May all sentient beings have happiness and the cause of happiness. May they be free of sorrow and the cause of sorrow. May they never be separated from happiness free of sorrow. May they abide in the equanimity free of both desire for friends and relatives and enmity towards enemies and strangers.

OFFERING

སྲས་བཅས་རྒྱལ་བའི་བསོད་ནམས་ཕུང་པོ་དང་།

SAE	CHE	GYAL WAI	SO NAM	PHUNG PO	DANG
Bodhisattvas	*together, with*	*Victors'*	*virtues, merit (the accumulation of merit)*	*heaps, vast amount*	*and*

By the power of the vast merit of the Buddhas and Bodhisattvas, and

སྒྲིབ་བྲལ་ཆོས་དབྱིངས་ཟབ་མོའི་བདེན་མཐུ་ཡིས།

DRIB	DRAL	CHO YING	ZAB MOI	DEN	THU	YI
obscurations (of the afflictions and their subtle traces)	*without*	*dharmadhatu, the sphere of all phenomena*	*profound*	*truth*	*power*	*of*

(the accumulation of wisdom)

The profound truth of the actuality of phenomena free of obscuration,

ཕྱོགས་འདིར་ནམ་མཁའ་མཛོད་ཀྱི་འབྱོར་པ་ལྟར།

CHOG	DIR	NAM KHA	DZO	KYI	JOR WA	TAR
direction	*here*	*sky's*	*treasure, store*	*of*	*wealth*	*similar*

Like wealth filling the sky treasury, may where we are

མཆོད་སྤྲིན་རྒྱ་མཚོས་གང་ཞིང་མཛེས་གྱུར་ཅིག།

CHO	TRIN	GYAM TSHO	GANG ZHING	DZE	GYUR CHIG
offering	*cloud**	*ocean#*	*becoming full*	*beautiful*	*must become*

*i.e. many and coming quickly
i.e. large and deep

Be beautifully filled with an ocean of offering clouds.

By the power of the vast merit of the Buddhas and Bodhisattvas, and the profound truth of the actuality of phenomena free of obscuration, may this place be beautiful, filled with an ocean of offering clouds like the wealth of the sky's treasury.

མཆོད་པའི་སྤྲིན་གཟུངས་བཟླ།

[Now recite the dharani of the offering cloud.]

DHARANI OF THE OFFERING CLOUD

ན་མོ་རཏྣ་ཏྲ་ཡཱ་ཡཿ ན་མོ་བྷ་ག་ཝ་ཏེ།

NA MO	RAT NA	TRA YA YA	NA MO	BHA GA WA TE
salutation	*jewels*	*three**	*salutation*	*perfect ones (Buddhas)*

* Buddha, Dharma, Sangha; guru, deva, dakini; dharmakaya, sambhogakaya, nirmanakaya

Salutation to the Three Jewels. Salutation to the Perfect Ones.

བཛྲེ་སཱ་ར་པྲ་མ་རྡ་ནི༔ ཏ་ཐཱ་ག་ཏཱ་ཡཿ

BEN DZE	SA RA	PRA MA DHA NI	TA THA GA TA YA
vajra. indestructible (sunyata)	*essence*	*great gift*	*all tathagatas, the Thus Gone Buddhas*

Indestructible essence – great gift! All the Thus Gone,

ཨརྷ་ཏེ༔ སམྱཀ་སཾ་བུདྡྷཱ་ཡཿ ཏདྱ་ཐཱ༔

AR HAT	SAM YAK SAM BUD DHA YA	TA DYA THA
vanquisher of the foe	*samyak samBuddhas fully enlightened Buddhas*	*it is like this*

The Vanquishers, the fully enlightened Buddhas – it is like this.

Salutation to the Three Jewels. Salutation to the Perfect Ones. Indestructible essence – great gift. All the Thus Gone, the Vanquishers, the fully enlightened Buddhas – it is like this.

ཨོཾ་བཛྲེ་བཛྲེ་

OM BEN DZE BEN DZE
original knowing indestructible, emptiness indestructible
Om. Indestructible,

མ་ཧཱ་བཛྲེ་མ་ཧཱ་ཏེ་ཛཱ་བཛྲེ༔

MA HA BEN DZE MA HA TE DZA BEN DZE
great indestructible great shining indestructible
Great indestructible, great shining indestructible.

མ་ཧཱ་བིདྱཱ་བཛྲེ་མ་ཧཱ་བོ་དྷི་ཙིཏྟ་བཛྲེ

MA HA BI DYA BEN DZE MA HA BO DHI TSIT TA BEN DZE
great awareness indestructible great bodhicitta, indestructible
Great awareness indestructible. Great indestructible awakened mind.

མ་ཧཱ་བོ་དྷི་མ་ནོ་ཏ༔

MA HA BO DHI MA NO TA
great enlightenment meaning
Great enlightenment meaning.

Om. Indestructible, great indestructible, great shining indestructible. Great awareness indestructible. Great indestructible awakened mind. Great enlightenment meaning.

ཨུདྦྷ་སཾ་ཀྲ་མ་ཎ་བཛྲེ་ཀརྨ༔

UD BHA SAM KRA MA NA BEN DZE KAR MA
come out by stages indestructible all deeds
Coming out by stages, indestructible activity.

ཨ་ཝ་ར་ཎི་བི་ཤུདྡྷ་ནི་བཛྲེ་ཡེ་སྭཱ་ཧཱ༔

A WA RA NI BI SHU DHA NI BEN DZE YE SWA HA
clarity very pure indestructible it is
Clarity very pure and indestructible. It is.

Coming out by stages, indestructible activity. Clarity very pure and indestructible. It is.

ཨོཾ་བཛྲ་དྷརྨ་ར་ཎི་ཏ། པྲ་ར་ཎི་ཏ།

OM BEN DZA DHAR MA RA NI TA PRA RA NI TA
original knowing indestructible dharma shining jewel vitality
Om. Indestructible shining wisdom. Vitality.

སཾ་པྲ་ར་ཎི་ཏ། སརྦ་བུདྡྷ་ཀྵེ་ཏྲ།

SAM	**PRA RA NI TA**	**SAR WA**	**BUD DHA**	**KSHE TRA**
complete	*vitality*	*all*	*buddha*	*realms*

Complete vitality. All buddha realms.

པྲ་ཙ་ལི་ཏི། པྲ་ཛྙཱ་པཱ་ར་མི་ཏ།

PRA TSA LI TI	**PRADZ NYA**	**PA RA MI TA**
knowing (the pure realms and wisdom itself)	*wisdom of emptiness*	*paramita, transcendental*

Knowing transcendental wisdom.

ནཱ་ད་སྭ་བྷཱ་ཝེ་བཛྲ་དྷརྨ་ཧྲི་ད་ཡ།

NA DA	**SWA BHA VE**	**BEN DZA**	**DHAR MA**	**HRI DA YA**
sound	*intrinsic*	*indestructible*	*dharma*	*heart, essence*

Sound, intrinsically indestructible dharma essence.

ས་ནྟོ་ཥ་ཎི་ཧཱུྃ་ཧཱུྃ་ཧཱུྃ་ཧོ་ཧོ་ཧོ་ཨ་ཁཾ་སྭཱ་ཧཱ།

SA NA TO SHA NI	**HUNG HUNG HUNG HO HO HO**	**A KHAM SWA HA**
satisfy (all beings)	*all come out (permanent flow)*	*filling the sky*

Satisfying all, arising endlessly, filling the sky.

Om. Indestructible shining wisdom. Vitality. Complete vitality. All buddha realms. Knowing transcendental wisdom. Sound, intrinsically indestructible dharma essence. Satisfying all, arising endlessly, filling the sky.

IMAGINING DEWACHEN

མི་མཛེད་འཇིག་རྟེན་འདི་ནས་ནུབ་ཕྱོགས་སུ།

MI JED	**JIG TEN**	**DI**	**NE**	**NUB**	**CHOG**	**SU**
many, numberless	*worlds*	*this (place)*	*from*	*western*	*direction*	*in*

In the western direction from here, beyond numberless worlds,

སངས་རྒྱས་ཞིང་མང་འདས་པའི་ཕ་མཐའ་ན།

SANG GYE	**ZHING**	**MANG**	**DAE PAI**	**PHA THA**	**NA**
buddha's	*realm*	*many*	*past, beyond*	*outside*	*at*

Past and on the far side of many Buddha realms,

རྒྱལ་སྲས་སྨོན་ལམ་གང་གའི་རྡུལ་སྙེད་དང་།

GYAL	SAE	MON LAM	GANG GAI	DUL	NYED	DANG
jinas (see appendix 1)	*bodhisattvas*	*aspiration*	*river Ganges*	*grains of sand*	*as many as*	*and*

Formed by an aspiration as vast as the sands of the river Ganges, to unite the good qualities of all the realms of the buddhas and bodhisattvas, and

རྒྱ་ཆེན་བསོད་ནམས་ཡེ་ཤེས་ཕུང་པོ་ལས།

GYA CHEN	SO NAM	YE SHE	PHUNG PO	LAE
vast, large	*merit (*	*wisdom of Amitabha)*	*heap)*	*from*

By a huge store of merit and wisdom

གྲུབ་པའི་ཞིང་མཆོག་ཕུལ་བྱུང་བདེ་བ་ཅན།

DRUB PAI	ZHING	CHOG	PHUL JUNG	DE WA CHEN
made, accomplished	*realm*	*excellent*	*very wonderful, perfect*	*Sukhavati, 'Happy'*

Is the excellent realm of the very wonderful Dewachen.

In the western direction from here, beyond the numberless worlds, past and on the far side of many Buddha realms, formed by an aspiration as vast as the sands of the river Ganges to unite the good qualities of all the realms of the buddhas and bodhisattvas, and by a huge store of merit and wisdom, is the excellent realm of the very wonderful Dewachen.

ལག་མཐིལ་ལྟར་མཉམ་ཐ་གྲུ་ཀུན་ནས་ཡངས།

LAG THIL	TAR	NYAM	THA DRU	KUN	NE	YANG
palm of the hand	*as*	*even, flat*	*large, spacious abundant, extent*	*all*	*from*	*vast*

Flat as the palm of your hand, it is vast and spacious in all directions.

རིན་ཆེན་རི་བོ་ནོར་བུའི་ནགས་ཚལ་དང་།

RIN CHEN	RI WO	NOR BUI	NAG TSHAL	DANG
jewel, precious things	*mountain*	*jewel*	*forest*	*and*

There are precious mountains and forests of jewels, along with

ལྷ་རྫས་མེ་ཏོག་ཚལ་དང་བདུད་རྩིའི་མཚོ།

LHA	DZE	ME TOG	TSHAL	DANG	DU TSI	TSHO
god	*articles*	*flower*	*grove*	*and*	*amrita, ambrosia, liberating elixir*	*lake*

(these groves and lakes are like those found in the gods' realms)

All that please the gods: flowers, groves, lakes of ambrosia and

དབྱངས་སྙན་སྤོས་ཆུའི་ཆུ་ཀླུང་འབབ་པ་དང་།

YANG	**NYEN**	**POE CHUI**	**CHU LUNG**	**BA PA**	**DANG**
sound, music melody	*sweet, pleasant*	*perfumed water*	*rivers*	*descend*	*and*

Flowing rivers of perfumed water making pleasant sounds, as well as

ནམ་མཁར་རྒྱུ་བའི་གཞལ་མེད་ཁང་པ་སོགས།

NAM KHAR	**GYU WAI**	**ZHAL ME KHANG PA**	**SOG**
sky	*moving*	*palaces*	*and so on*

(some rest on clouds and some are borne aloft by offering goddesses)

Divine palaces that move through the sky.

Flat as the palm of your hand, it is vast and spacious in all directions. There are precious mountains and forests of jewels, along with all that please the gods: flowers, groves, lakes of ambrosia and flowing rivers of perfumed water making pleasant sounds, as well as divine palaces that move though the sky.

གཞན་འཕྲུལ་འཆི་མེད་དགའ་བའི་གྲོང་ཁྱེར་ལྟར།

ZHAN TRUL	**CHI ME GA WAI**	**DRONG KHYER**	**TAR**
Zhan Trul Wong Zhed, the nicest of the 33 heavens	*Chime Gawa, the name of its city which is very beautiful and marvellous*	*city*	*as*

Like the city of Unending Joy in the heaven of Magic Form

ངོ་མཚར་བཀོད་པའི་ཁྱད་པར་འབྱམས་ཀླས་པའི།

NGO TSHAR	**KOE PAI**	**KHYE PAR**	**JAM LAE PAI**
wonderful	*built, constructed, designed*	*special, detailed*	*limitless, infinite*

Dewachen is wonderfully constructed with infinite special features.

སྙིང་པོ་བྱང་ཆུབ་ཤིང་རྒྱལ་མཛེས་པའི་དྲུང་།

NYING PO	**JANG CHUB**	**SHING**	**GYAL**	**DZE PAI**	**DRUNG**
at its centre point	*bodhi, enlightenment*	*tree*	*royal,*	*beautiful very fine*	*near*

At its centre, beside the beautiful and splendid Bodhi tree,

རིན་ཆེན་སེང་ཁྲི་པདྨ་བརྒྱན་པའི་སྟེང་།

RIN CHEN	**SENG**	**TRI**	**PAE MAE**	**GYAN PAI**	**TENG**
precious, jewelled	*lion*	*throne*	*lotus*	*adorned*	*on top of*

(a large lotus as a cushion)

Upon a precious lion throne adorned with a lotus

ས་གསུམ་ཆོས་ཀྱི་རྒྱལ་པོ་ཉག་གཅིག་པུ།

SA SUM	**CHO KYI**	**GYAL PO**	**NYAG CHIG PU**
*three levels**	*dharma's*	*lord*	*only one, sole*

** above the earth, on the earth and below the earth, i.e. everywhere.*

Is the one who is king of the dharma everywhere,

སྙན་གྲགས་ཆོས་ཀྱི་དབྱིངས་མཐར་ཁྱབ་པ་ཡི།

NYAN DRAG	**CHO KYI YING**	**THAR**	**KHYAB PA**	**YI**
fame	*dharmadhatu, all encompassing space*	*limit (beyond (time and space)*	*goes everywhere, pervading*	*of*

Whose fame has spread in all directions,

མགོན་པོ་འོད་ཟེར་དཔག་མེད་ཚེ་མཐའ་ཡས།

GON PO	**OE ZER**	**PA ME**	**TSHE**	**THA YAE**
protector, benefactor	*light rays (Amitabha)*	*countless, measureless*	*life*	*limitless (*Amitayus)*

* The two names refer to the same Buddha who has these two aspects.

Our great protector Measureless Light Limitless Life.

Like the city of Unending Joy in the heaven of Magic Form, Dewachen is wonderfully constructed with infinite special features. At its centre, beside the beautiful and splendid Bodhi tree, upon a precious lion throne adorned with a lotus, is the one who is king of the Dharma everywhere, whose fame has spread in all directions, our great protector Measureless Light Limitless Life.

ལྟ་བས་མི་ངོམས་མཚན་དཔེའི་དཔལ་འབར་ཞིང་།

TA WAE	**MI NGOM**	**TSHAN PEI**	**PAL**	**BAR ZHING**
looking, by	*not satisfied (i.e. always want to keep looking at him)*	*major and minor auspicious signs*	*splendour, glory*	*shining*

Endlessly attractive, you shine with the splendour of the auspicious major and minor marks, and

རི་རབ་རྒྱ་མཚོ་ཆེ་ལས་འཐོན་པ་བཞིན།

RI RAB	**GYAM TSHO**	**CHE**	**LE**	**THON PA**	**ZHIN**
Mt. Meru	*ocean*	*great*	*from*	*coming out*	*like*

Like Mt. Meru arising from the great ocean

རྣམ་མང་འཁོར་གྱི་ནང་ནས་མངོན་འཕགས་ཏེ།

NAM MANG	**KHOR**	**GYI NANG**	**NE**	**NGON PHAG**	**TE**
very many	*retinue, circle*	*inside*	*from*	*raised above*	*thus*

You are raised above the plentiful retinue that surrounds you.

བསོད་ནམས་ཉི་མ་བརྒྱ་པའི་གཟི་བརྗིད་ཀྱིས།

SO NAM	**NYI MA**	**GYA PAI**	**ZI JI**	**GYI**
*merit**	*sun*	*one hundred (very many)*	*tremendous, majestic*	*by*

*as the result of his accumulated merit

Due to your merit you shine with the majesty of a hundred suns and

རབ་འབྱམས་ཞིང་གི་དཀྱིལ་འཁོར་འགེང་བཞིན་དུ།

RAB JAM	**ZHING**	**GI**	**KYIL KHOR**	**GENG**	**ZHIN DU**
everywhere, infinitely vast	*realm*	*of*	*circle mandala*	*full*	*similar*

Your vast realm is like an infinite circle.

Endlessly attractive, you shine with the splendour of the auspicious major and minor marks, and like Mt. Meru arising from the great ocean, you are raised above the plentiful retinue that surrounds you. Due to your merit you shine with the majesty of a hundred suns and your vast realm is like an infinite circle.

དྲུག་ཅུ་རྩ་བཞིའི་ཡན་ལག་ཡོངས་རྫོགས་པ།

DRUG CHU TSA ZHI	**YAN LAG**	**YONG DZOG PA**
64	*branch, aspect*	*fully complete*

Using all the sixty-four branches of

ཚངས་པའི་དབྱངས་ཀྱིས་སྒྲ་ཀུན་ཟིལ་མནན་ནས།

TSHANG PAI	**YANG**	**KYI**	**DRA**	**KUN**	**ZIL NAN**	**NE**
Brahma, Hindu god of creation	*melodies*	*by*	*sound*	*all*	*overawe*	*then*

(all others become silent when they hear him)

Brahma's melodies you quieten all other sounds.

སྤྱན་རས་གཟིགས་དང་མཐུ་ཆེན་ཐོབ་པ་སྟེ།

CHEN RE ZI	**DANG**	**THU CHEN THOB PA**	**TE**
Avalokitesvara	*and*	*Vajrapani, Mahasthamaprapta*	*as*

Then to Chenrezi and Vajrapani,

རྒྱལ་སྲས་འཁོར་གྱི་གཙོ་བོ་རྣམ་གཉིས་སོགས།

GYAL SAE	**KHOR**	**GYI**	**TSHO WO**	**NAM NYI SOG**
Bodhisattva	*circle*	*of*	*chief, principal*	*two*

Your two principal Bodhisattvas, and

ཞིང་འདིར་པདྨོའི་སྐྱེ་གནས་བཟུང་བ་དང་།

ZHING	**DIR**	**PAE MOI**	**KYE**	**NE**	**ZUNG WA**	**DANG**
realm (Dewachen)	*here*	*lotus*	*birth*	*then*	*stay there*	*and*

To those who have taken lotus birth and stay in Dewachen, and

སངས་རྒྱས་ཞིང་མང་དག་ལས་ལྷགས་པ་ཡིས།

SANG GYE	**ZHING**	**MANG DAG**	**LE**	**LHAG PA**	**YI**
buddha	*realm*	*many*	*from*	*come, approach*	*by*

To those who come from many different buddha realms –

དག་པའི་འཁོར་ལ་གདམས་ངག་སྟོན་ཅིང་བཞུགས།

DAG PAI	**KHOR**	**LA**	**DAM NGAG**	**TONG CHING**	**ZHUG**
pure	*retinue, circle*	*to*	*instructions*	*teaching*	*stays*

To all your pure circle you give teaching and instructions.

Using all the sixty-four branches of Brahma's melodies you quieten all other sounds. Then to Chenrezi and Vajrapani, your two principal Bodhisattvas, and to those who have taken lotus birth and stay in Dewachen, and to those who come from many different buddha realms – to all your pure circle you give teaching and instructions.

གཟུགས་སྐུ་བདེ་ཆེན་ཞིང་ནས་མི་གཡོ་བཞིན།

ZUG KU	**DE CHEN**	**ZHING**	**NE**	**MI YO ZHIN**
body	*very happy*	*realm*	*from*	*not leave, not change*

You never leave this most happy realm.

མཁྱེན་བརྩེ་རིས་མེད་གདུལ་བྱའི་རྗེས་ཞུགས་པའི།

KHYEN	**TSE**	**RI ME**	**DUL JAI**	**JE ZHUG PAI**
knowledge	*compassion*	*impartial, equal*	*disciples*	*keep*

You support your disciples impartially with wisdom and compassion.

རྒྱལ་དང་དེ་སྲས་སྤྱོད་ཡུལ་བསམ་མི་ཁྱབ།

GYAL	**DANG**	**DE SAE**	**CHOD YUL**	**SAM MI KHYAB**
Victor (Amitabha)	*and*	*his Bodhisattvas*	*activities*	*inconceivable, measureless*

Victor, your activities and those of your Bodhisattvas are inconceivable.

དཔང་དུ་བགྱིས་ནས་གསོལ་འདིར་བརྩེ་བས་དགོངས།

PANG	**DU**	**GYI**	**NE**	**SOL**	**DIR**	**TSE WAE**	**GONG**
witness	*as*	*do*	*from*	*prayer*	*here*	*with compassion*	*hear, know about*

May you be my witness and hear this prayer with compassion.

You never leave this most happy realm. You support your disciples impartially with wisdom and compassion. Victor, your activities and those of your Bodhisattvas are inconceivable. May you be my witness and hear this prayer with compassion.

ཞེས་ཚོགས་ཞིང་མངོན་དུ་བྱས་ལ། རྩེ་གཅིག་ཏུ་བསྒོམ། དེ་ནས་ལངས་ལ་ཁ་ནུབ་ཏུ་བལྟ་བར་འོད་མདོ་ལས་གསུངས་པ་བཞིན་དུ་བྱས་ནས་ཕྱག་འཚལ་བཞིན་དུ།

Make all that has been described clear in your mind and meditate one-pointedly. Then, as is instructed in the Amitabha Sutra, face towards the west and make salutation.

REFUGE

བཅོམ་ལྡན་དེ་བཞིན་གཤེགས་པ་དགྲ་བཅོམ་པ།

CHOM DEN	DE ZHIN SHEG PA	DRA	CHOM PA
*bhagawan**	*tathagata#*	*enemy*	*vanquisher (Arhat)*

* finished all sin, having all good qualities, going from samsara: 'perfect ones'
#'thus gone' — gone in the same way as all the other Buddhas

Perfect one, Thus Gone, Vanquisher of the foe,

ཡང་དག་རྫོགས་པའི་སངས་རྒྱས་ཐུགས་རྗེ་ཅན།

YANG DAG	DZOG PAI	SANG GYE	THUG JE CHEN
very pure, complete	*perfect*	*Buddha*	*compassionate*

(Samyak Sambuddha, purified and with vast good qualities)

Compassionate complete and perfect Buddha

འོད་དཔག་མེད་མགོན་ཞབས་ལ་ཕྱག་འཚལ་ཞིང་།

OE PA ME	GON	ZHAB	LA	CHAG TSHAL ZHING
Amitabha	*lord, protector*	*feet*	*to, at*	*prostrate, making obeisance*

Amitabha, our protector, we prostrate at your feet.

བྱང་ཆུབ་སྙིང་པོ་ཇི་སྲིད་སྐྱབས་སུ་མཆི།

JANG CHUB	NYING PO	JI SI	KYAB SU CHI
bodhi, enlightenment	*heart, essence*	*until, for as long as*	*go for refuge (for the (sake of all beings)*

We go to you for refuge until we reach the heart of enlightenment.

Perfect one, Thus Gone, Vanquisher of the foe, compassionate complete and perfect Buddha Amitabha, our protector, we prostrate at your feet. We go to you for refuge until we reach the heart of enlightenment.

ཞེས་ལན་བདུན་བརྗོད། [Say this seven times]

SALUTATION

སྙིང་རྗེའི་མངའ་བདག་རྗེ་བཙུན་སྤྱན་རས་གཟིགས།

NYING JEI	**NGA DAG**	**JE TSUN**	**CHEN RE ZI**
compassion	*possessor, master, embodiment*	*noble, reverend*	*Avalokitesvara*

Noble Chenrezi, embodiment of compassion, and

མཐུ་ཆེན་ཐོབ་སོགས་རྒྱལ་སྲས་རྒྱ་མཚོ་དང་།

THU CHEN THO	**SO**	**GYAL**	**SAE**	**GYAM TSHO**	**DANG**
Vajrapani	*and the rest*	*victor*	*son, Bodhisattva*	*ocean*	*and*

Vajrapani and all the ocean of Bodhisattvas along with

གྲངས་ཡས་སློབ་མ་དུལ་བའི་དགེ་འདུན་ལ།

DRANG YAE	**LO MA**	**DUL WAI**	**GE DUN**	**LA**
numberless	*disciples*	*peaceful*	*sangha*	*to*

The numberless peaceful disciples within the Sangha –

གུས་པ་ཆེན་པོས་ཕྱག་འཚལ་སྐྱབས་སུ་མཆི།

GU PA	**CHEN POE**	**CHAG TSHAL**	**KYAB SU CHI**
reverence, respect and devotion	*great, with*	*make salutation*	*go for refuge*

With great devotion we make obeisance and take refuge in you.

Noble Chenrezi, the embodiment of compassion, and Vajrapani and all the ocean of Bodhisattvas along with the numberless peaceful disciples within the Sangha – with great devotion we make obeisance and take refuge in you.

ཞེས་ལན་བདུན་ནམ་གསུམ་བརྗོད། [Say the above verse seven or three times.]

OFFERINGS

མཆོད་ཡོན་མེ་ཏོག་བདུག་སྤོས་མར་མེ་དྲི།

CHOD YON	**ME TOG**	**DUG POE**	**MAR ME**	**DRI**
drinking water	*flowers*	*incense*	*lamp*	*perfumed water*

Drinking water, flowers, incense, lamps, perfumed water,

ཞལ་ཟས་སིལ་སྙན་ལ་སོགས་དངོས་བཤམས་དང་།

ZHAL ZAE	**SIL NYAN**	**LA SOG**	**NGO**	**SHAM**	**DANG**
food	*music, cymbals*	*the rest*	*actually*	*displayed*	*and*

Food, music and all that we actually display, as well as

གཟུངས་རིག་མོས་པ་ལས་བྱུང་མཆོད་པའི་སྤྲིན།

ZUNG RIG	**MOE PA**	**LAE**	**JUNG**	**CHO PAI**	**TRIN**
dharani, long mantra	*devotion, desire*	*from*	*arising*	*offering*	*cloud*

A cloud of offerings arising from devoted recitation of the dharani

ནམ་མཁའ་གང་བར་དམིགས་ཏེ་གུས་པས་མཆོད།

NAM KHA	**GANG WAR**	**MIG**	**TE**	**GU PAE**	**CHOD**
sky	*filling*	*imagine*	*then*	*reverence*	*offer*

Fill the sky. We imagine all this and offer it with devotion.

Drinking water, flowers, incense, lamps, perfumed water, food, music and all that we actually display, as well as clouds of offerings arising from devoted recitation of the dharani fill the sky. We imagine all this and offer it with devotion.

CONFESSION

འཁོར་ཚེ་ཐོག་མ་མེད་ནས་ད་ལྟའི་བར།

KHOR	**TSHE**	**THOG MA ME**	**NAE**	**DAN TAI**	**BAR**
samsara	*lives*	*beginningless*	*from*	*now*	*until*

From beginingless time up until now, in all our lives in samsara,

རང་བཞིན་བཅས་པའི་སྡིག་ལྟུང་བགྱིས་སོ་འཚལ།

RANG ZHIN	**CHE PAI**	**DIG**	**TUNG**	**GYI SO TSHAL**
*intrinsic**	*with rule#*	*sins*	*falls, broken vows*	*which we have done*

*things that are bad in themselves, like killing
#things which we are committed not to do e.g. no sex for monks or nuns.

We have broken our vows and have acted in ways that are intrinsically wrong and also made errors as defined by rules.

གནོང་འགྱོད་དྲག་པོས་མཐོལ་བཤགས་སླན་ཆད་ཀྱང་།

NONG	**GYOD**	**DRAG POE**	**THOL**	**SHAG**	**LAN CHAE**	**KYANG**
shame	*regret, sadness*	*intense*	*with hands held at heart*	*confess, request forgiveness*	*future, from now on*	*also*

With intense shame and regret we humbly confess this and request to be forgiven.

མི་བགྱིད་སྡོམ་སེམས་བརྟན་པོས་ཡང་དག་བཟུང་།

MI GYI	**DOM SEM**	**TAN POE**	**YANG DAG**	**ZUNG**
not do	*vows, obligation, moral system*	*firm, by*	*purely*	*hold, keep*

From now on we will not act in these ways but shall firmly maintain the purity of our moral obligations.

From beginingless time up until now, in all our lives in samsara, we have broken our vows and have acted in ways that are intrinsically wrong and also made errors as defined by rules. With intense shame and regret we humbly confess this and request to be forgiven. From now on we will not act in these ways but shall firmly maintain the purity of our moral obligations.

REJOICING AND REQUESTING

འཇིག་རྟེན་འཇིག་རྟེན་ལས་འདས་རང་གཞན་གྱི།

JIG TEN	**JIG TEN**	**LAE**	**DAE**	**RANG**	**ZHAN**	**GYI**
worldly (such as offerings, non-violence)	*world (emptiness, wisdom)*	*from*	*going*	*self*	*others*	*of*

All the virtues, both worldly and non-worldly, collected by ourselves and all others

དུས་གསུམ་དགེ་ཚོགས་ཀུན་ལ་རྗེས་ཡི་རང་།

DU	**SUM**	**GE**	**TSHOG**	**KUN**	**LA**	**JE YI RANG**
times	*three*	*virtues*	*collected*	*all*	*to*	*admire, rejoice with*
(past, present, future)		*(rejoicing in the virtue collected by others)*				

In the three times make us rejoice and feel happy.

ཕྱོགས་བཅུའི་འཇིག་རྟེན་སྒྲོན་མ་གང་བཞུགས་རྣམས།

CHOG	**CHUI**	**JIG TEN**	**DRON MA**	**GANG**	**ZHUG**	**NAM**
directions	*ten*	*world*	*lamp*	*whoever*	*staying*	*(plural)*
(i.e. everywhere)		*(Buddhas and Bodhisattvas)*				

All you lamps of the world staying in the ten directions,

བླ་མེད་ཆོས་ཀྱི་འོད་ཟེར་བསྐོར་བར་བསྐུལ།

LA ME	**CHO**	**KYI**	**OD ZER**	**KOR WAR**	**KUL**
unsurpassed (mahayana)	*dharma*	*of*	*light rays, bright*	*teach, turn the wheel*	*request, beseech*

We request you to please teach the unsurpassed illuminating Dharma.

All the virtues, both worldly and non-worldly, collected by ourselves and all others in the three times make us rejoice and feel happy. All you lamps of the world staying in the ten directions, we request you to please teach the unsurpassed illuminating Dharma.

PRAYING AND DEDICATING

ལྷར་བཅས་སྐྱེ་དགུའི་མགོན་པོར་ཡུན་རིང་དུ།

LHA	**CHE**	**KYE GUI**	**GON POR**	**YUN RING DU**
gods	*with*	*sentient beings*	*protector, benefactor*	*for long time*

We pray that the Protectors of gods and sentient beings

མྱ་ངན་མི་འདའ་བཞུགས་པར་གསོལ་བ་འདེབས།

NYA NGAN MI DA ZHUG PAR SOL WA DEB
not pass from sorrow, not die, not enter nirvana — stay — we pray

Will remain for a long time without passing into nirvana.

འདིས་མཚོན་དགེ་བས་མ་རྒན་སེམས་ཅན་ཀུན།

DI TSHON GE WAE MA GAN SEM CHEN KUN
by this example virtue, by old mothers sentient being all*
*all have been our mothers in past lives

By our virtues, including those arising from this practice, may all sentient beings, each one previously our own mother,

རྣམ་པ་ཀུན་མཁྱེན་ཡེ་ཤེས་ལ་འགོད་ཤོག།

NAM PA KUN KHYEN YE SHE LA GOD SHOG
fully omniscient original knowing to must get!

Gain fully omniscient original knowing.

We pray that the Protectors of gods and sentient beings will remain for a long time without passing into nirvana. By our virtues, including those arising from this practice, may all sentient beings, each one previously our own mother, fully gain omniscient original knowing.

ཅེས་ཚོགས་བསགས། In this way accumulate merit.

ASPIRATION

སླར་ཡང་སྨིན་པ་མེ་ཏོག་དང་བཅས་ཏེ། Then, holding a flower or some grain between your hands in prayer at your heart, say as follows:

འོད་མཚན་སྟོབས་བཅུ་མངའ་བ་སྲས་བཅས་ཀྱི།

OE TSHAN TOB CHU NGA WA SAE CHE KYI
Amitabha name powers ten has Bodhisattva together of

Amitabha with the ten powers, together with your Bodhisattvas –

མཚན་མཆོག་བརྗོད་དང་ཕྱག་འཚལ་མཆོད་པའི་མཐུས།

TSHAN CHOG JOD DANG CHAG TSHAL CHO PAI THU
names excellent saying and salutation offering power
(repeating their names again and again)

By the power of reciting your excellent names, making salutations and offerings, and

གང་ཞབས་དྲན་པའི་བྱང་ཆུབ་མཐའ་བར་དུ།

GANG	**ZHAB**	**DRAN PAI**	**JANG CHUB**	**THA**	**BAR DU**
whoever	*holy feet (Amitabha)*	*remember*	*bodhi, enlightenment*	*limit, end*	*until*

Keeping remembrance, until enlightenment is gained we will

དབང་པོ་ཚང་ཞིང་རིགས་མཐོར་སྐྱེ་བ་དང་།

WANG PO	**TSHANG ZHING**	**RIG THOR**	**KYE WA**	**DANG**
sense organ	*full*	*good family*	*born*	*and*

Be born with healthy organs in a good family, and

དབུལ་པོར་མི་འགྱུར་འཇིག་རྟེན་ཀུན་གྱིས་བཀུར།

WUL WOR	**MI GYUR**	**JIG TEN**	**KUN**	**GYI**	**KUR**
poor	*not become*	*worlds*	*all*	*by*	*respect, honour*

Free of poverty, be respected by all.

Amitabha with the ten powers[1] *together with your Bodhisattvas – by the power of reciting your excellent names and making salutations and offerings, and keeping remembrance of you, until enlightenment is gained we will be born with healthy organs in a good family, be free of poverty and be respected by all.*

འཆི་ཚེ་བདེ་གཤེགས་འཁོར་བཅས་མདུན་བཞུགས་ཤིང་།

CHI	**TSHE**	**DE SHEG**	**KHOR CHE**	**DUN**	**ZHUG SHING**
die	*when*	*Happily Gone (those who relied on Amitabha)*	*with their retinues*	*before me*	*staying**

*prevent them from falling to the lower realms

When we die, you the Happily Gone One with your retinue will stay in front of us ensuring that

སྐྱེ་བ་ཀུན་ཏུ་ཚངས་སྤྱོད་དངོས་པོ་ཐོབ།

KYE WA	**KUN**	**TU**	**TSHANG CHOD**	**NGO PO**	**THOB**
lives	*all*	*in*	*bhikshus, celibate*	*truly*	*get*

In all our lives we will live in purity.

རྟག་པར་བྱང་ཆུབ་སྤྱོད་ལ་དགའ་བ་དང་།

TAG PAR	**JANG CHUB**	**CHOD**	**LA**	**GA WA**	**DANG**
always	*bodhi, enlightenment*	*practice (mahayana)*	*to*	*liking*	*and*

Always being drawn to the activities that lead to enlightenment, and

གཟུངས་དང་ཏིང་འཛིན་བཟོད་ལ་ཡང་དག་ལྟ།

ZUNG	DANG	TING DZIN	ZO	LA	YANG DA	TA
memory from dharani practice	*and*	*samadhi, absorbed contemplation*	*patience*	*with*	*very pure*	*view*

With the very pure view leading to good memory and the patience of contemplation,

ཕྱིར་མི་ལྡོག་པའི་ས་བོན་འཇོག་པ་སོགས།

CHIR MI DOG PA	SA BON	JOG PA	SOG
not come back (not fall back into worldliness)	*seeds (of bodhicitta)*	*put*	*and develop*

We will plant the seed of never returning to worldliness.

When we die, you the Happily Gone One with your retinue will stay in front of us ensuring that in all our lives we will live in purity. Always being drawn to the activities that lead to enlightenment, and with the very pure view leading to good memory and the patience of contemplation, we will plant the seed of never returning to worldliness.

མདོར་ན་རྒྱལ་སྲས་ཆོས་ཀྱི་འབྱུང་གནས་ཀྱིས།

DOR NA	GYAL SAE	CHO	KYI	JUNG NAE	KYI
briefly	*bodhisattva*	*dharma*	*of*	*origin*	*by*

(He later becomes the Buddha Amitabha and generates the pure realm of Dewachen)

In brief, Bodhisattva Source of Dharma, you who

བཅོམ་ལྡན་འཇིག་རྟེན་དབང་ཕྱུག་རྒྱལ་པོའི་དྲུང་།

CHOM DEN	JIG TEN	WANG CHUG	GYAL POI	DRUNG
bhagawan	*world*	*powerful*	*king*	*before*

(name of Buddha, King Powerful in the World)

In front of the perfect one, Powerful King of the World,

ཞལ་བཞེས་སྨོན་ལམ་འགྱུར་བ་མི་མངའ་དང་།

ZHAL ZHE	MON LAM	GYUR WA	MI	NGA	DANG
took, made and accepted	**prayer of aspiration*	*change*	*not*	*possible*	*and*

*to gain enlightenment for the sake of others

Made your unchangeable aspiration, along with

གཞན་ཡང་རྗེ་བཙུན་སྤྱན་རས་གཟིགས་དབང་སོགས།

ZHAN	YANG	JE TSUN	CHEN RE ZIG WANG	SOG
others	*also*	*reverend*	*Avalokitesvara*	*and so on*

Reverend Chenrezi and the other

རྒྱལ་སྲས་སོ་སོའི་སྔོན་གྱི་ཐུགས་བསྐྱེད་དང་།

GYAL SAE	SO SOI	NGON GYI	THUG KYE	DANG
bodhisattva	*each*	*before, previous*	*took bodhisattva vows*	*and*

Bodhisattvas who have each formerly developed the altruistic aspiration for enlightenment, and

བདེན་གཟིགས་ཉན་ཐོས་ཆེ་རྣམས་བདེན་པ་དང་།

DEN	ZIG	NYAN THO	CHE	NAM	DEN PA	DANG
truth	*see*	*sravakas, listeners*	*great*	*(plural)*	*truth*	*and*

The truth of the great listeners who saw the truth, and

གཟུངས་དང་མདོ་སྡེའི་ཕན་ཡོན་ཚད་མེད་པ།

ZUNG	DANG	DO DEI	PHAN YON	TSHAE ME PA
dharani, mantra	*and*	*sutra, teaching*	*benefit*	*numberless*

The numberless benefits of the dharanis and sutras –

In brief, Bodhisattva Source of Dharma, you who made your unchangeable aspiration in front of the perfect one, Powerful King of the World, along with Reverend Chenrezi and the other Bodhisattvas who have each formerly developed the altruistic aspiration for enlightenment, and the truth of the great listeners who saw the truth, and the numberless benefits of the dharanis and sutras –

དཔང་དུ་མཛད་ནས་དེང་འདིར་བདག་ཅག་རྣམས།

PANG	DU	DZAD	NAE	DENG DIR	DAG CHAG NAM
guarantor, witness	*as*	*take*	*then*	*this time*	*we (by their power we gain the following blessings)*

With your support and validation

གནས་སྐབས་ཚེ་འདིར་ཚེ་རིང་ནད་མེད་ཅིང་།

NAE KAB	TSHE DIR	TSHE RING	NAD MED CHING
temporary	*this life*	*long life*	*free of sickness*

We shall have a long life free of sickness, and

མི་དང་མི་མིན་འཇིགས་པ་ཀུན་ལས་གྲོལ།

MI	DANG	MI MIN	JIG PA	KUN	LAE	DROL
human	*and*	*non-human (ghosts and so on)*	*fear*	*all*	*from*	*free*

Be free of all fears of humans and non-humans, and

དཔལ་འབྱོར་སྙན་གྲགས་གང་གཱའི་རྒྱུན་ལྟར་འབེབས།

PAL JOR	NYAN DRAG	GANG GAI	GYUN	TAR	BEB
wealth	*fame*	*Ganges*	*flow, current*	*as*	*flowing*

Have wealth and fame ceaseless as the flow of the River Ganges.

With your support and validation we shall have a long life free of sickness, and be free of all fears of humans and non-humans, and have wealth and fame ceaseless as the flow of the River Ganges.

ཤུགས་དྲག་བཅོས་མ་མིན་པའི་ཐར་འདོད་དང་།

SHUG	DRAG	CHO MA	MIN PAI	THAR	DOD	DANG
power, strength	*intense*	*artifice*	*without*	*liberation*	*desire, want*	*and*

With a very powerful and genuine desire for liberation

གཞན་ཕན་སྙིང་རྗེས་དྲངས་པའི་སེམས་བསྐྱེད་དང་།

ZHAN	PHAN	NYING JE	DRANG PAI	SEM KYE	DANG
others	*benefit*	*compassion*	*straight, true*	*develop bodhicitta*	*and*

We now develop both true bodhicitta to benefit others with compassion, and

འཁྲུལ་མེད་ངེས་དོན་རྟོགས་པའི་ལྟ་བ་སོགས།

TRUL ME	NGE DON	TOG PAI	TA WA	SOG
unconfused	*certain truth*	*awaken to*	*view*	*and so on*

The view that awakens the certain truth free of delusion.

ཐེག་མཆོག་ལམ་གནད་རྫོགས་པར་རྙེད་པ་དང་།

THEG CHOG	LAM	NAD	DZOG PAR	NYED PA	DANG
mahayana, best vehicle	*path*	*essential point*	*fully*	*get*	*and*

Fully gaining the key point of the mahayana path and

ཚེ་འཕོས་བདེ་ལྡན་ཞིང་དུ་སྐྱེ་བའི་མཚོན།

TSHE PHO	DE DAN ZHING	DU	KYE WAI	TSHON
when die	*Sukhavati, happy place*	*in*	*born*	*example, and so on*

Being guided to birth in Dewachen when we die,

ཇི་ལྟར་སྨོན་པའི་རེ་འབྲས་ཡིད་བཞིན་དུ།

JI TAR	MON PAI	RE	DRAE	YID ZHIN	DU
according to	*wish, desire*	*hopes*	*result*	*intend*	*as*

May our hopes and wishes be fulfilled perfectly,

གེགས་མེད་འཕྲལ་དུ་ཐོབ་པར་བྱིན་གྱིས་རློབས།

GEG ME	**TRAL DU**	**THOB PAR**	**JIN GYI LOB**
without obstruction or trouble	*immediate*	*gain*	*bless*

Immediately and without obstruction with your blessing.

With a very powerful and genuine desire for liberation we now develop both true bodhicitta to benefit others with compassion, and the view that awakens the certain truth free of delusion. Fully gaining the key point of the mahayana path and being guided to birth in Dewachen when we die, with your blessing may our hopes and wishes be fulfilled perfectly, immediately and without obstruction.

ཞེས་མེ་ཏོག་ནུབ་ཕྱོགས་སུ་འཐོར།

[Pray in this way then throw the flowers or grain towards the west.]

དེ་ནས་སེམས་བསྐྱེད་སྦྱང་བ་ནི།

PRACTISE DEVELOPING BODHICITTA

ཇི་ལྟར་བདེ་གཤེགས་ཁྱོད་སྐུ་ཇི་འདྲ་དང་།

JI TAR	**DE SHEG**	**KHYO**	**KU**	**JI DRA**	**DANG**
as it is, in that way	*Happily Gone (Amitabha)*	*you*	*body*	*like it is*	*and*

You who are Happily Gone, just as your body is, and

ཡང་དག་ཞིང་དང་འཁོར་དང་མཛད་པ་དང་།

YANG DAG	**ZHING**	**DANG**	**KHOR**	**DANG**	**DZAE PA**	**DANG**
very pure (Dewachen)	*realm*	*and*	*retinue*	*and*	*deeds*	*and*

Just as your very pure realm, retinue, deeds, and

མཚན་དང་སྐུ་ཚེ་དཔག་མེད་ཅི་འདྲ་བ།

TSHAN	**DANG**	**KU TSHE**	**PAG ME**	**CHI**	**DRA WA**
names	*and*	*lives*	*countless*	*as much*	*they are like*

Your names and measureless lives are,

བདག་སོགས་མ་འོངས་དེ་འདྲ་འགྱུར་བགྱིས་ནས།

DAG SOG	**MA ONG**	**DEN DRA**	**GYUR GYI**	**NAE**
we	*future*	*like that*	*become*	*then*

May we gain ones like this in the future.

ནམ་མཁའ་མཉམ་པའི་མ་གྱུར་རིགས་དྲུག་འགྲོ།

NAM KHA	NYAM PAI	MA	GYUR	RIG	DRUG	DRO
sky	*equalling*	*mother**	*become*	*realms, groups*	*six*	*beings*

*who are my mothers in all of the three times

All beings equalling the sky, each of whom has been our own mother in one or other of the six realms of samsara,

འཇིགས་རུང་སྲིད་པའི་ཆུ་བོར་བྱིང་བ་རྣམས།

JIG RUNG	SI PAI	CHU WOR	JING WA	NAM
fearful	*samsara's*	*river*	*sinking*	*(plural)*

All those who are sinking in the fearful river of samsara –

ཞི་འགོག་བདུད་རྩིའི་དབྱིངས་སུ་དབུགས་འབྱིན་པའི།

ZHI	GOG	DUD TSI	YING	SU	WUG JIN PAI
peaceful [nirvana)	*ending of suffering*	*amrita, liberating elixir*	*realm*	*in*	*encourage, fortify, inspire*

May we hearten them in this realm of the liberating elixir of sorrowless peace.

སེམས་མཆོག་བསྐྱེད་དོ་མི་ཉམས་འཕེལ་གྱུར་ཅིག།

SEM	CHOG	KYED DO	MI	NYAM	PHEL GYUR	CHIG
mind	*excellent*	*develop*	*no*	*decline*	*increase, spread*	*it must*

(mind fixed on gaining enlightenment in order to benefit others)

Developing this excellent bodhicitta, may it increase without decline.

Happily gone, may we in future gain bodies, realms, retinue, deeds, names and measureless lives just like yours. Then in this realm of the liberating elixir of sorrowless peace may we uplift all those who are sinking in the terrifying river of samsara, all our innumerable previous mothers who now wander in the six realms. Developing this excellent bodhicitta, may it spread and increase without decline.

ཅེས་ལན་གསུམ། [Recite this three times.]

སེམས་བསྐྱེད་འདོན་ལུགས་འདི་ནི་ལས་དང་པོ་པས་ཀྱང་བྱར་རུང་བས་འཇུག་བདེ་བ་ཞིག་ཡིན་ནོ།

[This system of developing bodhicitta is also suitable for those who are just starting in dharma, since it is easy to do.]

སྐབས་འདིར་འོད་དཔག་མེད་ཀྱི་གཟུངས་རིང་ཐུང་ཅི་རིགས་པ་བཟླ་ཞིང་།

[At this point recite the following short dharani of Amitabha, or the long one, as much as you can.]

ཨོཾ་ཨ་མི་དྷེ་ཝ་ཧྲཱིཿ

OM A MI DHE WA HRI

Amitabha grant blessing!

སྤྲོ་ན་འཕགས་པ་འདི་དཔག་མེད་ཀྱི་བཀོད་པའི་མདོ་འང་ཀློག།

[If you wish you can also read the 'Od-dPag-Med-Kyi-bKod-Pa'i-mDo, the Amitabhavyuha Sutra.]

RECEIVING BLESSINGS

རྩེ་གཅིག་བཟླས་པས་རྒྱལ་བ་འཁོར་བཅས་ཀྱི།

TSE CHIG	DAE PAE	GYAL WA	KHOR	CHE	KYI
one-pointed, unwavering	*recitation, by*	*Jina, Victor (Amitabha)*	*retinue*	*with*	*of*

By this one-pointed recitation the minds of you the Victor and your retinue

ཐུགས་དམ་རྒྱུད་བསྐུལ་སྐུ་ལས་འོད་ཟེར་བྱུང་།

THUG DAM	GYUD KUL	KU	LAE	OE ZER	JUNG
mind and vows	*move, invoke, stir*	*body*	*from*	*light rays (they merge into all beings)*	*arise*

Are moved and from your bodies rays of light arise by which

རང་གཞན་སྡུག་བསྔལ་མཐའ་དག་ཞི་བྱས་ནས།

RANG	ZHAN	DUG NGAL	THA DAG	ZHI	JAE	NAE
self	*others*	*suffering*	*all*	*pacify*	*finish*	*then*

All the sufferings of myself and all others are pacified and

སྨོན་དོན་ཡིད་བཞིན་འགྲུབ་པར་བྱིན་གྱིས་རློབས།

MON	DON	YI ZHIN	DRUB PAR	JIN GYI LOB
wish, desire	*meaning*	*according to wish*	*accomplish, come full, as*	*bless*

We are blessed with the fulfilment of whatever we desire.

By this one-pointed recitation, the minds of you the Victor and your retinue are moved and from your bodies rays of light arise by which all the sufferings of myself and all others are pacified and we are blessed with the fulfilment of whatever we desire.

གཟུགས་བུམ་ཡོད་ན་འོད་ཟེར་བསྡུ་འཕེབས་པ་བསྒྲུགས་ནས། སླར་ཡང་གཟུངས་ཅི་ནུས་བཟླ་ཞིང་རང་གཞན་ལ་ཁྲུས་བྱ། གང་ལྟར་ཡང་རྗེས་ལ།

[If doing the pot (Bum-Pa) of nectar with the recitation, then practise with light rays issuing from Amitabha and converging together into the pot. Then reciting the following dharani of offering as much as possible, bathe and purify oneself and all others with the transformed amrita nectar in the pot.]

DHARANI OF THE OFFERING CLOUD

ན་མོ་རཏྣ་ཏྲ་ཡཱ་ཡ༔ ན་མོ་བྷ་ག་ཝ་ཏེ།

NA MO *salutation* **RAT NA** *jewels* **TRA YA YA** *three** **NA MO** *salutation* **BHA GA WA TE** *perfect ones (Buddhas)*

* Buddha, Dharma, Sangha; guru, deva, dakini; dharmakaya, sambhogakaya, nirmanakaya

Salutation to the Three Jewels. Salutation to the Perfect Ones.

བཛྲེ་སཱ་ར་པྲ་མ་རྡ་ནི༔ ཏ་ཐཱ་ག་ཏཱ་ཡ༔

BEN DZE *vajra. indestructible (sunyata)* **SA RA** *essence* **PRA MA DHA NI** *great gift* **TA THA GA TA YA** *all tathagatas, the Thus Gone Buddhas*

Indestructible essence – great gift! All the Thus Gone,

ཨར་ཧ་ཏེ༔ སམྱཀ་སཾ་བུདྡྷཱ་ཡ༔ ཏ་དྱ་ཐཱ༔

AR HAT *vanquisher of the foe* **SAM YAK SAM BUD DHA YA** *samyak samBuddhas fully enlightened Buddhas* **TA DYA THA** *it is like this*

The Vanquishers, the fully enlightened Buddhas – it is like this.

Salutation to the Three Jewels. Salutation to the Perfect Ones. Indestructible essence – great gift. All the Thus Gone, the Vanquishers, the fully enlightened Buddhas – it is like this.

ཨོཾ་བཛྲེ་བཛྲེ་

OM *original knowing* **BEN DZE** *indestructible, emptiness* **BEN DZE** *indestructible*

Om. Indestructible,

མ་ཧཱ་བཛྲེ་མ་ཧཱ་ཏེ་ཛཱ་བཛྲེ༔

MA HA *great* **BEN DZE** *indestructible* **MA HA TE DZA BEN DZE** *great shining indestructible*

Great indestructible, great shining indestructible.

མ་ཧཱ་བིདྱ་བཛྲ་མ་ཧཱ་བོ་དྷི་ཙིཏྟ་བཛྲ

MA HA	**BI DYA**	**BEN DZE**	**MA HA**	**BO DHI TSIT TA**	**BEN DZE**
great	*awareness*	*indestructible*	*great*	*bodhicitta,*	*indestructible*

Great awareness indestructible. Great indestructible awakened mind.

མ་ཧཱ་བོ་དྷི་མ་ཎོ་ཏཱ༔

MA HA	**BO DHI**	**MA NO TA**
great	*enlightenment*	*meaning*

Great enlightenment meaning.

Om. Indestructible, great indestructible, great shining indestructible. Great awareness indestructible. Great indestructible awakened mind. Great enlightenment meaning.

ཨུད་བྷ་སཾ་ཀྲ་མ་ཎ་བཛྲ་སརྦ་ཀརྨ༔

UD BHA	**SAM KRA MA NA**	**BEN DZE**	**KAR MA**
come out	*by stages*	*indestructible*	*all deeds*

Coming out by stages, indestructible activity.

ཨ་ཝ་ར་ཎི་བི་ཤུདྡྷ་ཎི་བཛྲ་ཡེ་སྭཱ་ཧཱ༔

A WA RA NI	**BI SHU**	**DHA NI**	**BEN DZE YE**	**SWA HA**
clarity	*very*	*pure*	*indestructible*	*it is*

Clarity very pure and indestructible. It is.

Coming out by stages, indestructible activity. Clarity very pure and indestructible. It is.

ཨོཾ་བཛྲ་དྷརྨ་ར་ཎི་ཏ། པྲ་ར་ཎི་ཏ།

OM	**BEN DZA**	**DHAR MA**	**RA NI TA**	**PRA RA NI TA**
original knowing	*indestructible*	*dharma*	*shining jewel*	*vitality*

Om. Indestructible shining wisdom. Vitality.

སཾ་པྲ་ར་ཎི་ཏ། སརྦ་བུདྡྷ་ཀྵེ་ཏྲ།

SAM	**PRA RA NI TA**	**SAR WA**	**BUD DHA**	**KSHE TRA**
complete	*vitality*	*all*	*buddha*	*realms*

Complete vitality. All buddha realms.

པྲ་ཙ་ལི་ཏི། པྲ་ཛྙཱ་པཱ་ར་མི་ཏ།

PRA TSA LI TI	**PRADZ NYA**	**PA RA MI TA**
knowing (the pure realms and wisdom itself)	*wisdom of emptiness*	*paramita, transcendental*

Knowing transcendental wisdom.

ནཱ་ད་སྭ་བྷཱ་ཝེ་བཛྲ་དྷརྨ་ཧྲི་ད་ཡ།

NA DA SWA BHA VE BEN DZA DHAR MA HRI DA YA
sound intrinsic indestructible dharma heart, essence
Sound, intrinsically indestructible dharma essence.

ས་ནྟོ་ཥ་ཎི་ཧཱུྃ་ཧཱུྃ་ཧཱུྃ་ཧོ་ཧོ་ཧོ་ཨ་ཁཾ་སྭཱ་ཧཱ།

SA NA TO SHA NI HUNG HUNG HUNG HO HO HO A KHAM SWA HA
satisfy (all beings) all come out (permanent flow) filling the sky
Satisfying all, arising endlessly, filling the sky.

Om. Indestructible shining wisdom. Vitality. Complete vitality. All buddha realms. Knowing transcendental wisdom. Sound, intrinsically indestructible dharma essence. Satisfying all, arising endlessly, filling the sky.

[Then after that, again do the following refuge and implicit bodhicitta practice and the Seven Branch Practice (Salutation; offerings; confession; rejoicing; requesting teaching; praying they stay; dedicating) reciting them as much as possible.]

REFUGE

བཅོམ་ལྡན་དེ་བཞིན་གཤེགས་པ་དགྲ་བཅོམ་པ།

CHOM DEN DE ZHIN SHEG PA DRA CHOM PA
bhagawan tathagata# enemy vanquisher (Arhat)*
* finished all sin, having all good qualities, going from samsara: 'perfect ones'
#'thus gone' — gone in the same way as all the other Buddhas
Perfect one, Thus Gone, Vanquisher of the foe,

ཡང་དག་རྫོགས་པའི་སངས་རྒྱས་ཐུགས་རྗེ་ཅན།

YANG DAG DZOG PAI SANG GYE THUG JE CHEN
very pure, complete perfect Buddha compassionate
(Samyak Sambuddha, purified and with vast good qualities)
Compassionate complete and perfect Buddha

འོད་དཔག་མེད་མགོན་ཞབས་ལ་ཕྱག་འཚལ་ཞིང་།

OE PA ME GON ZHAB LA CHAG TSHAL ZHING
Amitabha lord, protector feet to, at prostrate, making obeisance
Amitabha, our protector, we prostrate at your feet.

བྱང་ཆུབ་སྙིང་པོ་ཇི་སྲིད་སྐྱབས་སུ་མཆི།

JANG CHUB NYING PO JI SI KYAB SU CHI
bodhi, enlightenment heart, essence until, for as long as go for refuge (for the sake of all beings)
We go to you for refuge until we reach the heart of enlightenment.

Perfect one, Thus Gone, Vanquisher of the foe, compassionate complete and perfect Buddha Amitabha, our protector, we prostrate at your feet. We go to you for refuge until we reach the heart of enlightenment.

ཞེས་ལན་བདུན་བརྗོད། [Say this seven times]

THE SEVEN BRANCH PRACTICE

SALUTATION

སྙིང་རྗེའི་མངའ་བདག་རྗེ་བཙུན་སྤྱན་རས་གཟིགས།

NYING JEI	NGA DAG	JE TSUN	CHEN RE ZI
compassion	*possessor, master, embodiment*	*noble, reverend*	*Avalokitesvara*

Noble Chenrezi, embodiment of compassion, along with

མཐུ་ཆེན་ཐོབ་སོགས་རྒྱལ་སྲས་རྒྱ་མཚོ་དང་།

THU CHEN THO	SO	GYAL	SAE	GYAM TSHO	DANG
Vajrapani	*and the rest*	*victor*	*son, Bodhisattva*	*ocean*	*and*

Vajrapani and all the ocean of Bodhisattvas along with

བགྲང་ཡས་སློབ་མ་དུལ་བའི་དགེ་འདུན་ལ།

DRANG YAE	LO MA	DUL WAI	GE DUN	LA
numberless	*disciples*	*peaceful, controlled*	*sangha*	*to*

The numberless peaceful disciples within the Sangha –

གུས་པ་ཆེན་པོས་ཕྱག་འཚལ་སྐྱབས་སུ་མཆི།

GU PA	CHEN POE	CHAG TSHAL	KYAB SU CHI
reverence, respect and devotion	*great, with*	*make salutation*	*go for refuge*

With great devotion we make obeisance and take refuge in you.

Noble Chenrezi, the embodiment of compassion, and Vajrapani and all the ocean of Bodhisattvas along with the numberless peaceful the disciples of the Sangha – with great devotion we make obeisance and take refuge in you.

ཞེས་ལན་བདུན་ནམ་གསུམ་བརྗོད། [Say the above verse seven or three times.]

OFFERINGS

མཆོད་ཡོན་མེ་ཏོག་བདུག་སྤོས་མར་མེ་དྲི།

CHOD YON	ME TOG	DUG POE	MAR ME	DRI
drinking water	*flowers*	*incense*	*lamp*	*perfumed water*

Drinking water, flowers, incense, lamps, perfumed water,

ཞལ་ཟས་སིལ་སྙན་ལ་སོགས་དངོས་བཤམས་དང་།

ZHAL ZAE	SIL NYAN	LA SOG	NGO	SHAM	DANG
food	*music, cymbals*	*the rest*	*actually*	*displayed*	*and*

Food, music and all that we actually display, as well as

གཟུངས་རིག་མོས་པ་ལས་བྱུང་མཆོད་པའི་སྤྲིན།

ZUNG RIG	MOE PA	LAE	JUNG	CHO PAI	TRIN
dharani, long mantra	*devotion, desire*	*from*	*arising*	*offering*	*cloud*

A cloud of offerings arising from devoted recitation of the dharani

ནམ་མཁའ་གང་བར་དམིགས་ཏེ་གུས་པས་མཆོད།

NAM KHA	GANG WAR	MIG	TE	GU PAE	CHOD
sky	*filling*	*imagine*	*then*	*reverence*	*offer*

Fill the sky. We imagine all this and offer it with devotion.

Drinking water, flowers, incense, lamps, perfumed water, food, music and all that we actually display, as well as a cloud of offerings arising from devoted recitation of the dharani fill the sky. We imagine all this and offer it with devotion.

CONFESSION

འཁོར་ཚེ་ཐོག་མ་མེད་ནས་ད་ལྟའི་བར།

KHOR	TSHE	THOG MA ME	NAE	DAN TAI	BAR
samsara	*lives*	*beginningless*	*from*	*now*	*until*

From beginingless time up until now, in all our lives in samsara,

རང་བཞིན་བཅས་པའི་སྡིག་ལྟུང་བགྱིས་སོ་འཚལ།

RANG ZHIN	CHE PAI	DIG	TUNG	GYI SO TSHAL
*intrinsic**	*with rule#*	*sins*	*falls, broken vows*	*which we have done*

*things that are bad in themselves, like killing
#things which we are committed not to do e.g. no sex for monks or nuns.

We have broken our vows and have acted in ways that are intrinsically wrong and also made errors as defined by rules.

གནོང་འགྱོད་དྲག་པོས་མཐོལ་བཤགས་སླན་ཆད་ཀྱང་།

NONG	GYOD	DRAG POE	THOL	SHAG	LAN CHAE	KYANG
shame	*regret, sadness*	*intense*	*with hands held at heart*	*confess, request forgiveness*	*future, from now on*	*also*

With intense shame and regret we humbly confess this and request to be forgiven.

མི་བགྱིད་སྡོམ་སེམས་བརྟན་པོས་ཡང་དག་བཟུང་།

MI GYI	DOM SEM	TAN POE	YANG DAG	ZUNG
not do	*vows, obligation, moral system*	*firm, by*	*purely*	*hold, keep*

From now on we will not act in these ways but shall firmly maintain the purity of our moral obligations.

From beginingless time up until now, in all our lives in samsara, we have broken our vows and have acted in ways that are intrinsically wrong and also made errors as defined by rules. With intense shame and regret we humbly confess this and request to be forgiven. From now on we will not act in these ways but shall firmly maintain the purity of our moral obligations.

REJOICING AND REQUESTING

འཇིག་རྟེན་འཇིག་རྟེན་ལས་འདས་རང་གཞན་གྱི།

JIG TEN	JIG TEN	LAE	DAE	RANG	ZHAN	GYI
worldly (such as offerings, non-violence)	*world (emptiness, wisdom)*	*from*	*going*	*self*	*others*	*of*

All the virtues, both worldly and non-worldly, collected by ourselves and all others

དུས་གསུམ་དགེ་ཚོགས་ཀུན་ལ་རྗེས་ཡི་རང་།

DU	SUM	GE	TSHOG	KUN	LA	JE YI RANG
times (past, present, future)	*three*	*virtues*	*collected*	*all*	*to*	*admire, rejoice with*

(rejoicing in the virtue collected by others)

In the three times make us rejoice and feel happy.

ཕྱོགས་བཅུའི་འཇིག་རྟེན་སྒྲོན་མ་གང་བཞུགས་རྣམས།

CHOG	CHUI	JIG TEN	DRON MA	GANG	ZHUG	NAM
directions (i.e. everywhere)	*ten*	*world (Buddhas and Bodhisattvas)*	*lamp*	*whoever*	*staying*	*(plural)*

All you lamps of the world staying in the ten directions,

བླ་མེད་ཆོས་ཀྱི་འོད་ཟེར་བསྐོར་བར་བསྐུལ།

LA ME	CHO	KYI	OD ZER	KOR WAR	KUL
unsurpassed (mahayana)	*dharma*	*of*	*light rays, bright*	*teach, turn the wheel*	*request, beseech*

We request you to please teach the unsurpassed illuminating Dharma.

All the virtues, both worldly and non-worldly, collected by ourselves and all others in the three times make us rejoice and feel happy. All you lamps of the world staying in the ten directions, we request you to please teach the unsurpassed illuminating Dharma.

PRAYING AND DEDICATING

ལྷར་བཅས་སྐྱེ་དགུའི་མགོན་པོར་ཡུན་རིང་དུ།

LHA	CHE	KYE GUI	GON POR	YUN RING DU
gods	*with*	*sentient beings*	*protector, benefactor*	*for long time*

We pray that the Protectors of gods and sentient beings

མྱ་ངན་མི་འདའ་བཞུགས་པར་གསོལ་བ་འདེབས།

NYA NGAN MI DA	ZHUG PAR	SOL WA DEB
not pass from sorrow, not die, not enter nirvana	*stay*	*we pray*

Will remain for a long time without passing into nirvana.

འདིས་མཚོན་དགེ་བས་མ་རྒན་སེམས་ཅན་ཀུན།

DI	TSHON	GE WAE	MA GAN	SEM CHEN	KUN
by this	*example*	*virtue, by*	*old mothers**	*sentient being*	*all*

*all have been our mothers in past lives

By our virtues, including those arising from this practice, may all sentient beings, each one previously our own mother,

རྣམ་པ་ཀུན་མཁྱེན་ཡེ་ཤེས་ལ་འགོད་ཤོག།

NAM PA	KUN KHYEN	YE SHE	LA	GOD SHOG
fully	*omniscient*	*original knowing*	*to*	*must get!*

Gain fully omniscient original knowing.

We pray that the Protectors of gods and sentient beings will remain for a long time without passing into nirvana. By our virtues, including those arising from this practice, may all sentient beings, each one previously our own mother, fully gain omniscient original knowing.

ཅེས་ཚོགས་བསགས། In this way accumulate merit.

ཡོན་ལག་བདུན་པ་སྔར་བཞིན་བཏང་མཐར།

[Having done the Seven Branch Practice as before say as follows:]

PRAYER

གདན་འཛོམས་རྒྱལ་བ་སྲས་བཅས་སྤྱན་སྔ་རུ།

DAN DZOM	GYAL WA	SAE	CHE	CHAN NGA RU
all present	*(Amitabha)*	*Bodhisattvas*	*together with*	*before*

Before you the Victor and all Bodhisattvas present here

ཕྱག་མཆོད་ཐུགས་དམ་བསྐུལ་སོགས་བགྱིས་པའི་མཐུས།

CHAG	CHOD	THUG DAM KUL	SOG	GYI PAI	THU
make salutation	*make offerings*	*move their minds*	*and so on*	*doing*	*power*

We bow and make offerings to move your minds. By the power of this

བདག་སོགས་གནས་སྐབས་བསམ་པ་ཀུན་འགྲུབ་ཅིང་།

DAG SOG	NAE KAB	SAM PA	KUN	DRUB CHING
we	*temporary, for the time being*	*thoughts, wishes*	*all*	*accomplishing*

May we be blessed that in the short term all our wishes are fulfilled, and

མཐར་ཐུག་རྫོགས་བྱང་ཐོབ་པར་བྱིན་གྱིས་རློབས།

THAR THUG	DZOG	JANG	THOB PAR	JIN GYI LOB
ultimate	*perfect,*	*bodhi, awakening*	*gain*	*bless*

Ultimately we gain perfect enlightenment.

Before you the Victor and all Bodhisattvas present here we bow and make offerings to move your minds. By the power of this may we be blessed with the immediate fulfilment of our wishes and the ultimate achievement of enlightenment.

གཞན་ཡང་རིས་མེད་རྒྱལ་བསྟན་དར་ཞིང་རྒྱས།

ZHAN YANG	RI ME	GYAL TAN	DAR ZHING	GYE
moreover	*of all schools*	*Victor's doctrines*	*vastly*	*spread*

Moreover may there be the blessing of all the schools of the Victor's doctrines spreading widely and

བསྟན་དགྲ་ནག་ཕྱོགས་ཀྲོལ་བ་མཐའ་དག་ཞི།

TAN	DRA	NAG CHOG	GOL WA	THA DAG	ZHI
doctrine	*enemies*	*wrong way, harmful things*	*strife, combat*	*fully, all*	*pacified*

All enemies of the doctrine and all negative paths and strife being fully pacified.

བསྟན་འཛིན་དམ་པའི་མགོན་རྣམས་ཞབས་པད་བརྟན།

TAN	DZIN	DAM PAI	GON	NAM	ZHAB PAE	TAN
doctrine	*holders*	*holy, excellent*	*protector, benefactor*	*(plural)*	*feet (i.e. life)*	*be firm*

May the lives of the excellent Protectors who maintain the holy doctrine be firm and

བསྟན་རྩ་དགེ་འདུན་འཕེལ་བར་བྱིན་གྱིས་རློབས།

TAN	TSA	GEN DUN	PHEL WAR	JIN GYI LOB
doctrine	*root*	*sangha*	*increase, as*	*bless*

May the Sangha, the root of the doctrine, increase.

Moreover may there be the blessing of all the schools of the Victor's doctrines spreading widely and all enemies of the doctrine and all negative paths and strife being fully pacified. May the lives of the excellent Protectors who maintain the holy doctrine be firm and may the Sangha, the root of the doctrine, increase.

དེས་མཐུས་ཡངས་པའི་རྒྱལ་ཁམས་བདེ་ཞིང་སྐྱིད།

DE	THU	YANG PAI	GYAL KHAM	DE ZHING	KYID
by that	*power*	*vast*	*kingdom (Dewachen)*	*happy*	*joyous*

By the power of this blessing, may the vast joyful kingdom

སྐྱེ་དགུ་ཐམས་ཅད་ལེགས་ལམ་དཔལ་ལ་སྦྱོར།

KYE GU	THAM CHE	LEG	LAM	PAL	LA	JOR
beings	*all*	*good*	*way*	*very fine*	*to*	*do, use, join*

Be enjoyed by all beings as their glorious excellent path.

ཕུན་ཚོགས་རྫོགས་ལྡན་ཟླ་བ་གསར་འཆར་བའི།

PHUN TSHOG	DZOG DEN	DA WA	SAR	CHAR WAI
all good things, everything pleasing	*complete (the happy first period of the aeon)*	*moon*	*new*	*rising*

With every felicity rising like the moon at the beginning of the aeon

དགེ་མཚན་ས་གསུམ་སྣང་བར་བྱིན་གྱིས་རློབས།

GE	TSHAN	SA	SUM	NANG WAR	JIN GYI LOB
virtue, auspicious	*sign, symbol*	*level (above, on, below the earth, i.e. everywhere)*	*three*	*appearance*	*bless*

May all that appears upon the earth and above and below it be the manifestation of virtue.

By the power of this blessing, may the vast joyful kingdom be enjoyed by all beings as their glorious excellent path. With every felicity rising

like the moon at the beginning of the aeon may all that appears upon the earth and above and below it be the manifestation of virtue.

ཞེས་གསོལ་བ་བཏབས། [Having prayed in this way,]

CONFESSION

གང་འདིར་བདག་ཅག་སྤྱོད་པ་དམན་པ་དང་།

GANG	DIR	DAG CHAG	CHO PA	MAN PA	DANG
whoever	*here*	*we*	*actions*	*low*	*and*

(This refers to mistakes made during practice.)

We have performed poorly and

དེ་བཞིན་རྫས་དང་བསམ་པ་མ་དག་སོགས།

DE ZHIN	DZE	DANG	SAM PA	MA DAG	SOG
similarly	*things*	*and*	*thoughts, ideas*	*not pure*	*and so on*

Have entertained objects and ideas that are not pure.

ནོར་ཞིང་འཁྲུལ་པ་ཅི་དང་ཅི་མཆིས་པ།

NOR ZHING	TRUL PA	CHI	DANG	CHI CHI PA
making mistakes	*confused*	*(plural)*	*and*	*whatever we have done*

Whatever mistakes and confusions we are responsible for

བརྩེ་ལྡན་རྣམས་ཀྱི་སྤྱན་སྔར་སྙིང་ནས་འཆགས།

TSE DAN NAM	KYI	CHAN NGAR	NYING	NAE	CHAG
those who are compassionate (Amitabha and other Buddhas and Bodhisattvas)	*of*	*in front*	*heart*	*from*	*confess*

We confess wholeheartedly in front of you.

We have performed poorly and have entertained objects and ideas that are not pure. We make heartfelt confession in front of you for all our mistakes and confusions.

ཞེས་གནོང་པ་བཤགས། [Confess your mistakes in this way]

ASPIRATION

དེ་ལྟར་ལེགས་གསུང་མདོ་ཡི་རྗེས་འབྲངས་ཏེ།

DE TAR	LEG	SUNG	DO	YI	JE TRANG	TE
like that	*well*	*spoken*	*sutra (the 'Od-mDo spoken by Shakyamuni)*	*of*	*following*	*thus, as*

Arranged in accordance with the well-spoken sutra,

ཞིང་མཆོག་སྦྱོང་བའི་ཆོ་ག་ཚུལ་བཞིན་དུ།

ZHING	CHOG	JONG WAI	CHO GA	TSHUL	ZHIN DU
realm	*excellent, supreme*	*coming*	*puja, ritual practice*	*method, system*	*according to*

This is the ritual method for reaching the excellent realm.

བསྒྲུབས་པའི་བསོད་ནམས་ཟླ་ལྟར་དཀར་བ་དེས།

DRUB PAI	SO NAM	DA	TAR	KAR WA	DE
practice	*merit*	*moon*	*as*	*white*	*by that*

(This practice creates enough merit for us to be born in Dewachen)

Practising in this way generates merit as white as the moon. Through this

འགྲོ་ཀུན་བདེ་ཆེན་ཞིང་དུ་སྐྱེ་བར་ཤོག།

DRO	KUN	DE CHEN ZHING	DU	KYE WAR	SHOG
beings	*all*	*Sukhavati, Dewachen*	*in*	*born*	*may they be, they must be*

May all beings be born in Dewachen.

This is the ritual method for reaching the excellent realm arranged according to the well-spoken sutra. Practising in this way generates merit as white as the moon. Through this may all beings be born in Dewachen.

ནམ་ཞིག་ཚེ་འདིའི་འདུ་བྱེད་སྡུད་པའི་ཚེ།

NAM ZHIG	TSHE	DI	DU JED	DUE PAI	TSHE
when	*life*	*this*	*compounded*	*gather in*	*that time*

(The constructs of our self and of our world are fading for us as we die.)

When this life is ending

བདེ་གཤེགས་སྐུ་ཡི་སྣང་བ་ལེགས་ཤར་ནས།

DE SHEG	KU	YI	NANG WA	LEG	SHAR	NE
Happily Gone (Amitabha)	*body*	*of*	*appearance, idea*	*well*	*arise (in my mind)*	*then*

May the body of the Happily Gone appear clearly for us.

དེ་མཐུས་ནད་གཅོད་སྡུག་བསྔལ་མི་འབྱུང་ཞིང་།

DE	THU	NAD	CHOD	DUG NGAL	MI	JUNG ZHING
that	*power, by (seeing Amitabha)*	*sickness*	*cut, end*	*suffering (of death)*	*not*	*arising*

By his power may all sickness cease and suffering not arise.

དགའ་ཞིང་སྤྲོ་བའི་ངང་ལ་འཕོ་བར་ཤོག།

GA ZHING	**TRO WAI**	**NGANG**	**LA**	**PHO WAR**	**SHOG**
happily	*happy, joyful*	*state*	*in*	*go (out from the body)*	*may we*

In a happy, joyful state we depart, leaving our body behind.

May the body of the Happily Gone appear clearly for us when this life is ending. By his power may all sickness cease and suffering not arise. In a happy, joyful state we depart, leaving our body behind.

ཤི་འཕོས་སྐྱེ་སྲིད་གཞན་གྱིས་མ་ཆོད་པར།

SHI PO	**KYE SI**	**ZHAN**	**GYI**	**MA**	**CHOD PAR**
when die	*birth (in samsara)*	*other*	*by*	*not*	*inhibited*

At death, without being interrupted by another birth in samsara

བདེ་ལྡན་ཞིང་དུ་པདྨའི་སྙིང་པོ་ལ།

DE DAN	**ZHING**	**DU**	**PAE MAI**	**NYING PO**	**LA**
happy	*realm*	*in*	*lotus*	*heart*	*in*

In the heart of a lotus in the realm of Dewachen

བརྫུས་ཏེ་སྐྱེས་ནས་རྒྱལ་བ་འོད་དཔག་མེད།

DZU TE	**KYE**	**NAE**	**GYAL WA**	**O PA ME**
magically	*born*	*then*	*Victor*	*Amitabha*

May we be miraculously born with the Victor Amitabha

དུས་ཀུན་མཐོང་བས་རབ་དགས་འཚོ་བར་ཤོག།

DU	**KUN**	**THONG WAE**	**RAB GAE**	**TSHO WAR**	**SHOG**
time	*all*	*see*	*very happy*	*stay, live*	*may*

Visible to us at all times so that we live very happily.

Without being interrupted by another birth in samsara at death may we be miraculously born in the heart of a lotus in the realm of Dewachen with the Victor Amitabha visible to us at all times so that we live very happily.

དེ་ལས་ཟབ་དང་རྒྱ་ཆེའི་གདམས་ངག་གི།

DE	**LAE**	**ZAB**	**DANG**	**GYA CHEI**	**DAM NGAG**	**GI**
him (Amitabha)	*from*	*deep*	*and*	*vast*	*instructions*	*of*

May we receive the ambrosia of the profound and vast instructions from him and

བདུད་རྩི་ཐོབ་ནས་རྒྱལ་སྲས་མཆོག་རྣམས་དང་།

DUD TSI	**THOB**	**NAE**	**GYAL**	**SAE**	**CHOG**	**NAM**	**DANG**
ambrosia (i.e. beneficial)	*get*	*then*	*Victor (Amitabha)*	*Bodhisattvas*	*excellent*	*(plural)*	*and*

With the Victor and the excellent Bodhisattvas

ལྷན་ཅིག་ཐེག་མཆོག་བགྲོ་བ་ལ་དབང་བས།

LHAN CHIG	**THEG CHOG**	**DRO WA**	**LA**	**WANG WAE**
together	*mahayana*	*discuss*	*as*	*empowered to allowed to*

May we be permitted to discuss the mahayana doctrines, and thus

ཐོས་པའི་ཆུ་གཏེར་ཉིན་བཞིན་འཕེལ་བར་ཤོག།

THO PAI	**CHU**	**TER**	**NYIN**	**ZHIN**	**PHEL WAR**	**SHOG**
hear	*water (i.e. ocean — very vast)*	*treasure*	*daily*	*as*	*increase*	*we must*

Hearing an ocean of teachings may our knowledge increase daily.

May we receive the ambrosia of the profound and vast instructions from him and be permitted to discuss the mahayana doctrines with the Victor and the excellent Bodhisattvas. In this way, by hearing an ocean of teachings may our knowledge increase daily.

སྐྱེ་མ་ཐག་ཏུ་མངོན་ཤེས་སྟོབས་ཐོབ་སྟེ།

KYE	**MA THAG TU**	**NGON SHE**	**TOB**	**THOB**	**TE**
birth	*immediately*	*foreknowledge*	*power*	*get*	*when*

Gaining foreknowledge and power immediately at birth,

བསམ་ཡས་ཞིང་དུ་སངས་རྒྱས་བལྟ་བ་དང་།

SAM YAE	**ZHING**	**DU**	**SANG GYE**	**TA WA**	**DANG**
beyond thoughts, numberless	*realms*	*in*	*Buddhas*	*see*	*and*

May we see the Buddhas who reside in inconceivable realms and

བསྙེན་བཀུར་བྱ་ཕྱིར་ཐོགས་པ་མེད་རྒྱུ་ཞིང་།

NYEN KUR	**JA**	**CHIR**	**THOG PA ME**	**GYU ZHING**
respectful service	*do*	*in order to*	*unimpeded, easily*	*going*

May we travel to them without impediment in order to render them respectful service

རྒྱལ་བ་ཀུན་གྱི་ཆོས་མཛོད་འཛིན་པར་ཤོག།

GYAL WA	**KUN**	**GI**	**CHO**	**DZOD**	**DZIN PAR**	**SHOG**
Victors	*all*	*of*	*Dharma*	*treasure, store*	*hold (i.e not forget)*	*may we*

And to access the Dharma treasures of all the Victors.

Gaining foreknowledge and power immediately at birth, may we see the Buddhas who reside in inconceivable realms and may we travel to them without impediment in order to render them respectful service and to access the Dharma treasures of all the Victors.

རླབས་ཆེན་ཞིང་གི་འབྱོར་བ་མཐོང་ནས་སུ།

LAB CHEN	**ZHING**	**GI**	**JOR WAR**	**THONG**	**NAE**	**SU**
great blessing	*realm*	*of*	*wealth, collection*	*see*	*then*	*at*
	(what its system is; how it is arranged)					

Seeing how well arranged is this great realm of blessing, and

རྣམ་དག་སྨོན་ལམ་དེ་འདྲའི་རྗེས་སློབ་ཅིང་།

NAM DAG	**MON LAM**	**DEN DRAI**	**JE**	**LOB CHING**
very pure (see Appendix I)	*aspiration*	*like that*	*after*	*studying*

Learning to develop the pure aspiration that gave rise to it,

མ་དག་ཞིང་དུ་རྒུད་པས་ཉེན་པ་ཡི།

MA DAG	**ZHING**	**DU**	**GUD PAE**	**NYEN PA**	**YI**
impure	*realm*	*in*	*trouble, deterioration*	*troubled, pained*	*of*
(samsara's root is ignorance and sin)					

For all beings who are troubled by the difficulties of the impure realms

འགྲོ་ཀུན་སྣ་ཚོགས་ཐབས་ཀྱིས་འདྲེན་པར་ཤོག།

DRO	**KUN**	**NA TSHOG**	**THAB**	**KYI**	**DREN PAR**	**SHOG**
beings	*all*	*many different*	*methods*	*by*	*guide (to a pure realm and enlightenment)*	*may we*

May we guide them with whatever methods are suitable.

Seeing how well arranged is this great realm of blessing, and learning to develop the pure aspiration that gave rise to it, may we guide all beings who are troubled by the difficulties of the impure realms using whatever methods are suitable.

མདོར་ན་ས་བཅུ་ལམ་ལྔའི་སྤང་རྟོགས་ཀུན།

DOR NA	**SA**	**CHU**	**LAM**	**NGAI**	**PANG**	**TOG**	**KUN**
in brief	*stages*	*ten*	*ways*	*five*	*things to be abandoned*	*things to be awakened to*	*all*
	(the stages and paths of a bodhisattva)						

In brief, achieving all the discardings and awakenings of the ten stages and five ways, and

ཕུལ་བྱུང་ཞིང་གི་ཁྱད་པར་ལ་བརྟེན་ནས།

PHUL JUNG *wonderful, perfect* **ZHING** *realm* **GI** *of* **KHYAE PAR** *special* **LA** *to* *(i.e. spiritual progress comes easily there)* **TEN** *power, rely on* **NAE** *then*

With the support of this uniquely wonderful realm,

མཐོང་བའི་ཆོས་ལ་མིག་འཕྲུལ་བཞིན་བགྲོད་དེ།

THONG WAI *seeing* **CHO** *dharma, phenomena* **LA** *to* **MIG TRUL** *miracle (i.e. instantaneously)* **ZHIN** *like* **DROD** *go* **DE** *that, thus*

May we miraculously travel to any site of dharma that we see.

བླ་མེད་མགོན་པོ་ཁྱེད་འདྲར་འགྱུར་བར་ཤོག།

LA ME *unexcelled* **GON PO** *protector* **KHYE** *you* **DRAR** *similar to* **GYUR WAR** *become* **SHOG** *may*

Thus may we become like you, our unexcelled Protector.

In brief, achieving all the discardings and awakenings of the ten stages and five ways, and with the support of this uniquely wonderful realm, may we miraculously travel to any site of Dharma that we see. Thus, may we become like you, our unexcelled protector.

ཅེས་དང་སྨོན་ལམ་གཞན་ཡང་བཀླག་པར་བྱའོ།

[At this point you can also recite other aspirations.]

ཚར་གྲངས་གསོག་ན་ཚོགས་བསགས་གསོལ་འདེབས་ལོ་ན་ལ་ཚར་གྲངས་བཟུང་ན་ནུང་མོད། ཆོག་ཡོངས་སུ་རྫོགས་པ་ལ་གྲངས་བཟུང་ན་བདེ་བ་ཅན་དུ་སྐྱེ་བའི་རྒྱུ་བཞི་ཚ་ཚང་བའི་སྙིང་ནས་ནུས་པ་ཐོན་པར་སྣང་བས་ཤིན་ཏུ་ལེགས། དེ་ལྟར་ཞག་བདུན་ལེགས་པར་རྩེ་གཅིག་ཏུ་འབད་ན་ངེས་པར་བདེ་བ་ཅན་དུ་སྐྱེ་བའི་ཚུལ་ནི་དྲི་མ་མེད་པའི་ལུང་དང་རིགས་པ་ལས་ཤེས་པར་མཛོད་ཅིག།ཅེས་ཚིག་ཉུང་ལ་དྲིལ་བས་ཁྱེར་བདེ། དོན་འདུས་ལ་གསལ་བས་གོ་སླ། གདུལ་བྱ་མཆོག་དམན་མེད་པས་སློ་ཡངས། ཁུངས་མདོ་སྡེ་དང་འབྲེལ་བས་བྱིན་རླབས་ཆེ། ཕྱག་ལེན་བསྡུས་ཆོག་ཏུ་བཀོད་པས་འཇུག་པ་བདེ་བའི་འོད་ཆོག་འདི་ཡང་བློ་གསལ་བསྟན་འཛིན་གྱིས་དར་དཀར་གྱི་སྐྱེས་དང་བཅས་ཏེ་བསྐུར་བ་ལྟར། འཇིགས་མེད་བསྟན་པའི་ཉི་མས་ལྷུགས་སྤྱག་དབྱུག་པའི་ཉ་བའི་ཤུན་གསེབ་ཏུ་བྲིས་པ་དགེ་ཞིང་བཀྲ་ཤིས། །།

If doing intensively then the refuge practice[2] and the Seven Branch Practice for accumulating merits[3] should be repeated many times.

If this whole ritual is done then one will fully gain the four causes for being born in Dewachen (see Appendix II). This will become clear through practice. You should know that if you practise in this way, strongly and one-pointedly for seven days then you will be born in Dewachen. So it is said in the Buddha's doctrines, and is known by true awareness.

This practice has few words and so is easy to do. With condensed meaning it is clear and easy to understand, and it can be practised by both excellent and ordinary disciples.

It is joined with (i.e. taken from and in harmony with) authentic sutras and so has great blessing.

This ritual for Amitabha is easy to do, being composed in a clear and evident system.

It was requested by *bLo-gSal bsTan-'Dzin* who offered a white scarf of silk. It was written by *'Jigs-Med bsTan-Pa'i Nyi-Ma* during a break in meditation on the full-moon day of the ninth month of the Iron-Tiger year [1890 CE].

Notes

1. སྟོབས་བཅུ་ The ten powers of a Bodhisattva: reflection, superior aspiration, application, discerning insight, prayer and aspiration, vehicle, conduct, transformation, enlightenment, turning the wheel of Dharma
2. *See* Page 212 with heading "Refuge".
3. *See* Page 213 with heading "The Seven Branch Practice"

བདེ་སྨོན་བསྡུས་པ་བཞུགས་སོ།
The Brief Prayer of Aspiration for Dewachen

བཅོམ་ལྡན་འདས་འོད་དཔག་མེད་ལ་ཕྱག་འཚལ་ལོ།

CHOM	**DEN**	**DAE**	**OE PA ME**	**LA**	**CHAG TSHAL LO**
finished all sin	*possessing all good qualities*	*going from samsara*	*Amitabha*	*to*	*salutation, obeisance*

Salutation to the Perfect Amitabha.

1. RECOLLECTING THE QUALITIES OF DEWACHEN

ཡང་ཡང་དྲན་ནོ་ཞིང་ཁམས་བདེ་བ་ཅན།

YANG YANG	**DRAN NO**	**ZHING KHAM**	**DE WA CHAN**
again and again	*remember*	*realm*	*Sukhavati, happiness*

Again and again we remember the realm of Great Happiness.

སྙིང་ནས་དྲན་ནོ་འདྲེན་པ་འོད་དཔག་མེད།

NYING	**NAE**	**DRAN NO**	**DREN PA**	**O PA ME**
heart	*from*	*remember*	*guide, leader*	*Amitabha, Infinite Light*

From the depths of our hearts we remember our guide, Infinite Light.

རྩེ་གཅིག་དྲན་ནོ་རྒྱལ་སྲས་རྒྱ་མཚོའི་འཁོར།

TSE CHIG	**DRAN NO**	**GYAL**	**SE**	**GYAM TSHOI**	**KHOR**
one-pointed	*remember*	*Victor*	*Bodhisattvas*	*ocean's*	*retinue*

One-pointedly we remember the Victor and his ocean-like circle of Bodhisattvas.

བྱིན་གྱིས་རློབས་ཤིག་སྐྱབས་མེད་སྐྱོབ་པའི་ཚོགས།

JIN GYI LO SHIG	**KYAB ME**	**KYOB PAI**	**TSHOG**
bless us!	*those who are without protection*	*protector*	*hosts (Amitabha and his circle)*

May this gathering of protectors of the unprotected grant us blessing.

Salutation to the perfect Amitabha. Again and again we remember the realm of Great Happiness. From the depths of our hearts we remember our guide, Infinite Light. One-pointedly we remember the Victor and his ocean-like circle of Bodhisattvas. Protectors of the unprotected, please gather here and bless us!

2. ACCUMULATION OF MERIT

ཐུགས་རྗེའི་བདག་ཉིད་མགོན་པོ་ཁྱེད་རྣམས་ལ།

THUG JEI	DAG NYID	GON PO	KHYE	NAM	LA
compassion's	*master, embodiment*	*protector, benefactor*	*you (Amitabha and his circle)*	*(plural)*	*to*

To you our benefactors, the embodiment of compassion,

གུས་པའི་ཕྱག་འཚལ་མཆོད་སྤྲིན་རྒྱ་མཚོས་མཆོད།

GU PAI	CHAG TSHAL	CHOD	TRIN	GYAM TSOE	CHOD
reverent	*salutation*	*offering*	*clouds*	*ocean*	*offer*

We make devoted salutation and offer oceans of offering clouds.

སྡིག་ལྟུང་ཀུན་བཤགས་དགེ་ལ་རྗེས་ཡི་རང་།

DIG	TUNG	KUN	SHAG	GE	LA	JE YI RANG
sins	*falls, lapses*	*all*	*confess*	*virtue (done by all the Buddhas and beings)*	*to*	*sympathetically rejoice*

We confess all our sins and lapses and rejoice in all virtue done by others.

ཆོས་འཁོར་བསྐོར་བཞིན་མྱ་ངན་མི་འདར་གསོལ།

CHO	KHOR	KOR	ZHIN	NYA NGAN	MI	DAR	SOL
Dharma (teach the Dharma)	*chakra*	*turn*	*also*	*sorrow*	*not (not die)*	*pass*	*pray, request*

We request you to teach the Dharma and not to enter nirvana.

To you our benefactors, the embodiment of compassion, we make devoted salutation and offer oceans of offering clouds. We confess all our sins and lapses and rejoice in all virtue done by others. We request you to teach the Dharma and not to leave us for nirvana.

3. DEVELOPING BODHICITTA

བདག་གིས་མཁའ་མཉམ་འགྲོ་བའི་དོན་སླད་དུ།

DAG	GI	KHA	NYAM	DRO WAI	DON	LAD DU
me	*by*	*sky*	*equal*	*beings*	*benefit*	*for the sake of*

For the sake of benefitting beings equalling the extent of the sky

ཡང་དག་རྫོགས་པའི་བྱང་ཆུབ་བསྒྲུབ་བྱའི་ཕྱིར།

YANG DAG	DZOG PAI	JANG CHUB	DRUB	JAI	CHIR
pure and perfect	*complete*	*bodhi, enlightenment*	*attain*	*do*	*in order to*

So that they may attain complete and perfect enlightenment,

སངས་རྒྱས་ཞིང་ཁམས་ཡོངས་སུ་སྦྱོང་བ་ཡི།

SANG GYE ZHING KHAM YONG SU JONG WA YI
Buddha realm fully produced of
(by their great merit, see appendix I*)*

Those who produced complete buddha realms must

རྣམ་ཐར་སྨོན་ལམ་རྒྱ་མཚོ་རྫོགས་གྱུར་ཅིག།

NAM THAR MON LAM GYAM TSHO DZOG GYUR CHIG
lives of the great aspiration ocean complete must become

Inspire our vast aspiration to be just like them!

For the sake of benefitting beings equalling the extent of the sky so that they may attain complete and perfect enlightenment, those who produced complete buddha realms must inspire our vast aspiration to be just like them!

4. DEDICATION AND ASPIRATION

འདིས་མཚོན་དགེ་བས་བདག་སོགས་ཡིད་ཅན་ཀུན།

DI TSHON GE WAE DA SO YI CHAN KUN
by this sign, example virtue, by we sentient beings all
(the merit gained from this practice)

By our virtue arising from this practice and all other causes may all beings be born

ཕྱི་མ་དག་པའི་ཞིང་ཁམས་བདེ་བ་ཅན།

CHI MA DA PAI ZHING KHAM DE WA CHEN
next, later (life) pure realm Sukhavati, Happy

In their next life in the pure realm of Dewachen

རྨད་བྱུང་ངོ་མཚར་བཀོད་པས་རབ་མཛེས་པར།

MAD JUNG NGO TSHAR KOE PAE RAB DZE PAR
wonderful amazing built, constructed very beautiful

Which is amazingly beautiful in its truly wonderful design.

སྐྱེས་ནས་ཐེག་མཆོག་དགའ་སྟོན་མྱོང་བར་ཤོག། །།

KYE NE THEG CHOG GA TON NYONG WAR SHOG
born then vehicle excellent (Amitabha's doctrines) joyous festival experience may we

Then may they experience the joyous festival of the excellent Mahayana.

By our virtue arising from this practice and all other causes may all beings be born in their next life in the pure realm of Dewachen which is amazingly beautiful in its truly wonderful design. Then may they experience the joyous festival of the excellent Mahayana.

[These four stanzas are the four causes of being born in Dewachen. See appendix 2]

ཅེས་པའང་དགེ་བའི་བཤེས་གཉེན་ཨོ་ཌི་ཡ་ནའི་ངོར་འཇིགས་མེད་བསྟན་པའི་ཉི་མས་སོ།།

[At the request of his virtuous friend called Oddiyana this was written by 'Jig-Med bsTan-Pa'i Nyi-Ma.]

ASPIRATION

འདི་ནས་ནུབ་ཀྱི་ཕྱོགས་རོལ་ན།

DI	NE	NUB	KYI	CHOG ROL	NA
here	*from*	*west*	*of*	*direction*	*in*

Far to the west of here

འོད་དཔག་མེད་པའི་ཞིང་ཁམས་ཡོད།

OE PA ME PAI	ZHING KHAM	YOE
Amitabha, Infinite Light	*Pure Land*	*is*

Is the pure land of Buddha Infinite Light.

སུ་ཞིག་དེ་ཡི་མཚན་འཛིན་པ།

SU ZHIG	DE	YI	TSHAN	DZIN PA
whoever	*that*	*of*	*name*	*remembers, holds in mind*

May whoever remembers his name

ཞིང་མཆོག་དེ་རུ་སྐྱེ་བར་ཤོག།

ZHING	CHOG	DE RU	KYE WAR	SHOG
realm	*best*	*there*	*born*	*may*

Be born there in his supreme pure land.

Far to the west of here is the pure land of Buddha Infinite Light. May whoever remembers his name be born there in his supreme pure land.

APPENDIX I

During a kalpa aeon long ago in the universe called Countless Worlds, *Mi-mJed 'Jig-rTen-Gyi-Khams,* the Universal Emperor Raja Chakravartin, was *rTsibs-Kyi-Mi-Khyud,* Wheel Rim. He had one thousand and twenty-two queens and each queen bore him one son. Each son had two male assistants and one female assistant.

The Raja Chakravartin had many ministers and they advised him that although the kingdom was very large and contained everything, it was impermanent and was bound to decline one day. They told him that there would be no financial resources available for going to a good place for their next lives.

The King listened to this advice from his ministers and then took the necessary action. With his queens, sons and ministers he approached the Buddha Ratna Garba, *Rin-Chen sNying-Po,* Precious Essence and took refuge and developed the bodhicitta altruistic intention towards enlightenment. Raja Chakravartin offered all that was under his power. He offered his wives and his sons and all his wealth, and similarly his sons' assistants and their mothers. All the others present made offerings of whatever they possessed, giving even their own bodies.

Buddha Ratna Garbha gave them bodhisattva ordination. He told them that now they had started to develop bodhicitta altruism and that they would get joy from this and would practise it further in the future. The King, Raja Chakravartin *rTsibs-Kyi-Mi-Khyud,* said, *"From today I will fully practise the deeds of a Bodhisattva and will keep my vows so that as a result in the future my realm will be the very highest most valuable place. Moreover, whoever remembers me and my name and realm or hears of them will not be born again but will come to my realm. If this does not occur then I will not become a Buddha."*

He acted according to that promise and kept his vows and then he became Buddha Amitabha (Opagme) with the realm of Sukhavati (Dewachen).

Why is it that he should gain the highest realm and that those who hear of it will go there? The reason is that all the Buddhas have formerly made and developed their altruistic intention towards enlightenment. When they did this they offered some flowers or jewels to the Buddhas. But Raja Chakravartin *rTsibs-Kyi-Mi-Khyud,* offered all his possessions, his kingdom, his queens and sons, even his own body, and so he made the highest offering. Moreover in his vow, his aspiration was vast, stating that whoever should hear of and remember him would arrive in his realm. His one thousand and twenty-two sons will become the one thousand and twenty-two Buddhas of the present Bhadrakalpa, the Good Aeon. The fourth of these Buddhas is our doctrine-giver, Lord Buddha, Sakyamuni. The mothers of each of his sons will be the mothers of the one thousand and twenty-two Buddhas. The two male assistants of each of the sons will become these Buddhas' chief assistants just as Sariputra and Maudgalayana were for Buddha Sakyamuni. The female assistants of the sons will be the stepmothers of each of the Buddhas, just as Prajapati Gotami was for Buddha Sakyamuni.

All details regarding these matters can be found in the Arya Bhadra Kalpa Mahayana Sutra, which gives information regarding the one thousand and twenty-two Buddhas including Buddha Shakyamuni. The Amitabha Vyuha Sutra gives a general outline of these occurrences.

APPENDIX II

The four causes for being born in Dewachen are as follows:

i) Without knowing of the good qualities, organisation and arrangements of Dewachen, people would feel no desire to go there at the end of this or future lives. For if one does not know whether Dewachen is good or bad, pleasant or unpleasant why would one try to go there? Therefore, the qualities of Dewachen must first be known, and these are briefly listed in the section of this text headed *Imagining Dewachen*[1] and in more detail in the section headed *The First Description* at the beginning of the Dechen Monlam prayer [2].

ii) If someone wishes to travel to another country she must make the necessary preparations to finance and organise her trip. Similarly, one who wishes to go to Dewachen must have the necessary 'fare' — her vast accumulations of virtues. Therefore, in order to collect these virtues The Seven Branch Practice[3] is given here and in the Dechen Monlam[4]. All these branches or parts should be practised very strongly and deeply and thus virtue will be generated. Without virtue one cannot reach Dewachen.

iii) Without generating the altruistic intention towards enlightenment (bodhicitta) one cannot reach Dewachen. No mention of Dewachen can be found in the Hinayana texts, since bodhicitta must be developed to go there and the development of bodhicitta is not found in the Hinayana texts. *The Development of Bodhicitta* is in this section and in the Dechen Monlam[5].

iv) In the first three causes, virtues have been collected by visualising the realm of Amitabha and its qualities in the first, by making The Seven Branch Practice in the second, and by developing bodhicitta in the third. As the fourth cause we dedicate whatever good results come from these virtues to all sentient beings. This is done in this text[6] and in the Dechen Monlam[7] which also describes the benefits they will enjoy.

Appendices written by C R Lama

Notes

1. See Imagining Dewachen, beginning on page 192
2. See The First Description, beginning on page 238
3. See The Seven Branch Practice, beginning on page 198
4. See Dechen Monlam prayer beginning on page 238
5. See Dechen Monlam prayer, beginning on page 238
6. See The Brief Prayer of Aspiration for Dewachen, beginning on page 226
7. See Dechen Monlam prayer, beginning on page 238

ཞལ་ཟས་ཚོགས་མཆོད་འབུལ་བ་ནི༔
Making Assembled Offerings of Food

ཚོགས་ཀྱི་ཞལ་ཟས་ཅི་འབྱོར་བཤམས༔

Set up whatever assembled offerings of food you have gathered.

རཾ་ཡཾ་ཁཾ་གྱིས་བསྲེགས་སྦྱངས་ཏེ༔

RAM	**YAM**	**KHAM**
fire	*air*	*water*

(By saying RAM, YAM KHAM once all impurities are burned up, blown away and washed out.)

ཨོཾ་ཨཱཿཧཱུྃ་གྱིས་བདུད་རྩིར་ན་བྱིན་གྱིས་བརླབས་ལ༔

OM	**AA**	**HUNG**
body	*speech (of Buddha)*	*mind*

(By saying OM AA HUNG three times the offerings are blessed as liberating elixir.)

དེ་ནས་ཚོགས་ལ་སྤྱན་དྲང་བ་ནི༔

Then invite the Victor and his retinue to the assembled offerings

ཕྱོགས་བཅུའི་ཞིང་ཁམས་རབ་འབྱམས་ནས༔

CHOG CHUI	**ZHING KHAM**	**RAB JAM**	**NAE**
ten directions	*realms*	*all, vast*	*from*

From infinite realms in the ten directions

རྒྱལ་བ་རྒྱ་མཚོའི་ལྷ་ཚོགས་རྣམས༔

GYAL WA	**GYAM TSHOI**	**LHA**	**TSHOG NAM**
Victor (Amitabha)	*ocean*	*gods*	*hosts*

Victor together with your ocean of deities

ལོངས་སྤྱོད་ཚོགས་ལ་སྤྱན་འདྲེན་གྱི༔

LONG CHO	**TSHOG**	**LA**	**CHEN DREN**	**GYI**
enjoyment	*assembled offerings*	*to*	*invite*	*therefore*

Are all invited to these enjoyable assembled offerings.

ཐུགས་དམ་ཚུལ་བཞིན་གཤེགས་སུ་གསོལ༔

THUG DAM	**TSHUL**	**ZHIN**	**SHEG SU SOL**
promise (to help others)	*system*	*according to*	*please come*

In accordance with your promise, please come here!

བཛྲ་ས་མ་ཡ་ཛཿཛཿ༔

BEN DZA	**SA MA YA**	**DZA**	**DZA**
vajra	*vows*	*come*	*come*

You must keep your vows! You must come here!

From infinite realms in the ten directions, Victor together with your oceans of deities are all invited to these enjoyable assembled offerings. In accordance with your promise, please come here! You must keep your vows! You must come here!

ཧྲཱིཿ རྒྱལ་བ་རྒྱ་མཚོ་འཁོར་བཅས་ལ༔

HRI	**GYAL WA**	**GYAM TSHO**	**KHOR CHE**	**LA**
seed of Amitabha	*Amitabha*	*ocean*	*with your retinue*	*to*

Hri. To you Amitabha with your oceans of Buddhas and all your circles

ཞལ་ཟས་ཚོགས་མཆོད་འབུལ་བ་ནི༔

ZHAL ZAE	**TSHOG**	**CHOD**	**BUL WA**	**NI**
food	*assembled offering*	*offering*	*make*	

We present these assembled offerings of food.

སྤོས་དང་སྨན་དང་དྲི་མཆོག་དང༔

POE	**DANG**	**MEN**	**DANG**	**DRI CHOG**	**DANG**
incense	*and*	*medicine*	*and*	*perfumes*	*and*

Incense, medicine, perfumes, and

བཟའ་བཏུང་གོས་རྒྱན་རོལ་མོ་དང༔

ZA	**TUNG**	**GO**	**GYEN**	**ROL MO**	**DANG**
food	*drink*	*clothes*	*ornaments*	*music*	*and*

Food, drink, clothes, ornaments, music, and

མར་ཐུད་ཞོ་དང་འོ་མ་ཁྲུམ༔

MAR	**THU**	**ZHO**	**DANG**	**O MA**	**TRUM**
butter	*soft cheese*	*curd*	*and*	*milk*	*cheese made from the milk of a cow that has just given birth*

Butter, soft cheese, curd, milk, and calf's cheese, along with

དཀར་གསུམ་མངར་གསུམ་མཆོད་པར་འབུལ༔

KAR	SUM	NGAR	SUM	CHO PAR	BUL
white (butter, milk, curd)	*three*	*sweets (sugar, honey, molasses)*	*three*	*offering*	*make*

The three white and the three sweet— we offer all these to you.

Hri. To you Amitabha with your oceans of Buddhas and all *your circles, we present these assembled offerings of food. Incense, medicine, perfumes, food, drink, clothes, ornaments, music, and butter, soft cheese, curd, milk, and cheese; and the three whites and the three sweets – we offer all these to you.*

འབྲས་ཆན་འབྲུ་ཆན་ཤིང་ཐོག་སོགས༔

DRE	CHAN	DRU	CHAN	SHING THOG	SOG
rice	*soft*	*grains*	*soft*	*fruit*	*and the rest*

Cooked rice, grains and fruit along with

ཟན་བཤོས་ཁུ་བའི་བྱེ་བྲག་དང༔

ZAN	SHO	KHUR WAI	JE DRAG	DANG
food, whole grain	*food in general*	*liquid food*	*many different*	*and*

Diverse whole foods, solid and liquid foods, and

བུ་རམ་སྦྲང་རྩི་ཇ་དར་དང༔

BU RAM	DRANG TSI	JA	DAR	DANG
molasses	*honey*	*tea*	*buttermilk*	*and*

Molasses, honey, tea, buttermilk and

ཁ་མངར་སྐྱུར་བ་ཚ་རྩུབ་སྣུམ༔

KHA	NGAR	KYUR WA	TSHA	TSUB	NUM
bitter	*sweet*	*sour*	*hot (like chilli)*	*intense (like garlic)*	*oil*

Bitter, sweet, sour, hot, intense, and oily tastes –

འདོད་ཡོན་སྣ་ཚོགས་མཆོད་པར་འབུལ༔

DOE YON	NA TSHOG	CHOD PAR	BUL
things that give pleasure to the senses	*many different*	*offering*	*make*

We offer all the many different items that please the senses.

བཞེས་ཏེ་དབང་དང་དངོས་གྲུབ་སྩོལ༔

ZHE	TE	WANG	DANG	NGO DRUB	TSOL
accept and eat	*then, thus*	*initiation, empowerment*	*and*	*attainment, enlightenment*	*give us*

Please accept them, then grant us empowerment and attainment.

ག་ན་ཙ་ཀྲ་པཱུ་ཙ་ཧོཿ

GA NA	**TSA KRA**	**PU TSA**	**HO**
assembled offerings	*wheel*	*puja, ritual ceremony*	*we give*

We present all these assembled offerings!

Cooked rice, grains and fruit along with diverse whole foods, solid and liquid foods, molasses, honey, tea, buttermilk and bitter, sweet, sour, hot, intense, and oily tastes – we offer all the many different items that please the senses. Please accept them and grant us empowerment and attainment. We present all these assembled offerings!

The Dechen Monlam

༄༅། །མཁས་གྲུབ་རཱ་ག་ཨ་སྱས་མཛད་པའི་རྣམ་དག་བདེ་ཆེན་ཞིང་གི་སྨོན་ལམ་བཞུགས་སོ།།

The Prayer of Aspiration to Reach the Very Pure Realm of Dewachen

by

The Scholar-Saint Raga Asya Karma Chags-Med

ཨོཾ་ཨ་མི་དྷེ་ཝ་ཧྲཱིཿ འདི་ཉིད་ཆགས་མེད་ཐུགས་དམ་མཛོད། ལག་པ་ན་ཡང་འབད་ནས་བྲིས། མང་པོ་འགྲོ་ལ་ཕན་པ་བསམས། དཔེ་གཙོད་འདོད་མི་གདའ་ན་ གཡོར། འདི་ལས་ཕན་ཡོན་ཆེ་བ་མེད། འདི་བས་ཟབ་པའི་གདམས་པ་མེད། ང་ཡི་ཆོས་ཀྱི་རྩ་བ་ཡིན། རང་གར་མ་བསྐྱུར་ཉམས་ལེན་འབུངས། འདི་ནི་མདོ་ལུགས་ཡིན་པའི་ཕྱིར། ལུང་མ་ཐོབ་ཀྱང་འདོན་ནི་རུང་།། །།

[Introduction by Karma Chags-Med]

Om Amidhewa Hri. This is the treasure of the doctrine that brings joy to Chag-Med. I have written this with my own hand thinking it might have some benefit by making many people happy. If someone would like to read this book without copying it, then they can borrow it. There is nothing more beneficial than this text. There are no instructions more profound than these. It is the root of my dharma. Do not treat it carelessly but practise it diligently. This text is written in the style of a sutra and so it is permissible to read it without having the authorisation[1].

THE FIRST DESCRIPTION

ཨེ་མ་ཧོ། འདི་ནས་ཉི་མ་ནུབ་ཀྱི་ཕྱོགས་རོལ་ན།

E MA HO	**DI**	**NAE**	**NYI MA**	**NUB**	**KYI**	**CHOG ROL**	**NA**
how amazing, wonderful	*here, this place*	*from*	*sun (i.e. to the west)*	*setting*	*of*	*direction*	*in*

Wonderful! Away from here in the direction of the setting sun,

གྲངས་མེད་འཇིག་རྟེན་མང་པོའི་ཕ་རོལ་ན།

DRANG ME	**JIG TEN**	**MANG POI**	**PHA ROL NA**
countless, numberless	*worlds (yet not too far away)*	*many's*	*beyond, on the other side*

Beyond a multitude of numberless worlds, and

ཅུང་ཟད་སྟེང་དུ་འཕགས་པའི་ཡུལ་ས་ན།

CHUNG ZAE	**TENG DU**	**PHAG PAI**	**YUL SA**	**NA**
little, slight	*above*	*noble*	*land*	*at*
		(India)		

Slightly elevated above the noble land of the Buddha

རྣམ་པར་དག་པའི་ཞིང་ཁམས་བདེ་བ་ཅན།

NAM PAR DAG PAI	**ZHING KHAM**	**DE WA CHEN**
very pure	*realm*	*Sukhavati 'happy'*

Is the very pure realm of Dewachen.

བདག་གི་ཆུ་བུར་མིག་གིས་མ་མཐོང་ཡང་།

DA GI	**CHU BUR**	**MIG**	**GI**	**MA**	**THONG**	**YANG**
my	*water bubble (i.e. physical organ)*	*eye*	*by*	*not*	*see*	*although*

Although it cannot be seen by my physical eye

རང་སེམས་གསལ་བའི་ཡིད་ལ་ལྷམ་མེར་གསལ།

RANG	**SEM**	**SAL WAI**	**YI**	**LA**	**LHAM MER**	**SAL**
my	*mind*	*clear*	*mental consciousness*	*for, in*	*brilliant*	*clear, shining*

It is bright and shining in my mind's clear perception.

Wonderful! Away from here in the direction of the setting sun, beyond a multitude of numberless worlds and slightly elevated above the noble land of the Buddha is the very pure realm of Dewachen. Although it cannot be seen by my physical eye, it is bright and shining in my mind's clear perception.

དེ་ན་བཅོམ་ལྡན་རྒྱལ་བ་འོད་དཔག་མེད།

DE NA	**CHOM DEN**	**GYAL WA**	**OE PA ME**
there	*Bhagawan**	*Victor, Buddha*	*Amitabha, 'measureless light'*

*he who has finished all sin, has great qualities, and is going from samsara. Perfect One.

There, at that place, is the perfect Buddha Amitabha

པདྨ་རཱ་གའི་མདོག་ཅན་གཟི་བརྗིད་འབར།

PAE MA RA GAI	**DOG**	**CHEN**	**ZI JI**	**BAR**
deep red jewel, the ruby, like the red lotus	*colour*	*has*	*splendid, magnificent tremendous personality*	*shining*

Who is radiant and majestic with the colour of a ruby red lotus.

དབུ་ལ་གཙུག་ཏོར་ཞབས་ལ་འཁོར་ལོ་སོགས།

U	**LA**	**TSUG TOR**	**ZHAB**	**LA**	**KHOR LO**	**SOG**
head	*on*	*usnisha, raised dome*	*feet*	*on*	*chakra, wheel*	*and so on*

On his head is the raised dome, on his feet the wheel symbols, and

མཚན་བཟང་སོ་གཉིས་དཔེ་བྱད་བརྒྱད་ཅུས་སྤྲས།

TSHAN	**ZANG**	**SO NYI**	**PE JE**	**GYAE CHU**	**TRAE**
signs	*good, auspicious*	*thirty-two*	*minor marks*	*eighty*	*adorned*
		(of a Buddha's body)			

He is adorned with the rest of the thirty-two auspicious signs and the eighty minor marks.

There, at that place, is the perfect Buddha Amitabha who is radiant and majestic with the colour of a ruby red lotus. On his head is the raised dome, on his feet the wheel symbols, and he is adorned with the rest of the thirty-two auspicious signs and the eighty minor marks.

ཞལ་གཅིག་ཕྱག་གཉིས་མཉམ་བཞག་ལྷུང་བཟེད་འཛིན།

ZHAL	**CHIG**	**CHAG**	**NYI**	**NYAM ZHAG**	**LHUNG ZE**	**DZIN**
face	*one*	*hand**	*two*	*meditation gesture*	*bhikshu's begging pot*	*holding*

*right hand on top of left and placed in his lap

He has one face and two hands resting in his lap for meditation while supporting a begging-bowl.

ཆོས་གོས་རྣམ་གསུམ་གསོལ་ཞིང་སྐྱིལ་ཀྲུང་གིས།

CHO	**GO**	**NAM**	**SUM**	**SOL ZHING**	**KYIL TRUNG**	**GI**
dharma	*cloth*	*kinds*	*three*	*wearing*	*asana* , posture*	*by*
(the three robes of a monk)						

*vajra or padma asana with left foot on right thigh and right foot on left thigh

Wearing the three Dharma robes he sits in lotus posture

པདྨ་སྟོང་ལྡན་ཟླ་བའི་གདན་སྟེང་དུ།

PAE MA	**TONG**	**DEN**	**DA WAI**	**DEN**	**TENG DU**
lotus	*thousand*	*having*	*moon's*	*seat, cushion*	*on top of*
(thousand petalled lotus flower)					

Upon a moon cushion on top of a thousand petalled lotus.

བྱང་ཆུབ་ཤིང་ལ་སྐུ་རྒྱབ་བརྟེན་མཛད་དེ།

JANG CHUB	**SHING**	**LA**	**KU GYAB**	**TEN DZAE**	**DE**
bodhi	*tree*	*at*	*his back*	*supporting, resting*	*he*

He sits with his back resting against the Bodhi Tree, and

ཐུགས་རྗེའི་སྤྱན་གྱིས་རྒྱང་ནས་བདག་ལ་གཟིགས།

THUG JEI	**CHEN**	**GYI**	**GYANG NAE**	**DAG**	**LA**	**ZIG**
compassionate	*eyes*	*by*	*from afar*	*me*	*to*	*looks*
					(and all sentient beings)	

With his compassionate eyes he looks at me from afar.

He has one face and two hands resting in his lap for meditation while supporting a begging- bowl. Wearing the three Dharma robes he sits in the lotus posture upon a moon cushion on top of a thousand petalled lotus. He sits with his back resting against the Bodhi Tree and from afar he looks at me with his compassionate eyes.

གཡས་སུ་བྱང་ཆུབ་སེམས་དཔའ་སྤྱན་རས་གཟིགས།

YAE	**SU**	**JANG CHUB SEM PA**	**CHEN RE ZI**
his right side	*at, on*	*Bodhisattva*	*Avalokitesvara*

On his right side is the Bodhisattva Chenrezi

སྐུ་མདོག་དཀར་པོ་ཕྱག་གཡོན་པད་དཀར་འཛིན།

KU	**DOG**	**KAR PO**	**CHAG**	**YON**	**PAE**	**KAR**	**DZIN**
body	*colour*	*white*	*hand*	*left*	*lotus*	*white*	*holding*

Who is white in colour and holds a white lotus in his left hand.

གཡོན་དུ་བྱང་ཆུབ་སེམས་དཔའ་མཐུ་ཆེན་ཐོབ།

YON	**DU**	**JANG CHUB SEM PA**	**THU CHEN THOB**
his left side	*at, on*	*Bodhisattva*	*Vajrapani, Mahasthamaprapta*

On his left side is the Bodhisattva Vajrapani

སྔོན་པོ་རྡོ་རྗེས་མཚན་པའི་པདྨ་གཡོན།

NGON PO	**DOR JE**	**TSHAN PAI**	**PAE MA**	**YON**
blue colour	*vajra*	*marked, having that symbol*	*lotus*	*left(hand)*

Who is blue in colour and holds a lotus with a vajra on it in his left hand.

གཡས་གཉིས་སྐྱབས་སྦྱིན་ཕྱག་རྒྱ་བདག་ལ་བསྟན།

YAE	**NYI**	**KYAB JIN**	**CHAG GYA**	**DAG**	**LA**	**TAN**
right (hand)	*both**	*refuge and protection*	*mudra, gesture*	*me*	*to*	*show*

*Chenrezi and Vajrapani

With their right hands they both show me the gesture of giving protection.

On his right is the Bodhisattva Chenrezi who is white in colour and holds a white lotus in his left hand. On his left is the Bodhisattva Vajrapani who is blue in colour and holds a lotus with a vajra on it in his left hand. With their right hands they both show me the gesture of giving protection.

གཙོ་བོ་གསུམ་པོ་རི་རྒྱལ་ལྷུན་པོ་བཞིན།

TSO WO	SUM PO	RI	GYAL	LHUN PO	ZHIN
chief, principle figure	*three*	*mountain (Mt. Meru)*	*king*	*heap*	*like, similar to*

These three main figures are like Mt. Meru, the king of mountains.

ལྷང་ངེ་ལྷན་ནེ་ལྷམ་མེར་བཞུགས་པའི་འཁོར།

LHANG NGE	LHAN NE	LHAN MER	ZHUG PAI	KHOR
impressive, vivid	*steadfast, calm and peaceful*	*magnificent brilliant*	*staying's, sitting's*	*retinue, circle*

Seated, they are vivid, distinct and brilliant with

བྱང་ཆུབ་སེམས་དཔའི་དགེ་སློང་བྱེ་བ་འབུམ།

JANG CHUB SEM PAI	GE LONG	JE WA	BUM
Bodhisattva's	*bhikshus, fully ordained*	*one million, or ten million**	*one hundred thousand*

*together they make one hundred thousand million or one million million and signify a huge quantity and so will be translated as 'a vast multitude'

Their retinue of a vast multitude of Bodhisattvas who are fully ordained monks.

ཀུན་ཀྱང་གསེར་མདོག་མཚན་དང་དཔེ་བྱད་བརྒྱན།

KUN	KYANG	SER	DOG	TSHAN	DANG	PE JAD	GYEN
all	*also*	*yellow*	*colour*	*auspicious signs (thirty-two)*	*and*	*minor marks(eighty)*	*adorned*

All are golden yellow in colour and are adorned with the auspicious signs and marks.

ཆོས་གོས་རྣམ་གསུམ་གསོལ་ཞིང་སེར་ལྷེམ་མེ།

CHO	GO	NAM	SUM	SOL ZHING	SER	TEM ME
Dharma	*clothes*	*kinds*	*three*	*wearing*	*yellow, golden*	*full*

(This completes the object of meditation, the Tsog-Shing.)

Wearing the three Dharma robes their radiant yellow is pervasive.

མོས་གུས་ཕྱག་ལ་ཉེ་རིང་ཁྱད་མེད་ཕྱིར།

MOE	GUE	CHAG	LA	NYE	RING	KHYAE	ME	CHIR
devotion	*reverence*	*salutation*	*to*	*near*	*far*	*difference*	*without*	*therefore*

For reverent and devoted salutation it makes no difference if the object is near or far, and so

བདག་གི་སྒོ་གསུམ་གུས་པས་ཕྱག་འཚལ་ལོ།

DAG GI	GO	SUM	GUE PAE	CHAG TSHAL LO
my	*doors (body, speech, mind)*	*three*	*devotion, with*	*make salutation, obeisance*

With my body, speech and mind I reverently make obeisance.

These three main figures are like Mt. Meru, the king of mountains. Seated, they are vivid, distinct and brilliant with their retinue of a vast multitude of Bodhisattvas who are fully ordained monks. All are golden yellow in colour and are adorned with the auspicious signs and marks. Wearing the three Dharma robes their radiant yellow is pervasive. For reverent and devoted salutation it makes no difference if the object is near or far, and so with my body, speech and mind I reverently make obeisance.

ཆོས་སྐུ་སྣང་བ་མཐའ་ཡས་རིགས་ཀྱི་བདག།

CHO KU	**NANG WA THA YAE**	**RIG**	**KYI**	**DAG**
dharmakaya	*Amitabha, Limitless Light*	*kula, family (Padma kula)*	*of*	*lord, master*

Dharmakaya Limitless Light, master of the family,

ཕྱག་གཡས་འོད་ཟེར་ལས་སྤྲུལ་སྤྱན་རས་གཟིགས།

CHAG	**YAE**	**OE**	**ZER**	**LAE**	**TRUL**	**CHEN RE ZI**
hand	*right*	*light*	*rays*	*from*	*emanates, manifests*	*Avalokitesvara*

Emanates Chenrezi from rays of light coming from this right hand, and

ཡང་སྤྲུལ་སྤྱན་རས་གཟིགས་དབང་བྱེ་བ་བརྒྱ།

YANG	**TRUL**	**CHEN RE ZI WANG**	**JE WA**	**GYA**
again (from the	*emanate, first Chenrezi)*	*Avalokitesvara*	*one or ten million*	*one hundred*

From this figure a vast multitude of Chenrezis arise as further emanations.

ཕྱག་གཡོན་འོད་ཟེར་ལས་སྤྲུལ་སྒྲོལ་མ་སྟེ།

CHAG	**YON**	**OE**	**ZER**	**LAE**	**TRUL**	**DROL MA**	**TE**
hand	*left*	*light*	*rays*	*from*	*emanates, manifests*	*Tara*	*then, thus*

Tara emanates from rays of light coming from his left hand, and

ཡང་སྤྲུལ་སྒྲོལ་མ་བྱེ་བ་ཕྲག་བརྒྱ་འགྱེད།

YANG	**TRUL**	**DROL MA**	**JE WA TRAG**	**GYA**	**GYE**
*again, further**	*emanates, comes out*	*Tara*	*one or ten million*	*one hundred*	*scatter, sent forth, spread out*

* from first Drolma

From this figure a vast multitude of Taras arise as further emanations.

ཐུགས་ཀྱི་འོད་ཟེར་ལས་སྤྲུལ་པདྨ་འབྱུང་།

THUG	KYI	OE	ZER	LAE	TRUL	PAE MA JUNG
heart (of Amitabha)	*of*	*light*	*rays*	*from*	*manifests, emanates*	*Padmasambhava*

Padmasambhava emanates from rays of light coming from his heart, and

ཡང་སྤྲུལ་ཨུ་རྒྱན་བྱེ་བ་ཕྲག་བརྒྱ་འགྱེད།

YANG	TRUL	UR GYAN	JE WA TRAG	GYA	GYE
again, further (from first Padmasambhava)	*emanated*	*Padmasambhava*	*one million or ten*	*one*	*come out, spread forth*

From this figure a vast multitude of Padmasambhavas arise as further emanations.

ཆོས་སྐུ་འོད་དཔག་མེད་ལ་ཕྱག་འཚལ་ལོ།

CHO KU	OE PA ME	LA	CHAG TSHAL LO
dharmakaya	*Amitabha*	*to*	*salutation*

Obeisance to you Dharmakaya Amitabha.

Dharmakaya Limitless Light, master of the family, emanates Chenrezi from rays of light coming from his right hand, and from this figure a vast multitude of Chenrezis arise as further emanations. Tara emanates from rays of light coming from his left hand, and from this figure a vast multitude of Taras arise as further emanations. Padmasambhava emanates from rays of light coming from his heart, and from this figure a vast multitude of Padmasambavas arise as further emanations. Obeisance to you Dharmakaya Amitabha.

སངས་རྒྱས་སྤྱན་གྱིས་ཉིན་མཚན་དུས་དྲུག་ཏུ།

SANG GYE	CHEN	GYI	NYIN	TSHAN	DU	DRUG	TU
Buddha	*eye*	*by, with*	*day (the whole twenty-four hours)*	*night*	*times,*	*six*	*in, during*

During all the six periods of the day and night, with your Buddha's eye

སེམས་ཅན་ཀུན་ལ་བརྩེ་བས་རྟག་ཏུ་གཟིགས།

SEM CHEN	KUN	LA	TSE WAE	TAG TU	ZI
sentient beings	*all*	*to*	*compassion/by, with*	*always*	*looking (sees the deeds of their bodies)*

You are continuously looking on all sentient beings with compassion.

སེམས་ཅན་ཀུན་གྱི་ཡིད་ལ་གང་དྲན་པའི།

SEM CHEN	**KUN**	**GYI**	**YI**	**LA**	**GANG**	**DRAN PAI**
sentient beings	*all*	*of*	*mind, mentation*	*to*	*whatever*	*remembrances, memories*

Whatever recollection of thoughts come and go in the minds of all beings

རྣམ་རྟོག་གང་འགྱུ་རྟག་ཏུ་ཐུགས་ཀྱིས་མཁྱེན།

NAM TOG	**GANG**	**GYU**	**TAG TU**	**THUG**	**KYI**	**KHYEN**
thoughts	*whatever*	*move*	*always*	*his mind*	*by*	*know*

They always fully known by your mind.

སེམས་ཅན་ཀུན་གྱིས་ངག་ཏུ་གང་སྨྲས་ཚིག།

SEM CHEN	**KUN**	**GYI**	**NGAG**	**TU**	**GANG**	**MAE**	**TSHIG**
sentient beings	*all*	*by*	*speech*	*with*	*whatever*	*say*	*words*

Whatever words are spoken by all sentient beings, they are

རྟག་ཏུ་མ་འདྲེས་སོ་སོར་སྙན་ལ་གསན།

TAG TU	**MA**	**DRE**	**SO SOR**	**NYEN**	**LA**	**SEN**
always	*not*	*mixing*	*each*	*his ear*	*with*	*hear*

Always heard by your ear, distinctly and unmixed.

ཀུན་མཁྱེན་འོད་དཔག་མེད་ལ་ཕྱག་འཚལ་ལོ།

KUN KHYEN	**OE PA ME**	**LA**	**CHAG TSHAL LO**
all knowing (omniscient)	*Amitabha*	*to*	*salutation, obeisance*

Obeisance to you omniscient Amitabha.

During the six periods of the day and night, with your Buddha's eye you are continuously looking on all sentient beings with compassion. Whatever thoughts and recollections arise in the minds of all beings, they are always fully known by your mind. Whatever words are spoken by all sentient beings, they are always heard by your ear, distinctly and unmixed. Obeisance to you omniscient Amitabha.

ཆོས་སྤངས་མཚམས་མེད་བྱས་པ་མ་གཏོགས་པ།

CHO	**PANG**	**TSHAM ME**	**JAE WA**	**MA TOG PA**
dharma	*abandoning*	*unlimited sins*	*done*	*with these exceptions only*

With the sole exception of those who have abandoned the Dharma or who have committed one of the five unlimited sins[2],

ཁྱེད་ལ་དད་ཅིང་སྨོན་ལམ་བཏབ་ཚད་ཀུན།

KHYE	**LA**	**DAE CHING**	**MON LAM**	**TAB**	**TSHE**	**KUN**
you	*to*	*faithful*	*prayer of aspiration*	*make*	*those who do*	*all*

Whoever prays to you with faith

བདེ་བ་ཅན་དེར་སྐྱེ་བའི་སྨོན་ལམ་འགྲུབ།

DE WA CHEN	**DER**	**KYE WAI**	**MON LAM**	**DRUB**
Sukhavati	*vthere*	*born*	*prayer of aspiration*	*get that result, accomplish*

Will attain their aspiration to be born in Dewachen.

བར་དོར་བྱོན་ནས་ཞིང་དེར་འདྲེན་པར་གསུངས།

BAR DOR	**JON**	**NAE**	**ZHING**	**DER**	**DREN PAR**	**SUNG**
the period just after death, in	*come to us*	*then*	*realm (Dewachen)*	*there*	*lead us*	*it is said**

*in the bDe-Ba-Chen-Gyi-Zhing-Khams-Yongs-Su-bKod-Pa'i-mDo, the Sukhavati Sutra which was spoken by Buddha Shakyamuni.

You will come in the period following their death and guide them to that realm — thus it is said in the Sutra.

འདྲེན་པ་འོད་དཔག་མེད་ལ་ཕྱག་འཚལ་ལོ།

DREN PA	**OE PA ME**	**LA**	**CHAG TSHAL LO**
guide, leader	*Amitabha*	*to*	*salutation, obeisance*

Obeisance to Amitabha our guide.

With the sole exception of those who have abandoned the Dharma and who have committed one of the five unlimited sins, whoever prays to you with faith will attain their aspiration to be born in Dewachen. You will come in the period following their death and guide them to that realm – thus it is said in the Sutra. Obeisance to Amitabha our Guide.

ཁྱེད་ཀྱི་སྐུ་ཚེ་བསྐལ་པ་གྲངས་མེད་དུ།

KHYE KYI	**KU TSHE**	**KAL PA**	**DRANG ME**	**DU**
your	*lifespan*	*kalpa, aeon*	*numberless*	*during, in*

For the duration of your lifespan of numberless aeons

མྱ་ངན་མི་འདའ་ད་ལྟ་མངོན་སུམ་བཞུགས།

NYA NGAN	**MI**	**DA**	**DA TAR**	**NGON SUM**	**ZHUG**
nirvana	*not*	*pass into*	*now*	*clearly visible*	*are, remain, be available for us*

(not cease from showing your present form)

You will not pass into nirvana, and now, at this time, you remain clearly manifest.

ཁྱེད་ལ་རྩེ་གཅིག་གུས་པས་གསོལ་བཏབ་ན།

KHYED	**LA**	**TSE CHIG**	**GU PAE**	**SOL TAB**	**NA**
you	*to*	*one-pointed*	*devotion, with*	*pray*	*if, when*

If we pray to you with one-pointed devotion, then,

ལས་ཀྱི་རྣམ་པར་སྨིན་པ་མ་གཏོགས་པའི།

LAE	**KYI**	**NAM PAR MIN PA**	**MA TOG PAI**
karma (bad)	*of*	*fully maturing*	*with only these exceptions (i.e. apart from their power)*

Excepting only for the maturation of life-ending karma,

ཚེ་ཟད་པ་ཡང་ལོ་བརྒྱ་ཐུབ་པ་དང་།

TSHE	**ZAE PA**	**YANG**	**LO GYA**	**THUB PA**	**DANG**
life	*finish*	*also*	*one hundred years*	*have that power, gain that*	*and*
(death)					

We will gain a lifespan of one hundred years, and

དུས་མིན་འཆི་བ་མ་ལུས་བཟློག་པར་གསུངས།

DU	**MIN**	**CHI WA**	**MA LU**	**DOG PAR**	**SUNG**
*time**	*without*	*death*	*without exception*	*averted, turned back*	*it is said (Sukhavati Sutra)*

*untimely i.e. 'accidental' due to fire, water and so on, and coming before the karmically determined maximum possible lifespan.

All causes of untimely death will be averted — thus it is said in the Sutra.

མགོན་པོ་ཚེ་དཔག་མེད་ལ་ཕྱག་འཚལ་ལོ།

GON PO	**TSHE PA ME**	**LA**	**CHAG TSHAL LO**
protector, benefactor	*Amitabha as Amitayus, Measureless Life*	*to*	*salutation, obeisance*

Obeisance to our benefactor Amitayus.

For the duration of your lifespan of numberless aeons you will not pass into nirvana, and now, at this time, you remain clearly manifest. If we pray to you with one-pointed devotion, then, excepting only for the maturation of life-ending karma, we will gain a lifespan of one hundred years, and all causes of untimely death will be averted – thus it is said in the Sutra. Obeisance to our benefactor Amitayus.

སྟོང་གསུམ་འཇིག་རྟེན་རབ་འབྱམས་གྲངས་མེད་པ།

TONG SUM	**JIG TEN**	**RAM JAM**	**DRANG ME PA**
*three thousand**	*worlds*	*vast, infinite*	*numberless*

*i.e. all the possibilities of samsara

Compared with making a gift of countless worlds full

རིན་ཆེན་གྱིས་བཀང་སྦྱིན་པ་བྱིན་པ་བས།

RIN CHEN	**GYI**	**KANG**	**JIN PA**	**JIN PA**	**BAE**
jewels	*by*	*fill*	*gift (to someone)*	*giving*	*compared with that (to the merit of that)*

Of vast infinitudes of gems,

འོད་དཔག་མེད་པའི་མཚན་དང་བདེ་བ་ཅན།

OE PA ME PAI	**TSHAN**	**DANG**	**DE WA CHEN**
Amitabha's	*name*	*and*	*Sukhavati*

If on hearing of Dewachen and the name of Amitabha,

ཐོས་ནས་དད་པས་ཐལ་མོ་སྦྱར་བྱས་ན།

THO	**NAE**	**DAE**	**PAE**	**THAL MO JAR**	**JAE**	**NA**
hear	*then*	*faith,*	*with*	*hold hands at heart as a sign of reverence*	*do*	*if, when*

One should feel faith and hold one's hand in reverence,

དེ་ནི་དེ་བས་བསོད་ནམས་ཆེ་བར་གསུངས།

DE NI	**DE WAE**	**SO NAM**	**CHE WAR**	**SUNG**
that	*compared with that*	*merit*	*greater*	*said (Sukhavati Sutra)*

Then the merit of this will be the greater — thus the Sutra says.

དེ་ཕྱིར་འོད་དཔག་མེད་ལ་གུས་ཕྱག་འཚལ།

DE CHIR	**OE PA ME**	**LA**	**GU**	**CHAG TSHAL**
*for that reason**	*Amitabha*	*to*	*reverence*	*salutation, obeisance*

*i.e. I want that great merit.

Therefore, we make reverent obeisance to you Amitabha.

Compared with making a gift of countless worlds full of vast infinitudes of gems, if on hearing of Dewachen and the name of Amitabha one should feel faith and hold one's hands in reverence, then the merit of this would be the greater – thus the Sutra says. Therefore we make reverent obeisance to you Amitabha.

གང་ཞིག་འོད་དཔག་མེད་པའི་མཚན་ཐོས་ནས།

GANG ZHIG	**OE PA ME PAI**	**TSHEN**	**THO**	**NAE**
whoever	*Amitabha's*	*name*	*hear*	*then*

Whoever hears the name of Amitabha, and

ཁ་ཞེ་མེད་པར་སྙིང་ཁོང་རུས་པའི་གཏིང་།

KHA ZHE ME PAR	**NYING**	**KHONG**	**RUE PAI**	**TING**
without hypocrisy, not just from the mouth	*heart*	*open*	*bone*	*depth*

Without hypocrisy, from the genuine depths of their heart

ལན་ཅིག་ཙམ་ཞིག་དད་པ་སྐྱེས་པ་ན།

LAN CHI	TSAM ZHIG	DAE PA	KYE PA	NA
once	*only*	*faith*	*born, arise*	*if*

Has faith arise just once,

དེ་ནི་བྱང་ཆུབ་ལམ་ལས་ཕྱིར་མི་ལྡོག།

DE NI	JANG CHUB	LAM	LAE	CHIR	MI	DOG
that	*bodhi, enlightenment*	*path*	*from*	*outside*	*no*	*turn, reverse (not depart from)*

Will never depart from the path to Buddhahood.

མགོན་པོ་འོད་དཔག་མེད་ལ་ཕྱག་འཚལ་ལོ།

GON PO	OE PA ME	LA	CHAG TSHAL LO
protector, benefactor	*Amitabha*	*to*	*salutation*

Obeisance to our benefactor Amitabha.

Whoever hears the name of Amitabha, and from the genuine depths of their heart has faith arise just once without hypocrisy, will never depart from the path to Buddhahood. Obeisance to our benefactor Amitabha.

སངས་རྒྱས་འོད་དཔག་མེད་པའི་མཚན་ཐོས་ནས།

SANG GYE	OE PA ME PAI	TSHAN	THO	NAE
Buddha	*Amitabha's*	*name*	*hear*	*then*

If anyone should hear the name of Buddha Amitabha then,

དེ་ནི་བྱང་ཆུབ་སྙིང་པོ་མ་ཐོབ་བར།

DE NI	JANG CHUB	NYING PO	MA	THOB	BAR
that (person)	*bodhi*	*heart, essence*	*not*	*get*	*until, for as long as*

Until enlightenment is gained,

བུད་མེད་མི་སྐྱེ་རིགས་ནི་བཟང་པོར་སྐྱེ།

BU MED	MI	KYE	RIG NI	ZANG POR	KYE
*woman**	*not*	*born*	*family*	*good in*	*born*

* In traditional patriarchal cultures being born as a woman was often an impediment to studying Dharma and practising meditation.

They will never be born as a woman. Born only in good families,

ཚེ་རབས་ཀུན་ཏུ་ཚུལ་ཁྲིམས་རྣམ་དག་འགྱུར།

TSHE RAB	KUN	TU	TSHUL TRIM	NAM DAG	GYUR
lives	*all*	*in*	*morality*	*very pure*	*have*

In all their lives they will keep very pure morality.

བདེ་གཤེགས་འོད་དཔག་མེད་ལ་ཕྱག་འཚལ་ལོ།

DE SHEG	**OE PA ME**	**LA**	**CHAG TSHAL LO**
Sugata, Happily Gone	*Amitabha*	*to*	*salutation*

Obeisance to Happily Gone Amitabha.

If anyone should hear the name of Buddha Amitabha then, until enlightenment is gained, they will never be born as a woman. Born only in good families, in all their lives they will maintain very pure morality. Obeisance to Happily Gone Amitabha.

OFFERINGS

བདག་གི་ལུས་དང་ལོངས་སྤྱོད་དགེ་རྩར་བཅས།

DA GI	**LU**	**DANG**	**LONG CHO**	**GE**	**TSER**	**CHE**
my	*body*	*and*	*wealth*	*virtues*	*root*	*together*

Our bodies, wealth and virtue together with

དངོས་སུ་འབྱོར་བའི་མཆོད་པ་ཅི་མཆིས་པ།

NGO SU	**JOR WAI**	**CHOE PA**	**CHI**	**CHI PA**
actually,	*collected, of*	*offerings*	*whatever*	*have*

Whatever material offerings we actually possess, and those

ཡིད་སྤྲུལ་བཀྲ་ཤིས་རྫས་རྟགས་རིན་ཆེན་བདུན།

YI	**TRUL**	**TA SHI DZAE TAG**	**RIN CHEN DUN**
mind, mentation	*manifested, emanated*	*the auspicious eight symbols**	*the seven precious things***

*mirror, medicine, curd, right-whorled conch shell, kusa grass, wood-apple, vermillion, and white mustard seed. **precious royal disc, jewel, queen, minister, elephant, horse, general.

Conjured up in our minds, such as the auspicious symbols and the seven precious items,

གདོད་ནས་གྲུབ་པ་སྟོང་གསུམ་འཇིག་རྟེན་གྱི།

DOE NAE	**DRUB PA**	**TONG SUM**	**JIG TEN**	**GYI**
from the beginning	*naturally present*	*three thousand (i.e. all)*	*worlds*	*of*

The billions of primordial worlds each with

གླིང་བཞི་རི་རབ་ཉི་ཟླ་བྱེ་བ་བརྒྱ།

LING ZHI	**RI RAB**	**NYI**	**DA**	**JE WA**	**GYA**
the four continents	*Mt. Meru*	*sun*	*moon*	*one or ten million*	*one hundred*

The four continents, Mt. Meru, and the sun and moon, all in countless numbers,

ལྷ་ཀླུ་མི་ཡི་ལོངས་སྤྱོད་ཐམས་ཅད་ཀུན།

LHA	**LU**	**MI**	**YI**	**LONG CHOD**	**THAM CHE**	**KUN**
gods	*nagas,*	*men*	*of*	*wealth,*	*all*	*all*
	snake gods			*luxuries*		

Together with all the wealth of gods, nagas and men –

བློ་ཡིས་བླངས་ཏེ་འོད་དཔག་མེད་ལ་འབུལ།

LO	**YI**	**LANG**	**TE**	**OE PA ME**	**LA**	**BUL**
intellect	*by*	*take,*	*then*	*Amitabha*	*to*	*offer*
		imagine				

All this we conceive in our mind and offer to Amitabha.

བདག་ལ་ཕན་ཕྱིར་ཐུགས་རྗེའི་སྟོབས་ཀྱིས་བཞེས།

DAG	**LA**	**PHAN**	**CHIR**	**THUG JEI**	**TOB**	**KYI**	**ZHE**
me	*to*	*benefit*	*in order to*	*compassion's*	*power*	*by*	*accept*

In order to benefit us with your compassion please accept this offering.

Our bodies, wealth and virtues, along with whatever material offerings we actually possess, and those conjured up in our minds, such as the auspicious symbols, the seven precious items, the billions of primordial worlds each with the four continents, Mt. Meru, and the sun and moon, all in countless numbers, together with all the wealth of gods, nagas and men – all this we conceive in our minds and offer to Amitabha. In order to benefit us please accept this offering with your compassion.

CONFESSION

ཕ་མས་ཐོག་དྲངས་བདག་སོགས་འགྲོ་ཀུན་གྱིས།

PHA	**MAE**	**THOE DRANG**	**DAG SOG**	**DRO**	**KUN**	**GYI**
father	*mother*	*principally*	*we*	*beings**	*all*	*by*

*those moving in samsara, who have also all been my own parents previously

Thinking principally of my own father and mother, I and all beings

ཐོག་མ་མེད་པའི་དུས་ནས་ད་ལྟའི་བར།

THOG MA ME PAI	**DU**	**NAE**	**DAN TAI**	**BAR**
beginingless	*time*	*from*	*now*	*up until*

From beginingless time up until now

སྲོག་བཅད་མ་བྱིན་བླངས་དང་མི་ཚངས་སྤྱོད།

SOG	**CHAE**	**MA JIN**	**LANG**	**DANG**	**MI TSHANG**	**CHO**
life	*cut*	*not given*	*taking*	*and*	*impure*	*conduct*
(i.e. kill)		*(i.e. stealing)*			*(bad sexual morality)*	

Have killed, taken what was not given, and misbehaved sexually –

ལུས་ཀྱི་མི་དགེ་གསུམ་པོ་མཐོལ་ལོ་བཤགས།

LU	KYI	MI GE	SUM PO	THOL LO	SHAG
body	*of*	*unvirtue, sin*	*three*	*with hands held in prayer*	*confess and request forgiveness and puriufication*

These three sins of the body, we humbly confess and request forgiveness.

རྫུན་དང་ཕྲ་མ་ཚིག་རྩུབ་ངག་འཁྱལ་བ།

DZUN	DANG	TRA MA	TSHIG TSUB	NGAG KHYAL WA
lying	*and*	*calumny, back-biting and divisiveness*	*rough speech, angry works*	*idle talk, useless conversations*

We have told lies, spread calumny, used rough speech and idle talk –

ངག་གི་མི་དགེ་བཞི་པོ་མཐོལ་ལོ་བཤགས།

NGAG	GI	MI GE	ZHI PO	THOL LO	SHAG
speech	*of*	*unvirtues, sins*	*four*	*humbly*	*confess and request forgiveness*

These four sins of speech we humbly confess and request forgiveness.

བརྣབ་སེམས་གནོད་སེམས་ལོག་པར་ལྟ་བ་སྟེ།

NAB SEM	NOE SEM	LOG PAR TA WA	TE
covetousness, desiring the possessions of others	*ill-will, malice*	*wrong view, deny karma and emptiness*	*thus*

We have coveted, borne ill-will, and held wrong views –

ཡིད་ཀྱི་མི་དགེ་གསུམ་པོ་མཐོལ་ལོ་བཤགས།

YI	KYI	MI GE	SUM PO	THOL LO	SHAG
mind	*of*	*unvirtues, sins*	*three*	*humbly*	*confess and request forgiveness*

These three sins of the mind we humbly confess and request forgiveness.

Thinking principally of my own father and mother, I and all beings from beginingless time up until now have killed, taken what was not given, and misbehaved sexually – these three sins of the body we humbly confess and request forgiveness. We have told lies, spread calumny, used rough speech and idle talk – these four sins of speech we humbly confess and request forgiveness. We have been covetous, have borne ill-will, and held wrong views – these three sins of the mind we humbly confess and request forgiveness.

ཕ་མ་སློབ་དཔོན་དགྲ་བཅོམ་བསད་པ་དང་།

PHA	MA	LOB PON	DRA CHOM	SAE PA	DANG
father	*mother*	*acharya, guru*	*vanquisher*	*kill*	*and*

Patricide, matricide, killing a dharma teacher or one who has vanquished, and

རྒྱལ་བའི་སྐུ་ལ་ངན་སེམས་སྐྱེས་པ་དང་།

GYAL WAI	KU	LA	NGEN SEM	KYE PA	DANG
Victor's Buddha's	*body*	*to*	*desire to harm**	*arise*	*and*

* causing the body of a Buddha to bleed

Carrying out a harmful intention towards the body of a Buddha –

མཚམས་མེད་ལྔ་ཡི་ལས་བསགས་མཐོལ་ལོ་བཤགས།།

TSHAM ME	NGA	YI	LAE	SAG	THOL LO	SHAG
*unlimited**	*five*	*of*	*actions, karma*	*collected*	*humbly, with hands at heart*	*confess*

*they mature immediately at death and bring the result of birth in hell.

The karma accumulated from these five unlimited sins we humbly confess and request forgiveness.

Patricide, matricide, killing a dharma teacher or one who has vanquished, and carrying out a harmful intention towards the body of a Buddha – the karma accumulated from these five unlimited sins we humbly confess and request forgiveness.

དགེ་སློང་དགེ་ཚུལ་བསད་དང་བཙུན་མ་ཕབ།

GE LONG	GE TSHUL	SAE	DANG	TSUN MA	PHAB
bhikshu, fully ordained monk	*upasaka, novice monk*	*kill*	*and*	*nun*	*take her virginity*

Killing a fully ordained monk or a novice, taking the virginity of a nun,

སྐུ་གཟུགས་མཆོད་རྟེན་ལྷ་ཁང་ཞིག་ལ་སོགས།

KU ZUG	CHOE TEN	LHA KHANG	SHIG	LA SOG
statues	*stupa*	*temple*	*destroy*	*and so on*

Destroying statues, stupas, temples and so on –

ཉེ་བའི་མཚམས་མེད་སྡིག་བྱས་མཐོལ་ལོ་བཤགས།

NYE WAI	TSHAM ME	DIG	JAE	THOL LO	SHAG
similar	*limitless*	*sins*	*done*	*humbly*	*confess*

These sins which we have done that are similar to the limitless sins, we humbly confess and request forgiveness.

Killing a fully ordained monk or a novice, taking the virginity of a nun, destroying statues, stupas, temples and so on – these sins which we have done that are similar to the limitless sins, we humbly confess and request forgiveness.

དཀོན་མཆོག་ལྷ་ཁང་གསུང་རབ་རྟེན་གསུམ་སོགས།

KON CHOG	LHA KHANG	SUNG RAB	TEN	SUM	SOG
*three jewels**	*temples*	*dharma*	*support*	*three*	*and so on*

*Buddha, Dharma, Sangha

We have taken the support of the Three Jewels, temples and scriptures

དཔང་ཞེས་ཚོད་བཙུགས་མནའ་ཟོས་ལ་སོགས་པ།

PANG	ZHE TSHAE TSUG	NA	ZOE	LA SOG PA
witness	*taken as*	*oath*	*eaten (i.e. not kept)*	*and so on*

As our witness when we made promises, and then we have broken our word –

ཆོས་སྤངས་ལས་ངན་བསགས་པ་མཐོལ་ལོ་བཤགས།

CHO	PANG	LAE	NGEN	SAG PA	THOL LO	SHAG
Dharma	*abandoning, forgetting*	*deeds, karma*	*bad*	*collected*	*humbly*	*confess*

The bad karma we have collected by abandoning the Dharma, we humbly confess and request forgiveness.

We have taken the three supports of the Three Jewels, temples, and scriptures as our witness when we made promises, and then we have broken our word – the bad karma we have collected by abandoning the Dharma we humbly confess and request forgiveness.

ཁམས་གསུམ་སེམས་ཅན་བསད་ལས་སྡིག་ཆེ་བ།

KHAM	SUM	SEM CHEN	SAE	LAE	DIG	CHE WA
realms	*three**	*sentient beings*	*kill*	*than (comparative)*	*sin*	*greater, bigger*

*desire, form, formless i.e. all of samsara

A sin greater than that of killing all the beings of the three worlds

བྱང་ཆུབ་སེམས་དཔའ་རྣམས་ལ་སྐུར་པ་བཏབ།

JANG CHUB SEM PA NAM	LA	KUR PA	TAB
Bodhisattvas	*to*	*insult, say bad things about*	*give*

Is to denigrate Bodhisattvas.

དོན་མེད་སྡིག་ཆེན་བསགས་པ་མཐོལ་ལོ་བཤགས།

DON ME	DIG	CHEN	SAG PA	THOL LO	SHAG
meaningless	*sins*	*great*	*collected*	*humbly*	*confess*

The meaningless great sins we have collected we humbly confess and request forgiveness.

A sin greater than that of killing all the beings of the three worlds is to denigrate Bodhisattvas. The meaningless great sins that we have collected, we humbly confess and request forgiveness.

དགེ་བའི་ཕན་ཡོན་སྡིག་པའི་ཉེས་དམིགས་དང་།

GE WAI	**PHAN YON**	**DIG PAI**	**NYE MIG**	**DANG**
virtues	*benefits, helpfulness*	*sin's*	*misery, punishment*	*and*

We hear of the benefits of virtue and the misery of sin, and of

དམྱལ་བའི་སྡུག་བསྔལ་ཚེ་ཚད་ལ་སོགས་པ།

NYAL WAI	**DUG NGAL**	**TSHE**	**TSHAD**	**LA SOG PA**
hell's	*suffering*	*life's*	*duration (i.e. very long)*	*and so on*

The duration of suffering in the hells,

ཐོས་ཀྱང་མི་བདེན་བཤད་ཚོད་ཡིན་བསམས་པ།

THO	**KYANG**	**MI DEN**	**SHAD TSHOD**	**YIN**	**SAM PA**
hear about these things	*but*	*untrue*	*only talk*	*is*	*think, believe*

But we do not believe this and think that it is only talk –

མཚམས་མེད་ལྔ་བས་ཐུ་བའི་ལས་ངན་པ།

TSHAM MED	**NGA**	**BAE**	**THU WAI**	**LAE**	**NGEN PA**
limitless	*five*	*compared*	*worse*	*karma*	*bad, evil, harmful*

This bad karma worse than the five unlimited sins,

ཐར་མེད་ལས་ངན་བསགས་པ་མཐོལ་ལོ་བཤགས།

THAR	**ME**	**LAE**	**NGEN**	**SAG PA**	**THOL LO**	**SHAG**
*freedom**	*without*	*actions*	*bad*	*accumulated*	*with hands held in reverence at the heart*	*confess, ask to be excused*

*it will not pass off by itself, we must struggle to be free of it

This bad karma we have collected which is so difficult to clear, we humbly confess and request forgiveness.

We hear of the benefits of virtue and the misery of sin, and of the duration of suffering in the hells, but we do not believe this and think that it is only talk – this bad karma worse than the five unlimited sins, this bad karma we have collected which is so difficult to clear, we humbly confess and request forgiveness.

ཕམ་པ་བཞི་དང་ལྷག་མ་བཅུ་གསུམ་དང་།

PHAM PA	**ZHI**	**DANG**	**LHAG MA**	**CHU SUM**	**DANG**
defeats	*four*	*and*	*remainder*	*thirteen*	*and*

The four defeats, the thirteen remainders,

སྤང་ལྟུང་སོར་བཤགས་ཉེས་བྱས་སྡེ་ཚན་ལྔ།

PANG TUNG	**SOR SHAG**	**NYE JAE**	**DE TSEN**	**NGA**
downfalls	*confessables*	*misdemeanours*	*classes*	*five*

The downfalls, the confessables and the misdemeanours – these five classes of

སོ་ཐར་ཚུལ་ཁྲིམས་འཆལ་བ་མཐོལ་ལོ་བཤགས།

SO THAR	**TSHUL TRIM**	**CHAL WA**	**THOL LO**	**SHAG**
*pratimoksha**	*morality*	*breaks, falls*	*hands held at the heart*	*confess*

*the outer vows of ordination

Failings in the vows of renunciate morality, we humbly confess and request forgiveness.

The four defeats, the thirteen remainders, the downfalls, the confessables and the misdemeanours – these five classes of failings in the vows of renunciate morality, we humbly confess and request forgiveness.

ནག་པོའི་ཆོས་བཞི་ལྟུང་བ་ལྔ་ལྔ་བརྒྱད།

NAG POI	**CHO**	**ZHI**	**TUNG WA**	**NGA**	**NGA**	**GYAE**
black	*dharmas*	*four**	*falls*	*five*	*five*	*eight*
				*(eighteen bodhisattva vows**)*		

* Abusing the pure dharma, praising evil dharmas, disturbing those who practise virtue, stopping the work of a faithful sponsor.

** Lapses in the five vows of the King, the five of the ministers and the eight of the people.

The four black dharmas, our downfalls in the eighteen bodhisattva vows, and

བྱང་སེམས་བསླབ་པ་ཉམས་པ་མཐོལ་ལོ་བཤགས།

JANG SEM	**LAB PA**	**NYAM PA**	**THOL LO**	**SHAG**
bodhisattva (mahayana bodhicitta)	*training, practice*	*lapses*	*with hands held at heart*	*confess*

Our lapses in the bodhisattva training, we humbly confess and request forgiveness.

The four black dharmas, our downfalls in the eighteen bodhisattva vows, and our lapses in the bodhisattva training, we humbly confess and request forgiveness.

རྩ་ལྟུང་བཅུ་བཞི་ཡན་ལག་སྦོམ་པོ་བརྒྱད།

TSA	**TUNG**	**CHUB ZHI**	**YAN LAG**	**BOM PO**	**GYAE**
root	*falls*	*fourteen*	*branch*	*big, important*	*eight*

The fourteen root downfalls and the eight major branch falls

གསང་སྔགས་དམ་ཚིག་ཉམས་པ་མཐོལ་ལོ་བཤགས།

SANG NGAG	DAM TSHIG	NYAM PA	THOL LO	SHAG
vajrayana, tantric	*oaths*	*lapses*	*with hands held at heart*	*confess*

These lapses in our tantric oaths, we humbly confess and request forgiveness.

The fourteen root downfalls and the eight major branch falls, these lapses in our tantric oaths, we humbly confess and request forgiveness.

སྡོམ་པ་མ་ཞུས་མི་དགེའི་ལས་བྱས་པ།

DOM PA	MA ZHU	MI GEI	LAE	JAE PA
vows	*not taken*	*unvirtues, sins*	*actions, karma*	*done*

Unvirtuous actions concerning which we may have taken no vows,

མི་ཚངས་སྤྱོད་དང་ཆང་འཐུང་ལ་སོགས་པ།

MI TSHANG CHO	DANG	CHANG	THUNG	LA SOG PA
sexual misconduct	*and*	*beer*	*drinking (getting drunk)*	*and so on*

Such as sexual misconduct and drinking alcohol –

རང་བཞིན་ཁ་ན་མ་ཐོའི་སྡིག་པ་སྟེ།

RANG ZHIN	KHA NA MA THOI	DIG PA	TE
natural (everyone knows they are wrong)	*what people hold to be wrong and bad*	*sins*	*then, thus*

All these actions which are naturally unwholesome and are generally held to be bad,

སྡིག་པ་སྡིག་ཏུ་མ་ཤེས་མཐོལ་ལོ་བཤགས།

DIG PA	DIG	TU	MA SHE	THOL LO	SHAG
sins	*sin*	*as*	*not know (or did not want to know)*	*in prayer*	*confess*

These sins which we did not know to be sins, we humbly confess and request forgiveness.

Unvirtuous actions concerning which we may have taken no vows, such as sexual misconduct and drinking alcohol – all these actions which are naturally unwholesome and are generally held to be bad, these sins which we did not know to be sins, we humbly confess and request forgiveness.

སྐྱབས་སྡོམ་དབང་བསྐུར་ལ་སོགས་ཐོབ་ན་ཡང་།

KYAB	**DOM**	**WANG KUR**	**LA SOG**	**THOB**	**NA**	**YANG**
refuge	*vows,*	*initiation*	*and so on*	*get*	*then*	*also, even*

Even with taking refuge and empowerment vows

དེ་ཡི་སྡོམ་པ་དམ་ཚིག་བསྲུང་མ་ཤེས།

DE YI	**DOM PA**	**DAM TSHIG**	**SUNG**	**MA**	**SHE**
these	*vows*	*oaths, binding words*	*protect, keep*	*not*	*know how to*

We did not know how to protect these vows and obligations.

བཅས་པའི་ལྟུང་བ་ཕོག་པ་མཐོལ་ལོ་བཤགས།

CHE PAI	**TUNG WA**	**PHOG PA**	**THOL LO**	**SHAG**
*order**	*falls*	*touched by (i.e. done)*	*with hands held at heart*	*confess*

*by Guru or Buddha not to do something

All these ways we have fallen short of the holy instructions, we humbly confess and request forgiveness.

Even with taking refuge and initiation vows, we did not know how to protect these vows and obligations. All these ways we have fallen short of the holy instructions, we humbly confess and request forgiveness.

འགྱོད་པ་མེད་ན་བཤགས་པས་མི་དག་པས།

GYOD PA	**ME**	**NA**	**SHAG PAE**	**MI**	**DAG PAE**
regret, repentance	*without*	*if*	*confession, by*	*not*	*purified, therefore*

If confession is made without repentance it will not be purifying, therefore,

སྔར་བྱས་སྡིག་པ་ཁོང་དུ་དུག་སོང་ལྟར།

NGAR	**JAE**	**DIG PA**	**KHONG DU**	**DUG**	**SONG**	**TAR**
previously	*done*	*sins*	*inside, in ones body*	*poison (i.e. fear that you will die)*	*gone*	*as*

Seeing these previously committed sins to be like poison we have eaten,

ངོ་ཚ་འཇིགས་སྐྲག་འགྱོད་པ་ཆེན་པོས་བཤགས།

NGO TSHA	**JIG TRAG**	**GYOD PA**	**CHEN**	**POE**	**SHAG**
shame	*fear*	*regret, remorse*	*great,*	*by/with*	*confess, ask forgiveness*

With shame, fear and great remorse, we humbly confess and request forgiveness.

If the confession is made without repentance it will not be purifying, therefore, seeing these previously committed sins to be like poison we

have eaten, with shame, fear and great remorse, we humbly confess and request forgiveness.

ཕྱིན་ཆད་སྡོམ་སེམས་མེད་ན་མི་དག་པས།

CHIN CHAE	**DOM**	**SEM**	**ME**	**NA**	**MI DAG PAE**
from this time on	*vows, intentions*	*remember to keep*	*without*	*if*	*not be purified, therefore*

If from this time on we are forgetful of our vows we shall not be purified, therefore

ཕྱིན་ཆད་སྲོག་ལ་བབས་ཀྱང་མི་དགེའི་ལས།

CHIN CHAE	**SOG LA BAB**	**KYANG**	**MI GEI**	**LAE**
from this time on	*under threat of death, forced to either sin or die*	*yet, even though*	*unvirtuous*	*action*

From now on, even if threatened with death,

ད་ནས་མི་བགྱིད་སེམས་ལ་དམ་བཅའ་བཟུང་།

DA	**NAE**	**MI GYI**	**SEM**	**LA**	**DAM CHA**	**ZUNG**
now	*from*	*not do*	*mind*	*as*	*vow, firm intention*	*hold*

We shall hold to our firm intention not to do any unvirtue.

བདེ་གཤེགས་འོད་དཔག་མེད་པ་སྲས་བཅས་ཀྱིས།

DE SHEG	**OE PA ME PA**	**SAE CHE**	**KYI**
Happily Gone, Buddha	*Amitabha*	*Bodhisattvas*	*by*

Happily Gone Amitabha with your Bodhisattvas,

བདག་རྒྱུད་ཡོངས་སུ་དག་པར་བྱིན་གྱིས་རློབས།

DAG	**GYU**	**YONG SU**	**DAG PAR**	**JIN GYI LOB**
my	*mind, character*	*fully*	*pure, as*	*bless*

Please bless our characters with complete purity.

If from this time on we are forgetful of our vows we shall not be purified, therefore, from now on, even if threatened with death, we shall hold to our firm intention not to do any unvirtue. Happily Gone Amitabha with your Bodhisattvas, please bless our characters with complete purity.

REJOICING AT THE VIRTUES OF OTHERS

གཞན་གྱིས་དགེ་བ་བྱས་པ་ཐོས་པའི་ཚེ།

ZHAN	**GYI**	**GE WA**	**JAE PA**	**THO PAI**	**TSHE**
others	*by*	*virtue*	*done*	*hear*	*when*

When hearing of the virtue done by others,

དེ་ལ་ཕྲག་དོག་མི་དགེའི་སེམས་སྤངས་ནས།

DE	**LA**	**TRAG DOG**	**MI GEI**	**SEM**	**PANG**	**NAE**
that (their virtuous action)	*to*	*jealousy*	*unvirtuous, sinful*	*mind*	*abandon, not do*	*then*

If jealous and unvirtuous thoughts are cast out and

སྙིང་ནས་དགའ་བའི་རྗེས་སུ་ཡི་རང་ན།

NYING	**NAE**	**GA WAI**	**JE SU**	**YI RANG**	**NA**
heart	*from*	*happily*	*subsequent, following*	*harmonic rejoicing*	*if*

From the heart there is happy rejoicing at their good fortune,

དེ་ཡི་བསོད་ནམས་མཉམ་དུ་ཐོབ་པར་གསུངས།

DE YI	**SO NAM**	**NYAM**	**DU**	**THOB PAR**	**SUNG**
that's	*merit*	*equal*	*as*	*get, as*	*said (Sukhavati Kshetra Sutra)*

Then a merit equal to theirs will be gained — thus it is said in the Sutra.

དེ་ཕྱིར་འཕགས་པ་རྣམས་དང་སོ་སྐྱེ་ཡིས།

DE CHIR	**PHAG PA NAM**	**DANG**	**SO KYE**	**YI**
therefore,	*aryas, Bodhisattvas*	*and*	*ordinary people, humans*	*by*

Therefore we rejoice in whatever virtues have been performed

དགེ་བ་གང་བསྒྲུབས་ཀུན་ལ་ཡི་རང་ངོ།

GE WA	**GANG**	**DRUB**	**KUN**	**LA**	**YI RANG NGO**
virtue	*whatever*	*gained, performed*	*all*	*to*	*rejoice sympathetically*

By Bodhisattvas and by ordinary people.

བླ་མེད་བྱང་ཆུབ་མཆོག་ཏུ་སེམས་བསྐྱེད་ནས།

LA ME	**JANG CHUB**	**CHOG**	**TU**	**SEM KYE**	**NAE**
unsurpassed, highest	*bodhi, enlightenment*	*excellent*	*to*	*develop the intention*	*then*

We rejoice in those who raise the highest thought of gaining unsurpassed enlightenment, and

འགྲོ་དོན་རྒྱ་ཆེན་མཛད་ལ་ཡི་རང་ངོ།

DRO	**DON**	**GYA CHEN**	**DZAE**	**LA**	**YI RANG NGO**
beings	*benefit*	*great*	*doing*	*to*	*sympathetically rejoice*

Who then greatly benefit sentient beings.

When hearing of the virtue done by others, if jealous and unvirtuous thoughts are cast out and from the heart there is happy rejoicing at their good fortune, then a merit equal to theirs will be gained – thus it is

said in the Sutra. Therefore we rejoice in whatever virtues have been performed by Bodhisattvas and by ordinary people. We rejoice in those who raise the highest thought of gaining unsurpassed enlightenment and who then greatly benefit sentient beings.

མི་དགེ་བཅུ་པོ་སྤངས་པ་དགེ་བ་བཅུ།

MI GE	**CHU PO**	**PANG PA**	**GE WA**	**CHU**
unvirtues	*ten**	*abandon*	*virtues*	*ten*

** listed in the section headed Confession*

Abandoning the ten unvirtues and practising the following ten virtues:

གཞན་གྱི་སྲོག་བསྐྱབ་སྦྱིན་པ་གཏོང་བ་དང་།

ZHAN GYI	**SOG**	**KYAB**	**JIN PA**	**TONG WA**	**DANG**
others'	*lives*	*protect*	*gifts, charity*	*give*	*and*

Protecting the lives of others and giving generously,

སྡོམ་པ་སྲུང་ཞིང་བདེན་པར་སྨྲ་བ་དང་།

DOM PA	**SUNG ZHING**	**DEN PAR**	**MA WA**	**DANG**
vows, morality	*protecting*	*truth*	*speaking*	*and*

Guarding one's morality and speaking truthfully,

འཁོན་པ་སྡུམ་དང་ཞི་དུལ་དྲང་པོར་སྨྲ།

KHON PA	**DUM**	**DANG**	**ZHI DUL**	**DRANG POR**	**MA**
disputes	*bring harmony to, settle*	*and*	*gently*	*directly, non-deviously*	*speak*

Settling disputes and speaking gently without deception,

དོན་དང་ལྡན་པའི་གཏམ་བརྗོད་འདོད་པ་ཆུང་།

DON DANG DEN PAI	**TAM**	**JOE**	**DOE PA**	**CHUNG**
meaningful	*talk*	*say*	*desires*	*small, few*

Talking meaningfully and having few desires,

བྱམས་དང་སྙིང་རྗེ་སྒོམ་ཞིང་ཆོས་ལ་སྤྱོད།

JAM	**DANG**	**NYING JE**	**GOM ZHING**	**CHO**	**LA**	**CHO**
*love**	*and*	*compassion#*	*meditating*	*Dharma*	*as*	*do*

*wanting others to be happy #actually removing the sorrows of others

Cultivating love and compassion and practising Dharma –

དགེ་བ་དེ་རྣམས་ཀུན་ལ་ཡི་རང་ངོ་།

GE WA	**DE NAM**	**KUN**	**LA**	**YI RANG NGO**
virtues	*these*	*all*	*to*	*sympathetically rejoice*

We rejoice in all these virtues done by beings.

Abandoning the ten unvirtues and practising the following ten virtues:

protecting the lives of others and giving generously; guarding one's morality and speaking truthfully; settling disputes and speaking gently without deception; talking meaningfully and having few desires; cultivating love and compassion and practising Dharma – we rejoice in all these virtues done by beings.

REQUESTING DHARMA TEACHING

ཕྱོགས་བཅུའི་འཇིག་རྟེན་རབ་འབྱམས་ཐམས་ཅད་ན།

CHOG	CHUI	JIG TEN	RAB JAM	THAM CHE	NA
directions (i.e. everywhere)	*ten*	*worlds*	*infinite, vast*	*all*	*in*

In all the infinite worlds that lie in the ten directions are you

རྫོགས་སངས་རྒྱས་ནས་རིང་པོར་མ་ལོན་པར།

DZOG	SANG GYE	NAE	RING POR	MA	LON PAR
complete, perfect	*Buddha (i.e. those who have not yet taught the Dharma)*	*then*	*long time*	*not*	*take, reach*

Who have recently gained perfect buddhahood.

དེ་དག་རྣམས་ལ་ཆོས་ཀྱི་འཁོར་ལོ་ནི།

DE DAG NAM	LA	CHO	KYI	KHOR LO	NI
them	*to*	*dharma (i.e. teaching the Dharma)*	*of*	*wheel*	*(emphasis)*

May you soon make a great turning of the wheel of Dharma –

རྒྱ་ཆེན་མྱུར་དུ་བསྐོར་བར་བདག་གིས་བསྐུལ།

GYA CHEN	NYUR DU	KOR WAR	DAG	GI	KUL
great	*quickly*	*turn*	*me*	*by*	*request, beseech*

We request this of you.

མངོན་ཤེས་ཐུགས་ཀྱིས་དེ་དོན་མཁྱེན་པར་གསོལ།

NGON SHE	THUG	KYI	DE	DON	KHYEN PAR	SOL
super-knowledge	*mind*	*by*	*that*	*meaning (i.e. my request)*	*know, understand*	*please, I pray*

With your minds' clairvoyance may you understand this request.

You who have recently gained perfect Buddhahood abide in all the infinite worlds that lie in the ten directions. May you soon make a great turning of the wheel of Dharma – we request this of you. With your minds' clairvoyance may you understand this request.

REQUESTING THEM NOT TO DIE

སངས་རྒྱས་བྱང་སེམས་བསྟན་འཛིན་དགེ་བའི་བཤེས།

SANG GYE	JANG SEM	TEN DZIN	GE WAI SHE
Buddhas	*Bodhisattvas*	*doctrine holders (those in the guru's lineage)*	*virtuous spiritual friends*

We pray that all you Buddhas, Bodhisattvas, doctrine holders and spiritual advisors

མྱ་ངན་འདའ་བར་བཞེད་ཀུན་དེ་དག་ལ།

NYA NGAN DA WAR	ZHE	KUN	DE DAG	LA
go from suffering, enter nirvana, die	*wish*	*all*	*then*	*to*

Who wish to pass from sorrow

མྱ་ངན་མི་འདའ་བཞུགས་པར་གསོལ་བ་འདེབས།

NYA NGAN	MI	DA	ZHUG PAR	SOL WA DEB
sorrow	*not*	*pass*	*stay*	*I pray*

Will remain here without passing away.

We pray that all you Buddhas, Bodhisattvas, doctrine holders and spiritual advisors who wish to pass from sorrow will remain here without passing away.

DEDICATION OF MERIT

འདིས་མཚོན་བདག་གི་དུས་གསུམ་དགེ་བ་རྣམས།

DI	TSHON	DA	GI	DU	SUM	GE WA NAM
by this	*example, sign**	*I (and all beings)*	*of*	*times (past, present, future)*	*three*	*virtues*

*the six preceding parts of the Seven Branch Practice, starting with salutation

We dedicate this virtue and all that we have collected in the three times

འགྲོ་བ་སེམས་ཅན་ཀུན་གྱི་དོན་དུ་བསྔོ།

DRO WA	SEM CHEN	KUN	GYI	DON DU	NGO
*movers**	*sentient beings#*	*all*	*of*	*benefit, help*	*dedicated, give*

*those rounding in samsara #this includes myself

To the benefit of all sentient beings moving in samsara.

ཀུན་ཀྱང་བླ་མེད་བྱང་ཆུབ་མྱུར་ཐོབ་ནས།

KUN	KYANG	LA ME	JANG CHU	NYUR	THOB	NAE
all of them	*also*	*unsurpassed*	*bodhi, enlightenment, buddhahood*	*quickly*	*get*	*then, thus*

May they all quickly attain unsurpassable awakening

ཁམས་གསུམ་འཁོར་བ་དོང་ནས་སྤྲུག་གྱུར་ཅིག།

KHAM *realms, spheres (desire, form, formless)* **SUM** *three* **KHOR WA** *samsara* **DONG NAE TRU** *upturned and emptied* **GYUR CHI** *must be!*

And thus completely empty the three levels of samsara.

We dedicate this virtue and all that we have collected in the three times to the benefit of all sentient beings moving in samsara. May they all quickly attain the unsurpassable awakening and thus may the three levels of samsara be emptied completely.

DIRECTING THE MERIT TO HELP BEINGS

དེ་ཡི་དགེ་བ་བདག་གཞན་མྱུར་སྨིན་ནས།

DE *that* **YI** *of** **GE WA** *virtue* **DAG** *me* **ZHAN** *other* **NYUR** *quickly* **MIN** *ripen* **NAE** *then*

*giving all virtue to others

May this virtue mature quickly for myself and all others so that

ཚེ་འདིར་དུས་མིན་འཆི་བ་བཅོ་བརྒྱད་ཞི།

TSHE *life* **DIR** *this* **DU MIN** *untimely* **CHI WA** *death* **CHOB GYE** *eighteen* **ZHI** *pacify*

In this life the eighteen causes of untimely death are inactive, and

ནད་མེད་ལང་ཚོ་རྒྱས་པའི་ལུས་སྟོབས་ལྡན།

NAE *sick* **ME** *without* **LANG TSO** *youthful* **GYE PAI** *healthy* **LU** *body* **TOB DAN** *powerful*

We gain healthy, youthful and powerful bodies, and

དཔལ་འབྱོར་འཛད་མེད་དབྱར་གྱི་གངྒ་ལྟར།

PAL JOR *wealth* **DZAE ME** *endless* **YAR** *summer (i.e. monsoon)* **GYI** *of* **GANG GA** *River Ganges* **TAR** *like*

Inexhaustible wealth like the flow of the Ganges in the summer rains.

བདུད་དགྲའི་འཚེ་བ་མེད་ཅིང་དམ་ཆོས་སྤྱོད།

DUD *maras** **DRAI** *enemies* **TSHE WA** *harm* **ME CHING** *without, free* **DAM** *holy,excellent* **CHO** *dharma* **CHO** *practice*

*demons who hinder the attainment of buddhahood

Being free of the harm of the maras and enemies, and practising the excellent Dharma,

བསམ་པའི་དོན་ཀུན་ཆོས་ལྡན་ཡིད་བཞིན་འགྲུབ།

SAM PAI	**DON**	**KUN**	**CHO DEN**	**YI ZHIN**	**DRUB**
thoughts, of (what we want)	*object*	*all*	*being in harmony with the Dharma*	*according to wish*	*accomplish*

May all our wishes be in harmony with the Dharma and all our intentions be accomplished.

བསྟན་དང་འགྲོ་ལ་ཕན་ཐོགས་རྒྱ་ཆེན་འགྲུབ།

TAN	**DANG**	**DRO**	**LA**	**PHAN THO**	**GYA CHEN**	**DRUB**
doctrines	*and*	*beings*	*to*	*benefit for others*	*great, vast*	*accomplish*

Greatly accomplishing the welfare of the teachings and of beings,

མི་ལུས་དོན་དང་ལྡན་པ་འགྲུབ་པར་ཤོག།

MI	**LU**	**DON DANG DEN PA**	**DRUB PAR**	**SHOG**
human	*body*	*meaningful**	*gain*	*must!*

* a body with the eighteen factors of the freedoms and advantages[3]

May we have a meaningful human existence.

May this virtue mature quickly for myself and all others so that in this life we are free of the eighteen causes of untimely death and we gain healthy, youthful and powerful bodies, and inexhaustible wealth like the flow of the Ganges in the summer rains. Being free of the harm of the maras and enemies, and practising the excellent Dharma, may all our wishes be in harmony with the Dharma and all our intentions be accomplished. Greatly accomplishing the welfare of the teachings and of beings, may we have a meaningful human existence.

THE JOURNEY TO DEWACHEN

བདག་དང་བདག་ལ་འབྲེལ་ཐོགས་ཀུན།

DAG	**DANG**	**DAG**	**LA**	**DREL THOG**	**KUN**
I	*and*	*me*	*to*	*connected*	*all*

(in particular all those I have had recent dealings with and in general all beings, each of whom has been my own mother in my countless past lives)

In front of myself and all those who are connected with me,

འདི་ནས་ཚེ་འཕོས་གྱུར་མ་ཐག།

DI	**NAE**	**TSHE**	**PO GYUR**	**MA THAG**
this life	*from*	*life*	*change*	*immediately*

(i.e. die)

As soon as we pass from this life,

སྤྲུལ་པའི་སངས་རྒྱས་འོད་དཔག་མེད།

TRUL PAI SANG GYE O PA ME
apparition buddha Amitabha
(a form of Amitabha emanates from Dewachen — it resembles him exactly)

May Buddha Amitabha's emanated form

དགེ་སློང་དགེ་འདུན་འཁོར་གྱིས་བསྐོར།

GE LONG GEN DUN KHOR GYI KOR
bhikshu, fully ordained monks Sangha, assembly retinue, circle by surrounded

Surrounded by his retinue of ordained Sangha

མདུན་དུ་མངོན་སུམ་འབྱོན་པར་ཤོག།

DUN DU NGON SUM JON PAR SHOG
before me clearly come may they, they must

Clearly appear.

May the emanated form of Buddha Amitabha surrounded by his retinue of ordained Sangha appear clearly in front of me and all those connected with me at the very moment of our death.

དེ་མཐོང་ཡིད་དགའ་སྣང་བ་སྐྱིད།

DE THONG YI GA NANG WA KYI
then see my mind happy happy, joyful

On seeing them may our minds be joyful, happy and

ཤི་བའི་སྡུག་བསྔལ་མེད་པར་ཤོག།

SHI WAI DUG NGAL MED PAR SHOG
death's suffering without may we be

Free of the sorrows of death.

བྱང་ཆུབ་སེམས་དཔའ་མཆེད་བརྒྱད་ནི།

JANG CHUB SEM PA CHED GYE NI
bodhisattva brother eight (emphasis)*

*Chenrezi, Chana Dorje, Jampa, Namkhai Nyingpo, Sayi Nyingpo, Kuntuzangpo, Dribpa Namsel, Jamyang

May the eight brother Bodhisattvas

རྫུ་འཕྲུལ་སྟོབས་ཀྱིས་ནམ་མཁར་བྱོན།

DZU TRUL TOB KYI NAM KHAR JON
miracle power by sky come

Miraculously appear in the sky before us and

བདེ་བ་ཅན་དུ་འགྲོ་བ་ཡི།

DE WA CHEN DU DRO WA YI
great happiness to going of

Show us the path to Dewachen and

ལམ་སྟོན་ལམ་སྣ་འདྲེན་པར་ཤོག།

LAM TON LAM NA DREN PAR SHOG
path, road show path guide, as may they, they must

Act as our guides along the way.

On seeing them, may our minds be joyful, happy and free of the sorrows of death. May the eight brother Bodhisattvas miraculously appear in the sky before us and show us the path to Dewachen and act as our guides along the way.

CUTTING OUR ATTACHMENT TO THIS WORLD

ངན་སོང་སྡུག་བསྔལ་བཟོད་གླགས་མེད།

NGAN SONG DUG NGAL ZOE LAG ME
states of woe sorrow bear, endure put up with, endure without*

*hells, insatiable ghosts, animals

In the states of woe the sufferings are unbearable, while

ལྷ་མིའི་བདེ་སྐྱིད་མི་རྟག་འགྱུར།

LHA MI DE KYI MI TAG GYUR
gods men's joy, happiness impermanent is

The happiness of gods and humans is impermanent –

དེ་ལ་སྐྲག་སེམས་སྐྱེ་བར་ཤོག།

DE LA TRAG SEM KYE WAR SHOG
that to fearful mind arise, come must! may it

May fear of these places arise in our minds!

In the states of woe the sufferings are unbearable, while the happiness of gods and humans is impermanent. May fear of these places arise in our minds!

ཐོག་མ་མེད་ནས་ད་ལྟའི་བར།

THOG MA ME NAE DAN DAI BAR
beginning (time immemorial) without from now up until

From beginningless time up until now

འཁོར་བ་འདི་ན་ཡུན་རེ་རིང་།

KHOR WA DI NA YUN RE RING
samsara this in very long time
(moving round and round)

We have wandered for so long in samsara.

དེ་ལ་སྐྱོ་བ་སྐྱེ་བར་ཤོག།

DE LA KYO WA KYE WAR SHOG
that to regret, sadness arise may it!
(pointless suffering)

May we feel regret at this!

From beginningless time up until now we have wandered for so long in samsara. May we feel regret at this!

མི་ནས་མི་རུ་སྐྱེ་ཆོག་ཀྱང་།

MI NAE MI RU KYE CHOG KYANG
human from human as born is possible but
(the human realm offers the best chances for gaining buddhahood)

It is possible for a human to be reborn as a human being, but even then

སྐྱེ་ག་ན་འཆི་གྲངས་མེད་མྱོང་།

KYE GA NA CHI DRANG ME NYONG
birth old age sickness death countless experience

There will be countless experiences of birth, old age, sickness and death.

དུས་ངན་སྙིགས་མར་བར་ཆད་མང་།

DU NGAN NYIG MAR BAR CHAE MANG
time bad degenerate, in difficulties, obstacles many
(the present period of the Kali Yuga)

In these degenerate evil times there are many difficulties.

མི་དང་ལྷ་ཡི་བདེ་སྐྱིད་འདི།

MI DANG LHA YI DE KYID DI
men, humans and gods of happiness this

The happiness of gods and men

དུག་དང་འདྲེས་པའི་ཟས་བཞིན་དུ།

DUG DANG DRE PAI ZAE ZHIN DU
poison and, with mixed food like

Is like food mixed with poison.

འདོད་པ་སྤུ་ཙམ་མེད་པར་ཤོག།

DOE PA	**PU**	**TSAM**	**ME PAR**	**SHOG**
desire (for them)	*one hair*	*even*	*without*	*may we be*

May we be without even a hair's worth of desire for such births!

It is possible for a human to be reborn as a human being, but even then there will be countless experiences of birth, old age, sickness and death. In these degenerate evil times there are many difficulties. The happiness of gods and men is like food mixed with poison. May we be without even a hair's worth of desire for such births.

ཉེ་དུ་ཟས་ནོར་མཐུན་གྲོགས་རྣམས།

NYE DU	**ZAE**	**NOR**	**THUN**	**DROG**	**NAM**
similarly	*food*	*wealth*	*pleasant*	*friends*	*(plural)*

In similar fashion, food, wealth and pleasant friends

མི་རྟག་སྒྱུ་མ་རྨི་ལམ་བཞིན།

MI TAG	**GYU MA**	**MI LAM**	**ZHIN**
impermanent	*maya, illusion*	*dream*	*like*

Are impermanent and illusory like a dream.

ཆགས་ཞེན་སྤུ་ཙམ་མེད་པར་ཤོག།

CHAG	**ZHEN**	**PU**	**TSAM**	**ME PAR**	**SHOG**
desire	*attachment, liking*	*one hair*	*even*	*without*	*may we be!*

May we be without even a hair's worth of longing for them.

In similar fashion, food, wealth and pleasant friends are impermanent and illusory like a dream. May we be without even a hair's worth of longing for them.

ས་ཆ་ཡུལ་རིས་ཁང་ཁྱིམ་རྣམས།

SA CHA	**YUL RIE**	**KHANG KHYIM**	**NAM**
earth	*province**	*house*	*(plural)*

*the land one is especially attached to

Our country, province and home

རྨི་ལམ་ཡུལ་གྱི་ཁང་ཁྱིམ་ལྟར།

MI LAM	**YUL**	**GYI**	**KHANG KHYIM**	**TAR**
dream	*country*	*of*	*house*	*as*

Are no more than our house in the land dreams.

བདེན་པར་མ་གྲུབ་ཤེས་པར་ཤོག།

DEN PAR	**MA DRUB**	**SHE PAR**	**SHOG**
truth, as	*not have*	*know*	*we must!*
(devoid of reality)			

We must know them to be devoid of reality.

Our country, province and home are no more than our house in the land of dreams. We must know them to be devoid of reality.

ཐར་མེད་འཁོར་བའི་རྒྱ་མཚོ་ནས།

THAR	**ME**	**KHOR WAI**	**GYAM TSHO**	**NAE**
liberation	*without*	*samsara's*	*ocean*	*from*
(i.e. very difficult to escape from)				

From this ocean of samsara which offers no liberation,

ཉེས་ཆེན་བཙོན་ནས་ཐར་པ་བཞིན།

NYE	**CHEN**	**TSON**	**NAE**	**THAR PA**	**ZHIN**
terrible	*very*	*prison*	*from*	*free, liberated*	*as, like*

As one who is freed from a most terrible prison,

བདེ་བ་ཅན་གྱི་ཞིང་ཁམས་སུ།

DE WA CHEN	**GYI**	**ZHING KHAM**	**SU**
Sukhavati, 'Happy'	*of*	*realm*	*in, to*

To the realm of Dewachen

ཕྱི་ལྟས་མེད་པར་འབྲོས་པར་ཤོག།

CHI	**TAE**	**ME PAR**	**DROE PAR**	**SHOG**
back	*look*	*without*	*escape, go there*	*may we!*
(over one's shoulder)				

May we escape without looking back!

As one who is freed from a most terrible prison, may we escape to the realm of Dewachen from this ocean of samsara which offers no liberation without a backward look.

COMING TO DEWACHEN

ཆགས་ཞེན་འཁྲི་བ་ཀུན་བཅད་ནས།

CHAG	**ZHEN**	**TRI WA**	**KUN**	**CHAE**	**NAE**
desire	*attachment, liking*	*entanglement, thraldom*	*all*	*cut*	*then*

Cutting all the thralls of desire and attraction,

བྱ་རྒོད་རྙི་ནས་ཐར་བ་བཞིན།

JA GOE	**NYI**	**NAE**	**THAR WA**	**ZHIN**
vulture (it flies high and fast)	*snare*	*from*	*freed*	*like*

Like a vulture freed from a snare,

ནུབ་ཀྱི་ཕྱོགས་ཀྱི་ནམ་མཁའ་ལ།

NUB KYI	**CHOG**	**KYI**	**NAM KHA**	**LA**
western	*direction*	*of*	*sky*	*to, in*

Travelling through the sky towards the west,

འཇིག་རྟེན་ཁམས་ནི་གྲངས་མེད་པ།

JIG TEN	**KHAM NI**	**DRANG ME PA**
world	*spheres*	*countless*

Across countless world spheres

སྐད་ཅིག་ཡུད་ལ་བགྲོད་བྱས་ནས།

KAE CHIG	**YU**	**LA**	**DROE JAE**	**NAE**
an instant	*moment*	*in*	*cross over, reach there*	*then*

May we pass in an instant and

བདེ་བ་ཅན་དུ་ཕྱིན་པར་ཤོག།

DE WA CHEN	**DU**	**CHIN PAR**	**SHOG**
Sukhavati, 'Happy'	*to*	*come*	*we must!*

Come to Dewachen

Cutting all the thralls of desire and attraction, like a vulture freed from a snare, may we traverse the western sky across countless worlds and arrive in an instant in Dewachen.

དེ་རུ་སངས་རྒྱས་འོད་དཔག་མེད།

DE RU	**SANG GYE**	**O PA ME**
there	*Buddha*	*Amitabha, 'Immeasurable Light'*

Here is Buddha Amitabha

མངོན་སུམ་བཞུགས་པའི་ཞལ་མཐོང་ནས།

NGON SUM	**ZHUG PAI**	**ZHAL**	**THONG**	**NAE**
manifestly (his real original form)	*sitting*	*face*	*see*	*then, by this*

Sitting before us — and we see his actual face!

སྒྲིབ་པ་ཐམས་ཅད་དག་པར་ཤོག།

DRIB PA	THAM CHE	DAG PAR	SHOG
obscurations	*all**	*purified*	*may they! they must!*

*of the afflictions and their subtle traces

May all our obscurations be purified!

Here is Buddha Amitabha sitting before us – and we see his actual face! May all our obscurations be purified.

སྐྱེ་གནས་བཞི་ཡི་མཆོག་གྱུར་བ།

KYE	NAE	ZHI	YI	CHOG	GYUR WA
birth	*place*	*four**	*of*	*best*	*is*

*heat and moisture (as for insect), egg, womb, and magically in a lotus flower

The best of the four ways of birth

མེ་ཏོག་པདྨའི་སྙིང་པོ་ལ།

ME TOG	PAE MAI	NYING PO	LA
flower	*lotus'*	*heart, centre*	*on, in*

Is magically within the heart of a lotus flower –

བརྫུས་ཏེ་སྐྱེ་བ་ལེན་པར་ཤོག།

DZU	TE	KYE WA	LEN PAR	SHOG
magical	*thus*	*birth*	*take*	*may we!*

(this is the mode of birth in Dewachen)

May we be born in this way!

སྐད་ཅིག་ཉིད་ལ་ལུས་རྫོགས་ནས།

KAE CHIG NYID	LA	LU	DZOG	NAE
in an instant	*in*	*body*	*fully developed*	*then*

With our bodies fully formed in an instant

མཚན་དཔེ་ལྡན་པའི་ལུས་ཐོབ་ཤོག།

TSHAN PE	DEN PAI	LU	THOB	SHOG
auspicious	*having*	*body*	*get*	*may we*

marks and signs of a Buddha's body

May these bodies display the auspicious marks and signs.

The best of the four ways of birth is magically within the heart of a lotus flower. May we be born in this way! With our bodies fully formed in an instant may these bodies display the auspicious marks and signs.

མི་སྐྱེ་དོགས་པའི་ཐེ་ཚོམ་གྱིས།

MI KYE	**DOG PAI**	**THE TSHOM**	**GYI**
not born	*fear, hesitation*	*doubt*	*by, due to*

Due to the hesitancy of doubting that one would be born there,

ལོ་གྲངས་ལྔ་བརྒྱའི་བར་དག་ཏུ།

LO DRANG	**NGAB GYAI**	**BAR**	**DAG TU**
years	*five hundred*	*until*	*all*

For a period of full five hundred years

ནང་དེར་བདེ་སྐྱིད་ལོངས་སྤྱོད་ལྡན།

NANG	**DER**	**DE KYID**	**LONG CHO**	**DEN**
inside (of the lotus bud)	*there*	*happiness*	*wealth, articles*	*having*

One will have happiness and all comforts within the lotus, and

སངས་རྒྱས་གསུང་ནི་ཐོས་ན་ཡང༌།

SANG GYE	**SUNG**	**NI**	**THO**	**NA YANG**
Buddha (Amitabha)	*speech*	*(emph.)*	*hear*	*but, and yet*

Hear the speech of Amitabha.

མེ་ཏོག་ཁ་ནི་མི་བྱེ་བས།

ME TOG	**KHA**	**NI**	**MI**	**JE WAE**
flower	*mouth (i.e petals)*		*not*	*open, separate*

Yet the mouth of the flower will not open and so

སངས་རྒྱས་ཞལ་མཇལ་ཕྱི་བའི་སྐྱོན།

SANG GYE	**ZHAL**	**JAL**	**CHI WAI**	**KYON**
Buddha (Amitabha)	*face*	*see, meet*	*delay*	*fault, defect*

There is the defect of delay in seeing the Buddha's face.

དེ་འདྲ་བདག་ལ་མི་འབྱུང་ཤོག།

DEN DRA	**DAG**	**LA**	**MI JUNG**	**SHOG**
like that	*I*	*to*	*not come*	*may we!*

May we not have that experience!

སྐྱེ་མ་ཐག་ཏུ་མེ་ཏོག་བྱེ།

KYE	**MA THAG**	**TU**	**ME TOG**	**JE**
birth	*immediately*	*at*	*flower*	*open*

May the flower open immediately at birth

འོད་དཔག་མེད་པའི་ཞལ་མཐོང་ཤོག།

OD PA ME PAI	ZHAL	THONG	SHOG
Amitabha's	*face*	*see*	*may we*

So that we see the face of Amitabha.

Due to the hesitancy of doubting that one would be born there, for a period of full five hundred years one will have happiness and all comforts within the lotus, and hear the speech of Amitabha. However the mouth of the flower will not open and so there is the defect of the delay in seeing the Buddha's face. May we not have that experience! May the flower open immediately at birth so that we see the face of Amitabha.

OUR ACTIVITIES IN DEWACHEN

བསོད་ནམས་སྟོབས་དང་རྫུ་འཕྲུལ་གྱིས།

SO NAM	TOB	DANG	DZU TRUL	GYI
merits	*power*	*and*	*miracle, magic*	*by*

Miraculously and by the power of our merit

ལག་པའི་མཐིལ་ནས་མཆོད་པའི་སྤྲིན།

LAG PAI	THIL	NAE	CHO PAI	TRIN
hand's	*palm*	*from*	*offering*	*cloud (i.e. vast and easily arising)*

From the palms of our hands may

བསམ་མི་ཁྱབ་པ་སྤྲོས་བྱས་ནས།

SAM MI KHYAB PA	TROE JAE	NAE
inconceivable, beyond the reach of mind	*come out, emanate*	*then*

Inconceivable clouds of offerings arise and

སངས་རྒྱས་འཁོར་བཅས་མཆོད་པར་ཤོག།

SANG GYE	KHOR CHE	CHO PAR	SHOG
Buddha (Amitabha)	*with his retinue*	*offer*	*may we*

May we then present them to the Buddha and his retinue.

དེ་ཚེ་དེ་བཞིན་གཤེགས་པ་དེས།

DE	TSHE	DE ZHIN SHEG PA	DAE
that	*time*	*the Tathagata (Amitabha)*	*by that*

When this happens may the Tathagata

ཕྱག་གཡས་བརྐྱང་ནས་མགོ་ལ་བཞག།

CHAG	YAE	KYANG	NAE	GO	LA	ZHAG
hand	*right*	*extend*	*then*	*(my)head*	*on*	*put (as blessing)*

Extend his right hand and place it on our heads.

བྱང་ཆུབ་ལུང་བསྟན་ཐོབ་པར་ཤོག།

JANG CHUB	LUNG TEN	THOB PAR	SHOG
bodhi, enlightenment	*prediction*	*get*	*may we!*

May we receive his prediction of our enlightenment.

Miraculously and by the power of our merit, inconceivable clouds of offerings arise from the palms of our hands so that we may offer them to the Buddha and his retinue. At that time may the Tathagata extend his right hand and place it on our heads. May we receive his prediction of our enlightenment.

ཟབ་དང་རྒྱ་ཆེའི་ཆོས་ཐོས་ནས།

ZAB	DANG	GYA CHEI	CHO	THO	NAE
deep	*and*	*large*	*Dharma*	*hear*	*then*

Hearing the profound and vast Dharma

རང་རྒྱུད་སྨིན་ཅིང་གྲོལ་བར་ཤོག།

RANG	GYU	MIN CHING	DROL WAR	SHOG
own	*mind*	*ripening*	*liberate*	*they must be!*

May our minds be ripened and liberated.

སྤྱན་རས་གཟིགས་དང་མཐུ་ཆེན་ཐོབ།

CHEN RAE ZI	DANG	THU CHEN THOB
Avalokitesvara	*and*	*Vajrapani*

May Chenrezi and Vajrapani,

རྒྱལ་སྲས་ཐུ་བོ་རྣམ་གཉིས་ཀྱིས།

GYAL	SAE	THU WO	NAM NYI	KYI
victor (bodhisattva)	*son*	*senior brother*	*two, both*	*by*

The two foremost Bodhisattvas,

བྱིན་གྱིས་བརླབས་ཤིང་རྗེས་བཟུང་ཤོག།

JIN GYI LAB SHING	JE ZUNG	SHOG
blessing	*hold us as disciples, take care of*	*may they*

Give us blessing and hold us as disciples.

Hearing the profound and vast Dharma may our minds be ripened and liberated. May Chenrezi and Vajrapani, the two foremost Bodhisattvas, give us blessing and hold us as disciples.

ཉིན་རེ་བཞིན་དུ་ཕྱོགས་བཅུ་ཡི།

NYIN RE ZHIN DU CHOG CHU YI
daily directions (i.e. everywhere) ten of

Each day, when countless

སངས་རྒྱས་བྱང་སེམས་དཔག་མེད་པ།

SANG GYE JANG SEM PA ME PA
Buddha Bodhisattvas measureless

Buddhas and Bodhisattvas of the ten directions

འོད་དཔག་མེད་པ་མཆོད་པ་དང་།

OE PA MEPA CHOE PA DANG
Amitabha offer and

Come to make offerings to Amitabha and

ཞིང་དེར་བལྟ་ཕྱིར་འབྱོན་པའི་ཚེ།

ZHING DER TA CHIR JON PAI TSHE
realm there look in order to come that time

To see his realm,

དེ་དག་ཀུན་ལ་བསྙེན་བཀུར་ཞིང་།

DE DA KUN LA NYEN KUR ZHING
these all to serving

May we serve all of them and

ཆོས་ཀྱི་བདུད་རྩི་ཐོབ་པར་ཤོག།

CHO KYI DU TSI THOB PAR SHOG
dharma of amrita, liberating elixir get may we

Receive the liberating elixir of the Dharma.

Each day when countless Buddhas and Bodhisattvas of the ten directions come to make offerings to Amitabha and to see his realm, may we serve them all and receive the liberating elixir of the Dharma.

རྫུ་འཕྲུལ་ཐོགས་པ་མེད་པ་ཡིས།

DZU TRUL THOG PA ME PA YI
miracles unimpeded by

Miraculously unimpeded,

མངོན་དགའི་ཞིང་དང་དཔལ་ལྡན་ཞིང་།

NGON GAI ZHING DANG PAL DEN ZHING
Joyous and Glorious***
* the name of Akshobya's pure realm in the east
** the name of Ratnasambhava's pure realm in the north

To the realms named Joyous, Glorious,

ལས་རབ་རྫོགས་དང་སྟུག་པོ་བཀོད།

LAE RAB DZOG DANG TUG PO KO**
Perfect Action and Densely Arrayed***
* the name of Amoghasiddi's pure realm in the south
** the name of Vairocana's pure realm in the centre

Perfect Action and Densely Arrayed

སྔ་དྲོ་དེ་དག་རྣམས་སུ་འགྲོ།

NGA DRO DE DAG NAM SU DRO
morning these to go

May we go in the morning.

མི་བསྐྱོད་རིན་འབྱུང་དོན་ཡོད་གྲུབ།

MI KYO RIN JUNG DON YO DRUB
Imperturbable, Akshobhya Jewel-born, Ratnasambhava Meaningful Accomplishment, Amoghasiddhi

There, from the Buddhas Akshobhya, Ratnasambhava, Amoghasiddhi,

རྣམ་སྣང་ལ་སོགས་སངས་རྒྱས་ལ།

NAM NANG LA SOG SANG GYE LA
Illuminator, Vairocana and so on Buddhas to

Vairocana and the other Buddhas

དབང་དང་བྱིན་རླབས་སྡོམ་པ་ཞུ།

WANG DANG JIN LAB DOM PA ZHU
empowerment and blessing vows request

May we request and receive empowerment, blessings and vows.

མཆོད་པ་དུ་མས་མཆོད་བྱས་ནས།

CHOE PA DU MAE CHOE JAE NAE
offerings many make offerings then

Presenting many offerings to them,

དགོང་མོ་བདེ་བ་ཅན་ཉིད་དུ།

GONG MO	**DE WA CHEN**	**NYI**	**DU**
evening	*Sukhavati 'Happy'*	*itself*	*to*

To Dewachen in the evening

དཀའ་ཚེགས་མེད་པར་སླེབས་པར་ཤོག།

KA	**TSHEG**	**ME PAR**	**LEB PAR**	**SHOG**
difficulty	*problems*	*without*	*come*	*we must!*

May we return without difficulty.

Miraculously unimpeded, may we go in the morning to the realms named Joyous, Glorious, Perfect Action and Densely Arrayed. In these realms, respectively from the Buddhas Akshobhya, Ratnasambhava, Amoghasiddhi, Vairocana and the other Buddhas may we request and receive empowerment, blessings and vows. Having presented many offerings to them, may we return without difficulty in the evening to Dewachen.

པོ་ཏ་ལ་དང་ལྕང་ལོ་ཅན།

PO TA LA	**DANG**	**CHANG LO CHAN**
Potala, where Chenrezi stays	*and*	*Alakavati, where Vajrapani stays*

Potala and Changlo Chan,

རྔ་ཡབ་གླིང་དང་ཨོ་རྒྱན་ཡུལ།

NGA YAB LING	**DANG**	**OR GYAN YUL**
Camaradvipa, where Padmasambhava is now at Zangdopalri	*and*	*the land of Oddiyana, where Padmasambhava was born*

Ngayab Ling and Orgyan Yul –

སྤྲུལ་སྐུའི་ཞིང་ཁམས་བྱེ་བ་བརྒྱར།

TRUL KUI	**ZHING KHAM**	**JE WA**	**GYAR**
nirmanakaya	*realms*	*one or ten million*	*hundred*

In an infinite number of these nirmanakaya realms reside

སྤྱན་རས་གཟིགས་དང་སྒྲོལ་མ་དང་།

CHEN RE ZI	**DANG**	**DROL MA**	**DANG**
Avalokitesvara	*and*	*Tara*	*and*

Chenrezi and Drolma,

ཕྱག་རྡོར་པད་འབྱུང་བྱེ་བ་བརྒྱ།

CHAG DOR	**PAE JUNG**	**JE WA**	**GYA**
Vajrapani	*Padmasambhava*	*one or ten million*	*one hundred*

Chana Dorje and Pema Jungnae, each one appearing in infinite numbers.

མཇལ་ཞིང་མཆོད་པ་རྒྱ་མཚོས་མཆོད།

JAL ZHING	**CHO PA**	**GYAM TSHOE**	**CHO**
see them, meet them	*offerings*	*ocean,(i.e. vast) amount//by*	*offer*

Seeing them, may we present oceans of offerings and

དབང་དང་གདམས་ངག་ཟབ་མོ་ཞུ།

WANG	**DANG**	**DAM NGAG**	**ZAB MO**	**ZHU**
empowerment	*and*	*instructions*	*profound*	*request*

Request and receive empowerments and profound instructions.

མྱུར་དུ་རང་གནས་བདེ་ཆེན་ཞིང་།

NYUR DU	**RANG**	**NAE**	**DE CHEN**	**ZHING**
quickly	*own*	*place*	*Sukhavati*	*realm*

Then to our own place, Dewachen,

ཐོགས་པ་མེད་པར་ཕྱིན་པར་ཤོག།

THOG PA ME PAR	**CHIN PAR**	**SHOG**
unimpeded, easily	*go, come back*	*we must*

May we return quickly without hindrance.

Potala and Changlo Chan, Ngayab Ling and Orgyan Yul, in an infinite number of these nirmanakaya realms reside Chenrezi and Drolma, Chana Dorje and Pema Jungnae, each one appearing in infinite numbers. Seeing them may we present an ocean of offerings and request and receive empowerments and profound instructions. Then to our own place of Dewachen, may we return quickly without hindrance.

ཤུལ་གྱི་ཉེ་དུ་གྲྭ་སློབ་སོགས།

SHUL GYI	**NYE DU**	**DRA**	**LOB**	**SOG**
*former place**	*friends, relatives*	*monks*	*teachers*	*and so on*

*from which we left for Dewachen

The friends, monks and teachers who remain in our old abode

ལྷ་ཡི་མིག་གིས་གསལ་བར་མཐོང་།

LHA YI	**MIG**	**GI**	**SAL WAR**	**THONG**
god's	*eye*	*by*	*clearly*	*see*

We can see clearly with the divine eye.

སྲུང་སྐྱོབ་བྱིན་གྱིས་རློབས་བྱེད་ཅིང་།

SUNG	**KYOB**	**JIN GYI LOB**	**JE CHING**
guarding	*protecting*	*blessing*	*doing*

May we guard, protect and bless them, and

འཆི་དུས་ཞིང་དེར་ཁྲིད་པར་ཤོག།

CHI	**DU**	**ZHING**	**DER**	**TRI PAR**	**SHOG**
death	*time*	*realm*	*there*	*conduct, lead*	*may we*
(when they die)			*(Dewachen)*		

At their death lead them here to Dewachen.

With the divine eye we can clearly see the friends, monks and teachers who remain in our old abode. May we guard, protect and bless them, and at their death lead them here to Dewachen.

བསྐལ་བཟང་འདི་ཡི་བསྐལ་པའི་ཡུན།

KAL ZANG	**DI**	**YI**	**KAL PAI**	**YUN**
*Bhadrakalpa**	*this*	*of*	*kalpas, aeon*	*time, duration*
			(i.e. a very long time)	

*the present good kalpa in which one thousand Buddhas will appear. Shakyamuni was the 4th

The duration of this aeon, the Good,

བདེ་བ་ཅན་གྱི་ཞག་གཅིག་སྟེ།

DE WA CHEN	**GYI**	**ZHAG**	**CHIG**	**TE**
Sukhavati	*of*	*day*	*one*	*thus*
		(24 hours)		

Is equal to that of one single day in Dewachen.

བསྐལ་པ་གྲངས་མེད་འཆི་བ་མེད།

KAL PA	**DRANG ME**	**CHI WA**	**ME**
kalpa, aeon	*countless*	*death*	*without*
(i.e. Dewachen kalpas)			

During numberless Dewachen aeons there is no death!

རྟག་ཏུ་ཞིང་དེར་འཛིན་པར་ཤོག།

TAG TU	**ZHING**	**DER**	**DZIN PAR**	**SHOG**
always, continuously	*realm (Dewachen)*	*that*	*hold, stay there*	*we must!*

May we always remain in this realm.

One single day in Dewachen is equal to the duration of the present aeon known as the Good.

བྱམས་པ་ནས་བཟུང་མོས་པའི་བར།

JAM PA	**NAE ZUNG**	**MO PAI**	**BAR**
*Maitreya**	*starting with, from him onwards*	*Mopa Thayae***	*until*

*the 5th Buddha of the Bhadrakalpa   ** Rochana, the 1000th Buddha of the Bhadrakalpa

From Maitreya up to Rochana,

བསྐལ་བཟང་འདི་ཡི་སངས་རྒྱས་རྣམས།

KAL ZANG	**DI**	**YI**	**SANG GYE NAM**
Bhadrakalpa	*this*	*of*	*Buddhas*

When the Buddhas of this Good Aeon

འཇིག་རྟེན་འདི་ན་ནམ་འབྱོན་ཚེ།

JIG TEN	**DI**	**NA**	**NAM**	**JON**	**TSHE**
world (in samsara)	*this*	*to*	*when*	*coming*	*time*

Come to this world, then

རྫུ་འཕྲུལ་སྟོབས་ཀྱིས་འདིར་འོངས་ནས།

DZU TRUL	**TOB**	**KYI**	**DIR**	**ONG**	**NAE**
miracle	*power*	*by*	*here*	*come (to this world from Dewachen)*	*then*

May we arrive here miraculously, and

སངས་རྒྱས་མཆོད་ཅིང་དམ་ཆོས་ཉན།

SANG GYE	**CHOD CHING**	**DAM**	**CHO**	**NYAN**
*Buddhas**	*offering*	*holy, excellent*	*dharma*	*hear*

** the ones in this Good Kalpa*

Making offerings to these Buddhas, may we hear the holy Dharma from them.

སླར་ཡང་བདེ་ཆེན་ཞིང་ཁམས་སུ།

LAR YANG	**DE CHEN**	**ZHING KHAM**	**SU**
again	*Sukhavati*	*realm*	*to*

Then, once again, to the realm of Dewachen

ཐོགས་པ་མེད་པར་འགྲོ་བར་ཤོག།

THOG PA ME PAR	**DRO WAR**	**SHOG**
unimpeded, easily and quickly	*go*	*may we!*

May we return without difficulty.

From Maitreya up to Rochana, when the Buddhas of this Good Aeon come to this world, then may we arrive here miraculously, and, making

offerings to these Buddhas, may we hear the holy Dharma from them. Then, once again, may we return without difficulty to the realm of Dewachen.

DESCRIPTION OF DEWACHEN

སངས་རྒྱས་བྱེ་བ་ཁྲག་ཁྲིག་བརྒྱ་སྟོང་ཕྲག།

SANG GYE	JE WA	TRAG TRIG	GYA TONG TRAG
Buddha	*ten million*	*a hundred thousand million*	*a hundred thousand*

Buddhas are infinite in number and they

བརྒྱད་ཅུ་རྩ་གཅིག་སངས་རྒྱས་ཞིང་ཀུན་གྱི།

GYAE CHU TSA CHIG	SANG GYE	ZHING KUN	GYI
eighty-one	*Buddha*	*realms*	*of*

Each have buddha realms, and

ཡོན་ཏན་བཀོད་པ་ཐམས་ཅད་གཅིག་བསྡོམས་པ།

YON TAN	KOE PA	THAM CHE	CHIG	DOM PA
good qualities	*built, decorated*	*all*	*one*	*united together (i.e. as Dewachen)*

All the good qualities of these realms are united together as one in

ཞིང་ཁམས་ཀུན་ལས་ཁྱད་འཕགས་བླ་ན་མེད།

ZHING KHAM	KUN	LAE	KHYAE	PHAG	LA NA ME
realm	*all*	*of*	*special*	*excellent*	*unsurpassed*

The realm unique amongst all others, the excellent, unsurpassed

བདེ་བ་ཅན་གྱི་ཞིང་དེར་སྐྱེ་བར་ཤོག།

DE WA CHEN	GYI	ZHING	DER	KYE WAR	SHOG
Sukhavati	*of*	*realm*	*there*	*born*	*may I be*

Realm of Dewachen. May we be born there!

Buddhas are infinite in number and they each have many buddha realms. The good qualities of all these realms unite together as the one realm unique amongst all others, the excellent, unsurpassed realm of Dewachen. May we be born there!

རིན་ཆེན་ས་གཞི་ཁོད་སྙོམས་ལག་མཐིལ་ལྟར།

RIN CHEN	SA ZHI	KHOE	NYOM	LAG THIL	TAR
jewel	*foundation, ground*	*surface*	*flat*	*palm of the hand*	*like*

The surface of its jewel foundation is flat like the palm of the hand, and

ཡངས་ཤིང་རྒྱ་ཆེ་གསལ་ཞིང་འོད་ཟེར་འབར།

YANG SHING	GYA CHE	SAL ZHING	OE ZER	BAR
wide	*vast*	*clear (i.e. shining brightly)*	*light rays*	*radiate*

Is wide, vast and brightly shining.

མནན་ན་ནེམ་ཞིང་བཏེགས་ན་སྤར་བྱེད་པ།

NAN	NA	NEM	ZHING	TEG	NA	PAR JE PA
push down	*if*	*goes down*	*and*	*lift up*	*if*	*comes up*

It is soft, subtle and responsive.

བདེ་འཇམ་ཡངས་པའི་ཞིང་དེར་སྐྱེ་བར་ཤོག།

DE	JAM	YANG PAI	ZHING	DER	KYE WA	SHOG
happy	*soft*	*wide, open*	*realm*	*there*	*born*	*may we be*

May we be born there in that pleasant, gentle, and spacious place.

The surface of its jewel foundation is flat like the palm of the hand. Wide, vast and brightly shining, it is soft, subtle and responsive. May we be born there in that pleasant, gentle and spacious place.

རིན་ཆེན་དུ་མ་ལས་གྲུབ་དཔག་བསམ་ཤིང་།

RIN CHEN	DU MA	LAE	DRUB	PAG SAM SHING
jewels	*many*	*from*	*made*	*wish granting trees*

There are wish-granting trees made of many jewels

ལོ་མ་དར་ཟབ་འབྲས་བུ་རིན་ཆེན་བརྒྱན།

LO MA	DAR ZAB	DRAE BU	RIN CHEN	GYEN
leaves	*silk*	*fruit*	*jewels*	*adorned*

That are adorned with leaves of silk and fruit of precious gems.

དེ་སྟེང་སྤྲུལ་པའི་བྱ་ཚོགས་སྐད་སྙན་སྒྲས།

DE TENG	TRUL PAI	JA	TSHOG	KAE	NYAN	DRAE
on it	*miraculous*	*birds*	*hosts*	*speech*	*sweet, pleasant*	*sound, say*

They host many miraculous birds singing sweetly and their sound

ཟབ་དང་རྒྱ་ཆེའི་ཆོས་ཀྱི་སྒྲ་རྣམས་སྒྲོགས།

ZAB	DANG	GYA CHEI	CHO	KYI	DRA NAM	DROG
deep	*and*	*vast*	*Dharma*	*of*	*sounds*	*make, speak*

Proclaims the profound and vast Dharma.

ངོ་མཚར་ཆེན་པོའི་ཞིང་དེར་སྐྱེ་བར་ཤོག།

NGO TSHAR	**CHEN POI**	**ZHING**	**DER**	**KYE WAR**	**SHOG**
wonderful	*very greatly*	*realm*	*there*	*born*	*may we be*

May we be born in that very marvellous land.

There are wish-granting trees made of many jewels that are adorned with leaves of silk and fruit of precious gems. They host many miraculous birds singing sweetly and their sound proclaims the profound and vast Dharma. May we be born in that very marvellous land.

སྤོས་ཆུའི་ཆུ་ཀླུང་ཡན་ལག་བརྒྱད་ལྡན་མང་།

POE	**CHUI**	**CHU LUNG**	**YEN LA**	**GYAE**	**DEN**	**MANG**
perfumed	*water*	*river*	*aspects*	*eight**	*having*	*many*

*softness, lightness, coolness, clears the throat, easy to digest, clarity, freshness, free of impurities

There are many rivers of fragrant water having the eight good qualities, and

དེ་བཞིན་བདུད་རྩིའི་ཁྲུས་ཀྱི་རྫིང་བུ་རྣམས།

DE ZHIN	**DUE TSI**	**TRU KYI**	**DZING BU NAM**
similarly	*amrita, liberating elixir*	*bathing*	*pools*

Bathing ponds of liberating elixir

རིན་ཆེན་སྣ་བདུན་ཐེམ་སྐས་ཕ་གུས་བསྐོར།

RIN CHEN	**NA DUN**	**THEM KAE**	**PHA GUE**	**KOR**
jewels, precious	*seven**	*steps*	*edge, border*	*surrounded*

*gold, silver, turquoise, coral, pearl, crystal and lead

With steps and borders of the precious seven.

མེ་ཏོག་པདྨ་དྲི་ཞིམ་འབྲས་བུར་ལྡན།

ME TOG	**PAE MA**	**DRI**	**ZHIM**	**DRE BUR**	**DEN**
flower (in the bathing ponds)	*lotus*	*smell*	*pleasing, sweet*	*fruit*	*having*

These ponds have lotus flowers, sweet-smelling and fruit-bearing,

པདྨའི་འོད་ཟེར་དཔག་ཏུ་མེད་པར་འཕྲོ།

PAE MAI	**OE**	**ZER**	**PAG TU ME PAR**	**TRO**
lotus	*light*	*rays*	*countless*	*radiate*

Which radiate countless rays of light

འོད་ཟེར་རྩེ་ལ་སྤྲུལ་པའི་སངས་རྒྱས་བརྒྱན།

OE	**ZER**	**TSE**	**LA**	**TRUL PAI**	**SANG GYE**	**GYAN**
light	*rays*	*top*	*at*	*miraculous*	*Buddhas*	*adorned*

Each adorned at its tip with miraculous Buddhas.

ཡ་མཚན་ཆེན་པོའི་ཞིང་དེར་སྐྱེ་བར་ཤོག།

YAM TSHAN	**CHEN POI**	**ZHING**	**DER**	**KYE WAR**	**SHOG**
wonderful, marvellous	*great*	*realm*	*there*	*born*	*may we be*

May we be born in that very wonderful place.

There are many rivers of fragrant water having the eight good qualities, and bathing ponds of liberating elixir with steps and borders of the precious seven. These ponds have lotus flowers, sweet-smelling and fruit-bearing, which radiate countless rays of light each adorned at its tip with miraculous Buddhas. May we be born in that very wonderful place.

མི་ཁོམས་བརྒྱད་དང་ངན་སོང་སྒྲ་མི་གྲགས།

MI KHOM	**GYAE**	**DANG**	**NGAN SONG**	**DRA**	**MI**	**DRAG**
difficult, unleisured states	*eight**	*and*	*states of woe (three lower realms)*	*sound*	*not*	*hear*

*hells, insatiable ghosts, animals, barbarian, border area, wrong views, stupid, long living gods

The sound of the eight difficult situations and the three lower realms does not reach there,

ཉོན་མོངས་དུག་ལྔ་དུག་གསུམ་ནད་དང་གདོན།

NYON MONG	**DUG**	**NGA**	**DUG**	**SUM**	**NAE**	**DANG**	**DON**
kleshas, afflictions	*poisons*	*five**	*poisons*	*three#*	*sickness*	*and spirits*	*evil*

*stupidity, anger, desire, pride and jealousy #the first three of the five poisons

To that realm untouched by the five afflicting poisons. Moreover sickness, evil spirits,

དགྲ་དང་དབུལ་ཕོངས་འཐབ་རྩོད་ལ་སོགས་པ།

DRA	**DANG**	**UL PHONG**	**THAB TSO**	**LA SOG PA**
enemies	*and*	*poor people*	*quarrelling, arguing*	*and so on*

Enemies, poverty, strife and

སྡུག་བསྔལ་ཐམས་ཅད་ཞིང་དེར་ཐོས་མ་མྱོང་།

DUG NGAL	**THAM CHE**	**ZHING**	**DER**	**THO**	**MA**	**NYONG**
sufferings	*all*	*realm*	*there*	*hear*	*not*	*experience*

All such sufferings are never even heard of there.

བདེ་བ་ཆེན་པོའི་ཞིང་དེར་སྐྱེ་བར་ཤོག།

DE WA CHEN POI	**ZHING**	**DER**	**KYE WAR**	**SHOG**
great joy	*realm*	*there*	*born*	*may we be!*

May we be born in that realm of great joy.

The sound of the eight difficult situations and the three lower realms does not reach there, to that realm untouched by the five afflicting poisons. Moreover sickness, evil spirits, enemies, poverty, strife and all such sufferings are never even heard of there. May we be born in that realm of great joy.

བུད་མེད་མེད་ཅིང་མངལ་ནས་སྐྱེ་བ་མེད།

BU ME ME CHING NGAL NAE KYE WA ME
woman without womb from born without

There are no women there and no birth from a womb as

ཀུན་ཀྱང་མེ་ཏོག་པདྨའི་སྦུབས་ནས་འཁྲུངས།

KUN KYANG ME TO PAE MAI BUB NAE TRUNG
all but flower lotus stem from born

All are born within lotus flowers.

ཐམས་ཅད་སྐུ་ལུས་ཁྱད་མེད་གསེར་གྱི་མདོག།

THAM CHE KU LU KHYAE ME SER GYI DO
all body body difference without yellow colour

There are no differences between bodies and all are golden in colour, each

དབུ་ལ་གཙུག་ཏོར་ལ་སོགས་མཚན་དཔེའི་བརྒྱན།

U LA TSUG TOR LA SOG TSHAN PE GYAN
head on ushnisha, raised dome and so on auspicious marks and signs adorned

Adorned with a raised dome on the head and all the other auspicious marks and signs.

མངོན་ཤེས་ལྔ་དང་སྤྱན་ལྔ་ཀུན་ལ་མངའ།

NGON SHE NGA DANG CHAN NGA KUN LA NGA
super knowledge five and eye** five all to have*

*divine eye, divine ear, knowledge of others thoughts, knowledge of how to perform miracles, and knowledge of one's previous lives ** flesh-, divine-, wisdom-, dharma-, and buddha-eye.

All have the five super-knowledges and the five eyes.

ཡོན་ཏན་དཔག་མེད་ཞིང་དེར་སྐྱེ་བར་ཤོག།

YON TAN PA ME ZHING DER KYE WAR SHOG
good qualities countless realm there born we must be

May we be born in that land of countless good qualities.

There are no women there and no birth from a womb as all are born within lotus flowers. There are no differences between bodies and all are golden in colour, each adorned with a raised dome on the head and all the other auspicious marks and signs. All have the five super-knowledges and the five eyes. May we be born in that land of countless good qualities.

རང་བྱུང་རིན་ཆེན་སྣ་ཚོགས་གཞལ་ཡས་ཁང་།

RANG JUNG	**RIN CHEN**	**NA TSHOG**	**ZHAL YAE KHANG**
self-arisen, self-occurring	*jewels*	*many different*	*palace, infinitude, mandala*

In the self-arisen divine palaces composed of diverse jewels

ཅི་འདོད་ལོངས་སྤྱོད་ཡིད་ལ་དྲན་པས་འབྱུང་།

CHI DOE	**LONG CHOE**	**YID**	**LA**	**DREN PAE**	**JUNG**
whatever is desired	*wealth, articles*	*mind*	*in*	*remember*	*comes*

Whatever wealth and luxury is wished for appears at the mere thought.

རྩོལ་སྒྲུབ་མི་དགོས་དགོས་འདོད་ལྷུན་གྱིས་གྲུབ།

TSOL	**DRUB**	**MI GOE**	**GOE**	**DOD**	**LHUN GYI DRUB**
effort	*effort, practice*	*not necessary*	*needs*	*desires*	*effortlessly arising*

Effort is not necessary and whatever one needs or desires comes easily.

ང་ཁྱོད་མེད་ཅིང་བདག་ཏུ་འཛིན་པ་མེད།

NGA	**KHYO**	**ME CHING**	**DAG**	**TU**	**DZIN PA**	**ME**
I	*you*	*without*	*self*	*at*	*grasping*	*without*

(not discriminating self and others)

Free from thinking ‘it is mine’ or ‘it is yours’ and without grasping at entities,

གང་འདོད་མཆོད་སྤྲིན་ལག་པའི་མཐིལ་ནས་འབྱུང་།

GANG	**DOE**	**CHOE**	**TRIN**	**LAG PAI**	**THIL**	**NAE**	**JUNG**
whatever	*like, desire*	*offering*	*clouds*	*hand’s*	*palm*	*from*	*arises*

Offering clouds of whatever is desired arises from the palm of one’s hand.

ཐམས་ཅད་བླ་མེད་ཐེག་ཆེན་ཆོས་ལ་སྤྱོད།

THAM CHE	**LA ME**	**THEG CHEN**	**CHO**	**LA**	**CHO**
all	*unsurpassed*	*mahayana*	*dharma*	*to*	*practise*

All beings there practise the unsurpassable mahayana Dharma.

བདེ་སྐྱིད་ཀུན་འབྱུང་ཞིང་དེར་སྐྱེ་བར་ཤོག།

DE KYI	**KUN**	**JUNG**	**ZHING**	**DER**	**KYE WAR**	**SHOG**
happiness	*all*	*source, arising*	*realm*	*there*	*born*	*may we be*

May we be born in that realm which is the source of all happiness.

In the self-arisen divine palaces composed of diverse jewels whatever wealth and luxury is wished for appears at the mere thought. Effort is not necessary and whatever one needs or desires comes easily. Free from thinking 'it is mine' or 'it is yours' and without grasping at entities, offering clouds of whatever is desired arise from the palm of one's hand. All beings there practise the unsurpassable mahayana Dharma. May we be born in that realm which is the source of all happiness.

དྲི་ཞིམ་རླུང་གིས་མེ་ཏོག་ཆར་ཆེན་འབེབས།

DRI	ZHIM	LUNG	GI	ME TOG	CHAR	CHEN	BEB
smell, scent	*pleasing*	*wind*	*by*	*flowers*	*rain*	*great*	*fall*

The pleasantly perfumed breeze rains down flowers.

ཤིང་དང་ཆུ་ཀླུང་པདྨོ་ཐམས་ཅད་ལས།

SHING	DANG	CHU LUNG	PAE MO	THAM CHE	LAE
tree	*and*	*river*	*lotus flower*	*all*	*from*

From all the trees, rivers and lotuses

ཡིད་དུ་འོང་བའི་གཟུགས་སྒྲ་དྲི་རོ་རེག།

YI DU ONG WAI	ZUG	DRA	DRI	RO	REG
attractive, fascinating	*form*	*sound*	*smell*	*taste*	*feeling, touch*

Fascinating forms, sounds, scents, tastes and textures arise

ལོངས་སྤྱོད་མཆོད་པའི་སྤྲིན་ཕུང་རྟག་ཏུ་འབྱུང་།

LONG CHO	CHOE PAI	TRIN	PHUNG	TAG TU	JUNG
wealth, pleasure	*offering*	*cloud*	*heap*	*always*	*arising*

Constantly as vast offering-clouds of all that is enjoyable.

བུད་མེད་མེད་ཀྱང་སྤྲུལ་པའི་ལྷ་མོའི་ཚོགས།

BU ME	ME	KYANG	TRUL PAI	LHA MOI	TSHOG
women	*without*	*although*	*miraculous*	*goddesses*	*hosts*

Although gender is absent there are hosts of miraculous goddesses,

མཆོད་པའི་ལྷ་མོ་དུ་མས་རྟག་ཏུ་མཆོད།

CHOE PAI	LHA MO	DU MAE	TAG TU	CHOD
offering	*goddesses*	*many*	*always*	*offer*

Offering goddesses proffering ceaseless delights.

The pleasantly perfumed breeze rains down flowers. From all the trees, rivers and lotuses fascinating forms, sounds, scents, tastes and textures arise constantly as vast offering-clouds of all that is enjoyable. Although gender is absent there are hosts of miraculous goddesses, offering goddesses proffering ceaseless delights.

འདུག་པར་འདོད་ཚེ་རིན་ཆེན་གཞལ་ཡས་ཁང་།

DUG PAR DOE TSHE RIN CHEN ZHAL YAE KHANG
stay, sit like when jewel palace, infinitude

When one desires to sit, there are divine palaces of jewels, and

ཉལ་བར་འདོད་ཚེ་རིན་ཆེན་ཁྲི་བཟང་སྟེང་།

NYAL WAR DOE TSHE RIN CHEN TRI ZANG TENG
sleep like when jewel couch excellent on

When one wishes to sleep there are excellent jewelled couches

དར་ཟབ་དུ་མའི་མལ་སྟན་སྔས་དང་བཅས།

DAR ZAB DU MAI MAL TAN NGAE DANG CHE
luxurious many's bedding pillow and so on

With much luxurious bedding, pillows and all that is required.

བྱ་དང་ལྗོན་ཤིང་ཆུ་ཀླུང་རོལ་མོ་སོགས།

JA DANG JON SHING CHU LUNG ROL MO SOG
bird and tree river music and so on

When one wishes to hear the sound of birds, trees, rivers, music and so on,

ཐོས་པར་འདོད་ཚེ་སྙན་པའི་ཆོས་སྒྲ་སྒྲོགས།

THO PAR DOE TSHE NYAN PAI CHO DRA DROG
hear like when pleasant, sweet dharma sound make, say

They offer the sweet sound of Dharma.

མི་འདོད་ཚེ་ན་རྣ་བར་སྒྲ་མི་གྲགས།

MI DOE TSHE NA NA WAR DRA MI DRAG
not like time when ear sound not hear

And when one does not wish this then one's ears will hear no sound.

བདུད་རྩིའི་རྫིང་བུ་ཆུ་ཀླུང་དེ་རྣམས་ཀྱང་།

DU TSI DZING BU CHU LUNG DE NAM KYANG
liberating elixir pond river these also

The rivers and bathing ponds of liberating elixir

དྲོ་གྲང་གང་འདོད་དེ་ལ་དེ་ལྟར་འབྱུང་།

DRO DRANG GANG DOE DE LA DE TAR JUNG
hot cold whichever like that (desire) to like that arise

Become hot or cold according to one's desire.

ཡིད་བཞིན་འགྲུབ་པའི་ཞིང་དེར་སྐྱེ་བར་ཤོག།

YI ZHIN	**DRUB PAI**	**ZHING**	**DER**	**KYE WAR**	**SHOG**
according to wish	*accomplishing, fulfilling*	*realm, place*	*there*	*born*	*we must be*

May we be born in that land where our wishes are always fulfilled.

When one desires to sit, there are divine palaces of jewels, and when one wishes to sleep there are excellent jewelled couches with much luxurious bedding, pillows and all that is required. When one wishes to hear the sound of birds, trees, rivers, music and so on they proffer the sweet sound of dharma and when one does not wish this then one's ears will hear no sound. The rivers and bathing pools of liberating elixir become hot or cold according to one's desire. May we be born in that land where our wishes are always fulfilled.

OUR PROGRESS TO ENLIGHTENMENT IN DEWACHEN

ཞིང་དེར་རྫོགས་པའི་སངས་རྒྱས་འོད་དཔག་མེད།

ZHING	**DER**	**DZOG PAI**	**SANG GYE**	**OE PA ME**
realm	*there*	*perfect*	*Buddha*	*Amitabha*

In that realm the perfect Buddha Amitabha

བསྐལ་པ་གྲངས་མེད་མྱ་ངན་མི་འདའ་བཞུགས།

KAL PA	**DRANG ME**	**NYA NGEN**	**MI**	**DA**	**ZHUG**
kalpa, aeon	*countless*	*sorrow*	*not*	*pass from (die, enter nirvana)*	*stay*

Will remain for countless aeons without passing into nirvana.

དེ་སྲིད་དེ་ཡི་ཞབས་འབྲིང་བྱེད་པར་ཤོག།

DE SI	**DE YI**	**ZHAB DRING**	**JE PAR**	**SHOG**
for as long as	*his*	*companion (i.e. always accompany him)*	*do*	*may we*

During that time may we always accompany him.

In that realm the perfect Buddha Amitabha will remain for countless aeons without passing into nirvana. During that time may we always accompany him.

ནམ་ཞིག་འོད་དཔག་མེད་དེ་ཞི་བར་གཤེགས།

NAM ZHI	**OE PA ME**	**DE**	**ZHI WAR**	**SHE**
when	*Amitabha*	*he*	*peace*	*goes (enters nirvana)*

When Amitabha passes into peace

བསྐལ་པ་གངྒཱའི་ཀླུང་གི་བྱེ་མ་སྙེད།

KAL PA	**GANG GAI**	**LUNG**	**GI**	**JE MA**	**NYE**
kalpa, aeons	*Ganges*	*river*	*of*	*sand*	*has*

His doctrine will remain for as many aeons

གཉིས་ཀྱི་བར་དུ་བསྟན་པ་གནས་པའི་ཚེ།

NYI	**KYI**	**BAR DU**	**TEN PA**	**NAE PAI**	**TSHE**
twice	*of*	*until, during*	*his doctrines*	*stay*	*time, span*

As twice the number of grains of sand in the River Ganges.

རྒྱལ་ཚབ་སྤྱན་རས་གཟིགས་དང་མི་འབྲལ་ཞིང་།

GYAL	**TSHAB**	**CHEN RE ZI**	**DANG**	**MI**	**DRAL ZHING**
Jina,(i.e. Amitabha)	*representative*	*Avalokitesvara*	*and*	*not*	*separating from*

During that time may we not be separated from his representative, Chenrezi, and

དེ་ཡི་ཡུན་ལ་དམ་ཆོས་འཛིན་པར་ཤོག།

DE YI	**YUN**	**LA**	**DAM**	**CHO**	**DZIN PAR**	**SHOG**
that	*period, duration*	*in*	*holy*	*dharma*	*hold, keep to*	*may we*

May we hold firmly to this holy dharma.

When Amitabha passess into peace his doctrine will remain for as many aeons, as twice the number of grains of sand in the River Ganges. During that time may we not be separated from his representative, Chenrezi, and may we hold firmly to this holy dharma.

སྲོད་ལ་དམ་ཆོས་ནུབ་པའི་ཐོ་རངས་ལ།

SOE	**LA**	**DAM**	**CHO**	**NUB PAI**	**THO RANG**	**LA**
twilight	*at*	*holy (i.e. Amitabha's doctrine)*	*dharma*	*decline*	*dawn*	*at*

This holy dharma of Amitabha will wane at dusk one day, then

སྤྱན་རས་གཟིགས་དེ་མངོན་པར་སངས་རྒྱས་ནས།

CHEN RE ZI	**DE**	**NGON PAR**	**SANG GYE**	**NAE**
Avalokitesvara	*that, him*	*perfect, manifest*	*Buddha*	*then*

At dawn the next day Chenrezi will attain perfect buddhahood

སངས་རྒྱས་འོད་ཟེར་ཀུན་ནས་འཕགས་པ་ཡི།

SANG GYE	**OE**	**ZER**	**KUN**	**NAE**	**PHAG PA**	**YI**
Buddha	*light*	*rays*	*all*	*from, by*	*glorious*	*of*

(Light rays from all the Buddhas will consecrate him.)

As Buddha Glorious from All Rays of Light

དཔལ་བརྩེགས་རྒྱལ་པོ་ཞེས་བྱར་གྱུར་པའི་ཚེ།

PAL	**TSEG**	**GYAL PO**	**ZHE JAR**	**GYUR PAI**	**TSHE**
splendour	*amassed*	*king*	*called*	*become*	*that time*

King of Amassed Splendour.

ཞལ་ཏ་མཆོད་ཅིང་དམ་ཆོས་ཉན་པར་ཤོག།

ZHAL TA	**CHOE CHING**	**DAM**	**CHO**	**NYAN PAR**	**SHOG**
see and serve him	*offering*	*holy*	*dharma*	*hear*	*may we*

From that time may we meet and serve him and hear the holy dharma.

This holy dharma of Amitabha will wane at dusk one day and at dawn the next day Chenrezi will attain perfect buddhahood as Buddha Glorious from All Rays of Light King of Amassed Splendour. From that time may we meet and serve him and hear the holy dharma.

སྐུ་ཚེ་བསྐལ་པ་བྱེ་བ་ཁྲག་ཁྲིག་ནི།

KU TSHE	**KAL PA**	**JE WA**	**TRAG TRIG**	**NI**
life span	*kalpa, aeon*	*ten million*	*one hundred thousand million*	*(emphasis)*

He will remain for a life span of

འབུམ་ཕྲག་དྲུག་ཅུ་རྩ་དྲུག་བཞུགས་པའི་ཚེ།

BUM TRA	**DRUG CHU TSA DRUG**	**ZHUG PAI**	**TSHE**
one hundred thousand	*sixty six*	*staying*	*time*

An incredible number of aeons.

རྟག་ཏུ་ཞབས་འབྲིང་བསྙེན་བཀུར་བྱེད་པ་དང་།

TAG TU	**ZHAB DRING**	**NYEN KUR**	**JE PA**	**DANG**
always	*accompany*	*service*	*do*	*and*

During that period may we always accompany and serve him, and

མི་བརྗེད་གཟུངས་ཀྱིས་དམ་ཆོས་འཛིན་པར་ཤོག།

MI JED	**ZUNG**	**KYI**	**DAM CHO**	**DZIN PAR**	**SHOG**
without forgetting	*hold*	*by*	*holy Dharma**	*hold, keep*	*may we!*

*the one taught by Chenrezi

Keep to his holy dharma without forgetting anything.

He will remain for a life span of an incredible number of aeons. During that period may we always accompany and serve him, and keep to his holy dharma without forgetting anything.

མྱ་ངན་འདས་ནས་དེ་ཡི་བསྟན་པ་ནི།

NYA NGAN DAE	**NAE**	**DE YI**	**TEN PA**	**NI**
pass into nirvana, go from suffering	*then*	*his*	*doctrines*	*(emphasis)*

After he passes into nirvana his doctrine

བསྐལ་པ་དུང་ཕྱུར་དྲུག་དང་བྱེ་བ་ཕྲག།

KAL PA	**DUNG CHUR**	**DRUG**	**DANG**	**JE WA TRA**
kalpa, aeon	*hundren million*	*six*	*and*	*ten million*

Will remain for an immense number of aeons.

འབུམ་ཕྲག་གསུམ་གནས་དེ་ཚེ་ཆོས་འཛིན་ཅིང་།

BUM TRAG	**SUM**	**NAE**	**DE TSHE**	**CHO**	**DZIN CHING**
hundred thousand	*three*	*stay*	*that time*	*dharma*	*holding, holder (this is the one who is in charge of that system of dharma)*

During that time his dharma will be held by

མཐུ་ཆེན་ཐོབ་དང་རྟག་ཏུ་མི་འབྲལ་ཤོག།

THU CHEN THOB	**DANG**	**TAG TU**	**MIN DRAL**	**SHOG**
Vajrapani, Mahasthamaprapta	*and*	*always*	*not separated from*	*may we*

Vajrapani. May we never be separated from him.

After he passes into nirvana his doctrine will remain for an immense number of aeons. During that time his dharma will be held by Vajrapani. May we never be separated from him.

དེ་ནས་མཐུ་ཆེན་ཐོབ་དེ་སངས་རྒྱས་ནས།

DE NAE	**THU CHEN THOB**	**DE**	**SANG GYE**	**NAE**
then	*Vajrapani*	*him*	*becomes Buddha*	*then*

Then when Vajrapani gains buddhahood as

དེ་བཞིན་གཤེགས་པ་རབ་ཏུ་བརྟན་པ་ནི།

DE ZHIN SHEG PA	**RAB TUN**	**TAN PA**	**NI**
Tathagata, Buddha, Thus Gone	*fully*	*stable*	*(emphasis)*

The Tathagata Fully Stable

ཡོན་ཏན་ནོར་བུ་བརྩེགས་པའི་རྒྱལ་པོར་གྱུར།

YON TAN	**NOR BU**	**TSEG PAI**	**GYAL POR**	**GYUR**
qualities	*jewels*	*amassed*	*King*	*becomes*

King of Amassed Jewels and Qualities

སྐུ་ཚེ་བསྟན་པ་སྤྱན་རས་གཟིགས་དང་མཉམ།

KU TSHE	**TEN PA**	**CHEN RE ZI**	**DANG**	**NYAM**
life span	*doctrine*	*Avalokitesvara*	*and*	*equal, same*

He will have a lifespan and doctrine equal to that of Chenrezi.

སངས་རྒྱས་དེ་ཡི་རྟག་ཏུ་ཞབས་འབྲིང་བྱེད།

SANG GYE	**DE YI**	**TAG TU**	**ZHAB DRING**	**JE**
Buddha (who was Vajrapani)	*him*	*always*	*accompany and serve*	*do*

May we always accompany this Buddha, and

མཆོད་པས་མཆོད་ཅིང་དམ་ཆོས་ཀུན་འཛིན་ཤོག།

CHOE PAE	**CHOE CHING**	**DAM**	**CHO**	**KUN**	**DZIN**	**SHOG**
offerings	*offering*	*holy*	*dharma*	*all*	*hold, keep*	*may we*

Presenting offerings, may we keep his holy Dharma.

Then when Vajrapani gains buddhahood as the Tathagata Fully Stable King of Amassed Jewels and Qualities he will have a lifespan and doctrine equal to that of Chenrezi. May we always accompany this Buddha and, presenting offerings, may we keep his holy dharma.

དེ་ནས་བདག་གི་ཚེ་དེ་བརྗེས་མ་ཐག།

DE NAE	**DAG GI**	**TSHE**	**DE**	**JE**	**MA THAG**
then, sometime	*my*	*life*	*that*	*after*	*immediately*

Then immediately at the end of our lives,

ཞིང་ཁམས་དེ་འམ་དག་པའི་ཞིང་གཞན་དུ།

ZHING KHAM	**DE**	**AM**	**DAG PAI**	**ZHING**	**ZHAN**	**DU**
realm (Dewachen)	*that*	*or*	*pure*	*realm*	*other*	*in*

In that realm or in some other pure realm

བླ་མེད་རྫོགས་པའི་སངས་རྒྱས་ཐོབ་པར་ཤོག།

LA ME	**DZOG PAI**	**SANG GYE**	**THOB PAR**	**SHOG**
unsurpassed	*perfect*	*buddhahood*	*gain*	*may I (and all beings)*

May we gain unsurpassable perfect buddhahood.

རྫོགས་སངས་རྒྱས་ནས་ཚེ་དཔག་མེད་པ་ལྟར།

DZOG	**SANG GYE**	**NAE**	**TSHE PA ME PA**	**TAR**
complete	*buddhahood*	*then*	*Amitayus (a form of Amitabha)*	*like*

Then in the manner of Amitayus, consequent on our enlightenment

མཚན་ཐོས་ཙམ་གྱིས་འགྲོ་ཀུན་སྨིན་ཅིང་གྲོལ།

TSHAN	**THO**	**TSAM**	**GYI**	**DRO**	**KUN**	**MIN CHING**	**DROL**
name	*hear*	*only*	*by*	*beings*	*all*	*ripening*	*liberated*

May all beings be ripened and liberated by simply hearing our name.

སྤྲུལ་པ་གྲངས་མེད་འགྲོ་བ་འདྲེན་པ་སོགས།

TRUL PA	**DRANG MED**	**DRO WA**	**DREN PA SOG**
emanations	*countless*	*beings*	*lead, guide*

With countless emanations may we guide beings and

འབད་མེད་ལྷུན་གྲུབ་འགྲོ་དོན་དཔག་མེད་ཤོག།

BAD ME	**LHUN DRUB**	**DRO**	**DON**	**PAG ME**	**SHOG**
without effort	*instantly*	*beings*	*benefit*	*numberless, measureless*	*may I*

Benefit countless beings instantly and without effort.

Then immediately at the end of our lives, may we gain unsurpassable perfect Buddhahood in that realm or in some other pure realm. Then in the manner of Amitayus, as a consequence of our enlightenment may all beings be ripened and liberated simply by hearing our name. With countless emanations may we guide beings and benefit countless beings instantly and without effort.

དེ་བཞིན་གཤེགས་པའི་ཚེ་དང་བསོད་ནམས་དང་།

DE ZHIN SHEG PAI	**TSHE**	**DANG**	**SO NAM**	**DANG**
Thus Gone, Tathagata, Buddha	*lifespan*	*and*	*merit*	*and*

Tathagata, you who have immeasurable lifespan,

ཡོན་ཏན་ཡེ་ཤེས་གཟི་བརྗིད་ཚད་མེད་པ།

YON TAN	**YE SHE**	**ZI JID**	**TSHAD ME PA**
good qualities	*wisdom, original knowing*	*splendid, majestic*	*measureless*

Merit, good qualities, original knowing and majesty,

ཆོས་སྐུ་སྣང་བ་མཐའ་ཡས་འོད་དཔག་མེད།

CHO KU	**NANG WA THA YAE**	**O PA ME**
dharmakaya	*Amitabha (limitless light)*	*Amitabha (measureless light)*

Dharmakaya Amitabha Limitless Light,

ཚེ་དང་ཡེ་ཤེས་དཔག་མེད་བཅོམ་ལྡན་འདས།

TSHE	**DANG**	**YE SHE**	**PA ME**	**CHOM DEN DAE**
life	*and*	*wisdom, original knowing*	*measureless*	*Bhagawan**

*finished with sin, going from the world, has good qualities. Perfect One

Perfect One with life and original knowing beyond measure,

གང་ཞིག་ཁྱེད་ཀྱི་མཚན་ནི་སུས་འཛིན་པ།

GANG ZHIG	**KHYE KYI**	**TSHAN NI**	**SU**	**DZIN PA**
whoever, somebody	*your*	*name*	*by whom*	*hold (remember and rely on)*

Whoever relies on your name,

སྔོན་གྱི་ལས་ཀྱི་རྣམ་སྨིན་མ་གཏོགས་པ།

NGON	**GYI**	**LAE**	**KYI**	**NAM MIN**	**MA TOG PA**
previous	*of*	*activity*	*of*	*fully mature*	*excepting only that*

Barring only the effects of the maturation of past karma,

མེ་ཆུ་དུག་མཚོན་གནོད་སྦྱིན་སྲིན་པོ་སོགས།

ME	**CHU**	**DUG**	**TSHON**	**NOE JIN**	**SRIN PO**	**SOG**
fire	*water*	*poison*	*weapons*	*yaksha*	*raksha*	*and so on*

Will gain protection from fire, water, poison, weapons, cruel spirits, cannibal demons and

འཇིགས་པ་ཀུན་ལས་སྐྱོབ་པར་ཐུབ་པས་གསུངས།

JIG PA	**KUN**	**LAE**	**KYOB PAR**	**TUB PAE**	**SUNG**
fear	*all*	*from*	*protected*	*ability*	*said**

*in the Sukhavati Kshetra Sutra

All that causes fear – thus it is said in the Sutra.

བདག་ནི་ཁྱེད་ཀྱི་མཚན་འཛིན་ཕྱག་འཚལ་བས།

DAG NI	**KHYE KYI**	**TSHAN**	**DZIN**	**CHAG TSHAL**	**WAE**
me	*your*	*name*	*hold (think of and rely on you)*	*salute*	*therefore*

I hold to your name and make obeisance, so

འཇིགས་དང་སྡུག་བསྔལ་ཀུན་ལས་སྐྱོབ་མཛད་གསོལ།

JIG	**DANG**	**DUG NGAL**	**KUN**	**LAE**	**KYOB DZAE**	**SOL**
fear	*and*	*sorrow*	*all*	*from*	*protect*	*I pray*

Please protect me from all fear and suffering!

Tathagata, you who have immeasurable lifespan, merit, good qualities, original knowing and majesty, Dharmakaya Amitabha Limitless Light, Perfect One with life and original knowing beyond measure, whoever relies on your name, barring only the effects of the maturation of past karma, will gain protection from fire, water, poison, weapons, cruel spirits, cannibal demons and all that causes fear – thus it is said in the Sutra. I hold to your name and make obeisance, so please protect me from all fear and suffering!

བཀྲ་ཤིས་ཕུན་སུམ་ཚོགས་པར་བྱིན་གྱིས་རློབས།

TA SHI	**PHUN SUM TSHOG PAR**	**JIN GYI LOB**
felicity, good luck, auspiciousness	*all good things, everything coming very nicely*	*blessing*

The blessing of felicity and everything pleasing,

སངས་རྒྱས་སྐུ་གསུམ་བརྙེས་པའི་བྱིན་རླབས་དང་།

SANG GYE	**KU**	**SUM**	**NYE PAI**	**JIN LAB**	**DANG**
Buddha	*kaya*	*three**	*getting*	*blessing*	*and*

*dharmakaya, sambhogakaya, nirmanakaya

The blessing of gaining the Buddha's three modes,

ཆོས་ཉིད་མི་འགྱུར་བདེན་པའི་བྱིན་རླབས་དང་།

CHO	**NYI**	**MIN**	**GYUR**	**DEN PAI**	**JIN LAB**	**DANG**
dharma	*itself*	*of*	*unchanging*	*truth*	*blessing*	*and*

The blessing of the truth of the unchanging Dharma essence, and

དགེ་འདུན་མི་ཕྱེད་འདུན་པའི་བྱིན་རླབས་ཀྱིས།

GEN DUN	**MI CHE**	**DUN PAI**	**JIN LAB**	**KYI**
sangha	*unchanging*	*harmony*	*blessing*	*by*

The blessing of the unwavering harmony of the Sangha —

ཇི་ལྟར་སྨོན་ལམ་བཏབ་བཞིན་འགྲུབ་པར་ཤོག།།

JI TAR	**MON LAM**	**TAB**	**ZHIN**	**DRUB PAR**	**SHOG**
like that	*prayer of aspiration (i.e. the Dechen Monlam)*	*made*	*like*	*accomplished*	*must be!*

By these blessings may this prayer of aspiration be accomplished!

དཀོན་མཆོག་གསུམ་ལ་ཕྱག་འཚལ་ལོ།

KON CHOG	**SUM**	**LA**	**CHAG TSHAL LO**
Triple Gem (Buddha, Dharma, Sangha)	*three*	*to*	*salutation, obeisance*

Obeisance to the Three Jewels.

ཏདྱ་ཐཱ། པཉྩེནྡྲི་ཡ་ཨཱ་ཝ་བོདྷཱ་ནི་ཡེ་སྭཱ་ཧཱ།

TA DYA THA **PAN TSAN DRI YA A VA BOD HA NI YE SVA HA**

It is like this. What we have prayed for must be attained!

སྨོན་ལམ་འགྲུབ་པའི་གཟུངས་སོ།

[This is the dharani for accomplishing the aspiration.]

The blessing of felicity and everything pleasing, the blessing of gaining the Buddha's three modes, the blessing of the truth of the unchanging Dharma

essence, and the blessing of the unwavering harmony of the Sangha – by these blessings may this prayer of aspiration be accomplished! Obeisance to the Three Jewels! It is like this. What we have prayed for must be attained!

དཀོན་མཆོག་གསུམ་ལ་ཕྱག་འཚལ་ལོ།

KON CHOG	**SUM**	**LA**	**CHAG TSHAL LO**
jewels	*three*	*to*	*salutation*

Obeisance to the Three Jewels.

ན་མོ་མཉྫུ་ ཤྲི་ཡེ།

NA MO	**MAN JU SHRI**	**YE**
salutation	*Manjusri*	*to*

Salutation to Manjushri.

ན་མོ་སུ་ཤྲི་ཡེ།

NA MO	**SU SHRI**	**YE**
salutation	*he who is divine, glorious*	*to*

Salutation to the divine.

ན་མཿཨུཏྟ་མ་ཤྲི་ཡེ་སྭཱ་ཧཱ།

NA MA	**UT TA MA**	**SHRI**	**YE**	**SWA HA**
salutation	*ultimate, very excellent*	*glory, god*	*to*	*so be it*

Salutation to the glorious ultimate. So be it.

Obeisance to the Three Jewels. Salutation to Manjusri. Salutation to the divine. Salutation to the glorious ultimate. So be it.

ཞེས་བརྗོད་ནས་ཕྱག་གསུམ་འཚལ་ན་འབུམ་ཐེར་དུ་འགྱུར་བར་གསུངས། དེ་ནས་རབ་བརྒྱ་ཕྲག། འབྲིང་ཅི་ནུས། ཐ་མ་འང་ཕྱག་བདུན་ཡན་འཚལ།

If after saying this you make three prostrations it will become equal to the performance of one hundred thousand prostrations – so it is said. It is best to make one hundred prostrations, middling to do as many as possible (about fifty), and minimal to do at least seven.

རབ་འདི་མ་ཆག་པ། འབྲིང་ལོ་ཟླ་ཙམ་མ་ཆག་པ། ཐ་མ་ནམ་ཁོམ་སྐབས་སུ་ཁ་ནུབ་ཏུ་ཕྱུ་ནས་བདེ་བ་ཅན་གྱི་ཞིང་ཁམས་ཡིད་ལ་དྲན་ཅིང་འོད་དཔག་མེད་ལ་ཐལ་མོ་སྦྱར་ཏེ་དད་པ་རྩེ་གཅིག་གིས་བརྗོད་ན། ཚེ་འདིར་ཚེའི་བར་ཆད་སེལ། ཕྱི་མ་བདེ་བ་ཅན་དུ་སྐྱེ་བར་ཐེ་ཚོམ་མེད་དོ། འོད་མདོ་ཞིང་བཀོད་མདོ་དང་། པདྨ་དཀར་པོ་འཆི་མེད་རྔ་སྒྲ་སོགས་ཀྱི་དགོངས་པ་ཡིན།

As for reading the Dechen Monlam, it is best to practise it daily without interruptions, middling to practise for some months or years without break. As a minimum, when the opportunity arises look in the western direction and, remembering the Pure Land of Dewachen, join your palms in devotion to Amitabha and recite with one-pointed faith. If you practise in any of these ways then the difficulties of this life will be removed and in the next life you will undoubtedly be born in Dewachen. This is the intention expressed in the Amitabha Sutra ('Od-mDo), the Kshetra Vibhu Sutra (Zhing-bKod), the Saddharma Pundarika Sutra (Pad-Ma-dKar-Po), the 'Chi-Med-rNga-sGra and so on.

ཞེས་དགེ་སློང་རཱ་ག་ཨ་སྱས་སྦྱར་བས་འགྲོ་བ་སེམས་ཅན་མང་པོ་བདེ་བ་ཅན་དུ་སྐྱེ་བའི་རྒྱུར་གྱུར་ཅིག།

This prayer was written by the Bhikshu Raga Asya.
May it be the cause of many beings being born in Dewachen.

The author of the Dechen Monlam, Chagme Raga Asya, was the Dharma brother of the great guru Rigdzin Chenpo Padma Trinlae of our Byangter lineage. When some Buddhist sects in Tibet brought in the Mongolian Chung Kar and his army and won victory in central Tibet, they thought that to destroy other Buddhist lineages and to kill their gurus was a service to the Dharma. At that time when Chung Kar caught Rigdzin Padma Trinlae of Dorje Drag monastery, he threw him in the river Brahmaputra, but he did not die and floated up again. When Chung Kar then asked him if there were any other lamas like him, he replied that there were none. Chung Kar said he had heard of another great lama called Raga Asya who was in the Chundo Shot, about three miles from Dorje Drag monastery. Then, Padma Trinlae saved his life by saying that, although Raga Asya was a scholar, his feet were crippled and so he could not do anything. Chung Kar further asked him how he, Padma Trinlae could be killed. Padma Trinlae replied that all his Dharma books should be put around his neck and then he should be put in the water. They did this and he was drowned. Seeing this, Chung Kar believed that he was an honest man and so did not bother to kill Raga Asya. Raga Asya heard of this and adopted a limp and thus has a connection with our Byangter lineage and so I made this translation with James Low.

C R Lama, 1976

Notes

1. ལུང་ Lung: permission to read and study a tantric text which is given by having it explained fully or at least read straight through once by someone who has in turn previously received such permission, and so on back through the lineage.

2. མཚམས་མེད་ The five unlimited sins which come to immediate fruition at death and lead to birth in the hells: matricide, patricide, killing an Arahat, causing a schism in the Sangha and wilfully causing a Tathagata to bleed.

3. The eighteen factors of a precious human birth consist of eight freedoms and ten opportunities. The eight freedoms are: freedom from birth in the hells, as an insatiable ghost, as an animal, as a long-living god, in an uncivilised tribe, with wrong views, in a non-buddhist land, and as a person with mental impairment.

   The ten opportunities are five concerning oneself: having a perfect human body, living where Dharma is practised, with all the five sense organs free of fault, innocent of the five boundless errors, and to have faith in the pure Dharma; along with the five opportunities dependent on others: that a perfect Buddha has arrived in this world, and taught the Dharma, which still remains, with practitioners engaged with it, and taught to disciples by compassionate gurus. [See Simply Being, ISBN 978 1907571015, page 7.]

༄༅།། གནམ་ཆོས་བདེ་སྨོན་བསྡུས་པ་ནི། Sky Dharma Aspiration for Dewachen

ཕྱོགས་དུས་རྒྱལ་བ་སྲས་བཅས་དགོངས༔

CHOG	**DU**	**GYAL WA**	**SAE**	**CHE**	**GONG**
(ten) directions	*(three) times*	*Victors, Buddhas*	*Bodhisattva*	*together*	*think of me*

Victors and Bodhisattvas of all directions and times, please pay heed to us!

ཚོགས་གཉིས་རྫོགས་ལ་རྗེས་ཡི་རང༔

TSHOG	**NYI**	**DZOG**	**LA**	**JE YI RANG**
accumulation (of merit and wisdom)	*two*	*completed (i.e. gained buddhahood)*	*to*	*I rejoice that they have (i.e. not jealous of them)*

We rejoice for those who have completed the two accumulations!

བདག་གི་དུས་གསུམ་དགེ་བསགས་པ༔

DAG	**GI**	**DU**	**SUM**	**GE**	**SAG PA**
me	*by*	*times (past, present, future)*	*three*	*virtue*	*accumulated*

All the virtue that we gather in the three times

དཀོན་མཆོག་གསུམ་ལ་མཆོད་པ་འབུལ༔

KON CHOG	**SUM**	**LA**	**CHO PA BUL**
jewels (Buddha Dharma, Sangha)	*three*	*to*	*offer*

We offer to the Three Jewels.

རྒྱལ་བའི་བསྟན་པ་འཕེལ་གྱུར་ཅིག༔

GYAL WAI	**TAN PA**	**PHEL**	**GYUR CHIG**
Jina's Buddha's	*doctrines*	*increase,*	*may they spread*

May the doctrines of the Buddha spread and flourish.

དགེ་བ་སེམས་ཅན་ཀུན་ལ་བསྔོ༔

GE WA	**SEM CHEN**	**KUN**	**LA**	**NGO**
virtue	*sentient beings*	*all*	*to*	*dedicate, give*

We dedicate our virtues to all sentient beings.

འགྲོ་ཀུན་སངས་རྒྱས་ཐོབ་གྱུར་ཅིག༔

DRO	**KUN**	**SANG GYE**	**THOB**	**GYUR CHIG**
beings	*all*	*buddhahood*	*get*	*may they*

May all beings gain buddhahood!

Victors and Bodhisattvas of all directions and times, please pay heed to us! We rejoice for those who have completed the two accumulations. All the virtue that we gather in the three times we offer to the Three Jewels. May the doctrines of the Buddha spread and flourish. We dedicate our virtues to all sentient beings. May all beings gain buddhahood!

དགེ་རྩ་ཐམས་ཅད་གཅིག་བསྡུས་ཏེ༔

GE	**TSA**	**THAM CHE**	**CHIG**	**DU**	**TE**
virtue	*roots*	*all*	*one*	*united*	*thus*

With all virtuous roots uniting as one

བདག་གི་རྒྱུད་ལ་སྨིན་གྱུར་ཅིག༔

DAG GI	**GYUD**	**LA**	**MIN**	**GYUR CHIG**
my (and all beings)	*mind, character*	*on*	*ripen, mature*	*may it*

May our minds be ripe and ready.

སྒྲིབ་གཉིས་དག་ནས་ཚོགས་རྫོགས་ཏེ༔

DRIB	**NYI**	**DAG**	**NAE**	**TSHOG**	**DZOG**	**TE**
obscurations	*two**	*purify*	*then*	*accumulations***	*complete*	*thus*

* afflictions and concepts ** merit and wisdom

With the two obscurations purified and the two accumulations complete,

ཚེ་རིང་ནད་མེད་ཉམས་རྟོགས་འཕེལ༔

TSHE RING	**NAE ME**	**NYAM**	**TOG**	**PHEL**
long life	*without sickness*	*meditation experiences*	*insight*	*increase*

With long life free of sickness, and with experience and insight increasing,

ཚེ་འདིར་ས་བཅུ་ནོན་གྱུར་ཅིག༔

TSHE	**DIR**	**SA**	**CHU**	**NON**	**GYUR CHIG**
life	*this here*	*stages of path*	*ten*	*get on*	*may they*

In this very life may we complete the Ten Stages.

With all virtuous roots uniting as one, may our minds be ripe and ready. With the two obscurations purified and the two accumulations complete, with long life free of sickness, and with experience and insight increasing, in this very life may we complete the Ten Stages!

ནམ་ཞིག་ཚེ་འཕོས་གྱུར་མ་ཐག༔

NAM ZHIG TSHE PHO GYUR MA THAG

when life change (i.e. die) immediately

When our lives end

བདེ་བ་ཅན་དུ་སྐྱེ་གྱུར་ཅིག༔

DE WA CHEN DU KYE GYUR CHIG

Sukhavati in born may

May we be born immediately in Dewachen.

སྐྱེས་ནས་པདྨའི་ཁ་བྱེ་སྟེ༔

KYE NAE PE MAI KHA JE TE

born then lotus mouth open then

At birth may the petals of the lotus open and

ལུས་རྟེན་དེ་ལ་སངས་རྒྱས་ཤོག༔

LU TEN DE LA SANG GYE SHOG

body that with buddhahood may I get

(i.e. become purified and possessed of all good qualities)

May we gain Buddhahood in that very body!

བྱང་ཆུབ་ཐོབ་ནས་ཇི་སྲིད་དུ༔

JANG CHUB THOB NAE JI SI DU

bodhi, enlightenment get then as long as (there are beings)

Having gained enlightenment, for as long as is necessary,

སྤྲུལ་པས་འགྲོ་བ་འདྲེན་པར་ཤོག༔

TRUL PAE DRO WA DREN PAR SHOG

send emanations beings lead, guide may

May we send emanations to guide beings.

When our lives end may we be born immediately in Dewachen. At birth may the petals of the lotus open and may we gain Buddhahood with that very body. Having gained enlightenment, for as long as is necessary, may we send emanations to guide beings.

ས་མ་ཡ་རྒྱ་རྒྱ་རྒྱ༔

SA MA YA GYA GYA GYA

Vows, Seal, Seal. Seal.

ཅེས་པ་འདི་ནི་སྤྲུལ་སྐུ་མི་འགྱུར་རྡོ་རྗེའི་གཏེར་མའོ།།

This is a Treasure of Tulku Migyur Dorje

སྨོན་ལམ་བསྡུས་པ་ནི། The Brief Prayer of Aspiration

ཨེ་མ་ཧོཿ

E MA HO
wonderful, amazing
Wonderful!

ངོ་མཚར་སངས་རྒྱས་སྣང་བ་མཐའ་ཡས་དངཿ

NGO TSHAR	**SANG GYE**	**NANG WA THA YAE**	**DANG**
marvellous	*Buddha*	*Amitabha, Limitless Light*	*and*

The marvellous Buddha Limitless Light with

གཡས་སུ་ཇོ་བོ་ཐུགས་རྗེ་ཆེན་པོ་དངཿ

YAE	**SU**	**JO WO**	**THUG JE CHEN PO**	**DANG**
his right	*on*	*lord*	*Mahakarunika, Chenrezi*	*and*

The blessed Great Compassion on his right and

གཡོན་དུ་སེམས་དཔའ་མཐུ་ཆེན་ཐོབ་རྣམས་ལཿ

YON	**DU**	**SEM PA**	**THU CHEN THOB**	**NAM**	**LA**
left	*on*	*sattva (Bodhisattva)*	*Vajrapani*	*(plural)*	*with*

Bodhisattva Great Strength on his left,

སངས་རྒྱས་བྱང་སེམས་དཔག་མེད་འཁོར་གྱིས་བསྐོརཿ

SANG GYE	**JANG SEM**	**PAG ME**	**KHOR**	**GYI**	**KOR**
Buddhas	*Bodhisattvas*	*numberless*	*retinue, circle*	*by*	*surrounded*

Together with a retinue of countless Buddhas and Bodhisattvas surrounding them,

བདེ་སྐྱིད་ངོ་མཚར་དཔག་ཏུ་མེད་པ་ཡིཿ

DE	**KYID**	**NGO TSHAR**	**PA TU ME PA**	**YI**
happy	*joyful*	*marvellous*	*measureless*	*of*

Are present in the realm of measureless marvellous happiness

བདེ་བ་ཅན་ཞེས་བྱ་བའི་ཞིང་ཁམས་དེར༔

DE WA CHEN	**ZHE JA WAI**	**ZHING KHAM**	**DER**
Sukhavati 'Happy'	*(called)*	*realm*	*there*

Known as Dewachen

Wonderful! The marvellous Buddha Limitless Light with the blessed Great Compassion on his right and Bodhisattva Great Strength on his left, together with a retinue of Buddhas and Bodhisattvas surrounding them, are present in the realm of measureless marvellous happiness known as Dewachen.

བདག་ནི་འདི་ནས་ཚེ་འཕོས་གྱུར་མ་ཐག༔

DAG NI	**DI**	**NAE**	**TSHE PHO**	**GYUR**	**MA THAG**
I	*this life*	*from*	*die, life*	*change*	*immediately*

Immediately on leaving this life,

སྐྱེ་བ་གཞན་གྱིས་བར་མ་ཆོད་པ་རུ༔

KYE WA	**ZHAN**	**GYI**	**BAR**	**MA CHOD PA**	**RU**
birth (in samsara)	*other*	*by*	*between*	*not interrupted*	*as*

Uninterrupted by a further birth in samsara,

དེ་རུ་སྐྱེས་ནས་སྣང་མཐའི་ཞལ་མཐོང་ཤོག༔

DE RU	**KYE**	**NAE**	**NANG THAI**	**ZHAL**	**THONG**	**SHOG**
there (in Dewachen)	*born*	*then*	*Amitabha, Limitless Light*	*face*	*see*	*we must*

May we be born there and see the face of Limitless Light.

Uninterrupted by a further birth in samsara, immediately on leaving this life, may we be born there and see the face of Limitless Light.

དེ་སྐད་བདག་གིས་སྨོན་ལམ་བཏབ་པ་འདི༔

DE KAE	**DAG**	**GI**	**MON LAM**	**TAB PA**	**DI**
these words	*me*	*by*	*prayer of aspiration*	*put, make*	*this*

With these words we make this aspiration, and

ཕྱོགས་བཅུའི་སངས་རྒྱས་བྱང་སེམས་ཐམས་ཅད་ཀྱིས༔

CHOG	**CHUI**	**SANG GYE**	**JANG SEM**	**THAM CHE**	**KYI**
directions (everywhere)	*ten*	*Buddhas*	*Bodhisattvas*	*all*	*by*

We pray that all the Buddhas and Bodhisattvas of the ten directions

གེགས་མེད་འགྲུབ་པར་བྱིན་གྱིས་བརླབ་ཏུ་གསོལ༔

GEG ME	DRUB PAR	JIN GYI LAB	TU	SOL
unobstructed	*accomplish*	*bless*	*as*	*pray*

Will bless us with its unobstructed accomplishment.

ཏདྱ་ཐཱ་པཉྩནྡྲི་ཡ་ཨ་ཝ་བོདྷ་ནི་ཡེ་སྭཱ་ཧཱ༔

TA DYA THA	PAN TSAN DRI YA	A VA BO DHA NI YE	SWA HA
it is like this	*what we have prayed for*	*come full*	*it must*

It is like this. What we have prayed for must be attained!

With these words we make this aspiration and we pray that all the Buddhas and Bodhisattvas in the ten directions will bless us with its accomplishment. It is like this. What we have prayed for must be attained!

ཞེས་པ་འདི་ནི་སྤྲུལ་སྐུ་མི་འགྱུར་རྡོ་རྗེ་དགུང་ལོ་བཅུ་གསུམ་གསེར་འཕྲུང་གི་ལོ་ས་ག་ཟླ་བའི་ཚེས་བདུན་ལ་གཙོ་འཁོར་རྣམས་ཀྱིས་ཞལ་གཟིགས་པའི་ཚེ་སྣང་བ་མཐའ་ཡས་ཀྱིས་དངོས་སུ་གསུངས་པའོ།། །།

Tulku Mingyur Dorje, at the age of thirteen, on the seventh day of the month of Saga Dawa (Vaisakh) in the fire-bird year, saw the faces of Amitabha and his retinue and at that time Buddha Limitless Light spoke this prayer.

བསྟན་པ་རྒྱས་པའི་སྨོན་ལམ།

The Prayer of Aspiration for the Spread of the Doctrine

དཀོན་མཆོག་གསུམ་དང་ཤཱཀྱའི་རྒྱལ།

KON CHOG	SUM	DANG	SHA KYAI GYAL
jewel (Buddha, Dharma, Sangha)	*three*	*and*	*Buddha Shakyamuni*

The Three Jewels and Buddha Shakyamuni,

རིགས་གསུམ་མགོན་དང་མ་ཕམ་པ།

RIG	SUM	GON	DANG	MA PHAM PA
kula, family	*three**	*protectors, lords*	*and*	*Maitreya*

* Manjushri, Avalokitesvara, Vajrapani

The protectors of the three families and Maitreya,

གནས་བརྟན་ཆེན་པོ་བཅུ་དྲུག་དང་།

NAE TEN	CHEN PO	CHU DRUG	DANG
sthaviras, elders	*maha, great*	*sixteen*	*and*

The sixteen great Elders and

པདྨ་འབྱུང་གནས་བདེན་སྟོབས་ཀྱིས།

PE MA JUNG NAE	DEN	TOB	KYI
Padmasambhava	*truth*	*power, strength*	*by*

Padmasambhava – by the power of their truth,

གསང་སྔགས་བསྟན་པ་དར་གྱུར་ཅིག།

SANG NGAG	TEN PA	DAR	GYUR CHIG
tantra vajrayana, guhyamantra	*doctrine*	*spread*	*may it*

May the tantric doctrines spread and flourish!

The Three Jewels and Buddha Shakyamuni, the protectors of the three families and Maitreya, the sixteen great Elders and Padmasambhava – by the power of their truth may the tantric doctrines spread and flourish!

བླ་མའི་སྐུ་ཚེ་བརྟན་པ་དང་།

LA MAI	**KU**	**TSHE**	**TEN PA**	**DANG**
guru's	*life*	*span*	*steady*	*and*

May the gurus' lives be long and

དགེ་འདུན་སྡེ་འཕེལ་ཐུགས་མཐུན་ཤོག།

GEN DUN	**DE**	**PHEL**	**THUG THUN**	**SHOG**
sangha	*group*	*increase*	*harmonious, friendly minded*	*they must*

May the sangha increase with friendly harmony.

བསྟན་པའི་འགལ་རྐྱེན་ཀུན་ཞི་ཞིང་།

TEN PAI	**GAL KYEN**	**KUN**	**ZHI ZHING**
doctrines	*difficulties, adverse conditions*	*all*	*pacifying, rendered harmless*

With all difficulties for the doctrines being pacified,

བཤད་སྒྲུབ་ཕྲིན་ལས་དར་རྒྱས་ཤོག།

SHED	**DRUB**	**TRIN LAE**	**DAR GYE**	**SHOG**
teaching, study	*practice*	*deeds*	*spread and increase*	*they must*

May study, teaching, practice and deeds spread and increase!

May the gurus' lives be long, and may the sangha increase with friendly harmony. With all difficulties for the doctrine being pacified, may study, teaching, practice and deeds spread and increase!

སྟོན་པའི་བསྟན་པ་ཡུན་རིང་གནས་གྱུར་ཅིག།

TON PAI	**TEN PA**	**YUN RING**	**NAE**	**GYUR CHIG**
teacher's, Buddha's	*doctrines*	*long time remain*	*stay,*	*they must*

May the doctrines of the teacher remain for a long time!

ཐེག་པའི་རྒྱལ་པོ་ཤིན་ཏུ་དར་གྱུར་ཅིག།

THEG PAI	**GYAL PO**	**SHIN TU**	**DAR**	**GYUR CHI**
*yana, vehicles**	*king*	*very much*	*spread*	*may it*

* methods for enlightenment (atiyoga)

May the king of the dharma vehicles spread widely!

བསྟན་པ་འཛིན་རྣམས་ཞབས་པད་བརྟན་གྱུར་ཅིག།

TEN PA	**DZIN NAM**	**ZHAB PAD**	**TAN**	**GYUR CHIG**
doctrine	*holders (guru)*	*feet (i.e. live for a long time)*	*steady*	*may they*

May the doctrine-holders live long and be healthy!

བསྟན་ལ་གནོད་རྣམས་མིང་ཙམ་སྟོང་གྱུར་ཅིག།

TEN	**LA**	**NOD NAM**	**MING**	**TSAM**	**TONG**	**GYUR CHIG**
doctrine	*to*	*troublemakers, demons*	*name*	*even, also*	*become empty, vanish*	*may they*

May the enemies of the doctrine vanish, even to the last trace of their name!

འགྲོ་ཀུན་སངས་རྒྱས་ཐོབ་པའི་རྒྱུར་གྱུར་ཅིག།

DRO	**KUN**	**SANG GYE**	**THOB PAI**	**GYUR**	**GYUR CHIG**
beings	*all*	*buddhahood*	*gain*	*cause**	*may it become*

* may the merit arising from these prayers be the cause for all beings gaining buddhahood.

May all beings gain buddhahood!

May the doctrines of the teacher remain for a long time! May the king of the dharma vehicles spread widely! May the doctrine-holders live long and be healthy! May the enemies of the doctrine vanish, even to the last trace of their name! May all beings gain buddhahood!

ལས་རབ་གླིང་པས་ལྷ་ལྡན་ཇོ་ཁང་དཀྱིལ་འཁོར་མཐིལ་དུ་རྟེན་འབྲེལ་ཉེས་སེལ་ཚོགས་འབུལ་
སྐབས་འཁོར་གདོང་སྤྲུལ་སྐུ་ཚུལ་ལོའི་ངོར་བྲིས།། །།

This was composed by Laerab Lingpa (Terton Sogyal) at the Central Mandala of the Jo Khang in Lhasa at the time of making one hundred thousand offerings of Ten Drel Nye Sel at the request of Khordong Tulku Tshullo (Tshultrim Zangpo).

༄༅། །སྔ་འགྱུར་བསྟན་པ་རྒྱས་པའི་སྨོན་ལམ་ཆོས་རྒྱལ་དགྱེས་པའི་ཞལ་ལུང་ཞེས་བྱ་བ། །

For the Flourishing of the Nyingma Teachings An Aspiration to Please the Dharma-King

དེ་ཡང་དུས་ཀྱི་ཐ་མར་རྩ་གསུམ་ལྷ་ཡི་ཐུགས་རྒྱུད་བསྐུལ་ནས་བསྟན་པའི་སྙིང་པོ་རིན་པོ་ཆེ་རྒྱས་པར་འགྱུར་ཅིག་སྙམ་དུ་ལན་གཅིག་ཙམ་སེམས་པ་ཡང་བསོད་ནམས་ཚད་མེད་པ་དང་ལྡན་ཅིང་། རྒྱལ་བའི་སྲས་ཀྱི་སྨོན་ལམ་ཡོངས་སུ་རྫོགས་ནས་སྐྱེ་བ་ཀུན་ཏུ་རྒྱལ་བའི་ཆོས་དང་ཆོས་ཀྱི་སྙིང་པོ་ཟབ་མོའི་ཐེག་པ་དང་འཕྲད་ནས་འཛིན་སྐྱོང་སྤེལ་བས་མྱུར་དུ་རྣམ་པ་ཐམས་ཅད་མཁྱེན་པའི་ཡེ་ཤེས་ལ་རེག་པ་འགྱུར་བའི་དགོས་པ་ཡོད་པས། སྐལ་བཟང་རྣམས་ཀྱིས་དུས་དུས་དང་། ཁྱད་པར་ཚོགས་མང་གི་སྐབས་སུ་འདི་ལྟར་སྨོན་ལམ་གདབ་པར་བྱ་སྟེ། །

In the final five hundred year period of the Dharma, to even once have the wish to move the minds of the deities who are the three roots (guru, deva, dakini) (encouraging them to help us), and to spread the precious essence of the doctrine (by reading this prayer) is virtue without measure. Moreover, truly practising this prayer of aspiration of the bodhisattvas, may we in all our lives meet with the Buddha's Dharma of the profound path of the essence of the dharma (atiyoga). Due to our cherishing it, practising it and spreading it to others, by the beneficial guidance of this prayer may all beings quickly gain enlightened wisdom regarding the actual and its appearances.

Whenever you feel moved to, and especially when many people gather together, make this aspiration:

ན་མོ། ཕྱོགས་བཅུའི་བདེ་བར་གཤེགས་པ་སྲས་དང་བཅས།

NA MO	**CHOG**	**CHUI**	**DE WAR SHEG PA**	**SAE**	**DANG CHE**
salutation	*directions (i.e. everywhere)*	*ten*	*sugatas, buddhas*	*sons, bodhisattvas*	*with*

Salutation! The buddhas and bodhisattvas of the ten directions, and

ཁྱད་པར་མཉམ་མེད་ཤཱཀྱའི་རྒྱལ་པོ་དང་།

KHYA PAR	**NYAM ME**	**SHA KYAI GYAL PO**	**DANG**
especially,	*unequalled*	*Buddha Shakyamuni*	*and particularly*

In particular the unequalled Shakyamuni, and

རྒྱལ་སྲས་བརྒྱད་དང་གནས་བརྟན་འཕགས་པའི་ཚོགས།

GYAL SAE	**GYAE**	**DANG**	**NAE TEN**	**PHAG PAI**	**TSHOG**
bodhisattva	*eight**	*and*	*staviras, elders*	*holy ones*	*assembly, host*

* Sayi Nyingpo, Namkai Nyingpo, Chenrezi, Chagna Dorje, Jampa, Dribpa Nampar Selwa, Kuntu Zangpo, Jampai Yang

The eight bodhisattvas, the elders and the hosts of the holy ones –

མཁྱེན་བརྩེའི་བདག་ཉིད་མཆོག་རྣམས་དགོངས་སུ་གསོལ།

KHYEN	**TSEI**	**DAG NYID**	**CHOG NAM**	**GONG SU SOL**
deep understanding, true knowledge	*compassion*	*those having*	*excellent ones*	*you must listen to me*

Most excellent ones, you who have true knowledge and compassion, please listen to me!

Salutation! Buddhas and bodhisattvas of the ten directions, and in particular unequalled Shakyamuni, along with the eight bodhisattvas, the elders and the hosts of the holy ones – most excellent ones, you who have true knowledge and compassion, please listen to me!

ཕན་བདེའི་འབྱུང་གནས་བསྟན་པའི་རིན་པོ་ཆེ།

PHEN	**DE**	**JUNG NAE**	**TEN PAE**	**RIN PO CHE**
benefit	*happiness*	*source*	*doctrines*	*precious*

The precious doctrines are the source of benefit and happiness.

སྟོན་དང་སེམས་དཔའ་འཕགས་པ་མཆོག་རྣམས་ཀྱིས།

TON	**DANG**	**SEM PA**	**PHAG PA**	**CHOG NAM**	**KYI**
teacher, Samantabhadra	*and*	*bodhisattvas, (Indrabhuti, Vajrapani and so on)*	*holy, noble*	*excellent ones*	*by*

The teacher and the bodhisattvas, the excellent holy ones,

ཡང་ཡང་དཀའ་བས་བཙལ་ཞིང་བརྣག་པའི་དོན།

YANG YANG	**KA WAE**	**TSAL ZHING**	**NAG PAI DON**
again and again, more to more	*difficult (like the difficulties faced by Tibetans going to India for the Dharma)*	*sought*	*great desire and aim (the enlightenment of all beings)*

Sought them with profound intent despite many difficulties.

མཚོ་སྐྱེས་རྒྱལ་བའི་བསྟན་པ་རྒྱས་གྱུར་ཅིག།

TSHO	**KYE**	**GYAL WAI**	**TEN PA**	**GYE**	**GYUR CHIG**
ocean (Padmasambhava)	*born*	*victor, buddha*	*doctrines*	*spread*	*they must*

The doctrines of the ocean-born buddha must spread and flourish!

The precious doctrines are the source of benefit and happiness. The teacher and the bodhisattvas, the excellent holy ones, sought them with profound intent despite many difficulties. The doctrines of the ocean-born buddha must spread and flourish!

མཁན་སློབ་ཆོས་རྒྱལ་སྤྲུལ་པའི་ལོ་པཎ་དང་།

KHAN	**LOB**	**CHO GYAL**	**TRUL PAI**	**LO**	**PAEN**	**DANG**
scholar, bodhisattva Shantarakshita	*Padmasambhava, acharya, teacher*	*dharma king, King Trisong Deutsan*	*apparitions of buddha*	*translators*	*Indian scholars (Vairocana)*	*and*

Shantarakshita, Padmasambhava, King Trisong Deutsan, and the translators and pandits who were emanations, and

བཀའ་གཏེར་རིག་འཛིན་བརྒྱུད་པ་ཡི་དམ་ལྷ།

KA	**TER**	**RIG DZIN**	**GYUE PA**	**YI DAM LHA**
*kama**	*terma#*	*adept, sage,*	*lineage*	*path deities*

(gods that are relied on for accomplishment)

*doctrines that were always available in the lineage # doctrines that have been hidden and then revealed

The adepts of the lineages of kama and terma, the path deities, and

མ་མགོན་གཟའ་དོར་བརྒྱུད་གསུམ་དྲེགས་པའི་ཚོགས།

MA	**GON**	**ZA**	**DOR**	**GYUE**	**SUM**	**DREG PAI**	**TSHOG**
Ekajati, Ma mo	*Mahakala*	*Rahula*	*Dorje Legpa*	*lineage*	*three*	*strong dharma protectors*	*hosts*

Ekajati, Mahakala, Rahula, Dorje Legpa and the hosts of strong protectors of the three lineages,

སྔ་འགྱུར་རྩ་གསུམ་ལྷ་ཚོགས་དགོངས་སུ་གསོལ།

NGA GYUR	**TSA SUM**	**LHA**	**TSHOG**	**GONG SU SOL**
nyingma, old translation school	*three roots (guru, deva, dakini)*	*gods*	*hosts*	*you must listen to me*

You, the divine hosts of gurus, deities, and dakinis of the old translation school, please listen to me!

Shantarakshita, Padmasambhava, King Trisong Deutsan, and the translators and pandits who were emanations, and the adepts of the lineages of kama and terma, the path deities, and Ekajati, Mahakala, Rahula, Dorje Legpa and the hosts of strong protectors of the three transmissions, you, the divine hosts of gurus, deities, and dakinis of the old translation school, please listen to me!

ཐུབ་བསྟན་མདོ་དང་སྔགས་ཀྱི་ཚུལ་མཐའ་དག།

THUB	**TEN**	**DO**	**DANG**	**NGAG**	**KYI**	**TSHUL**	**THA DAG**
buddha's	*doctrine*	*sutra*	*and*	*tantra*	*of*	*systems*	*all*

All the systems of the Buddha's doctrines, both sutra and tantra,

གངས་ཅན་ལྗོངས་སུ་བརྩེ་བས་དྲངས་གྱུར་པ།

GANG CHEN JONG	**SU**	**TSE WAE**	**DRANG GYUR PA**
Tibet	*in*	*by compassion*	*bring, lead*

Were compassionately brought to Tibet and

ཆེས་ཆེར་སྤེལ་བའི་རྡོ་རྗེའི་དམ་དགོངས་ནས།

CHE CHER	**PEL WAI**	**DOR JAI**	**DAM GONG**	**NAE**
very greatly, vastly	*spread*	*very strong*	*intention, free of doubts*	*then*

Spread everywhere with very strong resolve.

མཚོ་སྐྱེས་རྒྱལ་བའི་བསྟན་པ་རྒྱས་གྱུར་ཅིག།

TSHO KYE GYAL WAI TEN PA GYE GYUR CHIG

The doctrines of the ocean-born buddha must spread and flourish!

All the systems of the Buddha's doctrines, both sutra and tantra, were compassionately brought to Tibet and spread everywhere with very strong resolve. The doctrines of the ocean-born buddha must spread and flourish!

ཕྱོགས་དུས་རྒྱལ་བའི་སྐུ་གསུང་ཐུགས་རྡོ་རྗེ།

CHOG	**DU**	**GYAL WAI**	**KU**	**SUNG**	**THUE**	**DOR JE**
all directions	*all times*	*victors, buddha*	*body**	*speech***	*mind#*	*vajra,*

* nirmanakaya ** sambhogakaya # dharmakaya

The indestructible body, speech and mind of all the buddhas in all directions and times,

རིགས་གསུམ་སེམས་དཔའི་སྒྱུ་འཕྲུལ་རོལ་མོ་ཡིས།

RIG	**SUM**	**SEM PAI**	**GYU TRUL**	**ROL MO**	**YI**
kulas, families	*three**	*bodhisattvas*	*lila, illusory drama*	*sounds (teaching the dharma)*	*by*

*Buddha, Vajra and Padma families, and the bodhisattvas Manjushri, Vajrapani and Avalokitesvara who are aspects of the Buddha's three kayas or modes. They distill and manifest all the qualities of all the buddhas.

Is manifest as the bodhisattvas of the three families conveying the magical music of dharma bringing

གངས་ཅན་ཕན་བདེའི་ཉི་མ་གསལ་བར་མཛད།

GANG CHEN	**PHEN**	**DEI**	**NYI MA**	**SAL WA**	**DZAE**
Tibet	*benefit*	*happiness*	*sun*	*clear*	*make*

Happiness and benefit for Tibet, like the illuminating power of the sun.

མཚོ་སྐྱེས་རྒྱལ་བའི་བསྟན་པ་རྒྱས་གྱུར་ཅིག།

TSHO KYE GYAL WAI TEN PA GYE GYUR CHIG

The doctrines of the ocean-born buddha must spread and flourish!

The indestructible body, speech and mind of all the buddhas in all directions and times, is manifest as the bodhisattvas of the three families conveying the magical music of dharma, the bright sunshine bringing happiness and benefit to Tibet. The doctrines of the ocean-born buddha must spread and flourish!

རྒྱལ་དང་རྒྱལ་སྲས་འཕགས་པ་ཆེན་པོའི་ཚོགས།

GYAL	**DANG**	**GYAL**	**SAE**	**PHAG PA**	**CHEN POI**	**TSHOG**
victors	*and*	*victors*	*sons*	*noble*	*great*	*host*
		bodhisattvas				

The buddhas and bodhisattvas and the hosts of great noble ones

བསམ་བཞིན་སྤྲུལ་པའི་ཟློས་གར་ཉེར་བཟུང་ནས།

SAM ZHIN	**TRUL PAI**	**DOE GAR**	**NYER ZUNG**	**NAE**
according to wish, not due to compulsion	*apparational, manifesting*	*drama, show*	*appear, do*	*then*

(showing their illusory forms out of compassion for others, teaching and spreading the dharma)

Fulfil their intention by showing the illusory drama of their miraculous display, and

དྲི་མེད་རྒྱལ་བསྟན་ནོར་བུའི་རྒྱལ་མཚན་སྒྲེང་།

DRI ME	**GYAL**	**TEN**	**NOR BUI**	**GYAL TSHAN**	**DRENG**
without stain	*jina's, buddha's*	*doctrines*	*jewel*	*victory banner*	*hold up, raise aloft*

Raise aloft the jewel peak of the victory banner of the stainless buddha's doctrines.

མཚོ་སྐྱེས་རྒྱལ་བའི་བསྟན་པ་རྒྱས་གྱུར་ཅིག།

TSHO KYE GYAL WAI TEN PA GYE GYUR CHIG

The doctrines of the ocean-born buddha must spread and flourish!

The buddhas and bodhisattvas and the hosts of great noble ones fulfil their intention by showing the illusory drama of their miraculous

display and raise aloft the jewel peak of the victory banner of the stainless buddha's doctrines. The doctrine of the ocean-born buddha must spread and flourish!

ཐུན་མོང་ཐུན་མིན་གཞུང་ཀུན་རང་དབང་གིས།

THUN MONG	**THUN MIN**	**ZHUNG**	**KUN**	**RANG**	**WANG**	**GI**
general	*special*	*doctrines*	*all*	*own, self*	*power*	*by*

(the scholars of the old translation school)

Relying on their own abilities, all the doctrines , both general and special,

མ་ནོར་བསྒྱུར་ཞུས་གཏན་ལ་ཕབ་པ་ཡིས།

MA NOR	**GYUR**	**ZHU**	**TAN LA PHAB PA**	**YI**
without mistake	*translation (from Sanskrit to Tibetan)*	*editing*	*setting right, making corrections*	*by*

Were faultlessly translated, edited and corrected by the early Tibetan scholars and due to this

གངས་ལྗོངས་སྣང་བའི་སྒོ་ཆེན་ཐོག་མར་ཕྱེས།

GANG JONG	**NANG WAI**	**GO**	**CHEN**	**THOG MAR**	**CHE**
Tibet	*light (the dharma's light)*	*door*	*big*	*first (in King Trisong Deutsan's time)*	*opened*

The great door of light was first opened in Tibet.

མཚོ་སྐྱེས་རྒྱལ་བའི་བསྟན་པ་རྒྱས་གྱུར་ཅིག།

TSHO KYE GYAL WAI TEN PA GYE GYUR CHIG

The doctrines of the ocean-born buddha must spread and flourish!

Relying on their own abilities, all the doctrines, both general and special, were faultlessly translated, edited and corrected by the early Tibetan scholars and due to this the great door of light was first opened in Tibet. The doctrines of the ocean-born buddha must spread and flourish!

སྐལ་བཟང་གདུལ་བྱས་མདོ་དང་སྔགས་ཀྱི་ཚུལ།

KAL ZANG	**DUL JAE**	**DO**	**DANG**	**NGAG**	**KYI**	**TSHUL**
fortunate	*disciples**	*sutra*	*and*	*tantra*	*of*	*method*

* those who can be disciplined and who will be victorious

The fortunate ones were disciplined in the methods of sutra and tantra, and,

ཉམས་སུ་ལེན་ལ་གཞན་དྲིང་མི་འཇོག་པར།

NYAM SU LEN	**LA**	**ZHAN**	**DRING MI JOG PAR**
practice	*to*	*other*	*not going*

Not seeking after any other practices,

བཀའ་དང་དགོངས་པ་འགྲེལ་བའི་གཞུང་ཀུན་རྫོགས།

KA	DANG	GONG PA DREL WAI	ZHUNG	KUN	DZOG
oral teachings of the buddhas	*and*	*commentaries*	*texts*	*all*	*are full (in the translations)*

They completed translating all the texts of the Buddha's own teachings and their commentaries.

མཚོ་སྐྱེས་རྒྱལ་བའི་བསྟན་པ་རྒྱས་གྱུར་ཅིག།

TSHO KYE GYAL WAI TEN PA GYE GYUR CHIG

The doctrines of the ocean-born buddha must spread and flourish!

The fortunate ones were disciplined in the methods of sutra and tantra, and not seeking after any other practices, they completed translating all the texts of the Buddha's own teachings and their commentaries. The doctrines of the ocean-born buddha must spread and flourish!

བདེན་གསུང་བཀའ་ཡི་རྒྱ་མཚོ་ཆེན་པོ་ལ།

DEN	SUNG	KA	YI	GYAM TSHO	CHEN PO	LA
truth	*speaking*	*buddha's*	*of*	*ocean*	*great*	*to doctrines*

The great ocean of the doctrines of the speaker of truth

ཟབ་མོའི་ཆོས་གཏེར་ནོར་བུས་མངོན་པར་མཛེས།

ZAB MOI	CHO	TER	NOR BUE	NGON PAR	DZE
deep, profound	*dharma*	*treasure*	*jewels*	*very*	*beautiful*

Is made most beautiful by the jewels of the treasure of the profound dharma

མདོ་དང་སྔགས་ཀྱི་ལམ་བཟང་ཟུང་དུ་འབྲེལ།

DO	DANG	NGAG	KYI	LAM ZANG	ZUNG DU DREL
sutra	*and*	*tantra*	*of*	*good path*	*join together*

Which join together the good paths of sutra and tantra.

མཚོ་སྐྱེས་རྒྱལ་བའི་བསྟན་པ་རྒྱས་གྱུར་ཅིག།

TSHO KYE GYAL WAI TEN PA GYE GYUR CHIG

The doctrines of the ocean-born buddha must spread and flourish!

The great ocean of the doctrines of the speaker of truth is made most beautiful by the jewels of the treasure of the profound dharma, which join together the good paths of sutra and tantra. The doctrines of the ocean-born buddha must spread and flourish!

རྨད་བྱུང་ཟ་ཧོར་མཁན་པོའི་སྤྱོད་པ་དང་།

MAE JUNG	**ZA HOR KHAN POI**	**CHO PA**	**DANG**
wonderful, amazing	*Shantarakshita (yogachara)*	*deeds, conduct, way of acting*	*and*

The deeds of the amazing Shantarakshita, and

མཚུངས་མེད་དཔལ་ལྡན་ཀླུ་ཡི་ལྟ་བ་གཉིས།

TSHUNG ME	**PAL DEN**	**LU**	**YI**	**TA WA**	**NYI**
unequalled, unmatched	*glorious*	*Nagarjuna*	*of*	*view (madhyamika)*	*two*

The view of the unequalled glorious Nagarjuna –

ཟུང་འབྲེལ་བརྒྱུད་པའི་བཀའ་སྲོལ་ཕྱག་རྒྱས་བཏབ།

ZUNG DREL	**GYUE PAI**	**KA SOL**	**CHAG GYE**	**TAB**
joined together	*lineage*	*ritual system*	*seal (it is not possible to change it)*	*put*

These two joined together were sealed by the ritual system of the lineage.

མཚོ་སྐྱེས་རྒྱལ་བའི་བསྟན་པ་རྒྱས་གྱུར་ཅིག།

TSHO KYE GYAL WAI TEN PA GYE GYUR CHIG

The doctrines of the ocean-born buddha must spread and flourish!

The deeds of the amazing Shantarakshita, and the view of the unequalled glorious Nagarjuna – these two joined together were sealed by the ritual system of the lineage. The doctrines of the ocean-born buddha must spread and flourish!

ཟབ་མོའི་ནང་རྒྱུད་སྡེ་གསུམ་དགོངས་པའི་བཅུད།

ZAB MOI	**NANG GYUE**	**DE**	**SUM**	**GONG PAI**	**CHUE**
deep	*inner tantras*	*classes, groups*	*three**	*methods, thoughts, understanding*	*essence*

*Pa Gyud, Ma Gyud, Nyimed Gyud – father, mother and non-dual tantras, also Maha, Anu, Ati

By the essence of the understanding of the three classes of the profound inner tantras,

ཐུན་མིན་མན་ངག་གསང་བའི་ལམ་མཆོག་ནས།

THUN MIN	**MEN NGAG**	**SANG WAI**	**LAM**	**CHOG**	**NAE**
special	*deep method, instruction*	*secret, not generally available*	*path, way*	*excellent*	*from,with by*

The excellent secret path of special profound instructions,

འཇའ་ལུས་ཆོས་སྐུར་གཤེགས་པའི་ངོ་མཚར་འབར།

JA LU	**CHO KUR**	**SHEG PAI**	**NGO TSHAR**	**BAR**
rainbow	*dharmakaya*	*to go*	*wonderful*	*blazing, shining*

(one's body dissolving into a rainbow and vanishing)

There is the wonderful radiance of the rainbow body merging in the dharmakaya.

མཚོ་སྐྱེས་རྒྱལ་བའི་བསྟན་པ་རྒྱས་གྱུར་ཅིག།

TSHO KYE GYAL WAI TEN PA GYE GYUR CHIG

The doctrines of the ocean-born buddha must spread and flourish!

By the essence of the understanding of the three classes of the profound inner tantras, the excellent secret path of special profound instructions, there is the wonderful radiance of the rainbow body merging in the dharmakaya. The doctrines of the ocean-born buddha must spread and flourish!

རབ་འབྱམས་ཞི་ཁྲོའི་ཁྱབ་བདག་སྒྲུབ་སྡེ་བརྒྱད།

RAB JAM	**ZHI**	**TROI**	**KYAB DAG**	**DRUB DE GYAE**
infinitley vast	*peaceful*	*fierce, angry*	*pervading, chief and encompassing*	*kabgye, the eight great sadhana practices*

The eight great practices which span the infinite peaceful and wrathful deities,

བཀའ་བབ་རིག་འཛིན་སོ་སོའི་དགོངས་བཅུད་དང་།

KA BAB	**RIG DZIN**	**SO SOI**	**GONG**	**CHUE**	**DANG**
*authorised lineage**	*vidyadhara, awareness holder*	*each#*	*thoughts, understanding*	*essence*	*and*

* e.g. Humkara for Yang Dag # the original ones who first received the Kabgye teachings

The essences of the understanding of each of the authorised vidyadharas,

ཀུན་འདུས་པདྨའི་བཀའ་སྲོལ་གཅིག་ཏུ་འཁྱིལ།

KUN	**DU**	**PE MA**	**KA**	**SOL**	**CHIG**	**TU**	**KHYIL**
all	*assembling, encompassing*	*Padmasambhava**	*practice ritual*	*system*	*one*	*in,as*	*run together#*

* he received all the great sadhanas # like drops of quick silver

All flow together as one in the practice system of Padmasambhava who encompasses them all.

མཚོ་སྐྱེས་རྒྱལ་བའི་བསྟན་པ་རྒྱས་གྱུར་ཅིག།

TSHO KYE GYAL WAI TEN PA GYE GYUR CHIG

The doctrines of the ocean-born buddha must spread and flourish!

The eight great practices which span the infinite peaceful and wrathful deities, the essences of the understanding of each of the authorised vidyadharas, all flow together as one in the practice system of Padmasambhava who encompasses them all. The doctrines of the ocean-born buddha must spread and flourish!

རྒྱུ་དང་འབྲས་བུ་གསང་སྔགས་ཐེག་པ་ཆེན།

GYU	DANG	DRE BU	SANG NGAG THEG PA	CHEN
cause	*and*	*result*	*vajrayana, the tantric mantra system*	*great*

In the great vajrayana which covers both cause and result,

ཚང་ལ་མ་ནོར་རིག་འཛིན་བརྒྱུད་པའི་ལུང་།

TSHANG	LA	MA NOR	RIG DZIN	GYUE PAI	LUNG
complete	*and*	*not mixed with false things*	*vidyadhara*	*lineages **	*reading#*

* down until the present day # transmission of direct connection to the practice

The transmission of the practice of the lineage of vidyadharas is complete and unadulterated,

ཌཱ་ཀིའི་ཞལ་གྱི་དྲོད་རླངས་ཐོ་ལེ་བ།

DA KI	ZHAL	GYI	DROE	LANG	THO LE WA
dakinis	*mouth*	*of*	*heat*	*steam*	*still has*

(The practice method is still as correct today as when it was first heard from the dakinis by the vidyadharas)

Still possessing the warm moist breath of the dakinis' mouths.

མཚོ་སྐྱེས་རྒྱལ་བའི་བསྟན་པ་རྒྱས་གྱུར་ཅིག།

TSHO KYE GYAL WAI TEN PA GYE GYUR CHIG

The doctrines of the ocean-born buddha must spread and flourish!

In the great vajrayana which covers both cause and result, the transmission of the practice of the lineage of vidhyadharas is complete and unadulterated, still possessing the warm moist breath of the dakinis' mouths. The doctrines of the ocean-born buddha must spread and flourish!

རྡོ་རྗེ་འཆང་གི་དགོངས་དོན་བདུད་རྩིའི་བཅུད།

DOR JE CHANG	GI	GONG DON	DUE TSI	CHU
Vajradhara, dharmakaya	*of*	*original understanding, true method*	*amrita, liberating elixir*	*essence*

The amrita's essence of the truth of the presence of Vajradhara

མཁས་གྲུབ་བྱེ་བའི་ཞལ་ནས་སྙན་དུ་བརྒྱུད།

KHAE	**DRUB**	**JE WAI**	**ZHAL**	**NAE**	**NYAN DU**	**GYUE**
scholars	*siddhas, accomplished saints*	*all, numberless*	*mouth*	*from*	*hearing*	*lineage*

(each passing the teachings to his disciples)

Has been heard by the lineage from the mouths of numberless scholars and siddhas

རྟོག་གེ་ངན་པའི་རང་བཟོས་མ་བསླད་པ།

TOG GE	**NGAN PAI**	**RANG ZO**	**MA**	**LAE PA**
debaters	*bad*	*own ideas, constructions*	*not*	*mixed*

(own false ideas not in accordance with Buddha's teaching)

Without being mixed with the false constructions of the argumentative.

མཚོ་སྐྱེས་རྒྱལ་བའི་བསྟན་པ་རྒྱས་གྱུར་ཅིག།

TSHO KYE GYAL WAI TEN PA GYE GYUR CHIG

The doctrines of the ocean-born buddha must spread and flourish!

The amrita's essence of the truth of the presence of Vajradhara has been heard by the lineage from the mouths of numberless scholars and siddhas without being mixed with the false construction of the argumentative. The doctrines of the ocean-born buddha must spread and flourish!

གསེར་ཞིང་ནོར་བུའི་སྤྲས་པའི་ཡོན་གྱིས་ཀྱང་།

SER	**ZHING**	**NOR BUE**	**TRAI PAI**	**YON**	**GYI**	**KYANG**
gold	*land*	*jewels*	*put together*	*cost, value*	*by*	*also, yet*

Even the value of the golden foundation of the earth with all its jewels is not enough

མི་འགུགས་དབྱིངས་ཀྱི་མཁའ་འགྲོའི་ཐུགས་མཛོད་ཆོས།

MI GU	**YING**	**KYI**	**KHAN DRO**	**THUG**	**DZOE**	**CHO**
not get hold of	*dhatu, sunyata*	*of*	*dakinis*	*minds*	*treasure*	*dharma*

To secure the dharma treasure of the infinite dakini mind.

བརྩེ་བས་རྗེས་འཛུག་སྐལ་པ་ཁོ་ནར་བཀྲམ།

TSE WAE	**JE JUG**	**KAL PA**	**KHO NAR**	**RAM**
by compassion	*hold as disciple*	*fortunate one, those who get teaching*	*only*	*get, receive fully*

It is gained only by the fortunate ones who are held by the guru's compassion.

མཚོ་སྐྱེས་རྒྱལ་བའི་བསྟན་པ་རྒྱས་གྱུར་ཅིག།

TSHO KYE GYAL WAI TEN PA GYE GYUR CHIG

The doctrines of the ocean-born buddha must spread and flourish!

Even the value of the golden foundation of the earth with all its jewels is not enough to secure the dharma treasure of the infinite dakini mind. It is gained only by the fortunate ones who are held by the guru's compassion. The doctrine of the ocean-born buddha must spread and flourish!

ངོ་བོ་ཀ་ནས་དག་པའི་ཡེ་ཤེས་ལ།

NGO WO	**KA NAE**	**DAG PAI**	**YE SHE**	**LA**
essence, dharmakaya	*from the very beginning*	*pure*	*wisdom, original knowing*	*with, in, from*

With the wisdom of primordially pure actuality

རང་བཞིན་ལྷུན་གྱིས་གྲུབ་པའི་གདངས་ཤར་བས།

RANG ZHIN	**LHUN GYI DRUB PAI**	**DANG**	**SHAR WAE**
own nature, self-expression, sambhogakaya	*effortlessly arising*	*radiance, clarity*	*arise*

Its inherent quality of effortlessly appearing radiance shines forth.

བླུན་སྒོམ་སེམས་ལས་འདས་པའི་རྫོགས་པ་ཆེ།

LUN	**GOM**	**SEM**	**LAE**	**DAE PAI**	**DZOG PA CHE**
stupid, dull	*meditation*	*mind*	*from*	*pass beyond*	*dzogchen, great union, great perfection*

(not necessary to do repeated practice for clarity itself arises from the dharmadhatu)

This is the great completion which is beyond the reach of dull, contrived meditation.

མཚོ་སྐྱེས་རྒྱལ་བའི་བསྟན་པ་རྒྱས་གྱུར་ཅིག།

TSHO KYE GYAL WAI TEN PA GYE GYUR CHIG

The doctrines of the ocean-born buddha must spread and flourish!

With the wisdom of primordially pure actuality, its natural quality of effortlessly appearing radiance shines forth. This is the great completion which is beyond the realm of dull, contrived meditation. The doctrines of the ocean-born buddha must spread and flourish!

ཡོད་མེད་ཕྱོགས་རེར་ཞེན་པའི་དམིགས་གཏད་ཞིག།

YOE	ME	CHOG RER	ZHEN PAI	MIG TAE	ZHIG
have, being (real/ not real -) good/bad etc.)	*not have, not being*	*separate, take side, be partial (The view arising from Nagarjuna)*	*attachments to that*	*objects*	*finish, come loose by themselves*

Releasing reificatory fixation generating attachment to discriminations such as existing or not existing, and

མཐར་འཛིན་ལྟ་བའི་འཛིན་སྟངས་དྲུང་ནས་ཕྱུང་།

THAR	DZIN	TA WAI	DZIN TANG	DRUNG	NAE	CHUNG
limit	*holding **	*view*	*grasping system*	*root*	*from*	*come out*

*one particular point or extreme like permanence or non-continuity

Totally uprooting clinging to the view of extreme positions,

གཞི་ལམ་འབྲས་བུ་སྣང་སྟོང་ཟུང་དུ་འཇུག།

ZHI	LAM	DRAE BU	NANG	TONG	ZUNG DU JUG
ground	*way, path*	*result*	*ideas, appearance*	*emptiness, sunyata*	*fully coupled, completely joined, come together*

The base, path, and result are manifest in the union of appearance and emptiness.

མཚོ་སྐྱེས་རྒྱལ་བའི་བསྟན་པ་རྒྱས་གྱུར་ཅིག།

TSHO KYE GYAL WAI TEN PA GYE GYUR CHIG

The doctrines of the ocean-born buddha must spread and flourish!

Releasing reificatory fixation generating attachment to partiality towards polarised positions such as existing or not existing, and totally uprooting clinging to the view of extreme positions, the base, path, and result are manifest in the union of appearance and emptiness. The doctrines of the ocean-born buddha must spread and flourish!

དུས་གསུམ་རྒྱལ་བའི་དགོངས་པ་མཐར་ཐུག་དོན།

DU SUM	GYAL WAI	GONG PA	THAR THUG	DON
three times (past, (present, future)	*victors, buddhas*	*insight*	*highest one, final*	*meaning, original truth*

The ultimate meaning of the insight of the buddhas of the three times

ཟབ་ཞི་སྤྲོས་བྲལ་འོད་གསལ་འདུས་མ་བྱས།

ZAB	ZHI	TO DRAL	OE SAL	DUE MA JHE
deep	*peaceful*	*non-dual**	*shining, clear light*	*unconstructed, not made by anyone*

*free of all relative positions like beginning and ending

Is deep, peaceful, non-conceptual, uncompounded clear light.

རིག་སྟོང་མི་ཤིགས་རྡོར་རྗེ་གྲུབ་པའི་མཐའ།

RIG	TONG	MI SHIG	DOR JE	DRUB PAI THA
awareness	*emptiness*	*not destroyed*	*very strong*	*highest and most powerful view*

This is the indestructible, unwavering view of the inseparability of awareness and emptiness.

མཚོ་སྐྱེས་རྒྱལ་བའི་བསྟན་པ་རྒྱས་གྱུར་ཅིག།

TSHO KYE GYAL WAI TEN PA GYE GYUR CHIG

The doctrines of the ocean-born buddha must spread and flourish!

The ultimate meaning of the insight of the buddhas of the three times is deep, peaceful, non-conceptual, uncompounded clear light. This is the indestructible, unwavering view of the inseparability of awareness and emptiness. The doctrine of the ocean-born buddha must spread and flourish!

མང་དུ་ཐོས་པ་ལུང་གི་སྤྲིན་འཁྲིགས་ཤིང་།

MANG DU THOE PA	LUNG	GI	TRIN TRIG SHING
scholar, one who has heard much dharma teaching	*idea, books quotations*	*of*	*gathering clouds, i.e. very many*

Like gathering clouds, the learning of scholars

ཕ་རོལ་རྒོལ་འཇོམས་རིག་པའི་གློག་ཕྲེང་འབར།

PHA ROL	GOL	JOM	RIG PAI	LOG	TRENG	BAR
outside, non-buddhist	*debaters, contestant*	*destroy*	*vidyadhara's awareness*	*lightning*	*chain, stream*	*shining*

Releases the lightning stream of awareness which destroys the enemies of clarity

མན་ངག་གནད་ཀྱི་བདུད་རྩི་སྙིང་ལ་སིམ།

MEN NGAG	NAE	KYI	DU TSI	NYING	LA	SIM
deep teaching methods	*points*	*of*	*amrita, liberating elixir*	*mind, heart*	*in*	*absorbed, satisfied*

As the liberating elixir of the essential points of the deep instructions refreshes our minds.

མཚོ་སྐྱེས་རྒྱལ་བའི་བསྟན་པ་རྒྱས་གྱུར་ཅིག།

TSHO KYE GYAL WAI TEN PA GYE GYUR CHIG

The doctrines of the ocean-born buddha must spread and flourish!

Like gathering clouds, the learning of scholars releases the lightning of awareness which destroys the enemies of clarity as the liberating elixir of the essential points of the deep instructions refreshes our minds. The doctrines of the ocean-born buddha must spread and flourish!

རྨད་བྱུང་ཨ་ཏི་ཡོ་གའི་གསེང་ལམ་ནས།

MAE JUNG	**A TI YO GAI**	**SENG**	**LAM**	**NAE**
wonderful, amazing	*dzogchen*	*going inside (like a saw cutting)*	*path*	*then, from*

With the penetrating path of wonderful atiyoga,

མ་ལུས་རྒྱལ་བ་ཀུན་གྱིས་ཡེ་ཤེས་སྐུ།

MA LU	**GYAL WA**	**KUN**	**GYI**	**YE SHE**	**KU**
without exception	*victors*	*all*	*of*	*wisdom, original knowing*	*body, kaya*

The intrinsic wisdom body of all the buddhas without exception,

ཁྱབ་བདག་འཇམ་དཔལ་རྡོ་རྗེར་རབ་བསྒྲུབས་པ།

KYAB DAG	**JAM PAL**	**DOR JER**	**RAB DRUB PA**
pervading lord, dharmakaya	*Manjushri*	*Vajra*	*strongly practise*

The omnipresent indestructible Manjushri, will be fully achieved.

མཚོ་སྐྱེས་རྒྱལ་བའི་བསྟན་པ་རྒྱས་གྱུར་ཅིག།

TSHO KYE GYAL WAI TEN PA GYE GYUR CHIG

The doctrines of the ocean-born buddha must spread and flourish!

With the penetrating path of wonderful atiyoga, the intrinsic wisdom body of all the buddhas without exception, the omnipresent indestructible Manjushri, will be fully achieved. The doctrines of the ocean-born buddha must spread and flourish!

ཡང་དག་ཚད་མ་གསུམ་གྱི་ང་རོ་ཡིས།

YANG DAG	**TSAE MA**	**SUM**	**GYI**	**NGA RO**	**YI**
very pure, i.e buddhist	*logic methods**	*three*	*of*	*lion's roar*	*by*

*direct perception, inference, information from the Buddha,Guru and so on.

The lion's roar of the three very pure logical methods makes

ལྟ་དམན་རི་དྭགས་ཚོགས་རྣམས་སྐྲག་མཛད་པ།

TA MEN	**RI DA**	**TSHOG NAM**	**TRAG DZAE PA**
lesser views, those with less logic	*deer*	*hosts*	*become very afraid*

All those deer-like ones with lesser views become very afraid.

ཐེག་མཆོག་སེང་གེའི་སྒྲ་དབྱངས་ས་གསུམ་ཁྱབ།

THEG CHOG	**SENG GEI**	**DRA YANG**	**SA SUM**	**KYAB**
best vehicle, atiyoga	*lions*	*sound*	*three worlds**	*pervade, fill*

*gods, nagas and men, i.e. all of samsara

The lions' sound, the supreme vehicle, pervades the entire universe.

མཚོ་སྐྱེས་རྒྱལ་བའི་བསྟན་པ་རྒྱས་གྱུར་ཅིག།

TSHO KYE GYAL WAI TEN PA GYE GYUR CHIG

The doctrines of the ocean-born buddha must spread and flourish!

The lion's roar of the three very pure logical methods makes all those deer-like ones with lesser views become very afraid. The lion's sound, the supreme vehicle, pervades the entire universe. The doctrine of the ocean-born buddha must spread and flourish!

རྒྱལ་བསྟན་ཡོངས་སུ་རྫོགས་པའི་གོས་བཟང་རྩེར།

GYAL	**TEN**	**YONG SU DZOG PAI**	**GO**	**ZANG**	**TSER**
victors, buddhas	*doctrines*	*complete, fully perfect*	*cloth*	*good*	*top*
			(of the victory banner)		

At the top of the banner of the completely perfect buddha's doctrines

འོད་གསལ་རྡོ་རྗེ་སྙིང་པོའི་ཏོག་མཛེས་པ།

OE SAL	**DOR JE**	**NYING POI**	**TOE**	**DZE PA**
brilliant	*vajra (dzogpachenpo)*	*essence*	*top point, crest jewel (as at the top of a flagpole)*	*beautiful*

Is the beautiful crest jewel of the brilliant indestructible essence.

ཕྱོགས་ལས་རྣམ་པར་རྒྱལ་བའི་རྒྱལ་མཚན་མཐོ།

CHOG LAE	**NAM PAR GYAL WAI**	**GYAL TSHAN**	**THO**
everywhere	*completely victorious*	*victory banner*	*very high*

Raise high the victory banner that is completely victorious in all directions.

མཚོ་སྐྱེས་རྒྱལ་བའི་བསྟན་པ་རྒྱས་གྱུར་ཅིག།

TSHO KYE GYAL WAI TEN PA GYE GYUR CHIG

The doctrines of the ocean-born buddha must spread and flourish!

At the top of the banner of the completely perfect buddha's doctrines is the beautiful crest jewel of the brilliant indestructible essence. Raise high the victory banner that is completely victorious in all directions. The doctrines of the ocean-born buddha must spread and flourish!

བདག་སོགས་དེང་ནས་འགྲོ་བ་ཇི་སྲིད་དུ།

DAG SOG DENG NAE DRO WA JI SI DU

we (all beings in samsara) — from now — beings — as many as there are

From now on, we beings, as many as we are,

བསྟན་དང་བསྟན་པའི་སྙིང་པོ་ཡོངས་རྫོགས་པ།

TEN DANG TEN PAI NYING PO YONG DZOG PA

doctrines — and — doctrines (direct revelation) — essence, heart — must get fully, must be full

Must fully ripen through the teachings and their direct revelation.

མཁའ་ཁྱབ་ཞིང་དུ་འཛིན་སྐྱོང་སྤེལ་བ་ཡིས།

KHA KHYAB ZHING DU DZIN KYONG PEL WA YI

sky — pervading (i.e going everywhere) — in,as — holders of the buddha's doctrines — spread — by this

With those who exemplify the teaching spreading like the all-pervading sky,

མཚོ་སྐྱེས་རྒྱལ་བའི་བསྟན་པ་རྒྱས་གྱུར་ཅིག།

TSHO KYE GYAL WAI TEN PA GYE GYUR CHIG

The doctrines of the ocean-born buddha must spread and flourish!

From now on, we beings, as many as we are, must fully ripen through the teachings and their direct revelation. With those who exemplify the teaching spreading like the all-pervading sky, the doctrines of the ocean-born buddha must spread and flourish!

མདོར་ན་མཁས་བཙུན་གྲུབ་པའི་རྣམ་ཐར་གྱིས།

DOR NA KHAE TSUN DRUB PAI NAM THAR GYI

briefly — scholars — vow keepers — siddhas, accomplished practitioners — spiritual life stories — by

In brief, the lives of scholars, vow keepers and adepts demonstrate

རྒྱལ་བསྟན་སྤེལ་བའི་ཕྲིན་ལས་མཁའ་ཁྱབ་པའི།

GYAL TEN PEL WAI TRIN LAE KHA KHYAB PAI

victor's — doctrines — spread — deeds, activities — sky — pervade, spread everywhere

The activity of endlessly spreading the buddha's doctrines.

བསྟན་འཛིན་དམ་པས་ས་སྟེང་ཡོངས་གང་ནས།

TEN DZIN DAM PAE SA TENG YONG GANG NAE

doctrine — holders — holy — land — on, above — fully — fill — then

The holy doctrine holders must fill the earth then

མཚོ་སྐྱེས་རྒྱལ་བའི་བསྟན་པ་རྒྱས་གྱུར་ཅིག།

TSHO KYE GYAL WAI TEN PA GYE GYUR CHIG

The doctrines of the ocean-born buddha must spread and flourish!

In brief, the lives of scholars, vow keepers and adepts, demonstrate the activity of endlessly spreading the buddha's doctrines. The holy doctrine holders must fill the earth then the doctrines of the ocean-born buddha must spread and flourish!

དཔལ་ལྡན་བླ་མའི་སྐུ་ཚེ་རབ་བརྟན་ཅིང་།

PAL DEN	**LA MAI**	**KU TSHE**	**RAB**	**TEN CHING**
glorious	*guru's*	*life, heath*	*fully, very*	*firm (i.e. long life)*

With the glorious gurus having long healthy lives, and

བསྟན་པའི་སྦྱིན་བདག་མངའ་ཐང་དར་བ་ཡིས།

TEN PAI	**JIN DAG**	**NGA THANG**	**DAR WA**	**YI**
doctrines	*sponsors, patrons*	*very great, powerful*	*spread, arise*	*by*

The sponsors of the doctrines becoming great and powerful,

ཆོས་སྲིད་མི་ནུབ་ནོར་བུའི་རྒྱལ་མཚན་བསྒྲེངས།

CHO	**SI**	**MI NUE**	**NOR BUI**	**GYAL TSHEN**	**DRENG**
dharma	*influence, administration*	*not decline*	*jewels*	*victory banner*	*hoist, raise aloft*

The influence of the Dharma shall not decline and its jewelled victory banner will be hoisted high.

མཚོ་སྐྱེས་རྒྱལ་བའི་བསྟན་པ་རྒྱས་གྱུར་ཅིག།

TSHO KYE GYAL WAI TEN PA GYE GYUR CHIG

The doctrines of the ocean-born buddha must spread and flourish!

With the glorious gurus having long healthy lives, and the sponsors of the doctrine becoming great and powerful, the influence of the Dharma shall not decline and its jewelled victory banner will be hoisted high. The doctrines of the ocean-born buddha must spread and flourish!

ཅེས་རྒྱལ་བ་ཐབས་ཅན་གྱི་ངོ་བོ་དཔལ་ལྡན་སངས་རྒྱས་པདྨ་སྐྱེས་འཆི་མེད་མཚོར་འཁྲུངས་རྒྱལ་བའི་བསྟན་པ་སྤྱི་འགྱུར་རྙིང་མ་ཞེས་གྲགས་པ་འདི་ནི་རྒྱལ་བསྟན་ཡོངས་སུ་རྫོགས་པའི་ཕྱི་མོ་ཡིན་ཅིང་ཟབ་གནད་ཆེ་བ་དུ་མའི་ཁྱད་ཆོས་དང་། ལྷ་སྨོན་རྣམ་པར་དག་པ་རྒྱལ་བ་དགྱེས་པའི་ལམ་བཟང་མ་ནོར་བ་འདི་ངོ་ཤེས་ནས་ནོར་བུ་རིན་པོ་ཆེའི་ཏོར་བྱས་ཏེ་རྒྱལ་མཚན་གྱི་རྩེ་

ལ་མཆོད་པ་བཞིན་དུ་གང་ཟག་སྐལ་པ་དང་ལྡན་པ་རྣམས་ཀྱིས་འཆག་རྩོད་རྩོམ་གསུམ་གྱི་ཕྲིན་ལས་རླབས་པོ་ཆེས་ཕྱོགས་ཐམས་ཅད་དུ་དར་ཞིང་རྒྱས་པར་མཛད་པའི་ཐུགས་ཁུར་བཞེས་པ་དང་། དེ་ལྟ་བུའི་བཞེད་པ་ཡིད་བཞིན་དུ་འགྲུབ་པའི་རྟེན་འབྲེལ་སྨོན་ཚིག་ཏུ་རྙིང་བསྟན་ལ་ལྷག་བསམ་རྣམ་པར་དཀར་བ་མི་ཕམ་འཇམ་དབྱངས་རྣམ་རྒྱལ་རྒྱ་མཚོས་གནས་དུས་རྟེན་འབྲེལ་དགེ་བར་གུང་ཐུན་ལ་ཤར་མར་བྲིས་པ་དགེ་ལེགས་འཕེལ།།

The true essence of all the buddhas, glorious Buddha Padmasambhava the undying Ocean-born Victor, your doctrines are known as the Old Translation Nyingma. These buddha's doctrines are the completely perfect mother (of the Dharma in Tibet). They have the special quality of many very deep and important essential points, and having a very pure view and meditation they are the correct, good way which pleases the buddhas.

In the manner of polishing a precious jewel and offering it as the crest jewel of the victory banner, fortunate beings will read, debate and write about these teachings. By this great wave of activity they will act carefully to spread the doctrine in all directions.

With this hope, as a connecting aspiration for its being accomplished accordingly, Mipham Jamyang Namgyal Gyamtso, who is extremely fond of the Nyingma doctrines and wishes them well, quickly wrote down these words at midday at a time and place with auspicious connections.

༄༅།། འཇིག་རྟེན་བདེ་བའི་སྨོན་ལམ་བཞུགས།། །།

The Prayer of Aspiration for Happiness in the World

སྐྱབས་གནས་བསླུ་མེད་དཀོན་མཆོག་རྩ་བ་གསུམ།

KYAB	**NAE**	**LU ME**	**KON CHOG**	**TSA WA**	**SUM**
refuge shelter	*place*	*unfailing, undeceptive*	*jewels**	*roots*	*three***

*Buddha, dharma, sangha **guru, meditation deity, dakini

The three Jewels and the three Roots, our unfailing sources of refuge, and

ཁྱད་པར་འཇིག་རྟེན་མགོན་པོ་སྤྱན་རས་གཟིགས།

KHYAE PAR	**JIG TEN**	**GON PO**	**CHEN RE ZI**
especially	*world*	*protector, benefactor*	*Avalokitesvara*

Especially the benefactor of the world, Chenrezi, with

རྗེ་བཙུན་སྒྲོལ་མ་གུ་རུ་པདྨ་འབྱུང་།

JE TSUN	**DROL MA**	**GU RU**	**PAE MA JUNG**
reverend, noble	*Tara*	*guru, spiritual master*	*Padma Sambhava*

Jetsun Tara and Guru Padma Sambhava—

གསོལ་བ་འདེབས་སོ་ཐུགས་དམ་ཞལ་བཞེས་དགོངས།

SOL WA DEB SO	**THUG DAM**	**ZHAL ZHE**	**GONG**
we pray	*vows**	*taken, accepted*	*think of, remember (for our sake)*

*the vows they take to work for the benefit of others

We pray to you to think of the vows you have taken.

སྨོན་ལམ་ཡོངས་སུ་འགྲུབ་པར་བྱིན་གྱིས་རློབས།

MON LAM	**YONG SU**	**DRU PAR**	**JIN GYI LOB**
aspiration	*fully*	*accomplish*	*bless*

Please bless us with the full accomplishment of our aspiration.

Unfailing sources of refuge, the three Jewels and the three Roots, and especially Chenrezi, the benefactor of the world, with Jetsun Tara and Guru Padma Sambhava – we pray to you to think of the vows you have taken. Please bless us with the full accomplishment of our aspiration.

སྙིགས་དུས་འགྲོ་རྣམས་བསམ་སྦྱོར་ལོག་པ་དང་།

NYIG	DU	DRO NAM	SAM	JOR	LOG PA	DANG
evil, degenerate	*time*	*beings*	*idea*	*action*	*wrong, reversed*	*and*

In these present degenerate times, due to the causes and conditions of the wrong ideas and actions of all beings, and

ཕྱི་ནང་འབྱུང་བ་འཁྲུགས་པའི་རྒྱུ་རྐྱེན་གྱིས།

CHI	NANG	JUNG WA	TRUL PAI	GYU	KYEN	GYI
*outer**	*inner***	*elements*	*commotion, agitated confused*	*cause reason*	*condition,*	*by*

* the weather and the state of the world ** the constituents of our bodies

The commotion of elements in the world and in our bodies,

སྔར་མ་གྲགས་པའི་མི་ཕྱུགས་དལ་ཡམས་ནད།

NGAR	MA	DRAG PAI	MI	CHUG	DAL YAM	NAE
former time (i.e. new, unheard of)	*not*	*hear*	*humans*	*animals*	*disease, pestilence*	*sickness*

There are formerly unheard of diseases in humans and animals and

གཟའ་ཀླུ་རྒྱལ་གདོན་ནག་ཕྱོགས་འབྱུང་པོའི་གཟེར།

ZA	LU	GYAL	DON	NAG CHO	JUNG POI	ZER
*planets**	*nagas, snake gods*	*king# spirits*	*trouble-makers*	*black side, bad things*	*bhutas, demons*	*pressure, trouble*

*the spirits connected with them # ones who give orders

We are oppressed by the planets, snake gods, spirit-rulers, trouble-makers and evil demons.

In these present degenerate times, due to the causes and conditions of the wrong ideas and actions of all beings, and the commotion of elements in the world and in our bodies, there are formerly unheard of diseases in humans and animals and we are oppressed by the planets, snake gods, spirit-rulers, trouble-makers and evil demons.

བཙའ་སད་སེར་གསུམ་ལོ་ཉེས་དམག་འཁྲུག་རྩོད།

TSA	SAE	SER	SUM	LO	NYE	MAG TRUG	TSOE
red 'rust' on crops	*night frost*	*hail stones*	*three*	*harvest crop*	*bad, faulty*	*soldiers, fightings*	*dispute*

The crops are damaged by rust, night frost and hail, and there is war and dispute.

ཆར་ཆུ་མི་སྙོམས་གངས་ཆད་བྲ་བྱིའི་ཐན།

CHAR	**CHU**	**MI**	**NYOM**	**GANG CHAE**	**TRA CHAI**	**THAN**
rain	*river*	*not*	*equal*	*snow*	*a marmot-*	*famine,*
(i.e. too much or too little at the wrong time)				*avalanche*	*like rodent**	*drought*

* this animal eats all the grass roots and when in large numbers, they destroy all the cattle-grazing lands

Rains and water supply are not appropriate, there are snow avalanches and rodents destroy the pastures, bringing famine.

ས་གཡོས་མེ་དགྲ་འབྱུང་བཞིའི་འཇིགས་པ་དང་།

SA	**YOE**	**ME**	**DRA**	**JUNG**	**ZHI**	**JIG PA**	**DANG**
earth	*move*	*fire*	*enemies*	*elements**	*four*	*destroyed*	*and*

*earth, water, fire, air

There are earthquakes, fire and destruction by other hostile forms of the four elements.

The crops are damaged by rust, night frost and hail, and there is war and dispute. Rain and water supply are not appropriate, there are snow avalanches and rodents destroy the pastures, bringing famine. There are earthquakes, fire and destruction by other hostile forms of the four elements.

ཁྱད་པར་བསྟན་ལ་འཚེ་བའི་མཐའ་དམག་སོགས།

KHYAE PAR	**TAN**	**LA**	**TSE WAI**	**THA**	**MAG**	**SOG**
especially	*doctrine*	*to*	*trouble, harm*	*border*	*wars, soldiers*	*and so on*

In particular, there is trouble for the teachings due to border wars and so forth.

འཇིག་རྟེན་ཁམས་འདིར་གནོད་འཚེའི་རིགས་མཐའ་དག།

JIG TEN	**KHAM**	**DIR**	**NOD**	**TSEI**	**RIG**	**THA DAG**
world	*realm*	*here*	*harm*	*trouble*	*all kinds*	*all*

May all the many kinds of harm and trouble in this world

མྱུར་དུ་ཞི་ཞིང་རྩད་ནས་འཇོམས་གྱུར་ཅིག།

NYUR DU	**ZHI ZHING**	**TSAE**	**NE**	**JOM**	**GYUR CHIG**
quickly	*pacifying*	*root*	*from*	*destroy, finish*	*it must be!*
		(i.e. completely)			

Be quickly pacified and completely uprooted!

In particular, there is trouble for the teachings due to border wars and so forth. May all the many kinds of harm and trouble in this world be quickly pacified and completely uprooted.

མི་དང་མི་མིན་འགྲོ་བ་མཐའ་དག་གི།

MI	**DANG**	**MI MIN**	**DRO WA**	**THA DAG**	**GI**
humans	*and*	*non-humans, demons, tigers, etc.*	*beings*	*all*	*of*

For all beings, human and non-human,

རྒྱུད་ལ་བྱང་ཆུབ་སེམས་མཆོག་རིན་པོ་ཆེ།

GYUD	**LA**	**JANG CHUB SEM**	**CHOG**	**RIN PO CHE**
mind	*in*	*bodhicitta, altruistic intention towards enlightenment*	*excellent*	*precious*

May the precious, excellent bodhicitta arise naturally so that

ངང་གིས་སྐྱེས་ནས་གནོད་འཚེའི་བསམ་སྦྱོར་བྲལ།

NGANG	**GI**	**KYE**	**NE**	**NOD**	**TSEI**	**SAM**	**JOR**	**DRAL**
inherent potential	*by*	*arise*	*then*	*harm*	*troubles (killing, beating etc.)*	*thoughts*	*actions*	*without*

Free of harmful or troublesome thoughts and deeds,

ཕན་ཚུན་བྱམས་པའི་སེམས་དང་ལྡན་ནས་ཀྱང་།

PHEN	**TSHUN**	**JAM PAI**	**SEM**	**DANG DAN**	**NE**	**KYANG**
each	*other*	*loving, compassionate*	*mind*	*having*	*then*	*also*

They have minds full of love for each other.

འཇིག་རྟེན་ཁམས་ཀུན་བདེ་སྐྱིད་དཔལ་གྱིས་འབྱོར།

JIG TEN	**KHAM**	**KUN**	**DE**	**KYID**	**PAL GYI JOR**
world	*realms*	*all*	*happiness*	*joy*	*prosperity, wealth*

May all the world realms have happiness, joy and prosperity and

སངས་རྒྱས་བསྟན་པ་དར་རྒྱས་ཡུན་གནས་ཤོག།

SANG GYE	**TAN PA**	**DAR GYE**	**YUN NAE**	**SHOG**
Buddha	*doctrines*	*spread widely*	*endure long*	*they must*

May the doctrines of the Buddha spread far and remain for long.

For all beings, human and non-human, may the precious, excellent bodhicitta arise naturally so that free of harmful or troublesome thoughts and deeds, they have minds full of love for each other. May all the world realms have happiness, joy and prosperity and may the doctrines of the Buddha spread far and remain for long.

རྩ་གསུམ་རྒྱལ་བ་སྲས་བཅས་བདེན་པའི་སྟོབས།

TSA	**SUM**	**GYAL WA**	**SAE CHE**	**DEN PAI**	**TOB**
roots (guru, path deity [yidam], dakini)	*three*	*victors, buddhas*	*bodhisattvas*	*truth's*	*power*

By the power of the truth of the three roots, the buddhas, and the bodhisattvas,

འཁོར་འདས་དགེ་བའི་རྩ་བ་གང་མཆིས་དང་།

KHOR *samsara* **DAE** *nirvana* **GE WAI** *virtues* **TSA WA** *roots* **GANG** *what* **CHI** *have* **DANG** *and*

And whatever virtuous roots there are in samsara and nirvana, and

བདག་ཅག་ལྷག་བསམ་རྣམ་པར་དཀར་བའི་མཐུས།

DAG CHAG *we* **LHAG** *good* **SAM** *thoughts* **NAM PAR** *very, completely* **KAR WAI** *white, good* **THU** *power*

By the power of our excellent and very pure thoughts,

གསོལ་བཏབ་སྨོན་པའི་འབྲས་བུ་འགྲུབ་གྱུར་ཅིག། །།

SON TAB *prayed* **MON PAI** *aspiration, wish* **DRAE BU** *result, fulfilment* **DRUB** **GYUR CHIG** *it must be*

Our prayers and aspirations must be fulfilled!

By the power of the truth of the three roots, the buddhas and the bodhisattvas, and whatever virtuous roots there are in samsara and nirvana, and by the power of our excellent and very pure intentions, our prayers and aspirations must be fulfilled!

ཅེས་རྗེ་བླ་མ་འཇམ་དབྱངས་མཁྱེན་བརྩེའི་དབང་པོའི་ཞལ་སྔ་ནས་དེང་སང་དུས་ཀྱི་འཚུབ་འགྱུར་ཤིན་ཏུ་ཆེ་བའི་ཅི་ལྟར་འབྱུང་ཆ་མེད་པས་རྗེ་ཉིད་ནས་བོད་ཡུལ་སྨོན་ལམ་ཉིན་ཞག་རེར་ལན་དྲུག་རེ་མཛད་པ་ཡིན་པས་ཁྱོད་ནས་ཀྱང་དེ་ལྟར་གལ་ཆེ་བཀའ་རྩལ་ཕེབས་པ་ལྟར་བློ་གྲོས་མཐའ་ཡས་ཀྱིས་ཙ་འདྲ་རིན་ཆེན་བྲག་ཏུ་རྒྱལ་ཟླ་བའི་དཀར་ཕྱོགས་འགྲུབ་པའི་སྦྱོར་བ་དང་ལྡན་པའི་སྔ་དྲོའི་ཆར་རང་གི་བསླེལ་གསོས་སུ་བྲིས་པ་ཡ་ཐཱ་སི་དྡྷི་རསྟུ།།།།

The reverend guru ‘Jam-dByangs mKhyen-brTse’i-dBang-Po said that in the present times the situation is very bad and confused and that what will happen is unknown and so he himself prayed for the happiness of Tibet six times a day. He told me that it was very important that I also should pray in this way. Thus according to his order I, bLo-Gros mTha’-Yas wrote this at Tsandra Rinchen Drag in the first half of the Paush Month on the morning of an auspicious day from memory. The full result must be gained.

བསྟན་པ་རྒྱས་པའི་སྨོན་ལམ།

Aspiration for the Flourishing of Dharma

ཉེར་འཚེ་མ་ལུས་ཞི་བ་དང་།

NYER TSE	**MA LUE**	**ZHI WA**	**DANG**
difficulties, troubles	*without exception*	*pacify*	*and*

All difficulties without exception being pacified and

མཐུན་རྐྱེན་ནམ་མཁའི་མཛོད་བཞིན་དུ།

THUN	**KYEN**	**NAM KAI**	**DZO**	**ZHIN DU**
harmonious	*situations, reasons*	*sky's, infinitely vast*	*treasure*	*like*

With harmonious conditions like the treasure of the sky,

རྒྱལ་དབང་པདྨ་འབྱུང་གནས་ཀྱི།

GYAL	**WANG**	**PE MA JUNG NAE**	**KYI**
Jina, Victor	*lord*	*Padmasambhava*	*of*

The powerful Victor Padmasambhava's

བསྟན་པ་ཡུན་རིང་འབར་གྱུར་ཅིག།

TAN PA	**YUN RING**	**BAR**	**GYUR CHIG**
doctrine	*long life*	*shining*	*must*

Doctrines must live long and shine brightly!

ཨོཾ་ཨཱཿཧཱུྃཿབཛྲ་གུ་རུ་པདྨ་སི་དྡྷི་ཧཱུྃཿ

OM	**A**	**HUNG**	**BEN DZA**	**GU RU**	**PAE MA**	**SID DHI**	**HUNG**
Body	*Speech*	*Mind*	*indestructible*	*guru*	*Padmasambhava*	*accomplishment*	*give*

Indestructible three mode guru Padmasambhava, grant us accomplishment!

With all difficulties without exception being pacified, and harmonious conditions like the treasure of the sky, the powerful Victor Padmasambhava's doctrines must live long and shine brightly! Indestructible three mode guru Padmasambhava, grant us accomplishment!

པདྨ་ལས་འབྲེལ་རྩལ་(ཀློང་ཆེན་རབ་འབྱམས་)གྱིས་སོ།། །།

This was written by Padma Las-'Brel Tsal (kLong-Chen Rab-'Byams)

www.ingramcontent.com/pod-product-compliance
Lightning Source LLC
Chambersburg PA
CBHW040410110426
42812CB00012B/2517

* 9 7 8 1 7 3 9 9 3 8 1 0 9 *